The First Hundred Years of the Bureau of Labor Statistics, 1884-1984 [hy]

Joseph P. Goldberg and William T. Moye

353.008

D1041409

For sale by the Superintendent of Documents, U.S. Government Printing Office
Washington, D.C. 20402

[1985]

Library of Congress Cataloging in Publication Data

Goldberg, Joseph P., 1918–
  The first hundred years of the Bureau of Labor Statistics.

  (Bulletin / Bureau of Labor Statistics ; 2235)
  Bibliography: p.
  Includes index.
  1. United States. Bureau of Labor Statistics—History.
I. Moye, William T. II. Title. III. Series: Bulletin
(United States. Bureau of Labor Statistics) ; 2235.

HD8064.2.G65 1985   353.0083   85-11655
ISBN 0-935043-00-4
ISBN 0-935043-01-2 (pbk.)

Foreword

This volume reports on the first century of a government agency whose founders hoped that, by publishing facts about economic conditions, the agency would help end strife between capital and labor.

The Bureau's early work included studies of depressions, tariffs, immigrants, and alchoholism and many assignments to investigate and mediate disputes between labor and management. Most of these functions—especially those involving formulation of policy—passed on to other agencies. The Bureau today remains one of the Nation's principal economic factfinders.

This account of the Bureau's history is based on 4 years of research by two historians, Joseph P. Goldberg and William T. Moye. Dr. Goldberg holds degrees in history and economics from the City College of New York and Columbia University and has written extensively on the maritime industry, collective bargaining, labor law, and labor history. He has served as special assistant to the Commissioner of Labor Statistics since 1955. Dr. Moye holds degrees from Davidson College and the University of North Carolina and has been with the U.S. Department of Labor since 1976, specializing in the history of the Department and the Bureau of Labor Statistics.

In conducting their research, Drs. Goldberg and Moye had full access to the records of the Bureau and of the Department of Labor and also used the collections of the Library of Congress, the National Archives, and other public and private institutions. In addition, the authors conducted interviews with recent Commissioners and Secretaries of Labor and others familiar with the work of the Bureau. At the Archives, Jerry N. Hess and Joseph B. Howerton provided valuable assistance, as did Henry P. Guzda of the Department of Labor Historical Office.

Rosalie K. Epstein, the book's editor, worked closely with the authors in helping them fashion their voluminous research into a book-size manuscript.

Several expert readers helped improve the work through thoughtful critiques. They included Richard B. Morris, Gouverneur Morris Professor of History Emeritus, Columbia University; Professor Irving Bernstein, Department of Political Science, University of California, Los Angeles; Dr. Jonathan Grossman, Historian, U.S. Department of Labor, from 1962 to 1982; Dr. H.M. Douty, author and economic consultant; Dr. Herbert C. Morton, Director, Office of Scholarly Communications and Technology, American Council of Learned Societies; and several members of the staff of the Bureau of Labor Statistics.

Book design was supervised by Richard Mathews. Scenobia G. Easterly and Elizabeth M. Johnson assisted with manuscript preparation.

In writing the book, Drs. Goldberg and Moye had full freedom to interpret events in accordance with their judgments as historians, without conformance to an "official" view of institutional history. Given the perspective made possible by passing years, the authors offer broader evaluations of the Bureau's early history than of contemporary events.

Henry Lowenstern
Associate Commissioner, Office of Publications
Bureau of Labor Statistics

Contents

Chapter I.

Origins

When President Chester A. Arthur signed the bill creating the Bureau of Labor in the Department of the Interior on June 27, 1884, it was the culmination of almost two decades of advocacy by labor organizations that wanted government help in publicizing and improving the status of the growing industrial labor force.

Those two decades had seen vast changes in the American economy and society. A truly national economy was developing, epitomized by the transcontinental railroads. Industry was attracting increasing numbers of unskilled workers, recruited from among immigrants, freedmen, women, and children, into the urban centers. And, with the emergence of the industrial worker, unemployment, slum conditions, and labor unrest were on the rise.

The altruistic concerns of social reformers, largely directed against slavery in the pre-Civil War period, increasingly focused on ameliorating the conditions of American workers—men, women, and children. Some of these reformers supported the emerging national unions as aids to such amelioration. Further, they challenged the prevailing view that the primary role of government was to preserve order and protect property and that control of the economy was to be left to the captains of industry. They believed that the state should have an ethical and educational role, one that was indispensable to human progress.

It was in this era of ferment and demands for reform that the Bureau of Labor was born.

The campaign for a national labor agency

The campaign for a national labor agency had begun with the call for a Department of Labor at the 1867 convention of the short-lived National Labor Union.[1] In 1869, in response to the growing strength of a labor reform party in the State, Massachusetts established the first State bureau of labor statistics. But, under the leadership of labor activists, the new agency stirred controversy which almost destroyed it. In 1873, the governor appointed as chief Carroll D. Wright, a former State legislator who was not associated with the labor reformers, and Wright soon put the bureau on solid ground. Other States followed suit, and, within 10 years, 12 more States had established labor bureaus.

On the national scene, the Industrial Congress, later renamed the Industrial Brotherhood, carried on the fight but did not survive the depression years of the mid-1870's. Then, in 1878, the Knights of Labor adopted the preamble of the Brotherhood almost verbatim, calling for "the establishment of Bureaus of Labor Statistics" at the various levels of government.[2] That same year, a Select Committee of the U.S. House of Representatives held hearings on the causes of the general depression. In their testimony, Hugh McGregor, later a leader in the American Federation of Labor, and George E. McNeill, former Deputy Chief of the Massachusetts agency, called for a Federal Bureau of Statistics or Ministry of Labor to gather facts and figures.[3]

From its founding in 1881, the Federation of Organized Trades and Labor Unions, later reorganized as the AFL, joined the drive. At its first convention, the Federation urged the passage of an act establishing a national Bureau of Labor Statistics. The 1883 convention endorsed the creation of a Department of Industry and Statistics to collect "such facts as will tend to bring before the United States Congress each year the true condition of industry in all its departments."[4]

In Senate hearings on the relationship of capital and labor in 1883, union leaders testified in favor of a national Bureau of Labor Statistics. Samuel Gompers, chairman of the legislative committee of the Federation, felt that Congress should no longer be able to justify its inaction on labor matters by pleading ignorance of workers' conditions. A national Bureau "would give our legislators an opportunity to know, not from mere conjecture, but actually, the condition of our industries, our production, and our consumption, and what could be done by law to improve both [sic]." He cited the useful role of existing State statistical agencies as exemplified by a recent investigation of factory working conditions by the Massachusetts Bureau of Statistics of Labor under the direction of Carroll D. Wright.[5]

Wright appeared as an expert witness. He administered the Massachusetts Bureau, in his words, "as a scientific office, not as a Bureau of agitation or propaganda, but I always take the opportunity to make such recommendations and draw such conclusions from our investigations as the facts warrant." He stressed that the agency should be free of political influence. There was need for Federal "investigations into all conditions which affect the people, whether in a moral, sanitary, educational, or economic sense," thus adding "to the educational forces of the country a sure and efficient auxiliary." The resultant statistical progress of the Nation would indicate "its great progress in all other matters."[6]

In 1884, backed by the powerful Knights of Labor and the Federation, the establishment of a national Bureau was included in the platforms of both parties. In the same year, the House passed a bill establishing a Bureau of Labor, but in the Senate, Nelson W. Aldrich of Rhode Island secured an amendment putting the Bureau under the Department of the Interior. Attempts to ensure that the head of the agency would be identified with workers failed.

In the debate on the issue, Representative James H. Hopkins of Pennsylvania pointed out, "A great deal of public attention in and out of Congress has been given to the American hog and the American steer. I submit, Mr. Chairman, that it is time to give more attention to the American man."[7] Hopkins and Senators Henry W. Blair of New Hampshire and George F. Hoar of Massachusetts emphasized that the primary function of the new agency would be to collect information.

Southerners provided the main opposition. Senator Morgan of Alabama attacked "the disposition to pry into the affairs of the people" that had given rise to the desire to mount an "inquisition" on labor conditions.[8] Criticism was also forthcoming in editorials of *The New York Times*, which viewed the proposed new agency as "a fine bit of Congressional witlessness," arguing that the work could and should be done in some existing agency.[9]

Overwhelming majorities in both houses approved the establishment of the Bureau of Labor in the Department of the Interior, and the bill was signed by President Arthur on June 27. The statute provided for a Commissioner of Labor to be appointed by the President for a 4-year term, whose mission was to "collect information upon the subject of labor, its relation to capital, the hours of labor and the earnings of laboring men and women, and the means of promoting their material, social, intellectual and moral prosperity."

The new Bureau was a compromise arrangement, providing only factfinding authority and limited funds. Labor organizations had sought more; opponents had wanted less.

Appointing the first Commissioner

Activation of the new Bureau took an additional 6 months, however, as candidates for Commissioner presented themselves and others were offered. The process stirred considerable controversy, and the results set a permanent stamp on the Bureau.[10]

Initially, the candidates came from labor organizations. Terence V. Powderly, Grand Master Workman of the Knights of Labor, applied to Arthur for the position, arguing that the Knights were "the first and the only national organization" pressing for the Federal agency and the group primarily responsible for the establishment of the various State bureaus.[11] Through the Knights' *Journal of United Labor*, Powderly urged passage of resolutions supporting his candidacy. At a meeting with the President, he presented more than 1,500 petitions requesting his appointment.

Considering Powderly too controversial, Arthur looked for other candidates associated with labor. He turned to John Jarrett of the Iron and Steel Workers but dropped him because of the labor leader's political statements. Then he considered others, such as Miles S. Humphreys, a steel puddler who served in the Pennsylvania legislature and as Chief of the Pennsylvania Bureau of Statistics. Apparently the President even wrote nomination papers for John Fehrenbatch, former General Chief Engineer of the Brotherhood of Locomotive Engineers and, at the time, Supervising Inspector of Steamboats for the Ohio River District, only to withdraw his name because the Tenure of Office Act prohibited the holding of two Federal offices at one time.[12]

In the meantime, at its 1884 convention, the AFL passed a resolution to "respectfully but earnestly protest against the attitude assumed by President Chester A. Arthur in refusing to appoint a chief of the Labor Bureau of Statistics."[13]

The New York Times declared that the work "ought to be in the hands of some man of a judicial turn of mind who has no interest in the results to be shown other than that of presenting the absolute truth and such conclusions as spring naturally from the facts and figures."[14] The St. Louis *Globe Democrat* offered a more specific suggestion: "A Bureau of Labor Statistics which the new national institution would do well to take for a model has existed in Massachusetts for several years. . . . President Arthur, by the way, might have wisely put Colonel Wright in charge of the National Labor Bureau, with these inquiries in view on a broad scale."[15]

Wright's name had been presented to Arthur from several sources. One report to the President described Wright as "Chief of the Bureau of Labor Statistics. Not a labor man. Excellent statistician, but will not especially gratify Labor. Moderate Republican. No political aspirations."[16]

Finally, in January 1885, Arthur named Wright. *The New York Times* editorialized, "No better appointment could be made, and Mr. Wright's selection in the first place would have been much better than the attempt to win the favor of the labor organizations of the country by naming for the place someone prominently identified with them."[17]

Chapter II.

Carroll Wright: Setting the Course

Carroll D. Wright, the first Commissioner of the agency that came to be known as the Bureau of Labor Statistics, had little formal training or apparent inclination for labor statistics. Yet, by the turn of the century, he was the most widely known and respected social scientist in the Nation, and perhaps in the world. How did he come to play such a prominent role in his country's service? "Because," his biographer has responded, "to the confusion and misinformation surrounding labor reform, Wright brought high administrative ability, a nonpartisan interest in facts, and a humane idealism that dignified his character and work."[1]

Carroll Wright took office in January 1885 as head of the newly established Bureau of Labor. He was to lead the agency for the next 20 years. Over these years, government would play a more active role in social and economic affairs in response to the demands of labor, social reformers, and the growing Progressive movement, and the services of Wright's Bureau would be increasingly called upon. Although the Bureau would undergo several metamorphoses which reflected shifting political forces, Wright's leadership gave steady direction to its work in "conducting judicious investigations and the fearless publication of the results. . . ."

Wright was born in Dunbarton, New Hampshire, in 1840, the son of a Universalist parson and farmer. His early life gave no hint of his later career except for its heavy emphasis on religion and civic duty. Wright taught school while he studied at academies, and later read for the law. During the Civil War, at the age of 22, he enlisted in the New Hampshire Volunteers, making a distinguished record and receiving his commission as colonel in the fall of 1864. Ill health, which was to plague him periodically the rest of his life, cut short his service, and he returned to his old neighborhoods in Massachusetts and New Hampshire.

Wright established himself as a patent attorney in Boston with a residence in Reading, Massachusetts. He had a brief political career, winning a seat in the State Senate in 1871 and again in 1872, before declining renomination, as was the custom, in 1873. He sought nomination to Congress in 1874, 1876, and 1878, failing each time.

In the meantime, in 1873, Governor William B. Washburton appointed him Chief of the Massachusetts Bureau of Statistics of Labor, which, under earlier leadership, had become embroiled in controversy. Wright moved quickly to put the Bureau on a solid foundation of objectivity and impartiality, soon making an international reputation for himself and the agency.

As Chief, Wright investigated wages and prices, and supervised the Massachusetts Census of 1875 and the State section of the 1880 Federal Census. He also directed studies on such social problems as drunkenness, education of youth, and convict labor. He continued as head of the Massachusetts Bureau for 15 years, until 1888, a tenure which overlapped his Federal appointment for 3 years.

Self-trained, Wright pioneered in the development of the fields of economics and sociology in the United States. He contributed through statistical reports, papers, lectures, and new professional associations to the pragmatic approach to economic thinking, which had been limited to the narrower abstractions of classical economics. His optimistic view of human prospects made its mark on the direction of economic thought in the United States.[2]

Wright's views

A belief in the ability of man to study his situation and to devise ways to improve it put Wright in the forefront of the opposition to the prevailing doctrines of Social Darwinism. He has been linked to Lester Frank Ward, the great pioneer sociologist, in the "faith that mankind is intelligent enough, or may become so, to play a constructive part in the creation and organization of his social as well as of his physical environment."[3]

Wright expressed his ethical consciousness in a lecture delivered before the Lowell Institute in 1879 in which he attacked John Stuart Mill and others of the "old school" as urging, "Love thyself; seek thine own advantage; promote thine own welfare; put money in thy purse; the welfare of others is not thy business." In contrast, he spoke hopefully of the "new school" which sought "the amelioration of unfavorable industrial and social relations wherever found as the surest road to comparatively permanent material prosperity." The "new" would combine "with the old question the old school always asks, 'Will it pay?' another and higher query, 'Is it right?'" Wright would repeat this theme many times.[4]

Unrest in labor-management relations did not trouble Wright, who saw it as the basis of continuing improvement in the human condition. But it was the responsibility of government to provide information to educate those in the midst of the unrest. In the *Eighth Annual Report* of the Massachusetts Bureau (1877), Chief Wright explained, "Any means which the Legislature can adopt which will add to the information of the people on subjects which concern their daily lives are of untold value. . . . To popularize statistics, to put them before the masses in a way which shall attract, and yet not deceive, is a work every government which cares for its future stability should encourage and enlarge." In his 1886 presidential address to the American Social Science Association, he declared, "With the enlightenment of the workers of society, the reforms so much sought for will come as a natural consequence."[5]

Wright saw the benefits as well as the evils of the factory system. He praised the industrialist: "He is something more than a producer, he is an instrument of God for the upbuilding of the race."[6] At the same time he stated, "The evils of the factory system are sufficient to call out all the sentiments of justice and philanthropy which enable us to deal with wrong and oppression; all this I do not dispute, but I claim that, with all its faults and attendant evils, the factory system is a vast improvement upon the domestic system of industry in almost every respect."[7] He wrote, in *The Outline of Practical Sociology* in 1899, "Every material improvement by which society is permanently benefitted temporarily hurts somebody or disturbs some interest; every advance in civilization means the temporary discomfort, inconvenience, and loss, even, to some man or some set of men." The introduction of machines displaced some individuals; however, he argued, "Machines not only create new demands in old lines, they also create occupations that never existed prior to their introduction."[8] Thus, society as a whole benefitted.

In 1892, before the Buffalo Liberal Club, Wright declared, "In those countries where machinery has been developed to little or no purpose, poverty reigns, ignorance is the prevailing condition, and civilization consequently far in the rear." In "The Factory as an Element in Social Life," he stated, "The modern system of industry gives the skilled and intelligent workman an opportunity to rise in the scale of employment, in intellectual development, in educational acquirements, in the grade of services rendered, and hence in his social standing in his community."[9]

His views on the entry of women into the factory system were advanced for his time. Although initially he had felt that factory work would degrade women and disrupt the family, he later declared that the results of various investigations had caused him to change his mind. In one statement, he stressed the independence accruing to the working woman: "As woman has the power given her to support herself, she will be less inclined to seek marriage relations simply for the purpose of securing what may seem to be a home and protection. The necessity under which many young women live, of looking to marriage as a freedom from the bondage of some kinds of labor, tends, in my mind, to be the worst form of prostitution that exists. I cannot see much difference between a woman who sells her whole freedom and her soul to a man for life because he furnishes her with certain conveniences and one who sells her temporary freedom and her soul for a temporary remuneration, except this, that the former may be worse than the latter."[10]

He argued that working women had as high a moral standard "as any class in the community" and that "regular employment is conducive to regular living."[11]

In early expressions of his philosophy, Wright placed great faith in the power of the individual to bring about reforms. Increasingly, however, at a time of strong opposition to union organization and collective action, he supported both, although he did not accept all union demands. He threw out as "absurd" the claim on the part "of great employers that they can deal only with individual employees. . . ." Rather, "organizations must recognize organizations and the committees of the two must meet in friendly spirit for the purpose of fairly and honestly discussing the questions under consideration."[12] And he saw collective bargaining—"a new force comparatively, and one which expresses the most important principles of industrial management"—as the means for achieving what legislation or socialist revolution or unilateral trade union rules could not do to avoid strikes or satisfy strikers.[13]

While recognizing that strikes were sometimes necessary, Wright constantly urged the use of voluntary means to avoid or settle them. He favored mediation and conciliation but opposed compulsory arbitration, which he viewed as an indirect means of fixing wages and prices by law. Voluntary collective action, then, provided the "practical application of the moral principles of cooperative work."[14]

Wright did not believe, however, that resolution of the labor-management problem could be easily achieved. "The Bureau cannot solve the labor question, for it is not solvable; it has contributed and can contribute much in the way of general progress. The labor question, like the social problem, must be content to grow towards a higher condition along with the universal progress of education and broadened civilization. There is no panacea."[15]

Wright's frank expression of his views did not jeopardize his high standing with either labor or business interests. During his tenure as Commissioner in both Democratic and Republican administrations, and after his retirement, he was listened to with respect and was sought after as a commentator on the current scene.

Laying the foundation

After taking office in 1885, Wright moved quickly to establish professionalism and impartiality in the national Bureau, as he had in Massachusetts. He firmly spelled out the guidelines: Study all social and economic conditions; publish the results; and let the people, individually and collectively, assess the facts and act on them. Facts, not theories, were the foundation stones for constructive action. And facts were to be gained, according to Wright, "only by the most faithful application of the statistical method."[16]

Staff

He gathered a small force of investigators—capable, well-educated men and women who shared his views on the utility of public education for social reform. If, in the early years, some lacked formal training, as did Wright himself, others were fresh from European universities. The staff reflected Wright's broad interests and contacts with various academic, professional, and reform groups. Several went on to careers in other agencies or to academic pursuits, and some carried public administration into the territories gained during the national expansion of the 1890's.

Among these first staff members was Oren W. Weaver, who served as Chief Clerk from the Bureau's inception until his death in April 1900. Weaver had worked for Wright in Massachusetts, and Wright had recommended him for the post of Commissioner of the national Bureau. G.W.W. Hanger was Chief Clerk until 1913, when he left to become a member of the new Board of Mediation and Conciliation. Gustavus A. Weber, first a special agent and then head of the division of law and research work, went on to the Institute for Government Research, which was to become a part of The Brookings Institution. Other early staff members included William F. Willoughby and Elgin R.L. Gould. Willoughby, a graduate of Johns Hopkins, wrote extensively on foreign labor laws and U.S. factory legislation while at the Bureau, and later became Treasurer of Puerto Rico. Gould, who spent 5 years in Europe conducting several surveys for the Bureau, later played an important role in a number of political and social reform movements.

Wright also reached outside for assistance in special projects. Caroline L. Hunt conducted the fieldwork for a study of the Italians in Chicago, and Florence Kelley served as the expert in Chicago during an investigation of the slums of large cities.

At one time, John R. Commons also worked with Wright, on *Regulation and Restriction of Output* (XI Special Report, 1904). Commons later criticized Wright's method of leadership, writing that he had "developed the military organization of privates carrying out the detailed orders of their commander." The agents, he continued, "were remarkably accurate in copying figures and making calculations. . . . But they had no insight or understanding of what it was all about."[17]

But other contemporaries and associates of Wright evaluated his influence as broadly leavening in the developing social science field. Walter F. Willcox, in writing of the need to give practical assistance and experience to students of theoretical statistics, spotlighted "the group of young men who gathered around Carroll D. Wright" and complained that, after Wright's retirement, no agencies gave the "opportunity to get a training in statistics which would qualify one to rise to the most important statistical positions. . . ." And S.N.D. North declared of Wright, "His Bureau at Washington has been a university for the education of experts in statistics, in sociology, in economics, and in industrial studies."[18]

Conduct of studies

The principles underlying Wright's methods for the conduct of original studies were defined and applied early. These were: Firsthand data collection, voluntary reporting, and confidentiality of returns.

Wright explained his data collection methods: "The information under any investigation is usually collected on properly prepared schedules of inquiry in the hands of special agents, by which means only the information which pertains to an investigation is secured." The schedule would avoid the collection of "nebulous and rambling observations." Mail collection, though it might be used occasionally, was deemed a failure. "With properly instructed special agents, who secure exactly the information required, who are on the spot to make any explanation to parties from whom data are sought, and who can consult the books of accounts at the establishment under investigation, the best and most accurate information can be secured." The completed schedules were then scrutinized under strict supervision to ensure internal consistency. The final statistics were carefully checked and rechecked, as were the analytical results presented by the staff.[19]

Wright's British counterpart, Robert Giffen, head of the Bureau of Labour Statistics in the Board of Trade, sharply criticized Wright's methods, especially the use of field agents. Questioning the accuracy of their direct inquiries, Giffen declared in 1892, "I think I may say that there are no persons in the world whom I would trust with the kind of inquiries which some of the American agents make. . . ."[20]

Cooperation from businessmen was essential to the Bureau, since they were virtually the sole source of information on many subjects. Wright opposed making reporting mandatory to avoid the appearance of adversarial relations between the Bureau and business. And with voluntary reporting there were increasingly fewer refusals. Generally, agents were received in friendly fashion, even if information was refused, and substitutions were made for refusing establishments.

Cooperation was heightened by the businessman's knowledge that the Bureau maintained strict confidentiality regarding the identity of reporters. "The Bureau never allows the names of parties furnishing facts to be given in its reports," Wright assured respondents.[21]

Thus, in 1898, he wired a San Francisco businessman: "I pledge my word as a government officer that names of your plants and of city and State in which located shall be concealed. This will be done for all plants. If senator or representative should ask for these names, he should not have them."[22] E.R.L. Gould explained to the International Statistical Institute in 1891, "Impartiality, fair-dealing, and a respect for confidence bestowed have not only disarmed suspicion but engendered even willing cooperation."[23]

Wright's reputation for impartiality and objectivity gave him entree to the business community, through organizations such as the National Civic Federation and the National Association of Manufacturers. His contacts were helpful in the planning and conduct of studies. For example, in developing its studies of production costs, the Bureau sought the advice of producers in various industries.[24]

Similarly, his labor contacts helped smooth the way for the Bureau's investigators. When Wright found that unions did not always cooperate, Gompers urged cooperation. "Let there be light," Gompers wrote, "confident that impartial investigations create numberless sympathizers in our great cause."[25] Moreover, Gompers supported putting the census into the Bureau of Labor, advocated publication of a regular bulletin, and suggested topics for investigations.

Wright sought to expand the scope of the Bureau's coverage by joining forces with the State labor agencies. He was one of the founders of the National Association of Officials of the Bureaus of Labor Statistics and was its president throughout his term of office. He envisioned a nationwide network of collaborating State and Federal agents—" a powerful chain of investigators," he called it. He planned, he said in 1885, to ask Congress to authorize a system whereby the Federal Bureau could compensate State agencies for their assistance and to allow the Federal Bureau to place agents in States without bureaus.[26]

Although he had little success in carrying out joint studies with the States, the State bureaus drew increasingly on the Federal Bureau's experience, so that by 1900 the reports of work in progress in the States demonstrated a substantial degree of uniformity in inquiries covered.[27]

Achieving departmental status

While Wright was laying the foundation for his agency, forces were at work to expand its power and influence. The Knights of Labor under Terence Powderly had been active in the campaign to establish the Bureau. Early in 1886, Powderly asked President Cleveland to increase the powers of the Bureau and also to have the Commissioner investigate the railroad strike in the Southwest then in progress.[28] In April, Cleveland sent to Congress the first special message dealing with strictly labor matters, recommending that a mediation and arbitration commission be grafted onto the existing Bureau. Congress, however, adjourned without taking action.

Powderly persevered, and, at the Knights of Labor convention in October 1887, he urged establishment of a Department of Labor with its Secretary a member of the Cabinet. The next year, he scored a partial success. It was again a Presidential election year with labor difficulties on the southwestern railroads. In June 1888, Congress established a Department of Labor, independent but without Cabinet status. A separate statute, the Arbitration Act of 1888, authorized the Commissioner of Labor, with two ad hoc commissioners, to act as a board of inquiry in railroad disputes.

The growing reputation of the Bureau under Wright had contributed to its rise in status. Reflecting Wright's concerns, the act establishing the Department specifically called for studies of the domestic and foreign costs of producing goods, national trade and industrial activity, the causes and circumstances of strikes, and other special topics. The basic functions of the agency were not changed, but, for 15 years, it was to be more independent.

Any uncertainty regarding Wright's continuance in the new agency was soon dissipated. Although it was reported that the Knights of Labor and the Federation would oppose his retention because of his opposition to the Knights of Labor, his protectionist views, and his Republican associations, in fact, observers in the labor press commented favorably on Commissioner Wright, his staff, and the Bureau's endeavors.

The *National Labor Tribune* declared, "Inasmuch as Commissioner Wright conducted the Bureau with rare skill, energy, and impartiality and not as a politican, there does not seem to be any reason why there should be haste in changing."[29]

Powderly later wrote that President Cleveland had offered him the position but he had refused. At the time, however, in the *Journal of United Labor*, Powderly disclaimed all interest in the post of Commissioner. In fact, he declared that the campaign to boom him for the job was a conspiracy by his enemies to embarrass him and the Knights.[30]

Wright continued as Commissioner, now head of the Department of Labor. The Act of 1888 authorized 55 clerks and experts for the Department and substantially increased its appropriations. Until the early 1900's, Wright presided over the enlarged and independent operation largely without challenge.

A sister agency: Bureau of the Census

Wright took a prominent part in the establishment of a permanent Bureau of the Census in 1902. Until that time, each decennial census was conducted under temporary arrangements by a Superintendent of the Census appointed by the President. As early as 1884, during his service as Chief of the Massachusetts Bureau, Wright had testified before Congress on the benefits to be gained from the creation of a permanent census agency. Prominent academicians and Francis A. Walker, Superintendent of the 1870 and 1880 censuses, went beyond merely proposing a permanent agency; they proposed placing it in

Wright's Department for greater efficiency and to take it out of the political arena.[31]

Although there was support for a permanent agency, the 1890 census was still conducted under a temporary arrangement. But the impetus for a permanent agency increased in 1890, and the Secretary of the Interior recommended establishment of a permanent census office. In 1891, the Senate called for a report from the Secretary, and, in response, Robert P. Porter, then Superintendent of the Census, also suggested formation of a permanent agency. In his report, Porter included a letter from Wright supporting the idea.[32]

Widespread dissatisfaction with the conduct of the 1890 census, with especially sharp controversy in New York City, focused attention on the shortcomings of the periodic temporary arrangements. The immediate unhappiness was dissipated when, with the change of administrations and the resignation of Porter, Cleveland appointed Wright as Superintendent of the Census, a post he held concurrently with his leadership of the Department of Labor from 1893 until 1897.[33] Years later, in a eulogy on Wright, S.N.D. North, first head of the permanent Bureau of the Census in the Department of Commerce and Labor, stated that Cleveland appointed Wright "because no other available man was so conspicuously fitted" for the task.[34]

Calls for legislation continued. In 1892, the House Select Committee on the Eleventh Census held hearings on Porter's report and, in 1893, recommended a permanent Census Bureau, but Congress took no action.[35]

Two years later, the International Statistical Institute suggested studying ways to conduct a uniform worldwide census at the end of the century, and, in 1896, Congress directed Wright to correspond with various experts on the International Institute's suggestion and to report on the best organization for the upcoming 1900 canvass. Wright submitted his report with a draft of a bill providing for an independent office. He opposed putting the work in the Department of the Interior because the Secretary changed with each administration and appointments were subject to political pressures. In his view, the proposed office could include the activities of the Division of Statistics in the Department of Agriculture and of his Department of Labor, but he opposed such a transfer. When pressed on the question, he responded, "Personally, I should dislike very much to be put in charge of census duties." But he did admit that, from an administrative point of view, "the work of the Department of Labor and that of the Census Office could be carried along together."[36]

Bills were introduced, one drawn by Wright for an independent agency and one to place census work in the Wright-led Department of Labor. The House Committee on Appropriations, in February 1897, favorably reported the bill putting the work in the Labor Department, characterizing that agency as "admirably equipped for statistical work."[37] However, Congress took no action that session.

During the next session, Senator Henry M. Teller of Colorado commented, "The Census Office ought to be a bureau under some Department, and the Department of Labor is the proper place for this work." Then he offered an amendment putting the work in the Department of Labor, "out of which ought to grow in that Department a statistical force, and that Department ought to become the statistical department of this Government."[38]

Senator Henry C. Lodge of Massachusetts stated that he preferred that the Census Office be separate and independent but, "if it is to go anywhere," the Department of Labor was the natural choice. He opposed "jumbling it, with public lands, Indians, Pacific railroads, and every other kind of thing, into a department already absolutely heterogeneous and overloaded."[39]

Senator William B. Allison of Iowa favored putting the work in Interior. He pointed out that the Secretary of the Interior was a Cabinet officer. Moreover, in his view, it would not be fair to the Department of Labor as it would interfere with the work of that agency and the Department officials did not want the new work.[40]

Some Senators opposed the idea of a permanent Census Bureau as an extravagance.

In a compromise, in 1899, a Census Bureau was attached to the Department of the Interior specifically to conduct the 1900 census. In 1902, a permanent Census Bureau was formed and, a year later, transferred to the new Department of Commerce and Labor.[41]

In regard to Wright's statement that, "Personally, I should dislike very much to be put in charge of census duties," there is little but inference from surrounding events to explain his view. It may have been that, in serving 4 years as Superintendent of the Census while he was also Commissioner of Labor, he had had his fill of the administrative burdens and political pressures such a position would bring.

The Department of Commerce and Labor

The depression conditions of the 1890's led business interests to advocate a Cabinet-level department to further the growth of industry and foreign and domestic commerce. The National Association of Manufacturers, organized in 1895, had as a principal goal the formation of a Department of Commerce and Industry which would include the hitherto independent Department of Labor along with other agencies.[42] To counter the growing NAM drive, Gompers proposed a Cabinet-level Department of Labor for "a direct representative in the councils of the President."[43]

Congress also launched an initiative, creating the U.S. Industrial Commission in 1898 to investigate the Nation's many social and economic problems, including the growing role of corporate trusts, rising labor unrest bordering on class warfare, agricultural discontent, the vast influx of immigrants, and intensified competition in foreign markets. The commission reported in 1901 but produced little of significance.

The succession to the Presidency of Theodore Roosevelt in September 1901 brought into office an energetic and innovative leader who was prepared to meet the problems of the day through increased governmental activity. He sought to bridge the contending positions of business and labor, and in 1901, in his first State of the Union message, he recommended the creation of a Department of Commerce and Labor with power to investigate corporate earnings and to guard the rights of the workingman.

Roosevelt's enthusiasm for such a department, along with his party's control of Congress, made the matter a foregone conclusion, but the Democratic minority fought hard. Proponents of the bill, including Senator Marcus A. Hanna of Ohio, prominent in the National Civic Federation, saw no conflict between the interests of capital and labor and insisted that the concerns of labor would be well represented in such a department. All sides in the congressional debate praised Wright, and proponents urged that his role and that of his agency would only gain if transferred to the new department. The AFL and the unaffiliated railroad unions opposed the merger and supported instead the establishment of a Cabinet-level Department of Labor. Among labor groups, only the almost defunct Knights of Labor favored the merger.[44]

At the 1901 AFL convention, Gompers had argued that, on many questions of national importance, the Cabinet was deprived of labor representation and had to act without receiving advice on the workers' viewpoint. In January 1902, he wrote Senator William P. Frye of Maine, the President pro tempore of the Senate, that the proposed dual department would "minimize the importance of labor's interests and minimize the present Department of Labor. Against such a procedure, in the name of American labor, I enter my most solemn protest."[45]

At hearings on the bill, Thomas F. Tracy, an AFL representative, did not oppose a Department of Commerce but asked for a separate Department of Labor. H.R. Fuller, of the railroad brotherhoods, declared that a businessman "is not capable to speak for labor, even though he felt honestly disposed to do so." Andrew Furuseth, of the Seamen's Union, stated that the value of the existing department lay "in the absolute reliability of the information it furnishes. We do not believe it could remain that under the condition that is proposed."[46]

But the Federation and the brotherhoods did not give Wright and the Department of Labor their unqualified approval. Tracy expressed some reservations. "While they are not all that we would desire, while the Department is limited to a great extent and we would like to see the scope of the Department enlarged, the statistics and reports that are gathered in the Department of Labor are very beneficial and are very useful to the members of organized labor and are looked at very carefully and closely on many occasions."[47]

At these same hearings, businessmen presented their reasons for establishing a Department of Commerce. Theodore C. Search, of the National Association of Manufacturers, said the role of the agency would be "to assist in every feasible way in the extension of the export trade of our manufacturers." L.W. Noyes explained, "I can conceive of no other permanent and sure relief to this constantly recurring danger [depression] than the cultivation, establishment, and maintenance of foreign markets for our surplus, and labor will profit more by this department, through this means, than any other class of individuals."[48]

In the congressional debates, it was argued that the proposed organization would promote a more harmonious administration that would make for greater efficiency and service. Further, the new arrangement would provide increased facilities for the Commissioner of Labor. Indeed, the House report contended, under the new setup the Bureau would increase the scope of its activities and be more worthy of elevation to Cabinet status.

Southern Democrats constituted the major opposition. Their main point was that business and labor interests "naturally conflict. One wants what he can get, and the other wants to keep what he has, and, consequently, the two will always be in natural conflict." Further, the proposed grouping would place the labor agency "in an overshadowed and subordinate position." The minority on the House Committee reported that they feared "that distrust and suspicion will result in friction or create such relations as would seriously impair the usefulness and efficiency of the Department."[49]

Senator Hanna retorted that it would be unwise to recognize separate interests, "to divide this industrial question by raising the issue that one part of it is labor and the other part capital. Those interests are identical and mutual." Similar views were expressed in the House.[50]

The position of Wright and the Department on the legislation is difficult to determine. Senator Nelson stated his opinion that the opposition to the bill was "inspired from the inside of the Department of Labor." Yet Senator Lodge stated that, while he had not recently asked Wright, "I have certainly understood in the past that he favored that scheme." During the debate, Wright himself wrote, "I have declined to give any expression upon the proposed bill creating a Department of Commerce and Labor. This is in accordance with my long-continued practice of not making public statements relative to pending legislation, especially when that legislation bears upon this Department."[51]

The controversy was partially resolved by changing the agency's name to the Department of Commerce and Labor. President Roosevelt signed the bill on February 14, 1903, and named George B. Cortelyou the first Secretary. The Department of Labor became once more the Bureau of Labor, 1 of 18 agencies in the new Department. In 1904, it accounted for only 100 of the Department's 9,210 employees and about 1.5 percent of its appropriations.[52]

In his message to Congress in December 1904, Roosevelt reaffirmed the role of the Bureau of Labor in the new Department of Commerce and Labor, giving official recognition and praise to the developmental work of the Bureau under Carroll Wright. Further,

Roosevelt in effect proposed a quasi-policy status for the Bureau's ongoing factual studies, requesting that the Bureau provide Congress with information on the labor laws of the various States and be given "the means to investigate and report to the Congress upon the labor conditions in the manufacturing and mining regions throughout the country, both as to wages, as to hours of labor, as to the labor of women and children, and as to the effect in the various labor centers of immigration from abroad."[53]

This description of the scope of the Bureau's responsibilities coincided with Wright's formulation. Under the broad statutory authority, Wright held, "The Commissioner can undertake any investigation which in his judgment relates to the welfare of the working people of the country, and which can be carried out with the means and force at his disposal."[54] And in practice, Wright and the Bureau initiated most of the studies that were undertaken, although customarily the Commissioner sought either congressional or, later, departmental approval. But increasingly, there were demands from Congress, the White House, and, later, from social reform groups for specific studies even as the broad social studies of the early years continued.

The Bureau's work

During the 20 years of Wright's direction, the Bureau's investigations ranged widely over economic and social developments in the United States and also, for comparative purposes, in other industrial nations. Initially, studies were broadly conceived and directed at social issues such as marriage and divorce, temperance, and laboring women and children, but, with periodic economic depressions and a growing industrial labor force, the Bureau was called upon increasingly to deal with more strictly economic issues such as wages, hours of work, prices, and the cost of living. In addition, with the growth of unions and formal collective bargaining arrangements, the Bureau's reports and articles increasingly reflected these developments.

The Bureau's studies placed Wright and the agency in the forefront of the movement to develop quantitative methods for studying social and economic problems. Statistical concepts and techniques were developed and refined, although they remained rough hewn, reflecting the early stage of development of statistical methods.

The Bureau produced an impressive range and volume of studies considering the limited resources available. Publications during Wright's tenure included 20 annual reports, 12 special reports, several miscellaneous reports, and, for 9 years, the bimonthly *Bulletin*. But the failure of appropriations to keep pace with the demands on the agency posed a number of administrative problems, and Wright had to drop work he might otherwise have continued. While appropriations rose every year from 1885 to 1893, they did not approach the level of

Table 1. Appropriations for Bureau of Labor, 1885–1905
(in thousands)

Fiscal year ended June 30 —	Total[1]	Salaries
1885	$25	$25
1886	40	25
1887	96	53
1888	114	53
1889	139	85
1890	144	85
1891	150	86
1892	170	101
1893	192	101
1894	159	101
1895	170	101
1896	166	101
1897	172	101
1898	180	103
1899	173	103
1900	173	103
1901	177	103
1902	178	103
1903	184	106
1904	184	106
1905	184	106

[1]Includes salaries, per diem, rent, library, contingencies, and special and deficiency appropriations, but not allocations for printing and binding.

SOURCES: National Archives Record Group 257, Bureau of Labor Statistics, Appropriations Ledger, 1887–1903. Legislative, Executive, and Judicial Appropriations.

1893 during the rest of his term. Table 1 shows the annual funding by fiscal year during Wright's tenure.

In 1892, Wright could say that Congress "has been very liberal." The Department, he continued, "has met with the most generous confidence on the part of Congress and of the President and been aided in all reasonable ways in bringing its work to a high standard of excellence."[55] By 1896, however, congressional demands had grown beyond the Bureau's resources and Wright asked for more funds, declaring, "I am now struggling under two investigations Congress has ordered, and to carry out the third one, which Congress has already ordered, I have not force enough." Little improvement had occurred by 1902, when Wright testified, "I have not asked for any increase of special agents since the office was established, and I may say further that there has been no increase in the salary appropriations since 1892. It was then $101,000, and it is now $102,000. That is the only increase in 10 years in the salary list of my Department."[56]

The first report: Industrial Depressions
The Bureau's first annual report (1886) was on industrial depressions. The study originated in concern over the depressed conditions of the mid-1880's and the accompanying labor unrest, particularly in the railroad industry. The report surveyed depressions from 1830 on, covering the United States, Great Britain, France, Belgium, and Germany through information obtained directly by 20 Bureau agents in the United States and Europe. Workers' wages and living costs in the foreign industrialized countries were included. The ongoing depression was analyzed in terms of "alleged causes," and a catalog of "suggested remedies" was presented. Among the remedies, Wright suggested that capital and labor "treat with the other through representatives" in disputes, and that "the party which declines resort to conciliatory methods of arbitration [is] morally responsible for all effects growing out of the contest." The report noted the advantages of mechanization, although asserting that in the short run the displacement of labor contributed to "crippling the consuming power of the community."[57]

The study was a test case, as Wright later described it, conducted under the "critical watchfulness of friend and foe, and with the idea prevailing among labor organizations that the duty of the new office was in the nature of propagandism, and not of the educational func-

tions of gathering and publishing facts." Wright pointed to the successful conclusion and acceptance of the report. He saw it as
innovative in bringing out for "the first time, the relation of nations to
each other as producers and the various influences bearing upon
discontent."[58]

Gompers cited figures from the report at the 1887 AFL convention, referring to "one of the most important facts with which the
labor movement has to grapple. The displacement of labor by machinery in the past few years has exceeded that of any like period in our
history."[59]

A leading contemporary economist found in this first report "a
mass of information of very considerable value," while noting two
mild criticisms: The subject was too broad and diverse and the statistics were not sufficiently analyzed.[60]

In his conclusions, Wright emphasized overproduction/under-
consumption and speculative investment. Later, such students of the
business cycle as Alvin H. Hansen praised Wright's comments on the
relation between investment—notably in canals and railroads—and
business fluctuations. Hansen referred to Wright's "penetrating
insight into the changing character of modern industry."[61]

The persistent depression of the early 1890's gave rise to another
important Bureau study, which looked into whether machines were
depressing wages and causing widespread unemployment. In 1894, a
joint resolution of Congress called on the Commissioner to investigate
the effect of machinery on costs of production, productivity, wages,
and employment, including comparisons with manual labor. The
study took almost 4 years of difficult work. Agents observed current
machine methods for an article's production and then, with greater
difficulty, attempted to secure information on the "hand" production
of the same article. The report provided information on the production time required and the total costs under the two methods.

In carefully qualified conclusions, Wright suggested the benefits
contributed by the introduction of machinery to rising wages and
broadened employment opportunities. "The general tendency of
wages since the introduction of power machinery and the employment of women and children in its operation has been upward, but it
will be difficult to decide positively whether such increase is due
absolutely to the use of machinery, or to a higher standard of living, or
to the increased productivity of labor supplemented by machinery, or

to all these causes combined, or to other causes." He found further that "there has been a larger increase in the number of persons required for the production of the articles considered, in order to meet present demands, than would have been necessary to meet the limited demands under the hand-labor system."[62]

Strike investigations and industrial relations studies
Turbulence on the railroads, an industry crucial to the economic development of the country, led to both congressional and Bureau investigations. For an early Bureau study, *Strikes and Lockouts* (1887), Bureau agents collected information on the Missouri and Wabash strike of 1885 and the Southwest strike of 1886, and Wright offered the material to the congressional committee investigating the disturbances. Later, Wright devoted an entire annual report to railway labor, the first U.S. study to deal with labor turnover.[63]

Further studies on strikes and lockouts were published in 1894 and 1901, presenting exhaustive treatments of strikes during the 19th century. The 1887 and 1894 reports included estimates of the losses to management and labor because of lost worktime. A union periodical expressed the criticism in 1895 that "statistics of losses sustained through strikes by labor are carefully noted, but no estimates are given of the gains made by labor," and called on the Commissioner of Labor to "so far forget himself as to do a little statistical work from an employee's rather than employer's standpoint."[64]

The 1901 report contained additional information, including results of strikes ordered by unions as against those not so ordered. This time, the same union periodical welcomed the report for showing that "the United States Government says that only 36.19 percent of all strikes in 20 years failed, and that most of the wages lost in strikes is subsequently made up by extra work, and that with the increase in labor unions, has come an increase in successful strikes."[65]

In 1904, with President Roosevelt's encouragement, Wright investigated violence in Colorado mining areas. Drawn-out labor disturbances had caused the governor to call out the State militia, and the Western Federation of Miners demanded Federal intervention. Wright's lengthy report covered some 25 years and 13 strikes in the region and contained an account of the violations of civil law and constitutional rights of the State's striking miners.[66]

The Bureau studied many other aspects of industrial relations in addition to the causes and effects of strikes. From the mid-1890's on, it published extensively on new developments in collective bargaining and State and foreign social legislation and practices such as accident prevention; workmen's compensation; insurance against sickness, accidents, old age, and invalidity; and union welfare and benefit plans.

One of the most innovative studies was the special report, *Regulation and Restriction of Output*, published in 1904. Conducted under the direction of John R. Commons, the study covered union management relations in the United States and England, particularly in the building trades and in the iron and steel, cigar, boot and shoe, and coal industries. It discussed both employers' objectives of stable conditions, fair prices, and fair wages, and workers' efforts, working through unions, to improve wages, working conditions, and skills. It pointed out the restrictive practices of employers, unions, and nonunion workers.[67]

Wright's role in dispute settlement

On several occasions, Wright was called upon in his capacity as Commissioner of Labor to participate in the settlement of disputes. The railroad strikes of the 1880's had led to passage of the Arbitration Act of 1888. In addition to providing for voluntary arbitration, it empowered the President to establish committees of three, with the Commissioner of Labor as Chairman, to investigate disputes threatening interstate commerce, make recommendations, and publish a report. In 1894, President Cleveland appointed Wright to the investigating commission on the Pullman strike, and its reports and recommendations bore the imprint of Wright's growing awareness of the importance of labor organizations in balancing employer domination to achieve stability and continuity through agreement.

The strike began in May 1894, when the recently organized workers at the Pullman factory near Chicago walked out, primarily because town officials insisted on maintaining rent levels on the company-owned homes despite wage reductions and layoffs following the depression of 1893. The American Railway Union led by Eugene V. Debs, which had advised against the strike, sought arbitration. When Pullman refused, the union voted to boycott Pullman sleeping cars. The general managers of the railroads retaliated by importing strikebreakers. Management also began to attach mail cars to the sleepers so that refusal to service the Pullmans would constitute interference with the mails. The managers thus painted the strike as a fight between anarchy and law and sought Federal Government intervention.

President Cleveland and Attorney General Richard Olney obtained an injunction against the strikers, and regular troops were sent in to enforce it. In July, after the strike was broken, the President invoked the Arbitration Act of 1888 and appointed an investigating commission consisting of Wright, John D. Kernan of New York, and Nicholas E. Worthington of Illinois. The commission took extensive testimony in Chicago and Washington before reporting in November.[68]

Samuel Gompers, along with Debs and others, appeared before the commission. Gompers stated his views on strikes when Wright asked him whether sympathetic strike action, such as that in the Pullman strike, was justifiable when it could "paralyze, to any degree, the commercial industry of the country." Gompers replied, "I believe that labor has the right. . . to endeavor to improve its condition. . . . If industry or commerce is incidentally injured, it is not their fault; the better course and the most reasonable course would be for employers to grant the reasonable requests labor usually makes and thus avert the disaster of commerce or industry that you have mentioned." The social losses of widespread unemployment, both persistent and intermittent, were greater than disadvantages from strikes, he insisted, citing Wright's earlier reports. He opposed legislation for arbitration, fearing it would lead to compulsory arbitration, with labor at a disadvantage.[69]

In its recommendations, the Wright-chaired commission cited the quasi-public nature of railroad corporations as permitting the exercise of congressional authority over strikes. It urged employers to recognize unions, stressing that their interests were reciprocal, though not identical. It proposed a permanent commission to investigate and make recommendations in disputes having a major impact on the public, with enforcement by the courts. And it advised that "yellow dog" contracts be outlawed.[70]

Gompers praised the commission's report as trailblazing in an era of employer opposition to union organization, although he implicitly disagreed about special legislation for mediation and arbitration in the railroad industry, which the railroad unions supported. He wrote, "Whatever may be the ultimate result of United States interference between the railroad managers and the road laborers of this country, we have confidence that none today will refuse to bestow a generous meed of praise on Carroll D. Wright and his companion commissioners for their lucid and conscientious report on the Chicago strike of 1894."[71]

The commission's recommendations became the basis for legislation dealing with railroad disputes that had a major impact on the public. Wright helped draft and publicly supported the pertinent bills under congressional consideration between 1895 and 1898.[72] Addressing the charge that the proposed measures contemplated compulsory arbitration, he pointed out that they sought, first, conciliation or mediation. Only if these failed to bring about agreement was there provision for seeking a board of arbitration, with the award final only "if the parties coming before it agree it shall be."[73]

In the congressional debates in 1897, Representative Constantine Erdman introduced a letter from Wright stating, "Instead of contemplating involuntary servitude, the bill, it seems to me, places labor and capital on an equality as to the enforcement of contracts." Citing protections against yellow dog contracts and blacklists, Wright explained, "Practically, this is a bill of rights that the workingman, so far as railways are concerned, can not claim at present."[74] But Wright did not leave any illusions about this being a panacea: "The bill, should it become a law, will not solve any phase of the labor problem, nor prevent strikes entirely, but it will do much to steady the forces involved and afford a powerful and even effective balance wheel in interstate controversies."[75]

The resulting Erdman Act of 1898 revised the 1888 statute by providing for voluntary arbitration and establishing a board of mediation and conciliation composed of the Commissioner of Labor and the Chairman of the Interstate Commerce Commission. Operations of the board were limited since it could function only on the request of the parties, nor did the act include provisions for investigatory committees as found in the earlier act. Yellow dog contracts were prohibited, a provision later voided by the Supreme Court. The arbitration provisions of the act were never utilized, but the board of mediation was called upon later; Wright's successor, Charles P. Neill, was very actively engaged.

Wright also figured prominently in the anthracite coal strike of 1902, in which he emerged as Roosevelt's labor adviser. Roosevelt's handling of this strike contrasted with Cleveland's actions in the Pullman strike, introducing the Roosevelt policies of seeking to reduce the impact of strikes, of recognizing the right of unions to organize, and of urging the public airing of issues. Wright and Gompers helped to ensure impartiality on the part of the Federal Government in the investigation of the strike, the dispute-resolving machinery, and the findings and recommendations.

The miners had walked out in May when the operators refused to negotiate a new contract. Wright acted as intermediary between Roosevelt and Gompers in discussions of means of settling the strike. In June, Roosevelt directed Wright to investigate the situation, and the Commissioner prepared a report and recommendations for settling the dispute. Although pleased to have the factfinding report, the Mine Workers criticized Wright for not visiting the fields and attacked some of his suggestions. The strike dragged on into the fall.[76]

Frustrated and running out of patience, Roosevelt called the parties to meet with him. Subsequently, with the miners willing to accept arbitration, Roosevelt prevailed on the mine operators to cooperate, and he appointed a commission. Wright acted initially as recorder, later as a member of the commission and as umpire in the continuing conciliation process. His earlier recommendations were apparent in the commission's report settling the strike.

Roosevelt's appointment of Wright to explore the anthracite dispute was welcomed, with one expression that: "No man in this country—and probably there is no man living—has more persistently and intelligently applied himself to the study of labor problems and their remedy than has Colonel Wright." Later, however, as permanent umpire of disputes under the board of conciliation established by the commission's award, he was criticized by the United Mine Workers and Gompers for unfavorable awards.[77]

Studies on working women and children

Wright's early and continuing concern about the impact of changing industrial developments on the family, and particularly on the employment of women and children, was reflected in a series of landmark studies. He had conducted the survey *Working Girls in Boston* in 1884, before leaving Massachusetts. In 1888, the new national Bureau issued *Working Women in Large Cities*, which covered 17,000 "shop girls" engaged in light manual or mechanical work in factories and stores, representing about 7 percent of such employment in 22 cities.

Notably, the survey was conducted in large measure by women agents of the Department, evidence also of the changing role of women. Of these agents, Wright's report said, "The result of the work of the agents must bear testimony to the efficiency of the women employed by the Department, and to the fact that they are capable of taking up difficult and laborious work. They have stood on an equality in all respects with the male force of the Department, and have been compensated equally with them."[78]

The study reported on the wages, expenditures, health, moral standards, work environment, family backgrounds, and marital status of the women. Commenting on the new opportunities and earnings of women, Wright observed, "A generation ago women were allowed to enter but few occupations. Now there are hundreds of vocations in which they can find employment. The present report names 343 industries in which they have been found actively engaged. . . . By the progress or change in industrial conditions, the limit to the employment of women has been removed or at least greatly extended, and their opportunities for earning wages correspondingly increased and the wages themselves greatly enhanced. . . ." He noted, however, that women were willing to work for lower wages than men.[79]

Depression conditions in the 1890's raised the question of whether women and children were replacing men, and Wright received congressional authorization for a study of industrial establishments. In pointing out the need for the study, he noted the doubling of the number of women in gainful employment since the 1870 census and the "serious economical and ethical question as to the reasons for such a vast increase."[80]

The scope of the 1895-96 survey was characterized as covering "specifically the employment and wages of women and children in comparison with the employment of men in like occupations, how far women and children are superseding men, and the relative efficiency of men, women, and children when employed in doing like work." Agents visited over a thousand establishments, mainly in manufacturing industries, in 30 States. Current data were collected for almost 150,000 men and women employed during the survey period, while information for some week at least 10 years earlier was collected for 100,000 workers. The published tables provided information on the occupations, hours worked, and comparative earnings of men, women, and children of "the same grade of efficiency," and the reasons usually given for the employment of women and girls. The data confirmed the continued rapid increase of women in manufacturing employment. Comparisons of average earnings of men, women, and children in the same occupation and grade of efficiency showed that men earned over 50 percent more than women, and that children earned substantially less than adult workers.

One academician criticized the report, arguing that its emphasis on manufacturing created a downward bias in reflecting the employment of women and girls, since the vast majority were employed in nonmanufacturing industries. Such coverage, the sociologist contended, would have shown a much greater increase in the employment of women and girls.[81]

In the early years of the new century, Wright directed another of the landmark studies on the employment of children, *Child Labor in the United States* (Bulletin 52, 1904). Hannah R. Sewall and Edith Parsons investigated conditions for children under 16 years of age through visits with employers, parents, and youth.

Wright also gave considerable attention to the training of youth. He explained the growing need: "Training in trade schools in the United States is intended to supply the place of the old-time apprenticeship, which has nearly disappeared under the conditions of present-day industry." He had studied vocational education back in Massachusetts and, in fact, participated in surveys there after leaving the Bureau. While he was Commissioner, two of the Bureau's annual reports focused on industrial schools.[82]

Urban and ethnic studies

Several Bureau studies reported on problems of the burgeoning urban centers. One of these was conducted during the depression of the early 1890's, when Congress directed the Bureau to study the slums of the major cities. Wright noted the reasons for the study: "The popular idea is that the slums of cities are populated almost entirely by foreigners, and by foreigners of a class not desirable as industrial factors and who do not assimilate with our people." He added, "The alleged tendency of colored people to crowd into cities becomes a part of this wide subject and emphasizes the necessity of the investigation."[83] In 1894, the Bureau issued *The Slums of Baltimore, Chicago, New York, and Philadelphia*, which gave figures on nativity, illiteracy, occupations, earnings, and health and presented information on liquor, saloons, and arrests.

On the liquor issue, Wright had stated earlier, "You cannot discuss the labor question from either the ethical or economical side without consideration of the temperance question."[84] He was a member of the "Committee of Fifty," a group of prominent citizens headed by Seth Low studying the liquor problem, and planned a major Bureau study to supplement the committee's work. In 1897, the Bureau's *Economic Aspects of the Liquor Problem* reported on production and consumption, traffic, revenues, and the practices of employers in the liquor industry.

In *The Housing of the Working People* (1895), the Bureau presented data on sanitary laws, building regulations, public intervention, and model buildings in the United States and Europe. The role of building and loan associations, cooperative methods for saving, and home financing available to wage earners also were subjects of Bureau studies.

In the late 1890's, Wright turned his attention to other municipal problems. One report dealt with public ownership of public utilities, which was favored by reformers. The report, Wright stated, was intended to provide clarification, not "material for local contention." In 1899, at the direction of Congress, the Bureau began the annual series, "Statistics of Cities," which surveyed conditions in cities with a population of at least 30,000. This work occupied a disproportionate amount of the Bureau's time, and, when the Bureau of the Census was established, Wright succeeded in having the work transferred. Even so, Wright claimed a constructive influence for the data. "The annual publication of these statistics. . . has stimulated many cities to reform their methods of accounting, and this. . . has already had most beneficial results."[85]

Ethnic studies of the condition of Negroes and of newly arrived immigrant groups were among Wright's important contributions. Wright's interest in the status of Negroes under the conditions of Reconstruction and migration to the cities had been evident in his study of Negroes as part of the Massachusetts Census of 1875. He had sought to conduct a major study of Negro labor when the Bureau was established, but had failed to receive authorization.[86] However, in the late 1890's, he provided assistance for and published a number of regional studies of the condition of blacks in cities and agricultural areas. W.E.B. Du Bois was notable among the black sociologists conducting the studies, contributing three of the nine articles published in the Bureau's *Bulletin* between 1897 and 1903.

In 1901, when Representative Leonidas F. Livingston of Georgia introduced a bill appropriating funds for Negro studies in the Department, Wright explained that he certainly had no objections and that, in fact, the Bureau had been conducting such work for several years: "Professor Du Bois, whom I presume you know, has done excellent work along this line, and I hope to be able to continue him."[87] However, after the relocation of the Bureau to the new Department of Commerce and Labor, Wright noted obstacles. In August 1903, he wrote Du Bois, "I do not believe it will be possible for us in the near future to take up the question of the Lowndes County Negroes. This is a financial question with us at the present time." [88]

Apparently Wright finally found a means of funding a major study of Negroes after he left office. He headed the Department of Economics and Sociology at the newly formed Carnegie Institution which, in 1906, added a division called The Negro in Slavery and Freedom.[89]

About the time Wright launched the black studies in the Bureau, he also directed investigations of the Italian community. The 1890's had witnessed an increased influx of Italians into the cities and also a rise in violence, to an extent set off by "native" fear of the so-called "mafia." In fact, the whole issue of immigration and importation of contract labor continued to arouse considerable passion.[90] *The Italians in Chicago: A Social and Economic Study* (1897), based on materials collected by Caroline L. Hunt under Wright's supervision, presented the general economic conditions of the Italian community. It also provided data on literacy, nativity, diet, size of family, weekly earnings, and unemployment and gave some comparisons with the earlier study of slum conditions. An 1897 *Bulletin* article, "The Padrone System and Padrone Banks," also dealt with the Italian community.

Many of the subjects of these early Bureau studies were later to come under the jurisdiction of other government agencies. The Census Bureau took up the statistics of cities; savings and loan associations came under the Bureau of Corporations in the new Department of Commerce and Labor; and women and children were to be represented by their own agencies in the Cabinet-level Department of Labor before too long.

Tariff studies and price and wage statistics

The enactment of the McKinley tariff in 1890 gave rise to several Bureau studies and stimulated groundbreaking work in the development of statistical methods and data on wages, prices, and the cost of living. In 1891, to determine the effect of the new tariff law, the Senate Committee on Finance, headed by Nelson W. Aldrich of Rhode Island, called on Wright to collect data on prices, wages, and hours of work, and hired Roland P. Falkner of the University of Pennsylvania to analyze the material. There was the "constant demand from legislators and economic students for reliable statistics in regard to the course of prices and wages in the United States," for, the committee report stated, "Without them it has been impossible to judge even with approximate accuracy of the progress of the people of the country and the changes which have taken place from time to time in their condition."[91]

Wright's activities had already anticipated the need. The Act of 1888 elevating the Bureau to departmental status had specifically called for studies of "the cost of producing articles at the time dutiable in the United States" and "the effect of the customs laws." [92] Bureau studies of the cost of production in the iron and steel, coal, textile, and glass industries in the United States and abroad were already well underway. Along with wage data for workers in these industries, cost-of-living and budget information was collected. The term "cost of living" referred to family expenditures, and thus the study sought to reflect the standard of living supported by the actual levels of family income. In all, 8,544 families were covered. Of these, 2,562 were viewed as "normal" families, defined as families consisting of a husband and wife, up to five children under the age of 15, and without other dependents or boarders.

Two reports prepared by the Bureau for the Aldrich Committee became landmark sources of data on prices and wages. Some wholesale price data were assembled for the preceding half century; for the 28 months preceding September 1891, prices were collected for 218 articles in 7 cities. Retail price collection was limited to the 28-month period, covering 215 commodities, including 67 food items, in 70 localities. Wage data were also assembled for the preceding half century in 22 industries; for the 28-month period, the data covered 20 general occupations in 70 localities and specialized occupations in 32 localities.

Falkner's methodological innovations related to weighting and indexing the price and wage data. Indexing techniques, although known, had not been used to any extent in analyzing economic phenomena. To weight the wholesale and retail price indexes, Falkner used the family expenditure patterns developed in the Bureau's cost of production studies, supplemented by additional budgets developed for the Senate committee. The wage indexes, however, were based on unweighted data.[93]

The academic community was generally pleased with the recognition accorded professional statistical and economic analysis by the Aldrich Committee, although some found fault with Falkner's methods. The *Quarterly Journal of Economics* referred to the wholesale price statistics as a "monument of thorough and skillful statistical work" and a "careful and complete investigation of the course of prices." Frank W. Taussig wrote, "The skill and judgment of Commissioner Wright have yielded results whose importance and interest to the economist can hardly be overstated. . . ." Yet Richmond Mayo-Smith criticized Falkner's method for risking distortion in the general wholesale price index by placing "undue emphasis upon certain kinds of commodities" in order to utilize family expenditures as weights.[94]

Frederick C. Waite said of the two reports, "Together they constitute the most valuable contribution to the history of American economic conditions that has yet appeared." However, Waite criticized Wright and Falkner for making "a series of fallacious deductions." Waite complained that the wage index was based on too few occupations and too few returns—and all of them collected in the Northeast. He further alleged problems in the methodology in that Falkner should have used a multiyear base instead of the single year 1860 and that he should have weighted the wage data in making the index.[95] And, in further comment, some critics did not see that the reports would resolve the disputes surrounding the tariff question.

The work on wholesale prices, begun for the Aldrich Committee, was developed further by Falkner and the Bureau in 1900 and thereafter. They directed their efforts towards overcoming the undue representation of consumer goods arising from the use of the weights determined from the family expenditure studies. In 1900, in revising his indexes, Falkner maintained the weighting system based on family expenditures, but sought to improve the price representation of specific commodities. However, criticism of his use of family expenditure weights continued; Taussig commented that these were better suited to retail prices.[96]

The Bureau's own Wholesale Price Index, covering 1890 to 1901, appeared in 1902, marking the Bureau's entry into the field of current economic measures. Although the Bureau sought to link its effort as much as possible to the earlier work, the index of 1902 was based on an entirely new survey and concept. Because a weighting system based on national consumption patterns was not deemed feasible, and weighting by family expenditures was held to miss too many manufactured items, the Bureau used "a large number of representative staple articles, selecting them in such a manner as to make them, to a large extent, weight themselves."[97] A subsequent revision in 1914, however, turned to computing the weights "from the aggregate values of commodities exchanged year by year," utilizing the 1909 Census of Manufactures.[98]

To lay the groundwork for an index of retail prices, the Bureau conducted a massive survey of family expenditures during 1901-03, 10 years after the Aldrich study. Unlike the earlier surveys, which had covered workers' families in specific industries and areas, the new survey aimed to be representative of the conditions of workers in the whole country. Special agents of the Bureau visited 25,440 families of wage earners and of salaried workers earning up to $1,200 a year in the principal industrial centers in 33 States. Native—including Negro—and foreign-born families were included, without reference to industry. The agents recorded one year's expenditures on food, rent, principal and interest on homes, fuel, lighting, clothing, furniture, insurance, taxes, books and newspapers, and other personal expenditures. They also obtained information on earnings of family members.

Detailed data on income and expenditures of 2,500 families provided a basis for determining the relative expenditures, or weights, for the principal items entering into the cost of living. In particular, weights were determined for the principal articles of food consumed.

The Bureau also obtained information on prices for the period 1890 to 1903 from 800 retail merchants for the same items and localities as those reflected in the budgets of the expenditure survey. This was the first known collection of retail price data covering a period as long as 3 years.

With the expenditure and price data, the Bureau prepared its first weighted retail price index: "Relative Retail Price of Food, Weighted According to the Average Family Consumption, 1890 to 1902 (base of 1890-1899)." It provided monthly quotations of 30 principal items of food and summarized them in terms of "average price of the article" and "relative price," presenting these as averages and as weighted by consumption. Coverage was soon expanded to over 1,000 retail establishments in 40 States. The index was maintained through 1907.[99]

Wage data were collected as part of the same set of surveys. Previously, the agency's wage work had been sporadic and for specific purposes. In releasing the results of the study in 1904, in *Wages and Hours of Labor*, the Bureau explained that it had undertaken "a very painstaking and complete investigation which would result in thoroughly representative figures for a period of years [1890 to 1903] and which would serve as the basis for the regular annual collection and presentation of data from the establishments covered."

The study covered 519 occupations, "only the important and distinctive occupations which are considered representative of each industry," in 3,475 establishments in 67 manufacturing and mechanical industries. The voluminous data included actual and relative wages and hours by occupation; relative wages by industry; and relative wages and hours for all industries covered, weighted according to census data for aggregate wages in each industry. The new series appeared formally in 1905, as "Wages and Hours of Labor in Manufacturing Industries, 1890 to 1904," but covered fewer industries and occupations than the original study.[100]

The wage and retail price survey results were placed in juxtaposition in an article in the Bureau's *Bulletin* in July 1904, with the observation that, "taking 1903, it is seen that hourly wages were 16.3 percent above the average of 1890-1899, while retail prices of food were 10.3; making the increase in purchasing power of the hourly wage, 5.4 percent."

There were sharp reactions to this conclusion from labor organizations, politicians, and academicians, coming as it did at a time of industrial unrest and strikes due to layoffs, wage reductions, and reduced purchasing power following the panic of 1903—and the Presidential campaign of 1904. Representative William S. Cowherd of

Missouri, of the Democratic Congressional Committee, attacked the Bureau's results and charged Wright with veiling the truth by manipulating figures to meet party necessities. The *Journal* of the United Mine Workers complained of methodological problems, arguing that the Bureau should show not only the daily wage but also the number of days worked. The *Official Journal* of the Amalgamated Meat Cutters and Butcher Workmen castigated Wright and the wage and cost-of-living figures, alleging that the summary "appears to have been edited solely for political purposes and, to that end, has so many misleading statements that, as a bulletin concerning labor matters, it is entirely unworthy and inaccurate."[101]

The *Machinists' Monthly Journal* of the International Association of Machinists roundly attacked the figures: "It will take more than the figures given by the Honorable Carroll D. Wright in the July *Bulletin* of the Bureau of Labor to convince the housewives of the nation that wages have increased in proportion to the increase in prices."[102] Ernest Howard wrote in the *Political Science Quarterly*, "The effort made by the Bureau of Labor to find an approximate compensation for the rise of retail prices in the wage increase among certain classes of labor, most highly organized and aggressive, cannot be accepted as representative of the general labor experience."[103]

More moderate views came from two other sources. Wesley C. Mitchell spoke favorably of the improvements in wage data under Wright, especially in classified wage tables and index numbers. Later, he upheld the "high character" of the Bureau's index numbers, specifically in contrast to a Census report that showed different trends. Nevertheless, even Mitchell warned of shortcomings. The new tables, he said, had met "with more favor than they merit" because they continued Falkner's "most serious error"—lack of an adequate system of weights. The National Civic Federation gave a balanced perspective on the issue under the caption "Statistics That Do Not Apply." Commenting that "partisan motives, sharply accentuated by a Presidential campaign, have caused both attack and defense of these data," it pointed out that the Bureau had not intended that the observations apply to the immediate situation. The statistics "share the fault, perhaps inevitable, of all governmental statistics. They may enlighten in retrospect, but as to the immediate present, they are out of date."[104]

International influences

Wright's interest in developments abroad was apparent early in his career. As Chief of the Massachusetts Bureau, he visited England in 1881 to collect material for a factory study. Later, as Commissioner of the Federal Bureau, he sent members of his staff to Europe and obtained the services of experts studying abroad to collect information for studies.

Wright's reputation and his example, as well as the example of the State bureaus, influenced the rise of labor agencies in the European countries. At an Industrial Remuneration Conference in London in January 1885, several speakers pointed to the American experiments. Charles Bradlaugh, M.P., maintained "there could not be any fair arbitration satisfactory to the men until we had bureaux of the statistics of labour similar to those which had existed for 17 years in Massachusetts, which had been established in Connecticut, and in which an experiment had been made to some extent in Washington." Sir Rawson Rawson, President of the Royal Statistical Society, hoped the conference would impress the government with the importance of following the example of "the American government or the government of Massachusetts."[105]

The influence of the U.S. agency was formally recognized in a resolution of the 1891 convention of the International Statistical Institute in Vienna, which expressed the desire "that the governments may be willing to create Bureaus of Labor on the plan of those of the United States, where these offices do not exist, either creating a distinct Bureau or utilizing the organization of existing bureaus of statistics." National bureaus of labor statistics were established in quick succession during the 1890's and early 1900's in France (1891), Britain (1893), Spain (1894), Belgium (1895), Austria (1898), Germany, Italy, and Sweden (1902), and Norway (1903). Other countries, like Denmark (1895) and the Netherlands (1895), established central statistical offices which also collected statistics on labor.[106]

During hearings before the British Royal Commission on Labour in 1892, Elgin R.L. Gould, a special agent of Wright's agency, was called upon to testify. Gould had been in Europe to attend a session of the International Statistical Institute and to collect information for several Bureau studies, and he gave a thorough picture of the philosophy and organization of the agency under Wright. One outcome of the commission's activities was the prompt establishment of the new British Labour Department.[107]

Shortly after its establishment, the British agency exerted a reciprocal influence on its American counterpart when it began publication of the monthly *Labour Gazette*, which Wright used as an example to justify congressional authorization of a similar publication. In a letter to Representative Lawrence E. McGann, Wright endorsed the House bill providing for a bulletin, "especially as foreign Governments are now doing precisely what your bill aims to accomplish. The English Department of Labor, which was established only recently, is now publishing, very successfully and with great acceptance to the industrial interests of the country, a labor gazette."[108] Congress approved publication of a bulletin in 1895.

Wright was active in the early international efforts of economists, social reformers, and government labor officials to provide a bridge between trade union concerns, particularly about working conditions, and national government approaches to labor policy. The first conference held under such informal welfare reform auspices was the Congress for International Labor Legislation in Brussels in 1897. Wright and W.F. Willoughby of the Bureau staff attended these first discussions of international cooperation "in the formulation of labor standards and uniform presentation of reports and statistics regarding enforcement."[109]

In 1900, Wright attended the Congress of Paris, an outgrowth of the Brussels meetings. From the Paris conference developed the International Labour Office, established at Basel in 1901, and the International Association for Labor Legislation, which first met at Basel that same year. The next year, Wright helped organize an American section of the International Association. From 1903 to 1909, the Bureau carried $200 in its budget to support the work of the Labour Office, which received generally greater support from European governments.[110]

The Commissioner also belonged to the International Statistical Institute and the International Institute of Sociology. He was made an honorary member of the Royal Statistical Society of Great Britain and the Imperial Academy of Science of Russia, and a corresponding member of the Institute of France. In 1906, the Italian government honored him and, in 1907, France bestowed on him the Cross of the Legion of Honor for his work in improving industrial conditions.

Wright's other activities

While at the Bureau and after he left, Wright was active in many pursuits. He served as president of the American Social Science Association (1885-1888), the International Association of Governmental Labor Officials (1885-1905), and the American Statistical Association (1897-1909). He also served as president of the American Association for the Advancement of Science (1903) and was active in the Washington Academy of Sciences. He was also president of the Association for the Promotion of Profit Sharing, a short-lived group established in 1893 to promote industrial partnership between employers and workers through profit sharing.

Shortly before leaving the Bureau, he was superintendent of the Department of Social Economy at the Louisiana Purchase Exposition, St. Louis World's Fair (1904). He also served on the Massachusetts Committee on Relations Between Employer and Employee, whose report favored profit sharing, arbitration, child labor restrictions, workmen's compensation, and revision of the laws on injunctions.[111]

From 1895 to 1904, Wright was honorary professor of social economics at the Catholic University of America—where he met the young professor of political economy, Charles P. Neill, who was to succeed him as Commissioner of Labor Statistics. For some of the period he also lectured at Columbian University, later to become George Washington University. He served on the board of trustees of the newly established Carnegie Institution of Washington and, in 1904, became head of its new department of economics and sociology. Meanwhile, in 1902, he had become the first president of Clark College, charged with organizing the undergraduate program for the innovative institution.

After leaving the Bureau, he served as chairman of the Massachusetts Commission on Industrial and Technical Education. At the same time, he helped found and served as president of the National Society for the Promotion of Industrial Education and was active on several committees of the National Civic Federation.[112]

Retirement

Carroll Wright retired from government service at the end of January 1905—the 20th anniversary of his joining the new Bureau of Labor in the Department of the Interior. Near the close of his tenure, Wright reaffirmed his view of the agency's role: "To my mind, all the facts which have so far been gathered and published by the Bureau bear, either directly or indirectly, upon the industrial and humanitarian advance of the age, and are all essential in any intelligent discussion of what is popularly known as the 'labor question.'" He stressed that labor statistics should relate to the "material, social, intellectual, and moral prosperity of society itself," rather than solely to narrow fields. In response to those who called on the Bureau to become "the instrument of propagandism" in the interest of reform, Wright replied, "Whenever the head of the Bureau of Labor attempts to turn its efforts in the direction of sustaining or of defeating any public measure, its usefulness will be past and its days will be few." He continued: "It is only by the fearless publication of the facts, without regard to the influence those facts may have upon any party's position or any partisan's views, that it can justify its continued existence, and its future usefulness will depend upon the nonpartisan character of its personnel."[113]

Wright died in February 1909 at the age of 69.

Chapter III.

Charles Neill:
Studies for Economic
and Social Reform

On December 12, 1904, President Roosevelt appointed Charles P. Neill to succeed Carroll Wright as Commissioner of the Bureau of Labor, effective February 1, 1905. The active role already emerging for the Bureau under Wright in the early years of the Roosevelt administration intensified under Neill as Roosevelt increasingly used the Bureau to further the reform efforts of the Progressive movement. In 1908, the President wrote, "Already our Bureau of Labor, for the past 20 years of necessity largely a statistical bureau, is practically a Department of Sociology, aiming not only to secure exact information about industrial conditions but to discover remedies for industrial evils."[1]

As a major figure in the conservative wing of the Progressive movement, Roosevelt was concerned with the social problems of the working population brought on by the increasing industrialization of the economy and the growth of large-scale enterprises. This concern reflected both a sincere interest in reducing the ill effects of industrialization and a desire to forestall the possible alternatives of social instability and radicalism. In relations between capital and labor, neither "government of plutocracy" nor of "mob" was to be controlling.[2]

Roosevelt regularly expressed his concern with labor problems in his annual messages to Congress. His policy, innovative for the times, was for limited government involvement in labor-management relations to protect the interests of the public. He saw unions and their federations as accomplishing "very great good. . . when managed with forethought and when they combine insistence upon their own rights with law-abiding respect for the rights of others." The role of the Department of Commerce and Labor was to secure fair treatment for both labor and capital.[3]

For Roosevelt, the Bureau of Labor's investigatory activities and reports were of great value in furthering his goals. In his 1904 message to Congress, he called attention to the positive role of government accomplished "merely by giving publicity to certain conditions," and praised the Bureau of Labor for doing excellent work of this kind "in many different directions."[4]

The Bureau retained its broadened role even after Taft took office in 1909. Thus in 1911, in describing the Bureau's activities, Neill wrote of "the practical nature of the work which the Federal Government is trying to do to assist in exposing conditions which are dangerous to the life and health of wage-earners and to furnish the basis for sound legislation for the improvement of these conditions."[5]

Demands for legislation mounted during the early years of the century as the growing strength of labor unions was challenged by the concerted action of large corporations. Responding to gains by the American Federation of Labor and especially the United Mine Workers, the National Association of Manufacturers and the Citizens' Industrial Association launched a vigorous campaign for the open shop. At the same time, the United States Steel Corporation drove the remnants of the iron and steel workers' union from its plants.

In defense against these antiunion moves, the AFL increased its political activities. In 1906, it presented "Labor's Bill of Grievances," calling labor's principal demands to the attention of the President and the leaders of the House and Senate. Among the demands were legislation for an 8-hour workday, elimination of the competition of convict labor, relief from the mounting flow of immigration, exemption of unions from the antitrust laws, and relief from injunctions, which were increasingly sought by employers to prevent union action in labor disputes.

In the factories and mines, a militant new union, the Industrial Workers of the World, emerged to challenge the AFL from the left. Originating in western mining areas, the IWW took up the cause of the unorganized and unskilled, largely immigrant, work force in the factories of the East. Confrontations of workers, strikebreakers, police, and militia often erupted into violence.

In the turmoil of the times, Neill, as Roosevelt's ally in reform efforts, became embroiled in considerable controversy. Although the Commissioner forcefully defended his agency against charges of partisanship, declaring that it sought objectivity and balance, his experience provided something of an object lesson, warning of the hazards of being closely identified with particular government policies.

The second Commissioner

Charles Patrick Neill was born in Rock Island, Illinois, in 1865 and was reared in Austin, Texas. He attended the University of Notre Dame and the University of Texas before graduating summa cum laude from Georgetown University in 1891. He then became an instructor at Notre Dame. In 1895, he returned to the East Coast to finish his doctorate at Johns Hopkins, receiving the Ph.D. in 1897. In the meantime, he served as an instructor at Catholic University in Washington, D.C. He was appointed Professor of Political Economy in 1900, a post he held until he came to the Bureau of Labor in 1905. It was at Catholic University that Neill met Carroll Wright, who was teaching there while serving as Commissioner of Labor.

Before the House Committee on Agriculture in 1906, Neill briefly summarized his early years: "I was engaged in business as a clerk from the time I was 10 years old to 20, including occupation as a newsboy, a clerk, and other things. I have been a student from the time I was 20 until I was 30, and a teacher from that time on." He had also worked at the University of Chicago settlement house at the gate of the stockyards.[6]

Neill was active in charitable organizations in Washington before his entry into government service, and was associated with the "new era" of professionalism in welfare work in that city. In 1900, President McKinley appointed him to the newly created Board of Charities for the District of Columbia, which chose him as its vice president.[7]

Neill also participated in the educational activities of the District's Civic Center, which sponsored studies of housing conditions, especially of alley dwellings, and of sanitary conditions in the schools, and which played an important role in the enactment of child labor and compulsory education laws—causes in which he was prominent as Commissioner.[8]

Neill first came to Roosevelt's attention in 1902, when Carroll Wright recommended him for a post on the staff of the commission set up to mediate the anthracite coal strike. Roosevelt commented in his autobiography, "The strike, by the way, brought me into contact with more than one man who was afterward a valued friend and fellow-worker. On the suggestion of Carroll Wright, I appointed as assistant recorder to the Commission Charles P. Neill, whom I afterward made Labor Commissioner to succeed Wright himself. . . ." [9] In 1903, Roosevelt appointed Neill to the new Board of Conciliation and Arbitration for the anthracite industry, where he served first as accountant and later as umpire, replacing Wright.

When Roosevelt was looking for a new Commissioner of Labor, a number of influential men supported Neill for the position. One of them, Edward A. Moseley of the Interstate Commerce Commission, wrote Marshall Cushing of the National Association of Manufacturers, "I believe he is the sort of man that should be appointed to a position of that kind not only because he is a political economist, but will be able to hold the balance with a steady hand." The *Review of Reviews*, while commenting that it would be difficult to fill Wright's place in government and academic reputation, remarked, "The new Commissioner brings good credentials for his work."[10]

Neill's views

Neill's early writings and speeches reflected the view that the betterment of society could come only from the moral improvement of the individual. He saw the task of the social worker as one of developing the psychic fortitude of the poor: "We may say what we will about environment. The struggle of the poor is the struggle of the interior psychical forces against external environment. Any society is only as strong as the individual members make it."[11]

By the time he became Commissioner, he had broadened his view: "It is true poverty is perfectly compatible with sanctity, but when this happens it is the unusual. Those of you who have seen something of low standards of living amid poor material surroundings know how almost impossible it is to bring up children with decent moral standards. To raise the standards of living, both material and moral, we must begin with the food, clothing, and shelter. . . . There are certain possibilities in higher standards of living which the individual cannot attain by himself. This requires State action. There must be certain united action to allow the individual to reach the highest standard of living possible."[12]

Neill emphasized the collective social conscience, especially after becoming Commissioner. In a 1906 article, "Child Labor in the National Capital," he summarized his ideas as follows: "Whose is the responsibility? For whom do these children work? The truth is these child victims are working for us. They are working for me, and they are working for you. We enjoy cheaper products because the rights of children are outraged in order to furnish cheap labor. We cannot turn around and lay the blame entirely on the greed of the employer. Whatever shameful conditions of child labor exist, it is due just as much to a lack of conscience in the community at large as it is to any greed on the part of particular employers."[13]

Neill did not agree with those who believed that capital and labor were "necessary allies and natural friends." On the contrary, he argued that industrial disputes were inherent in the very nature of the economic system. However, he stated, "That strife may be tempered and kept within reasonable limits. . . . The best hope of industrial peace between these two groups lies in educating each to the realization that antagonistic interests can be compromised and treaties of peace arranged better before than after a test of strength has been made by an appeal to force."[14]

He saw unions as an avenue for tempering the conflict. "We must either develop a satisfactory process by which, through some form of trade unionism and collective bargaining, the burdens of industry shall be lightened and the wealth constantly created by the joint toil of brain and arm shall be more widely distributed amongst those who cooperate in its production, or we shall find ourselves face to face with the menace of Socialism in one form or another."[15]

The Bureau's investigative work

During his first year in office, Neill concentrated on completing studies Wright had begun. But the President soon asked him to undertake several major new investigations on issues of immediate concern.

Packinghouse conditions

For over a decade, reformers had been demanding Federal legislation to require the accurate labeling of preserved foods, beverages, and drugs. Germany and other European countries had roundly condemned American preserved meat and packinghouse products. Veterans of the Spanish-American War remembered none too fondly the "embalmed beef" of the quartermaster. Such legislation had passed the House only to die in the Senate, and Roosevelt urged its adoption in his message to Congress in December 1905.[16]

Early in 1906, Upton Sinclair published *The Jungle*, which exposed the unsanitary practices of the Chicago packers and stirred public indignation. Roosevelt called for action. The Bureau of Animal Industry of the Department of Agriculture, which maintained a staff of inspectors at the stockyards, immediately launched an investigation. The President directed Neill to make an independent inquiry: "I want to get at the bottom of this matter and be absolutely certain of our facts when the investigation is through." Neill, along with James Bronson Reynolds, a reformer from New York City, spent 2½ weeks gathering information and then submitted a report to Roosevelt, who praised him for his work. In addition, not satisfied with the report of the Animal Industry Bureau, Roosevelt asked Neill to revise it.[17]

Based on these reports, Roosevelt ordered the Department of Agriculture to prepare a bill establishing more stringent meat inspection procedures. Senator Albert J. Beveridge introduced the proposal in May. The so-called Beveridge Amendment quickly passed the Senate, where the packers made no fight. The press reported that the packers "were willing to agree to almost any kind of legislation" to prevent publication of the Neill-Reynolds report.[18]

However, Representative James W. Wadsworth of New York, Chairman of the Committee on Agriculture, mounted a vigorous opposition in the House. Thereupon, Roosevelt released both reports. As he transmitted the Neill-Reynolds report, he declared, "The conditions shown by even this short inspection to exist in the Chicago stockyards are revolting. It is imperatively necessary in the interest of health and decency that they should be radically changed. Under the existing law it is wholly impossible to secure satisfactory results." The Neill-Reynolds report had described the poor lighting and ventilation facilities; the "indifference to matters of cleanliness and sanitation" demonstrated by the privies provided for men and women; and the uncleanliness in handling products.[19]

The packers retorted in congressional hearings that their procedures were sanitary and wholesome but that they would favor more efficient and expanded inspection. Nevertheless, their defenders in the House treated Neill harshly when he came to testify, prompting him to complain, "I feel like a witness under cross-examination whose testimony is trying to be broken down."[20]

In the meantime, the press reported vigorous activities at the packinghouses where "carpenters and plumbers and kalsominers by the score are at work on alterations." Nevertheless, a great outcry continued in both American and foreign newspapers. On June 19, Congress agreed to a meat inspection bill, and the President signed it on June 30, the same day he signed the Pure Food Law.[21]

Violations of the 8-hour law

At the same time that Roosevelt ordered Neill into Chicago on the meatpacking investigation, he asked the Commissioner to investigate alleged abuses of the law limiting contractors on Federal Government work to an 8-hour day for their laborers and mechanics. The AFL charged that contractors disregarded the 8-hour law with impunity. In response, Roosevelt wrote to Frank Morrison, Secretary of the AFL: "At our interview yesterday, I requested you to bring to my attention any specific cases of violation of the 8-hour law. . . . I shall at once forward them to Mr. Neill, of the Labor Bureau, and direct him to investigate them and report direct to me. . . . My belief is that you will find that with Commissioner Neill personally supervising the enforcement of the law all complaints will be met."[22]

After a thorough inquiry, Neill reported to the President in August that the law was rarely obeyed. In September, referring to the Neill memorandum, Roosevelt issued executive orders putting into effect the Commissioner's suggestions for improving notification and enforcement procedures. Roosevelt asked Neill to continue his review of enforcement by the contracting agencies and the courts. A year later, Neill reported that most contractors continued to have their employees work 10 hours a day.[23]

The *Butchers' Journal* of the Amalgamated Meat Cutters and Butcher Workmen declared, "Charles P. Neill, National Commissioner of Labor, has come out flat-footed against the greedy and grasping contractors on government work and in a letter to President Roosevelt he shows up the contractors in their true light and condemns their persistent efforts to violate the 8-hour law on all government work."[24]

The *Machinists' Monthly Journal* of the International Association of Machinists thought politics to be at the root of the President's action: "Whether the sudden feverish desire on the part of the Federal authorities to see that the provisions of the 8-hour law are strictly enforced has anything to do with the recent decision of the organized forces of labor to enter the political field can best be determined by the workers themselves."[25]

Immigration laws

Immigration laws figured prominently among labor's grievances, because the unions viewed existing laws as providing draftees for business to restrain wages and prevent unionization. Roosevelt frequently called on Neill to conduct inquiries, and the issue occasionally found Neill, who supported restriction of immigration, at odds with his superior, Secretary of Commerce and Labor Oscar Straus, a founder of the Immigrants' Protective League and a proponent of an open immigration policy.

In June 1906, Roosevelt asked Neill to prepare confidential reports on the immigration situation, with the assistance of the Commissioner General of Immigration. Neill also surveyed conditions surrounding Japanese immigration into the San Francisco area.[26]

Roosevelt also called on Neill, as well as Straus, when the actions of the State of South Carolina under the Immigration Act of 1903 were questioned. The act had made it unlawful to pay for the transportation of aliens or to assist or encourage the importation of aliens by advertising in foreign countries or otherwise. The ban on advertising, however, did not apply to State governments, and South Carolina established a Department of Agriculture, Commerce, and Immigration to encourage immigration into the State. The State Commissioner induced several hundred aliens to migrate, with the understanding that their passage would be paid from a fund made up of a State appropriation and individual and corporate contributions. Organized labor charged that mill owners supplied the funds, thereby skirting the letter of the law in hope of obtaining cheap labor.

When the Solicitor of the Department of Commerce and Labor upheld South Carolina, Roosevelt called on Straus to review the matter thoroughly, because "many of the people most affected sincerely believe that it is the end of any effort to stop the importation of laborers under contract in the Southern States, and that this means further damage to laborers in the Northern States." Roosevelt also advised Straus that he was consulting with Neill, who had "exceptional advantages in the way of keeping in touch with the labor people and of knowing their feelings as well as their interests."[27]

The Immigration Act of 1907 was intended to close the loophole. However, a conference called by the President on the interpretation of the act produced divergent views. Straus commented in his diary, "Commissioner Neill gave a narrow view of the whole situation which, however, the President did not adopt." Roosevelt then appointed a committee, with Neill as a member, to study immigration into the South and directed that all reports of violations of contract labor laws should be filed with the Commissioner.[28]

The 1907 act also created a commission to study the whole question of immigration, and the President appointed Neill to it. Neill wrote later, "When the Immigration Commission was created in the spring of 1907, I was, against my personal wishes, drafted into service. I had a good deal to do with the planning of the work of the Commission in the beginning, and during the entire period of its existence, I was in close touch with its work." He helped direct the statistical work and the southern investigation and supervised the general work in Washington, at least in the earlier years of the commission. A number of Bureau personnel worked with the commission as well, including Fred C. Croxton, who served as its chief statistician.[29]

The new act also set up a Division of Information within the Bureau of Immigration. Terence Powderly, former leader of the Knights of Labor, was appointed Chief of the Division, whose function was to distribute immigrants to sections of the country where there were jobs available. Originally, the AFL had viewed this function as permitting "workmen lawfully coming to the United States. . . a more intelligent choice of location in which to seek employment. . .

and if administered fairly [as] calculated to be of least injury to labor."[30]

In a period of widespread unemployment, however, the activities of the Division of Information in helping immigrants find jobs came in for much criticism. The AFL argued that the Department of Commerce and Labor should devote its energies solely to meeting the problem of the domestic unemployed. Neill reaffirmed an earlier view that "it is useless to talk about any plan to distribute immigrants, other then the single plan of offering higher wages in the places that want them than they are getting in the places that they are now or in offering them opportunities to take up land that make the opportunities actual and really within their reach."[31]

In September 1909, Neill wrote President Taft, calling his attention to union charges that immigrants were being used to break the unions: ". . . the immigration figures are rapidly mounting up to what they were during the high tide of immigration 2 years ago, and the labor organizations are convinced that a number of the large corporations are determined to take advantage of the abundance of labor and the incoming immigrants to break the power of the unions before there is a full return to prosperity and such a scarcity of labor as would give an advantage to the organizations."[32]

Neill also expressed concern about the influx of Orientals into Hawaii. A major section of the third report of the Commissioner of Labor on Hawaii (1906) was entitled "Orientalization of Laboring Population and Its Results." Neill wrote that "as long as Oriental labor is available, it will be practically impossible to build up a typical American commonwealth." Besides, he continued, pointing to the plantation regimen, "It will always be impossible to secure any body of self-respecting Caucasian laborers who will work under those conditions." Neill reported in 1911 that competition had increased between American and Japanese workers, and that the territorial government and businessmen had attempted to attract Caucasian labor from the mainland, with only slight success.[33]

Strike investigations
In the festering industrial unrest of the period, Neill and the Bureau were called upon to investigate many labor disputes, particularly in the steel, mining, and textile industries, which were later viewed as landmarks in the history of industrial relations. The Bureau's reports

on these disputes were comprehensive. In addition to noting the immediate causes of the dispute, they discussed the new developments on the labor scene—the role of immigrant labor, the rise of the IWW, and the growth of the open shop and company unions. Further, they dealt with the corporate structure of the industry, its business practices, and the impact of new technology on the work force.

Steel was one of the most strife-ridden industries. In 1909, Neill was asked to investigate a strike called by unorganized workers, many of them recent immigrants, at the Pressed Steel Car Company of McKee's Rock, Pennsylvania, when the company altered the wage system and refused to post rates of pay. The workers' other grievances included the compulsory use of company stores, extortion by foremen, and a speedup of work. Moreover, the Austrian consul complained that employment agencies were importing immigrants as strikebreakers. The IWW gave advice and direction to the strikers, marking its entry into the East.[34]

The AFL noted Neill's report on the strike when it directed its executive board to obtain the report "for the purpose of framing national legislation for the proper supervision of the employment agencies."[35]

At the same time, when the United States Steel Corporation announced that all its plants would operate on an open shop basis, the Amalgamated Association of Iron, Steel and Tin Workers struck in protest at a company subsidiary, the American Sheet and Tin Plate Company, the only remaining unionized mill of U.S. Steel. During the unsuccessful year-long strike, the AFL provided organizing support and presented grievances to President Taft and Congress, calling for an investigation of the activities of U.S. Steel.

Neill reported to Taft on the "bitterness in labor circles" aroused by the company positions in the two steel strikes. He suggested to Taft that, to avoid increasing bitterness, a study of labor conditions in the steel industry be undertaken and announced immediately. Taft replied that he had no objection to such a study, "but I do not wish it advertised. . . . I am not in favor of grandstand performances in advance."[36]

In February 1910, another walkout by several thousand unorganized workers at the Bethlehem Steel Company over the extension of overtime and Sunday work prompted the Secretary of Commerce and Labor to direct the Bureau to investigate. Ethelbert Stewart of the

Bureau's staff led the study. He reported that at least half the company's workers were required to work 12 or more hours a day, with no premium for overtime or Sunday work, and that a 7-day workweek was common. No grievance procedure was available to the unorganized workers, he reported, and "time-bonus" payments stimulated a speedup in work.[37]

The *Machinists' Monthly Journal* described the report as providing "reliable information founded upon exact data, carefully and scientifically collected," and called on the union's members to give all possible publicity to the facts in the report. Charles Schwab, Bethlehem Steel's president, protested that the report was unfair in failing to clarify that these conditions existed throughout the American steel industry. Following a meeting with Schwab and the Secretary of Commerce and Labor, Neill affirmed that the "shocking" conditions prevailed in the industry generally, but that U.S. Steel had recently ordered Sunday work reduced to a minimum.[38]

A month after the publication of the report on Bethlehem Steel, the Senate authorized the Bureau to examine working conditions in the iron and steel industry. The Bureau's 4-volume study, published over a 2-year span, was based on information obtained through personal visits and mail questionnaires to plants employing about 90 percent of the industry's workers, the majority of whom were recent immigrants. The study covered wages, hours of work, and accidents. It reported continued 6- and 7-day workweeks of 12-hour days: One-third of the 150,000 workers in blast furnaces, steel works, and rolling mills were working 7 days a week, and one-fifth were working 84 hours or more a week. The report questioned the need for Sunday work in view of the recent action of U.S. Steel in abolishing most Sunday work. The report also called attention to the dilution of skills in the industry as mechanical developments spread, adding to the already large proportion of unskilled workers.[39]

In commenting on the study, the Machinists' *Journal* stated, "Gratifying in the extreme and profitable in every way is the report. . . because of the additional light it throws upon the terrible conditions under which men have to work in that industry." Pointing out the inadequacy of craft unions for dealing with the employers, the *Journal* continued, "There is only one remedy and that is thorough and perfect organization. Not the organization of a little aristocracy composed of the less than one-twentieth of these workers who receive fifty cents an hour and over, but the complete organization of every worker in the industry along the broadest, the most liberal and democratic lines imaginable. . . ."[40]

Gompers cited excerpts from the report to reply to "public opinion" that labor was well-treated in the industry. Later, in his autobiography, he wrote, "Dr. Neill performed a very comprehensive and valuable piece of work which caused the officials of the steel corporations to 'cuss' him and gnash their teeth."[41]

The Bureau continued to focus considerable attention on the outbreaks of industrial violence characteristic of the period. A congressional resolution of June 1911 called on the Bureau to investigate conditions in Westmoreland County, near Pittsburgh, where a strike had been going on in the bituminous coal mines for over a year. The Bureau reported that union efforts at organization had been blocked by the mine operators for two decades and that the introduction of machinery had increased the number of unskilled jobs for which immigrants were employed.[42]

One of the most dramatic industrial disputes of the period began in the textile mills of Lawrence, Massachusetts, in January 1912. The immediate cause of the strike was a reduction in earnings announced by the American Woolen Company in response to a new State law reducing the limit on working hours for women and children from 56 to 54 hours a week. The strike was marked by violent confrontations between strikers and the police and militia. Although Congress held hearings, the Bureau conducted its own investigation and prepared a report, which commented on the strike "started by a few unskilled non-English-speaking employees" that developed into an organized action of 20,000 workers led by the IWW. It noted that wage increases were obtained.[43]

Friends of President Taft objected to giving publicity to the poor wages and working conditions in the highly protected textile industry for fear of exposing the weakness of the argument that high tariffs kept American wages high. However, the Senate called for the Bureau report, and published it as a Senate Document.[44]

The widespread industrial unrest prompted concerned citizens to petition Taft to form a commission to make a thorough investigation of laboring conditions in the country. In a message to Congress, Taft supported the idea, explaining that recent investigations had been "fragmentary, incomplete, and at best only partially representative."

The country needed, he said, a comprehensive, nationwide study. Neill expressed a similar view in congressional testimony, stating that the Bureau was too small to undertake such a task. But Taft delayed in making appointments and Woodrow Wilson subsequently named the members—after Neill had left the government and the Department of Labor had been established.[45]

Neill's mediation activities

Although the President and Congress called upon Neill for many tasks, mediation of labor disputes proved to be his major and most absorbing public work. As Commissioner, he helped settle some 60 railway controversies, and his involvement in railroad labor relations extended into World War I, when he served on the first Railway Board of Adjustment.

The Erdman Act of 1898 had provided for a board of mediation for railroad disputes, with the Commissioner of Labor as a member, but the act's procedures had been asked for only once during Wright's tenure. In December 1906, the Southern Pacific Railroad Company applied to the board when it found itself threatened by a jurisdictional dispute between two railway unions. Although one of the unions was skeptical at first about the board's role, it viewed the final result favorably, finding that "Mr. Neill applied himself with such diligence to the task of bringing about an adjustment that he was soon familiar with every detail of the controversy. He was absolutely fair to all interested."[46] Within a month, the unions agreed to an arbitration panel. This success, coupled with the broadening scope of railroad collective bargaining agreements, spurred use of the act's machinery.

Neill noted that, in the beginning, the companies viewed him with some suspicion since they presumed him to be pro-labor because of his position. But, he said, "After the first case or two, why, they became convinced of my fair-mindedness." He further explained, "There is no occasion to charge either side, as a rule, with unfairness. . . . It is human nature to want to be fair. But it is also human nature to be self-centered. Therefore, each side has an entirely different conception of what is fair."[47]

His colleague on the mediation board, Judge Martin A. Knapp, chairman of the Interstate Commerce Commission, stated that the function of the mediators "is to aid a friendly settlement. . . . For this reason, it has been the conception of those who have acted in this capacity that their duty is not to determine what settlement they think ought to be made, but to find out what settlement can be made."[48]

As originally viewed, the Erdman Act provided a tool for dealing with disputes between a single railroad and its operating employees, but the railroad brotherhoods turned to concerted action, in which they organized and negotiated with management on a broader regional basis. This greatly complicated procedures and took considerably more of Knapp's and Neill's time while threatening a more extensive public impact if mediation failed.

In addition, legislation was proposed in 1912 to extend coverage under the Erdman Act to coal companies in interstate commerce and to railway shop craft workers. Widening the board's scope would make further demands on the time of the Commissioner of Labor.

Thus, in his report for 1912, the Secretary of Commerce and Labor stated that the Commissioner needed some relief and recommended an independent board of conciliation and arbitration, to be named by the President and confirmed by the Senate. This reflected Neill's concern that, if the Erdman Act were expanded or if he and Knapp were to undertake cases not properly falling under the letter of the act, "It would be absolutely necessary to create some other machinery."[49] And in testimony before Congress that year, Neill emphasized that the suggested expansion would require a new mechanism, declaring, "It has been impossible for me to give proper attention to this work and even begin to perform my legitimate duties in the Bureau of Labor. . . . I might add that I would not, under any conditions, be willing to continue to attempt to carry on the work under this act and the work of the Bureau of Labor both."[50]

Early in 1913, under the pressure of disputes on eastern railroads, Knapp and Neill worked with a committee from the National Civic Federation and representatives of the major railroads and the railroad brotherhoods to develop a plan for a separate, permanent board of mediation. Within the year, Congress passed the Newlands Act, which set up a separate Board of Mediation and Conciliation. From that time on, Commissioners of the Bureau were no longer occupied with the time-consuming task of mediating labor disputes.

Work in industrial safety and health

Under Neill, the Bureau was a leading force in the movement to improve industrial safety and health conditions. In 1908, the Bureau highlighted the lack of information on industrial accidents by publishing an article by Frederick L. Hoffman, a consulting statistician for the Prudential Insurance Company, in which he wrote, "Thus far, no national investigation of the subject of industrial accidents has been made to determine the true accident risk in industry, and the statistical data extant are more or less fragmentary and of only approximate value."[51] To fill some of the gaps, the Bureau published reports on railway employee accidents, fatal accidents in coal mining, and accident experience in other countries.

In addition, Bureau staff developed information on occupational accidents as part of larger studies. Lucian W. Chaney, the Bureau's expert on accident prevention, prepared *Employment of Women in the Metal Trades*, a study of accidents to machine operators, as volume XI of the Bureau's massive study on working women and children. In 1912, the Bureau published Chaney's *Accidents and Accident Prevention* as volume IV of its report on working conditions in the iron and steel industry. Chaney had taken 2 years to collect the data. This publication was the first in a continuing annual series on industrial accidents in iron and steel.

Both Neill and Chaney played important roles in the early years of the National Safety Council. At the First Cooperative Safety Congress in 1912, both were appointed to the Committee on Permanent Organization, whose function was "to organize and to create a permanent body devoted to the promotion of safety and to human life." The next year, Neill delivered a paper in which he advocated that the National Council for Industrial Safety become a clearinghouse that would circulate information about accidents and maintain a roster of lecturers. In the speech he declared, "I doubt if there is a commercial nation today, laying any claim to an elementary civilization, that has been maiming and mangling and killing those who attempt to earn their bread in the sweat of their faces with as little apparent regret and as little thought as we do in the industrial centers of the United States."[52]

The Bureau's interest in industrial hygiene paralleled its concern with industrial accidents. In 1908, the Bureau published an article on the subject by George M. Kober, professor at the Georgetown University Medical School. In the same year, an article by Hoffman, "Mortality from Consumption in Dusty Trades," gave impetus to the fight against tuberculosis.

The Bureau also gave increased attention to the problem of exposure to industrial poisons. As late as 1908, the report of the Lucerne Conference of the International Association for Labor Legislation included the following comment on the state of protective legislation in the United States: "The protection of the worker from industrial poisons and dust has hitherto made little progress in the United States. No material on the subject was available and the American Section could do nothing except bring to the notice of the Governments of the various States the petition of the International Association requesting the compulsory notification by doctors of cases of industrial poisoning."[53]

In 1904, when the president of the International Association had written Secretary Cortelyou, head of the Department of Commerce and Labor, about a conference to consider, among other things, the use of white phosphorus in the production of matches, Cortelyou replied, "I have the honor to state that the Federal Government has no jurisdiction in such matters. They belong definitely and specifically to the several States."[54] Subsequently, in September 1906, Germany, Denmark, France, Italy, Luxembourg, Switzerland, and the Netherlands signed a convention on the prohibition of the use of white phosphorus in the manufacture of matches. In December 1908, the British Parliament passed the White Phosphorus Matches Prohibition Act.

Neill and the Bureau were instrumental in arousing American concern over phosphorus poisoning. In 1909, the Bureau cooperated with the American Association for Labor Legislation in a study of the effects of white phosphorus in match production. John B. Andrews, secretary of the association, summed up the results: "The investigation of 15 of our 16 match factories during the year 1909 proved conclusively that, in spite of modern methods and precautions, phosphorus poisoning not only occurs in this country but exists in a form so serious as to warrant legislative action to eliminate the disease."[55]

The Secretary of Commerce and Labor wrote Neill, "While this report will no doubt make some stir, I am satisfied that the truth of this condition ought to be known, especially since we seem to be behind other countries in giving attention to so serious a condition. If the matter is to be published, kindly urge it as much as possible in order that it may receive attention as early as conditions admit of."[56]

After publication of the report, legislation was introduced to ban phosphorus matches from interstate commerce. The campaign sought to encourage production of matches by the more modern ses-quisulphide process, but this faced three problems: The Diamond Match Company (also known as the "match trust") held the patent on the process; the technology was more expensive; and the match industry was localized and not easily subject to Federal regulation under the commerce clause. Therefore, supporters of the legislation argued the need for a heavy tax to discourage use of phosphorus by eliminating the economic incentive. In his 1910 message to Congress, President Taft recommended such an approach.[57]

In the meantime, Diamond moved to sell rights to other companies who wished to use the sesquisulphide process. In January 1911, it relinquished the patent to three trustees: Neill, E.R.A. Seligman of Columbia University, and Jackson Ralston, an attorney for the American Federation of Labor. On January 27, the trustees surrendered the patent.

Since the industry could not be forced to adopt the new process, efforts to tax phosphorus matches continued. Finally, in 1912, Congress passed a law that provided for the tax, ending the phosphorus poisoning problem so far as matches were concerned, but not in other industries.[58]

The Bureau also focused considerable attention on the problem of lead poisoning, beginning with three articles in the *Bulletin* in July 1911. Based on personal investigation of 22 factories, Alice Hamilton, later a professor at Harvard Medical School, wrote on the white-lead industry in the United States. John Andrews wrote on deaths from industrial lead poisoning reported in New York State in 1909 and 1910. And Sir Thomas Oliver, leader of the British crusade against the employment of women in white-lead processes, contributed an article on lead poisoning and lead processes in European countries. In 1913, the Bureau published Hamilton's tentative findings on the effects of lead in the painters' trade.

Neill's activities included participation both at home and abroad in efforts to establish occupational health standards. The American Association for Labor Legislation, of which he was a member, took several steps in the field of occupational health in addition to the work on phosphorus, such as organizing the National Commission on Industrial Hygiene (1908) and calling the First National Conference on Industrial Diseases (1910). The conference wrote a Memorial to the President which recommended some greatly expanded national efforts.[59]

Industrial education

The Bureau had published studies on industrial education in 1892 and 1902, but in 1908 there was intensified interest from the AFL, which corresponded with educators, academicians, and social workers on the subject. In that year, a committee was formed which included Neill, union officials, and representatives of public interest groups. At the committee's request, the Bureau conducted another study.

The AFL termed the Bureau's effort, published in 1910, the "most comprehensive study of the whole subject. . . that has ever been made in the United States." The study provided support for legislative proposals by the AFL for Federal aid to the States for industrial education on the basis that, as Gompers wrote, "Industrial education, like academic education, is becoming a public function and. . . should be paid for by public funds."[60] Legislation did not come until 1917, however.

Social insurance

The Bureau's educational work in the field of social insurance also began under Wright, who, as early as 1893, had published a study of compulsory insurance in Germany. Under Neill, the Bureau continued to provide information on European and also American practices. In 1908, a study by Lindley D. Clark reported on U.S. employers' legal liability for injuries to their employees, and the Bureau's annual report for that year consisted of a study of workmen's insurance and benefit funds in the United States. A companion report published in 1909 dealt with workmen's insurance and compensation systems in Europe.

It was in the field of workmen's compensation that the Bureau exercised, for 8 years, a statutory administrative function. In May 1908, Congress passed a law providing compensation for injuries to certain artisans and laborers employed by the Federal Government, the first workmen's compensation act in the United States. Administration of the law was assigned to the Department of Commerce and Labor, and the Secretary turned over most of these duties to the Bureau, including the examination and approval of claims. The coverage of the act was later widened so that by 1913 the compensation system covered about 95,000 civilian government employees. The Bureau retained this responsibility until 1916, when Congress established the Federal Employees' Compensation Board.

A sidelight on the compensation system the Bureau administered is provided by a 1913 magazine article by a former Bureau employee. He noted, first, that the Government treated its employees badly: "The economic and social value of the welfare work of large corporations need not be exaggerated, but it is a sad fact that the Federal Government has done less of it (outside the Isthmian Canal) than many of the soulless corporations." Second, he noted that, although the Federal act was the first compensation law in this country, several States had subsequently enacted programs that were far superior. Further, he charged that the Bureau had done little to implement improvements.[61]

The Federal Government's efforts to establish a pension system for its employees led to several Bureau studies. In examining various proposals, the Senate asked the Bureau for information on domestic and foreign retirement plans. In response, the Bureau prepared a study of 219 municipal retirement systems and 22 railroad programs. The Bureau also commissioned a report by an outside expert on civil service retirement programs in Great Britain, New Zealand, and Australia.

The study on working women and children

During 1907, with much encouragement from the AFL and welfare reform organizations, Neill and the Bureau embarked on a massive study of the working conditions of women and children. The investigation joined two campaigns, one for limitation of child labor and the other to improve the conditions of the increasing number of working women.

In his annual messages for 1904 and 1905, Roosevelt had pressed for such a study, with special emphasis on child labor and its regulation by the States.

Social reformers from Chicago pushed for an investigation of women's working conditions, and Mary McDowell and Jane Addams met with Roosevelt in 1905 to ask for a study. Several women's organizations took up the cause and drew up a proposed bill. In January 1906, Neill wrote to Sophonisba Breckinridge of Chicago, "The President is very much in earnest in this matter and has said to me since you were here that he is quite anxious to do anything he can to help secure the investigation."[62]

In the appropriations hearings on the study, the Commissioner stated, "If there were conditions of prime importance affecting the family life and morals and citizenship, due to industrial conditions, the national government has just as much interest in finding that out as it has in finding out what is the total amount in savings banks or what is the general increase of street railways, or nine hundred and ninety-nine other things for which large sums of money are expended in the Census. Here are matters. . . of tremendous sociological importance."[63]

The movement toward the study proceeded at the same time that proposals were introduced in Congress to limit child labor. A bill introduced by Senator Albert J. Beveridge prohibited the interstate transportation of the products of factories or mines employing children under 14 years of age. A bill proposed by Senator Henry C. Lodge applied only to the District of Columbia.

Neill, who had been campaigning for a child labor law in the District, wrote to the President, arguing that, "If Congress has the power to pass legislation of this kind, some bill embodying the principle of the Lodge or the Beveridge Bill should be passed. . . . Child labor is indefensible from any view point whatever, and is a blot on the civilization that tolerates it." Either bill, he explained, "would serve both to protect the markets of any State from being made the dumping ground for the products of child labor in other less advanced States, and would assure to the manufacturers of more progressive States a protection against the competition of child labor States in outside markets."[64] Neither bill won committee approval. However, Congress finally passed a bill applying only to the District of Columbia which prohibited the employment of youth under 16, with some exceptions. Roosevelt signed the limited measure in May 1908.

There was even opposition to the conduct of a study. Congressional opponents questioned whether the national government had the authority to investigate, contending that Congress lacked authority to legislate on the subject.[65]

Another set of arguments was directed at limiting the scope of the study. Neill was asked, "Is not all this information that you can gather already to be had right here in the Census Bureau—the number of women and children employed and the average wages they receive per annum?"[66]

Supporters of the measure responded that the Census Bureau could provide some numbers but not the "thorough investigation as to the effects of the employment of women and children upon their health and upon the social conditions of the people."[67]

In January 1907, Congress directed the Secretary of Commerce and Labor to conduct the investigation, later stipulating that the Census Bureau should do the work. With continuing uncertainty over the status and conduct of the investigation, the National Civic Federation established a commission of its own, made up of representatives of manufacturers and the AFL, to investigate the extent and menace of child labor, expressing concern that "it would be most unfortunate to have the result of the investigation be a lot of misleading figures and exaggerated statements of conditions which would simply serve as socialist propaganda."[68]

Roosevelt wrote to Secretary Straus that the Bureau of Labor should have the work: "I cannot too strongly state that in my judgment the investigation will be shorn of a very large part of the good results we have a right to expect from it, if it is not confided to the Bureau of Labor."[69] Straus then wrote, "Both the Director of the Census and the Commissioner of Labor agree with me thoroughly" that the investigation should be carried out by the Bureau of Labor. In the end, the Bureau of Labor was permitted to conduct the study.[70] For each of two consecutive years, the Bureau received $150,000 for the investigation.

Eager to have the cooperation of employers, Neill assured the National Association of Manufacturers, as he had Congress, that there were no preconceived notions guiding the conduct of the study and that its purpose was solely to gather facts. The study would take into account the conditions and practices of the "best class of manufacturers" and avoid the misrepresentation that would result from describing only the worst conditions. "There is no desire to discover the harrowing or unearth the sensational. . . ." "When the important facts have all been brought out, there will be found to be evils to be corrected," Neill went on to say. "I believe that then it will be found that the members of this association are just as ready as any body of men in the country to see that justice is done."[71]

The AFL and representatives of welfare organizations offered their assistance in the investigation, and the National Child Labor Committee provided the Bureau with the material it had collected over a period of 3 years. As the investigation proceeded, AFL representatives met with Neill to suggest setting up a division in the Bureau to deal specifically with the conditions of working women and children.[72]

The Bureau encountered many problems in the conduct of the study. Although Bureau agents took great care to verify the ages of children under 16, as reported by children and mill officers, there were difficulties in obtaining age information in the southern mills, and frequently, it was reported, working children were hidden from Bureau agents.[73] In addition, there were complaints by mill operators about the time required to respond to the questions of the agents.

Neill's designation of a southerner to conduct the study of the textile mills was challenged very early by the study's supporters. McDowell wrote Neill, "I saw Miss Addams. . . and from her learned that the cotton industry had been assigned to a southerner. . . . I did hope so much that you were going to be free to give a body of facts that would stand the test of criticism, but already I hear rumors that the cotton industry investigation is discredited. This may be unfair, but natural."[74] Then, when the study finally was published, Neill was attacked from the other side as having slandered the South.

Work on the study began in 1907 and continued through 1909. The inquiry was substantially confined to States east of the Mississippi, partly because the social and industrial problems dealt with were found mainly in the East, and partly because of the limitations of time and money. One aspect of the study dealt with employment of women and children in the four industries in which they made up a significant proportion of the work force—cotton, glass, men's readymade garments, and silk—and also with employment of women in stores and factories, in the metal trades, and in laundries. Two studies dealt with child labor problems, focusing on the reasons for leaving school and on the relationship between employment and juvenile delinquency. Three studies gave historical accounts of child labor legislation, women in industry, and trade unionism among women. Three reports dealt with health questions: Infant mortality in Fall River, causes of death among cotton-mill operatives, and hookworm disease, particularly in the southern cotton-mill communities. The remaining studies included a survey of family budgets of cotton-mill workers, the connection between occupation and criminality among women, and State enforcement of labor laws and factory inspection laws. In all, 19 volumes of studies were published.

Among the leading findings of this landmark report was the disparity between the North and the South in the employment of children. In the textile mills of the South, where the legal age limit was 12, there were many children at work; there were far fewer in New England. However, in Pennsylvania, although the age limit was 16, enforcement was lax, and a large number of children were at work in the silk mills.

The study showed that, in a substantial number of cases, children's earnings were essential to meet pressing necessity. But in many other cases, both in the South and elsewhere, families would not have suffered hardship if child labor were forbidden. The report concluded that, to a considerable extent, child labor seemed to be due "to indifference or active hostility to the schools on the part of both parents and children."[75]

Another finding concerned the growing substitution of women for men in industry. The report brought out the paradox that "a process of substitution has been going on by which men have been gradually taking the leading role in industries formerly carried on chiefly in the home and considered distinctly feminine, such as spinning and weaving and garment making and knitting. As the women have been more or less dispossessed in their specialities, they have either gone into work formerly considered men's, such as the printing trade, or entered newly established industries which had not been definitely taken over by either sex. In both cases they are usually found doing the least skilled or poorest paid work."[76]

Among the many pioneering aspects of the study was the development of new techniques for analyzing economic and social phenomena. The first standard budgets prepared by the Bureau were developed for the purpose of evaluating the living conditions of the cotton-mill workers in Fall River and the South in 1908-09. Actual weekly earnings and expenditures for a year were obtained for representative cotton-mill families. From these the Bureau prepared standard budgets for a "fair standard of living," including some allowance for comfort, and a "minimum standard of living of bare essentials," on which families were living and apparently maintaining physical efficiency.

Commissioner Neill noted: "These standards, it should be emphasized, are the standards found to be actually prevailing among cotton-mill families of the several communities studied, and are not standards fixed by the judgment either of the investigators or of the Bureau of Labor."[77]

The diet of the Federal prison in Atlanta was compared with the expenditures for food of the cotton-mill families. The comparison indicated that—for both Fall River and southern families—at least half had expenditures at a standard less than the prison diet.[78]

The study results influenced the establishment of the Children's Bureau, achieved in 1912 after several years of effort by supporters. Neill had favored its establishment as a separate agency rather than have his Bureau assume the added responsibilities. The intensive studies required of a Children's Bureau would not duplicate the work of the Bureau of Labor, he said.

Pressure also developed to make special provision for women's studies. The AFL, for example, called for a special unit in the Bureau of Labor—to be headed by a woman—that would conduct studies relating to the condition of women in the United States. The Bureau established such a section in 1911 under the direction of Marie L. Obenauer, who published a series of studies on hours and earnings of women in selected industries in Chicago, the District of Columbia, Maryland, California, and Wisconsin.

Controversy over the study findings

In 1912, during congressional debate on the establishment of the Children's Bureau, southern Senators charged that the study on women and children presented an unfair picture of southern conditions. In addition, a former Bureau agent charged that Neill had suppressed his survey of conditions in southern mills. The agent's report, which he later published on his own, held that conditions under industrialization, even if not very good, represented an improvement over the conditions in the rural areas from which the mill workers had migrated.[79]

Although the Bureau had not published the agent's study, Senator Lee S. Overman of North Carolina referred to sections of it as presenting an "obscene and. . . scandalous" picture of southern rural conditions. A month later, the Senator criticized as "odious" the Bureau's report on family budgets of cotton-mill workers. A Washington newspaper had reported the study under the headline, "Southern Mills Bad as Prisons (Bureau of Labor Report)—Families ill fed, poorly clad, and ignored by every class of society—children all drudges."[80]

Neill responded to these criticisms, both as they occurred and later. To charges that he had been unfair to the South, Neill replied, "I designedly placed this under charge of special agent Walter B. Palmer, himself born, reared, and educated in the South and known to me to be southern in every respect." Furthermore, Neill said, he had directed that the southerners on the project staff were to be assigned to the cotton textile study.

The Commissioner also pointed out that the study covered virtually all the best mills as well as the worst, stating, "I desired to be able to point out that good conditions could be maintained on a commercial and practical basis by the fact that they did exist in mills that were being profitably conducted." He stated further that he had been so anxious to avoid any appearance of focusing attention on the South that he had hoped to present the data by State, without dividing them by region, but that clear differences between the northern and southern States in age limits, working hours, and the ethnic composition of the work force required presentation by region.[81]

Neill summed up: The agents "were not sent south to write up sensational material any more than they were sent north to do so. . . . If the results were sensational, it was due to the facts and not to any desire on the part of the Bureau to make them sensational."[82]

There was much support for the conduct and findings of the investigation. In the Senate, William E. Borah of Idaho, sponsor of the Children's Bureau proposal, contested Overman: "But the fact remains that a vast amount of the facts were based upon real investigations and brought forth a number of things which were startling to the country. I do not know whether there are things in them that are untrue or not; but I know from investigations of my own, which have resulted since I took charge of this measure, a great many of those things reported to be true are true."[83]

The *Survey* commented on the first publications, "No greater service could be done the various movements against child labor, against the night employment of women, against unsanitary shop conditions and for higher wages, better hours, more conserving methods of work, than to secure a wide distribution and reading of these encyclopedic books."[84]

Warren M. Persons, in the *Quarterly Journal of Economics*, wrote, "The first three volumes issued by the Bureau of Labor on *Woman and Child Wage-Earners in the United States* set a very high standard of excellence for the series. . . . The investigations seem to have been as careful as they were extensive."[85]

Gompers, in his report to the 1911 AFL convention, declared, "The results of this investigation have fully justified the action of the American Federation of Labor in behalf of such an inquiry being made."[86]

The National Child Labor Committee also took some pride of sponsorship: "We may fairly claim a large share of responsibility. . . . We promoted the bill which secured the appropriation for this investigation and have placed all our available information at the disposal of the United States Bureau of Labor."[87]

But criticism of Neill's conduct of the study persisted and reappeared when President Taft asked Congress to reconfirm Neill as Commissioner in 1913.

The Bureau's statistical work

Neill continually sought to improve the quality of the Bureau's statistical work. One of his first activities upon becoming Commissioner was to visit the Bureau's agents in the field. He had heard, he said, "serious charges affecting the integrity" of their work, and reports of "a large degree of loafing and considerable drinking." "I made a trip through the country visiting practically every agent in the field and made inquiries in proper quarters concerning the character of their work."[88]

Collection of data on prices and wages was the primary activity of the field agents; for this, it was essential to be assured of the representativeness of the stores selected for obtaining prices and of the establishments selected for obtaining wages. The stores were to be those patronized by workers. In his trips to the field, Neill visited many stores to be sure the selection had been the proper one.

As a check on the validity of the agents' work, Neill decided to switch the territories and industries to which they were assigned. The agents protested that this would undermine the value of the personal relationships they had established with store proprietors and of their familiarity with the characteristics of the industry. Neill felt that certainty of the quality of the primary material collected overshadowed these considerations, and he went ahead with the reassignments.

Neill sought to take the Bureau's price and wage reports out of the climate of political campaigns. These reports had been published in alternate years, a pattern which had placed them "at the beginning of a political campaign and. . . a subject of discussion in the campaign. This led to attacks upon the report and the charge that it was prepared for political purposes, and attempts were made to discredit the integrity of the work." He decided to change the time of publication to nonelection years. "In this way we felt that it received consideration as a serious scientific study and would not be subject to the charge of being a political document."[89]

In 1908, Neill undertook an extensive revision and reorganization of the Bureau's statistical work. He halted the collection of data on retail prices and wages, partly because of the heavy demands on the Bureau's resources arising from the study on women and children, but also because he felt there were serious shortcomings in the concepts and techniques. Collection of retail price data was resumed in 1911 and wage data in 1912; information for the missing years was gathered retroactively. In the interim, Fred C. Croxton developed new techniques for data collection and supervised the reorganization of the field staff. [90]

When retail price collection was resumed, the new series covered 39 cities in 32 States, generally the cities with the largest population in each region, representing two-fifths of the urban population and one-fifth of the total population. One innovation was the arrangement whereby retail merchants furnished price information by mail directly to the Bureau each month. Retail dealers selected were those selling largely to the families of American, English, Irish, German, and Scandinavian wage earners. Neighborhood stores predominated; few downtown stores were included, no cut-rate stores were priced, and chain stores were included only where they were so numerous as to be an important factor in the city's trade. The grade of articles quoted was that sold in each city in the stores patronized by wage earners.

The Bureau cautioned that it had not "attempted to quote prices for an article of identical grade throughout the 39 cities. For almost every article, this would be absolutely impossible, as the grade varies not only from city to city but also from firm to firm within the same city, and the grade even varies to some extent from month to month within the same store."[91]

The Bureau presented "Relative Retail Prices of Food" for the 15 leading food items, representing approximately two-thirds of the expenditure for food by the average workingman's family. The relatives were presented in two forms—a simple average of the relative prices for the 15 items, and as indexes weighted according to the workingmen's expenditure patterns in 1901.

As Neill summarized the results of the reorganization of retail price collection, the information was secured from "a larger number of stores, is therefore more representative, is submitted monthly, and is more accurate, and what is more the collection of this field data from a large number of stores is now carried on at probably one-third or possibly one-fourth the cost of the former work."[92]

Regular publication of wage data was not resumed until after Neill left office. But in March 1913 he described the new data collection system. One of the changes was to have the agents specialize in certain industries, whereas formerly they had covered many. Also, they were to become more familiar with the nature of the work in the various occupations. "Under the new system which we devised, the agents are required to make a careful study of systems and occupations in the industries to which they were assigned." Neill went on to point out, "The importance of this is suggested by the fact that. . . methods of production in the United States frequently change, so that, while the name remains, the real character of the occupation has undergone radical change, and this fact should be reflected in the reports on these occupations."[93]

The series on industry wages and hours launched in 1913 reflected the improvements developed under Neill, including the application of statistical techniques for weighting and for constructing indexes. Further, successive reports on individual industries were made more comparable through provision of data for identical establishments and well-defined occupations, with weights based on the number of workers at each rate. Similarly, the work on union scales of wages in seven industries was systematized. The studies covered the cities included in the Bureau's survey of food prices, with indexes for wages and hours derived by weighting each city by the number of union employees in the city.

Wholesale price collection, begun under Wright in 1902, was maintained throughout Neill's term. The Bureau priced about 250 articles on an annual basis, generally in the New York market. At this time the wholesale index was not weighted, in the technical sense. Rather, the Bureau simply priced "a large number of representative staple articles, selected in such a manner as to make them to a large extent weight themselves." The quotations were collected partly from the standard trade journals and partly from different firms, or from chambers of commerce, by correspondence. The same source was used year after year so as to maintain the same standard.

Strikes and Lockouts was published as the Bureau's 1907 annual report. It provided data for the 1901-05 period on the number of employees involved in each strike, the duration of the strike, and the cause. It also indicated how the settlement was reached—whether by joint agreement or arbitration—and included a summary of the preceding 25 years. As with price and wage data, collection of strike statistics was suspended in 1908, and no further information on strikes was collected until 1914.

There were several efforts during this period to reorganize and coordinate statistical work on a broader scale, both within the Department of Commerce and Labor and throughout the Federal establishment. In connection with one such effort—the Interdepartmental Statistical Committee set up by executive order in 1908—Neill pointed out in answer to the committee's survey that, within the same Department, both the Bureau of Labor and the Bureau of Statistics published wholesale prices—even of the same commodities. He concluded, "The subject of wholesale prices, however, cannot be classed within the province of the Bureau of Labor; logically, it should be transferred to the Bureau of Statistics, provided a sufficient force be given that Bureau to keep this annual investigation at its present standard, or better, to extend and improve it."[94]

The committee took no action on Neill's suggestion. Nor did other attempts to coordinate the government's statistical work come to fruition during Neill's tenure.

Administration

Neill continued most of the top leadership from Wright's administration, including Chief Clerk G.W.W. Hanger, Charles Verrill, and Gustavus Weber. Ethelbert Stewart continued as one of the principal members of the field staff.

Neill had to deal with several personnel problems during his tenure. No retirement system was yet in force for Federal workers, and the Bureau found itself with a large number of elderly employees. Neill explained, "The Bureau has been, and still is, hampered in its work by having a number of employees who have been long in the service and reached an age when their usefulness in the work of the Bureau is considerably impaired."[95] At the same time, the Bureau lost some of its best staff members because of low salaries.

In 1908, in line with a governmentwide directive to improve efficiency, the Bureau moved to put its personnel system on a merit basis and instituted efficiency ratings for its employees. On the basis of these, Neill made a number of promotions and demotions, which led some employees to charge him with unfairness and discrimination. The Secretary of Commerce and Labor found the charges to be groundless, but they came up again 5 years later at Neill's reconfirmation hearing.[96]

Sufficient funding was a chronic problem. The many special studies the President and Congress called for, along with the reluctance of Congress to provide additional funds, strained the Bureau's resources. Regular appropriations remained at close to the same level during Neill's 8 years; extra funds were granted only for the largest studies. (See table 2.) As noted earlier, Neill suspended some of the Bureau's regular data collection programs partly because of the demands of other, more pressing work.

Table 2.   Appropriations for Bureau of Labor, 1906–13
(in thousands)

Fiscal year ended June 30 —	Total[1]	Salaries
1906	$184	$106
1907	173	107
1908	[2]323	107
1909	[2]323	107
1910	173	107
1911	176	107
1912	[3]191	103
1913	[4]270	103

[1]Includes salaries, per diem and etc., library, and medical examinations, but not allocations for printing and binding.

[2]Includes $150,000 for the study on working women and children.

[3]Includes a deficiency appropriation of $20,000 for special work.

[4]Includes $100,000 for the Industrial Commission.

SOURCES: National Archives Record Group 257, Bureau of Labor Statistics, Appropriations Ledger, 1887–1903. Legislative, Executive, and Judicial Appropriations.

The Bureau revised its publications program at about the time it introduced its revised price and wage series. Neill had already halted publication of the voluminous annual and special reports, relying on the bimonthly *Bulletin* to present more timely information. Since 1895, the *Bulletin* had presented original work, digests of State reports, summaries and digests of foreign labor conditions and statistical papers, and summaries of current legislation and court decisions. Under the new plan, the Bureau produced the *Bulletin* at irregular intervals, with each issue devoted to one of nine subject areas.

International activities

Neill continued Wright's interest and participation in international activities. In 1910, he served as the delegate of the U.S. Government to the Paris International Conference on Unemployment and as a delegate of the American Association for Labor Legislation to the Lugano Conference of the International Association. In that year as well, the annual U.S. appropriation for the unofficial International

Labor Office, carried in the Bureau budget, was increased from $200 to $1,000.

In 1912, Neill presented a paper at the International Conference on Unemployment. The same year, President Taft appointed him a government representative to the Fifth International Congress of Chambers of Commerce and Commercial and Industrial Associations.

Reconfirmation

Neill's second term as Commissioner expired on Feb. 1, 1913, in the midst of the transition from the Taft to the Wilson administration. Taft had sent Neill's name to the Senate for reconfirmation in January, but Democratic capture of the White House and Congress had prompted partisan debate over all Taft appointments. The influence of southern Democrats in the Senate created an additional obstacle for Neill, as his study of working conditions for women and children in the South remained a sore point.

On March 4, his last day in office, Taft reluctantly signed the bill creating the new Department of Labor. On March 8, President Wilson sent Neill's nomination forward. With reconfirmation before the Senate, two former Bureau employees submitted "Summary of Charges Preferred Against Charles P. Neill" in the name of "a large majority of the employees of the Bureau of Labor (irrespective of party affiliation)." They called for a "thorough and impartial investigation by the U.S. Senate," explaining that "such an investigation will show extravagance, maladministration, woeful waste of public funds, lack of executive ability, evasion of the Civil Service law, cruelty and injustice to the employees of said Bureau—especially towards Democrats and old soldiers."[97]

At about the same time, another former employee wrote to the new Secretary of Labor, William B. Wilson, charging that the previous Secretary had not satisfactorily answered his earlier allegations against Neill. The protestor concluded, "Neill has been the most daringly incompetent public official that has ever been foisted upon an unsuspecting labor contingent or an ambitious President."[98]

When President Wilson sent the nomination forward in March, Senator Benjamin R. Tillman of South Carolina wrote the Secretary that his appointment of Neill "would be a very unwise one to make," citing Neill's alleged bias against the South. Overman joined Tillman in opposition. To this allegation, they added the charge that Neill had demoted or fired Democrats and replaced them with Republicans.[99]

At Neill's insistence, Secretary Wilson launched a full investigation. A. Warner Parker, Law Officer of the Bureau of Immigration, conducted the inquiry, holding hearings and making independent studies. The complainants, along with Neill and the supervisory staff of the Bureau, testified fully.

The investigation again completely absolved Neill. Parker found no basis for the charge of unfairness to the South. Nor did he find political partisanship in the staff demotions, pointing out that no "cruelty and injustice" had been involved but that Neill had carried out a plan under a Presidential Order. Further, Parker stated that the Bureau had devoted more time and thought to carrying out the reclassification than was generally true in government.

The charge of maladministration had specified that investigations had been started "at great expense and then abandoned." One of the studies referred to was a report on Negroes in Lowndes County, Alabama, by W.E.B. Du Bois. Parker stated that the project had not been abandoned and that Neill viewed the work as "a report of great value." However, Parker stated, it "contained many of Professor Du Bois' personal opinions and also other matter not suitable for a government publication. . . . Press of other work in the Bureau has prevented either Dr. Neill or his chief editor from reviewing the work and editing out the objectionable parts."

As to charges that Neill had been away from his office an excessive amount of time, Parker found them exaggerated, noting that Neill's absence arose from the statutory procedures for railroad mediation under the Erdman Act. Further, in regard to Neill's administration of the Bureau, Parker wrote, "I was in a position to witness his remarkable familiarity with details, evidenced by the manner in which he could promptly respond to each and every call upon him for records, data, and information."

Thus, Parker concluded, "In closing this report, the evidence accompanying which I feel fully vindicates Dr. Neill of every charge preferred directly or impliedly in the papers turned over to me, I wish to add that Dr. Neill welcomed the investigation."[100]

Neill received many expressions of support during the reconfirmation proceedings. In January, the Executive Council of the AFL resolved that "Hon. Chas. P. Neill has served faithfully and ably in the capacity as Commissioner of Labor, and that his reappointment be strongly urged." The railway brotherhoods also urged Neill's confirmation.[101]

The Washington *Times* declared, "To defeat Dr. Neill's confirmation now would be equivalent to telling the sweat shop employers of the country that they have nothing to fear."[102] Alexander J. McKelway of the National Child Labor Committee wired the President: "Failure to confirm Neill would alienate the countless friends of the reform of child labor and woman labor abuses in the nation."[103]

Neill also received support because of his activities in railroad mediation under the Erdman Act, especially because his commission had expired in the middle of mediation proceedings involving the eastern roads. Before leaving office, Taft had written Senator Borah, pointing out that since February 1 Neill had been powerless to perform his Erdman functions. The President concluded, "The failure to confirm him may very well carry responsibility for serious consequences."[104] Ralph M. Easley of the National Civic Federation telegraphed Secretary Wilson: "The Federation never makes political recommendations but it felt that the public exigencies required the reappointment of Dr. Neill. His experience and tact in handling the railroad problems is required at the present time as never before."[105]

Not all of Neill's opposition came from the South. In a letter to President Wilson, a Massachusetts manufacturer wrote, "He has evidently felt it necessary to suppress all reports that do not agree with his preconceived ideas concerning labor conditions."[106]

President Wilson fought for his nominee. On March 21, he wrote Tillman, apparently basing his comments on Parker's preliminary report. "Whatever mistakes Dr. Neill may have made in judgment, he was certainly not guilty of the charges preferred against him." Wilson continued, "Circumstances have arisen which make it extremely desirable that I would appoint Dr. Neill in recess in order to make use of his services in arbitrating a pending controversy between the railroad switchmen and the 20 odd railroads that center in Chicago." The next day, the President made the appointment.[107]

Tillman had already dropped serious opposition, awaiting only a face-to-face meeting with the Commissioner to confirm his new position. He had "learned the kind of work he is doing and the kind of people who are attacking him," Tillman said. Also, the Senator explained somewhat enigmatically, "I learned this morning that he was born in Texas and is southern to the backbone in his prejudices and feelings."[108] On May 1, the Senate voted to consent to the appointment.

Resignation

Two weeks after his reconfirmation, however, Neill tendered his resignation and took a position with the American Smelting and Refining Company to organize and conduct their labor department. In his letters of resignation to the President and the Secretary, Neill wrote that it was "impossible for me to make the financial sacrifice required to continue in the Government." He took the step, he said, "with extreme regret and only because my personal affairs at this time require it."[109]

Secretary Wilson received the letter with "a deep sense of loss." He commented, "Your wide experience and sound judgment of industrial affairs would have been of great value to me in organizing the Department of Labor and directing its initial efforts in the proper channels."[110]

It was a testimonial to the nonpartisan character of the work of the Commissioner and the Bureau that, particularly in the face of the charges, the new Democratic administration was prepared to have Neill continue his service. Although the Bureau assumed its role in the new Department of Labor without his leadership, in many ways Neill had prepared it for its new functions.

Later years

Neill's career following his resignation was a full one, including many activities he had begun as Commissioner. Among these were mediation in the coal and railroad industries and work on the Railway Board of Adjustment.

Neill's work at the American Smelting and Refining Company has been described in the company's history: "Following the long-established Guggenheim policy of engaging the best qualified experts, C.P. Neill, who had been Labor Commissioner under the Theodore Roosevelt, Taft, and Wilson administrations, was engaged to direct the welfare and safety work. He was made chairman of the Labor Committee with Franklin Guiterman and William Loeb, Jr., as associates."[111] Neill resigned from the company in 1915 to become manager of the Bureau of Information of the Southeastern Railways, a post he held until his retirement in 1939.

Neill remained active in National Civic Federation projects directed at labor-management cooperation, mediation, and arbitration. When the Federation undertook a survey of industrial and social conditions, it named Neill as a member of both the Committee on Plan and Scope and the Child Labor Committee.[112] During the railroad and coal strikes of 1922, he was involved in Federation activities to bring the parties together. In October 1922, as part of the settlement of the coal strike, President Harding appointed Neill to a commission to investigate both the bituminous and anthracite industries and report to Congress.[113]

Neill continued his work as umpire for the Anthracite Board of Conciliation until 1928. At the 50th anniversary dinner of the Board, J.B. Warriner, of the Lehigh Navigation Coal Company and long-time operator member of the Board, recalled, "Charles P. Neill, the first long-term umpire, was a learned and scholarly man, keen and able, broad minded and liberal. He stands very high in my mind."[114]

Neill also continued to be active in civic and social welfare work, particularly concerning women and children. In January 1920, the Supreme Court of the District of Columbia named him to the Board of Education for a term expiring June 30, 1921.[115] In November 1921, when the National Council of Catholic Women opened the National Catholic School of Social Service in Washington, a graduate school affiliated with Catholic University, Neill became its first director. During the 1920's, Neill also served as a member of the Department of Social Action of the National Catholic Welfare Council.[116]

Charles Patrick Neill died in October 1942.

Chapter IV.

Royal Meeker:
Statistics in Recession
and Wartime

R oyal Meeker, the new Commissioner of Labor Statistics, faced a different situation in August 1913 from that of his predecessors. The Bureau of Labor Statistics was now part of the newly established Cabinet-level Department of Labor. The Secretary of Labor, rather than the Commissioner, was labor's primary point of contact. Thus, Meeker's dealings with organized labor were more circumscribed than was the case for Neill or Wright.

The influences on Meeker and the Bureau came from a variety of sources. In the early years, concern with unemployment in a deepening recession led the Bureau to begin studies on the subject and, in 1916, to start a regular series of reports on industrial employment. The Bureau also encouraged the activities of State and municipal public employment offices and the efforts of Secretary of Labor William B. Wilson to establish a national employment service.

Upon U.S. entry into the war in April 1917, government programs for increasing production, mobilizing the labor force, maintaining peaceful labor-management relations, and stabilizing prices and wages influenced the work of the Bureau. With statistics now used in planning war programs, the Bureau was called upon to expand its conceptual and technical work in the fields of prices and wages. This led notably to the development of a cost-of-living index. The necessary resources were provided by Presidential allocations from special war funds.

Meeker and the Bureau cooperated effectively with the War Industries Board's Central Bureau of Planning and Statistics, established to monitor and coordinate the mushrooming statistical activities of the war agencies.

The demands on the Bureau continued after the armistice, particularly for information on living costs. But the special funding from the President was now terminated, and the Bureau's budget was cut as Congress sought to return expenditures to "normal" following the war emergency.

When Meeker resigned in 1920, the Bureau had established a substantial place for itself as a provider of widely utilized economic data and had become a prototype of the modern statistical agency.

The third Commissioner

Royal Meeker was born in 1873 in Susquehanna County, Pennsylvania. As a young man, Meeker worked "on the farms of Pennsylvania and Iowa, in the lumber woods of Pennsylvania, in the foundries, machine shops, and factories, and at casual employments in several States"—all apparently before his graduation from Iowa State College in 1898.[1] He moved on to Columbia University as a graduate student under E.R.A. Seligman from 1899 to 1903, then spent a year at the University of Leipzig before returning to his native Pennsylvania as a professor of history, political science, and economics at Ursinus College during 1904 and 1905. He published his dissertation, "History and Theory of Shipping Subsidies," in 1905 and received his Ph.D. from Columbia the following year.

Meeker's association with Woodrow Wilson began in 1905, when he applied to Wilson, then president of Princeton, for a position as preceptor in economics. He obtained the appointment and taught, among other subjects, money and banking and transportation. He was named assistant professor in 1908.

He was also associated with Wilson in charitable and welfare activities. Meeker served on the executive committee of the New

Jersey Conference of Charities and Correction while Wilson served as a vice president. Also, he served on the Board of Managers of the New Jersey State Reformatory for Women while Wilson was Governor of New Jersey.[2]

After the election of 1912, Meeker offered his services to the President-elect, suggesting, among other things, a survey of the economic community on the banking reform issue. In this connection, he helped prepare a questionnaire and compiled the results for Wilson. In March 1913, the new President wrote Meeker of the findings, "They are most useful to me, and I warmly appreciate all the trouble you have taken in getting this material together."[3]

In June 1913, Secretary of Labor Wilson recommended Meeker to the President for the post of Commissioner of Labor Statistics. The President urged his acceptance: "I hope with all my heart we shall see you here a great deal."[4] Upon Meeker's nomination, *The New York Times* described him as "a close friend of President Wilson," who "has given much attention to labor problems." The *Times* also reported that he was frequently consulted by "Wilson Administration leaders on the currency question." The reference to labor problems may have been an overstatement, for Meeker had said little on the subject before his appointment.[5]

When offered the position, Meeker went to New York to talk with his predecessor, Charles P. Neill. Writing of the meeting, Meeker said that Neill "strongly advised me to tackle the job" but that he also "expressed the belief that the functions of the Commissioner are too many and incompatible." The role of the Commissioner in mediating and conciliating disputes in the railroad industry definitely caused Meeker to pause. He wrote Secretary Wilson, "I feel then that unless I can be assured that the Commissioner of Labor Statistics will be relieved of the duties of mediator in the disputes covered by the Erdman Act, I must ask you to withdraw my name from consideration as Commissioner."[6]

Nevertheless, Meeker wrote the Secretary, "I know the work is hard and the responsibility great; but I should deem it an honor and a pleasure to serve under you and President Wilson no matter what the task." Passage of the Newlands Act, which created a new agency for mediation of labor disputes, cleared the way for Meeker's acceptance, and the President transmitted the nomination to the Senate on July

22. The Senate confirmed the appointment on August 11, and Meeker was sworn in the following day.[7]

Meeker's views

Meeker, like Neill, was associated with the Progressive movement for governmental activism to achieve reform. In 1910, he wrote, "Before all else, the average American must be startled out of his stupefying faith in the divinely ordained destiny of his country. The policy of drift cannot possibly bring the ship of state to any desirable haven, and the sooner the crew are made aware of this, the better."[8]

Meeker carried over into his work as Commissioner his belief in the positive role of government. It was his duty, he said, "to turn the searching light of publicity into the farthest and darkest corners of industry, to make known the successes of enlightened policies of dealing with labor, to show up wrongdoers, whether they be employers of workers or workers of employers, to aid every endeavor to raise the ethical standards that obtain in the dealings between employer and employee, to bring about kinder feelings between master and man, and to foster the spirit of cooperative endeavor throughout all industry." For Meeker, the Bureau's role was crucial to ensuring that "the old policies of antagonism, belligerency, and warfare must give way to the policies of cooperation, mutual understanding, and peace." [9]

Linking morality and business gain, Meeker stressed the need for constructive approaches for dealing with the human factor in industry. As he expressed it, "The dissemination of information bearing on labor, the presentation of the facts which will enable employers to contrast the statistical results of the different systems and methods of dealing with labor, is of the utmost importance and benefit to business." The Bureau's publications "have aided business immeasurably by showing that the employer who deals justly with his workers can produce better goods and services at lower prices than the employer who depends for his profits upon low wages, long hours, and bad working conditions." [10]

But much remained to be done. He wrote, "Managers generally seem to regard the workman as a peculiar kind of peripatetic machine which installs and removes itself when and where needed without cost to the employer, needs no oil or attention, and scarcely ever is worth conserving or safeguarding because so easily replaceable when broken or worn out."[11]

Meeker viewed unemployment as one of the great hazards of life and felt that government had a larger responsibility toward the unemployed than merely "handing out bread and soup. . . ." He favored the establishment of a nationwide system of public employment offices with "the responsibility for the furnishing of suitable employment for all the unemployed, not merely jobs to the jobless, but economically paying jobs—jobs that pay an American living wage to American workingmen."[12]

Meeker set forth his views on this issue in his 1919 testimony supporting a national employment system: "I take it that every man and woman born in the United States is entitled to the privilege of earning a living, and that his job or her job should not be dependent upon any private fee-charging agency whatsoever. . . . It should be the first and foremost policy of our National Government to see to it that every potential worker is an actual worker every working day of the year outside needed vacation time."[13]

He was also concerned with protecting workers against other hazards. Asserting that "social insurance against property losses" was more common in this country than "insurance against personal hazards of workers or those in the lower income groups," Meeker argued that the laboring man should be protected against the hazards of accident, illness, unemployment, invalidity and old age, and death. He came to view such insurance as one of the necessities of life, just like food, clothing, and shelter—and as "essentially a public function" which "should be operated as a social enterprise." "I do not happen to be a socialist," he declared, "but, if it is socialism to provide adequate protection to the lives, health, and well-being of our working population, then let us have some more of the same."[14]

In Meeker's view, workmen's compensation provided not only a rightful and proper protection for the laborer but also an economic benefit to business and to society at large. Accidents had always occurred in industry, but the workers had had to shoulder the burden of this cost of production. However, said Meeker, the advent of workmen's compensation had wrought a miracle. Because compensation laws prompted safer and more efficient production methods—as managers sought to avoid the cost of claims—they encouraged generally better business practices. And the bitterest critics of compensation had become its strongest friends.[15]

Meeker's recommendations for workmen's compensation could be summed up in two words—compulsory and universal. The plans should be funded by the States and operated as a State monopoly or a State-controlled mutual benefit society from which all private casualty companies were excluded. And the plans should cover occupational poisons and diseases and compensate for permanent disabilities.[16]

He laid out six "minimum requirements" for the system. First, industry and government should concentrate on preventing accidents. When injuries occurred, the worker must be assured of adequate medical, surgical, and hospital care to cure or restore him as completely as possible. The injured worker should receive adequate compensation for himself and his family. When ready to return to work, he should be retrained, if necessary, for suitable employment. He should then be placed in an appropriate job. And, at proper intervals, he should be reexamined to make sure that the injury had responded to treatment.[17]

Meeker had expressed definite views on child labor before becoming Commissioner, apparently influenced by his work in the charities and prisons of New Jersey. Although, like his predecessor, he opposed child labor on moral grounds, Meeker recognized some fundamental economic necessities. Thus, while supporting restrictions on child labor, he also preached the need to improve education and training. In requiring school attendance and prohibiting factory work for children, society must also assure the quality of their education. "We must be sure that our schools are at least as good educational institutions as our factories," Meeker warned.[18]

Meeker advocated a strong, state-controlled school system. In an article in *The New York Times* in April 1913, he called for the compulsory public education of all children through the intermediate grades. All would be "busy preparing for the great business of living," with some beginning to learn trades, others, engineering professions or general culture.[19] He believed that many of the community's problems with crime and pauperism could be traced to an inadequate school system. As part of the remedy, he suggested vocational education, arguing that proper training in conjunction with counseling would help alleviate unemployment problems by giving guidance and resources to the unskilled.[20]

He favored some form of compulsory civic service for youth and proposed that, as "an antidote and partial substitute for militarism," all youth on completion of secondary or technical school be required to enter the service of the state for a period, serving in private employ-ment, government factories, farms, and mines. In addition to aiding youth "to find themselves and to select more intelligently a vocation in life," such service would diminish industrial strife by "giving sons and daughters of luxury a saving knowledge of blisters, backaches, and hunger, the first fruits of manual labor."[21]

Meeker supported government action to protect workers, view-ing the state of trade union organization as inadequate. However, he considered unions to be beneficial institutions, at one time even pro-posing that the state oblige "every laboring man to belong to a union, discriminating against non-unionism to the extent of actually prohibit-ing it. . . . Wages and hours of labor would not be fixed by inflexible statutory enactment, but by bargaining between employers and employees in approximately equal terms."[22]

Shortly before he left office in 1920, Meeker warned of the growing bitterness in labor-management relations, lamenting the inability to carry over the cooperative relationships of the war years into peacetime. He cited the British experience of securing worker representation on joint industrial councils and works committees. At home, he saw the resumption of employer opposition to unions and little prospect for continuing such wartime efforts as worker represen-tation on shop committees. "We are today exactly where the British were about 30 years ago," he stated. Meeker's conclusion was more an appeal: "Before abandoning ourselves completely to pessimism and despair, we should at least try the experiment of giving the workers a real voice and responsibility in management."[23]

Securing the Bureau's place

Meeker entered the Bureau at a time when government agencies were proliferating in response to specialized demands. One of his continu-ing concerns was to secure a clear jurisdiction for the Bureau, both within the new Department of Labor and in the growing Federal establishment. At the same time, he sought to establish cooperative arrangements so as to avoid duplication and provide uniformity in the statistical work of government agencies.

The Bureau in the Department of Labor

Meeker maintained effective relations throughout his tenure with Secretary of Labor William B. Wilson and Assistant Secretary Louis F. Post and, during the war years, with Special Assistant Felix Frankfurter. To a degree, this was helped by the early establishment of the Department Committee on Correlation, under Post, to coordinate the activities of the bureaus within the Department and to work with other departments and commissions on matters relating to labor.

In the new Department, the Bureau retained its old responsibilites for labor-associated statistics. In addition, it was given some oversight of the statistical work of other bureaus. Also, the Committee on Correlation set up agreements and procedures to avoid disputes between the Department's agencies. BLS negotiated one such agreement with the Children's Bureau on statistics relating to wage-earning children and another with the Secretary's Office on procedures for administering the Federal workmen's compensation system.[24]

During the period, several bills were introduced to create a Bureau of Labor Safety in the Department of Labor, one as early as July 1913.[25] Both the interest of the Department and BLS in the field of safety and their reluctance to see a new agency established were apparent in their correspondence with Congress on the bills. In August 1913, Secretary Wilson wrote Rep. David J. Lewis, Chairman of the House Committee on Labor, that "much useful work would be performed" by such a bureau but emphasized that the Bureau of Labor Statistics had "for a long time" studied accident statistics, accident prevention, and compensation, and had issued many reports and bulletins on the subject. The proposed new bureau was not established.[26]

Meeker also faced an active campaign by women's groups to establish a separate agency to deal with women's issues. BLS had had a women's division since 1911, but its studies had been limited by the failure of Congress to make appropriations for the work. Further, the women's advocates wanted an agency which would actively promote social reform rather than merely present statistical information. In 1916, Zip S. Falk, Executive Secretary of the Consumers League of the District of Columbia, wrote Secretary Wilson that women wanted to show "the human story of wage earning women." The Bureau, she said, published its reports in "an exclusively statistical form." And Edith Abbott wrote that the Bureau's 19-volume report on working women and children constituted a superior collection of facts, but a "commission inquiry would in all probability have been vastly more useful in promoting improvements in the condition of the working women and children." Abbott cited the New York State Factory Investigation Commission as an example of what she and her friends wanted—constructive publicity, not just dry facts. [27]

Initially, Secretary Wilson and the Bureau opposed the creation of a separate agency. Ethelbert Stewart, Meeker's second in command, argued that the Bureau of Labor Statistics had had a women's division for several years and that establishment of a separate agency would cause "duplication or conflict of jurisdiction." Besides, he said, women's concerns were part of general labor issues. The better procedure, he explained, would be to create by statute a women's division within BLS and to appropriate sufficient funds.[28]

At first, Secretary Wilson supported the Bureau's position, but the arguments of the women's advocates apparently impressed him, for he soon changed his mind. Upon "mature consideration," Wilson wrote to Rep. Lewis, "there is a vast field for investigation and study which specially and peculiarly affects women in industry which could be more effectively handled under the immediate direction of women than under the direction of men."[29]

The House Committee recommended passage of a bill to establish a separate agency, finding that the lack of statutory support had made for limited funding of the women's division in BLS and uncertainty over its continued existence, finally resulting in successive resignations from the position of division chief.[30]

Meeker reluctantly altered his views. In 1916 he wrote to Mary Van Kleeck, "As Congress seems disinclined to grant larger appropriations and larger salaries in the Bureau of Labor Statistics, I think the only thing for the women of the country to do in order to bring about the proper consideration of women in industry is to advocate the establishment of a Women's Bureau."[31]

Congress failed to act, however, and Meeker sought funds for special studies of women in industry and to create the statutory position of chief of the women's division, but with little success. In July 1918, Secretary Wilson established the Woman in Industry Service as part of the War Labor Administration, and, in 1920, with Meeker's full support, Congress created the separate Women's Bureau.[32]

The Bureau in the Federal establishment

Shortly after taking office, Meeker wrote Joseph P. Tumulty, private secretary to the President, asking for an appointment with Wilson to discuss his plans for the Bureau. He wanted to know if the Bureau's program "trespasses upon the preserves of any other department or bureau." He also expressed concern that Congress might create additional bureaus and commissions in disregard of the already existing bureaus.[33]

For several years, Meeker complained to congressional committees about duplication of work by government agencies. In 1914, he pointed out to the House Appropriations Committee, "There are no less than five governmental agencies that are commissioned by law to investigate the cost of living." And he wrote the President that Congress had ordered the Commerce Department to investigate the cause of rising food prices, emphasizing that only BLS collected retail prices on a regular basis and that, in fact, Commerce had turned to BLS for assistance. A little later, Meeker criticized Commerce for publishing material on wholesale prices: "The work that they do is but a small segment of the work that we are doing in wholesale prices."[34]

On several occasions, the Bureau complained of intrusions by the Treasury Department's Public Health Service. Stewart charged that the Public Health Service had begun studies of occupational diseases 5 or 6 years after the Bureau had done similar work for the study on women and children. He called the action "a deliberate infringement" and "an act of trespass" upon the functions of the Bureau of Labor Statistics. Before the Senate Appropriations Committee, both Meeker and Stewart criticized the Public Health Service: "They are not well fitted to do that thing. . . . Their statistics are extremely inaccurate and unreliable because they do not know the occupations."

In 1918, Meeker cautioned Secretary Wilson about an Executive Order proposed by the Secretary of the Treasury concerning the functions of the Public Health Service, alerting Wilson to the potential threat to Bureau programs. Yet during the war, the Bureau joined with the Public Health Service in a study of health problems arising from industrial poisons. Despite his continuing concerns, Meeker saw "no reason why there should not be full and cordial cooperation between the Bureau of Labor Statistics and the Public Health Service."[35]

Meeker also fought for a role for the Bureau in developing resources for industrial education. In February 1914, he wrote Tumulty that Congress had established a commission to investigate the field and also noted that the National Society for the Promotion of Industrial Education sought a separate investigation. In view of those activities, he wanted to make the President aware of the Bureau's efforts on the subject. As "the only Federal agency that has ever made a comprehensive study of industrial and vocational education and guidance," his Bureau deserved the work, Meeker argued, pointing out that BLS had made the pioneering studies and had invented the terminology.[36]

Ethelbert Stewart expressed like concerns in writing the Secretary about the new Federal child labor law. He stated that parents must be convinced that they would profit by keeping their children in school because of the child's increased earning power. This meant that schools must make the hope a reality. Training should reflect employment opportunities, and the Department of Labor should have the functions of developing both the national employment offices and the vocational training resources.[37]

Early in 1915, at the President's instruction, Meeker wrote a confidential memorandum outlining the major cases of overlapping and duplication in the Federal establishment. He listed six agencies competing with BLS: The Bureau of Mines of the Department of the Interior, for accidents in the iron and steel industry; the Bureau of Foreign and Domestic Commerce of the Department of Commerce, for wages and prices; the Public Health Service, for occupational health and diseases; the Forest Service and the Bureau of Chemistry of the Department of Agriculture, for industrial poisons; and the Bureau of Education, for vocational education.[38] In 1917, the Secretary of Labor pointed out several of these in his report to Congress on harmonizing the work of the various government agencies.[39]

Meeker used various forums to stress the importance of cooperation. In 1914, he told the National Safety Council, "We must get governmental agencies to work together. I regard that as my principal job." At the American Economic Association meeting in December 1914, he commented, "I sincerely hope that the proposed joint committee of the Economic Association and the Statistical Society to advise with the statistical Bureaus of the government will be appointed. Unnecessary duplication of statistical work should be eliminated, and the statistical methods used should be standardized and made uniform."[40]

The Bureau and State agencies

Meeker tried to improve communications with and among State agencies as well. He wanted to make the Bureau "the center for the dissemination of useful information regarding developments in the industrial field, to cooperate with the State agencies, and to secure their cooperation in making labor studies. . . ."[41] "I have, it seems to me, a very excellent plan which covers cooperation between my Bureau and the various State agencies that deal with labor matters. . . . You do the work, and I will reap the glory," he suggested to the Association of Governmental Labor Officials in 1915. More seriously, he declared his intention to eliminate duplication, to develop information where it was lacking, and to establish uniform statistical definitions and methods.[42]

When unemployment became a major public concern in 1914, the Bureau began a continuing cooperative relationship with the American Association of Public Employment Offices and regularly published its proceedings. In addressing the association, Meeker cited the need for national and local information on the employed and unemployed, including industrial and occupational detail. He suggested that the States were better able to obtain and furnish such information and indicated the kinds of information to be sought from trade unions and employers.[43] In 1916, shortly after the Bureau began its employment series, it arranged with the New York State Department of Labor for the mutual use of the employment data collected by that agency.

The Bureau's work: Meeker's first term

Price indexes

One of Meeker's first projects was revision of the index numbers of retail and wholesale prices. He later commented, "Long before I took charge of the Bureau, I had become very suspicious of the Bureau's index numbers, especially its retail price index. . . . Before I had got settled in the saddle, I set about to revise and recalculate the index numbers published by the Bureau." He called upon his fellow economists; Irving Fisher and Wesley C. Mitchell were among the few who responded with helpful suggestions. He later thanked them especially: "Had it not been for the sympathy, encouragement, and counsel of Professors Mitchell and Fisher, I should not have had the courage to carry out the recasting of the Bureau's index numbers."[44]

The Bureau expanded retail price coverage in 1914. To obtain a more realistic measure of changes in workers' living costs, it increased the number of food items priced and added several cloth and clothing items. By 1917, retail prices were collected in 46 cities, as against 39 formerly; for 28 food items, as against 15 earlier; for the new category of dry goods, 8 items; and, in addition, for anthracite and bituminous coal and gas for domestic use.

Also, the method of computation of the indexes was altered by shifting the base from 1890-1900 to the most recent year and developing a chain index, making year-to-year comparisons easier. Actual prices, rather than averages of relative prices (percentages), were now used in determining relative change. The Bureau explained the reason for the new method: "When averages of averages of relative prices are thus piled up, it becomes difficult to comprehend the meaning of the final average." Under the new system, "A percentage based on average or aggregate *actual* prices of a commodity reflects more accurately the changes in the cost of that commodity."[45]

The wholesale price index underwent a parallel revision. In 1914, the Bureau increased the number of price quotations to 340, defined the commodities more accurately, and included more markets. Previously unweighted, the index was now weighted by value (price multiplied by quantity marketed) based on the 1909 censuses of manufactures and agriculture. Indexes were rebased and computed in the same fashion as for retail prices. The Bureau published its new wholesale price index in 1915, along with Wesley C. Mitchell's classic essay, "The Making and Using of Index Numbers."

The influences of both Fisher and Mitchell were apparent in the price index revisions. Fisher advocated chain indexes as more easily comparable than those on fixed bases. Also, Fisher believed that the wholesale price index could be computed from a relatively small number of commodities. Mitchell agreed that chain indexes were more accurate than fixed-base measures and that the series should be an aggregate of actual prices weighted according to the quantities marketed. However, he differed with Fisher about the size of the survey field: "The more commodities that can be included in such an index number the better, provided that the system of weighting is sound."[46]

Years later, before the American Statistical Association, Meeker recommended further improvements in the wholesale index: "In my view, the best way to achieve the 'best index number' is, first, to secure more trustworthy and more representative prices from (1) producers and (2) jobbers and wholesalers, and, secondly, to obtain more accurate statistics and estimates of quantities of goods produced, imported, exported, and consumed." [47]

Meeker early showed an interest in developing an international system of price statistics. In January 1914, the Bureau wrote to the Senate Appropriations Committee that negotiations were underway with England, France, and Canada. In March, Meeker wrote the President, "Plans for putting international statistics upon a common basis have proceeded so far that I think it highly desirable that I go to Europe to confer in person with the leading statisticians there." He made the trip, but the outbreak of war in Europe prevented any further work on the project.[48]

Wage studies

Shortly after resuming its program of industry wage studies, the Bureau was collecting payroll data for all industries that employed at least 75,000 workers. The Bureau surveyed nine major industry groups: Cotton, wool, and silk; lumber, millwork, and furniture; boots and shoes; hosiery and knit goods; iron and steel; cigars; men's clothing; slaughtering and meatpacking; and steam railroad cars.

The 1913 study on the cotton, wool, and silk industries gave hourly wage rates and nominal full-time hours per week. The 1914 study for the same industries added data on full-time weekly earnings. Moreover, in line with revisions in the retail and wholesale price indexes, the weighting system for the wage indexes was changed. The new industry relative was constructed as an aggregate compiled directly from employment data rather than as a relative of relatives.

Another innovation in the wage studies was the collection of data on the extent and regularity of employment. In a study of the hosiery industry, the Bureau introduced the concept "variation in employment during the year," appearing in other industry studies as "fluctuations in employment during the year" and "volume of employment."

Productivity measures also were introduced. A study of the lumber and millwork industry in 1915 presented output per one-man hour, cost per one-man hour, and cost per 1,000 board feet produced for logging and saw mill operations. For the boot and shoe industry, data were presented on "time and labor cost, by occupations in the manufacture of 100 pairs of welt shoes, the rate of wages or earnings per hour, and the number of pairs worked on per hour."

In 1913, the Bureau published union scales of wages and hours for 1907 to 1912 for more than 40 trades in 39 important industrial cities. The material consisted of time rates as stipulated in written agreements and trade union records made available to Bureau agents by local union officials. Later, the series was expanded to cover 56 cities in 35 States for 11 industry groups, and over 100 trades and occupations. The Bureau also constructed index numbers of wages in the trades and occupations covered, which it compared to retail food price indexes as a cost-of-living measure.

In addition to its regular reports, the Bureau was called upon for special wage studies. In 1914, workers in fish canneries around Seattle requested an investigation of wage conditions which the Bureau had to refuse because of a lack of funds. That same year, the Bureau gathered data on wages and conditions in street railways when a strike in Indianapolis pointed up the lack of available information. During the summer and fall of 1915, the Bureau conducted a special investigation for the Joint Committee on Printing. The Joint Committee was considering pay scales at the Government Printing Office, and the Bureau surveyed wages and hours from employer payroll records in the printing and binding trades in 179 establishments in 26 cities and presented those findings along with the union wage rates for the same occupations and the same cities.[49]

Cost-of-living studies
When Meeker came to the Bureau, retail price data were being used to set wage rates for some government work, as, for example, at the Government Printing Office and the Washington Navy Yard. In testifying on the data, Meeker said, "In order to settle upon what is a fair and reasonable wage, it is necessary to know what a dollar will buy and this is the most accurate information available to both trades-union men and to employers. . . ." However, since the Bureau had last collected expenditure data in 1901-03, the existing budget information

was obsolete: "It is, in my judgment, extremely necessary that, as soon as possible, provision be made for a new budget survey."[50]

In 1914, the Senate Committee on Education and Labor reported in favor of authorizing the Department of Labor to develop information on the cost of living in the District of Columbia. Meeker had indicated that the proposed survey would cover only nongovernment workers, and that existing Bureau resources would not be adequate for the study.[51] The Senate did not take further action, however. In 1916, Meeker testified that a survey would be helpful in determining a minimum wage level but that it would also help answer the pressing question: "What does it cost the American family to live?"[52] Finally, in December 1916, Congress appropriated $6,000 for the investigation.

The first phase of the study consisted of the collection of data on budgets of 2,110 families in the District during the first half of 1917. In the second phase, the Bureau studied the income and expenditures of 600 white women earning wages of under $1,100 a year. As the third phase, in cooperation with the Office of Home Economics of the Department of Agriculture, the Bureau conducted a dietary study of 31 families.[53]

Beginning in October 1917, the *Monthly Labor Review* carried a series of articles presenting the findings, one of which was that ". . . a very considerable proportion of the low-income families of Washington do not buy enough food to maintain the family members in health and strength." Among the wage-earning women, the Bureau found that the majority "were not only working at distressingly low wages, but a very large proportion of them were women who had been wage earners for many years." William F. Ogburn, after an intensive examination of 200 of the budgets, declared that an average family of man, wife, and three children under the age of 10 needed an income of at least $1,155 to say out of debt.[54] The Bureau published a cost-of-living index for the District in 1919, and, in 1921, added it to the list of cities included in the national index.

Industrial relations

The Bureau investigated several major labor disputes during Meeker's early days in office. Secretary Wilson called on Ethelbert Stewart in the fall of 1913 to mediate a coal mining dispute involving the Rockefeller interests in Colorado. Later the same year, Meeker sent Walter B. Palmer, who had investigated earlier troubles in Colorado and

Pennsylvania, into Michigan for information on a copper strike led by the Western Federation of Miners. But such assignments became infrequent once the new Mediation and Conciliation Service was fully organized and were not a regular Bureau function as they were under Neill.

The Bureau continued to report extensively on collective bargaining developments. From 1913 through 1916, it published five bulletins on the subject; four of these were on collective bargaining in New York City—three on the garment industry and one on the building trades.

In 1915, the Bureau resumed publication of data on the number of strikes and lockouts, including causes and results, based on public sources.

Employment and unemployment

Meeker's deep concern for the problems of employment and unemployment reflected the growing awareness that the United States lagged far behind other industrial countries in dealing with unemployment as a broad social and economic problem. As Neill had stated in 1912 at an international conference on unemployment, "The subject of unemployment has, up to the present time, received but a limited amount of attention in this country."[55]

The recession of 1913-14 spurred the Bureau to consider studies on unemployment. In early 1914, Meeker met with Gompers and Morrison of the AFL about possible projects on unemployment which the Bureau could undertake. But later in the year Meeker had to inform Gompers that the Bureau had done no work because Congress had failed to provide funds.[56] In requesting appropriations, Meeker had testified: "We have not anything that is worth the paper it is written on on the question of unemployment in this country, and, my heavens, it is up to this Bureau. . . to find out the facts."[57]

During the winter of 1914-15, however, the Committee on Unemployment formed by Mayor John P. Mitchell called upon the Bureau for a series of field surveys of unemployment in New York City. The committee had collected data from employers on the number employed in a week of December 1914 and for the corresponding week of December 1913. At about the same time, the Metropolitan Life Insurance Company, in cooperation with the Mayor's Committee, had surveyed its industrial policyholders in Greater New York. At the request of the committee, with personnel borrowed from the U.S. Immigration Bureau and the New York City Tenement House Inspection Service, the Bureau covered over 100 city blocks and some 3,700 individual tenement houses in January and February 1915. It found an unemployment rate of 16.2 percent, which approximated the 18-percent rate reported by Metropolitan. The results were published by the Bureau in *Unemployment in New York City, New York.*[58]

Meeker then contracted with Metropolitan for studies in 16 cities in the East and Middle West and in 12 Rocky Mountain and Pacific Coast cities. In August and September 1915, at the urging of the Mayor's Committee, both the Bureau and Metropolitan conducted surveys in New York City for a second time. The results of this work were presented in 1916 in a Bureau publication, *Unemployment in the United States.*[59]

Meeker declared of the program: "These studies constitute the beginning of what should be carried as a regular series of reports. . . . The Bureau of Labor Statistics should be in a position to give the fullest information to employers, employees, and the public as to numbers employed and unemployed." And he complained of congressional parsimony: "It is a great pity that no provision has yet been made for the collection and publication of statistics of unemployment by the Federal Bureau of Labor Statistics."[60]

Meeker gave several reasons for the continuing unemployment, foremost among them being immigrant labor which had, he said, poured into the country and had caused congestion in many labor markets. Furthermore, he argued, many corporations followed the deliberate policy of keeping "40 men waiting in line outside the gates of their plants for every possible job that might be open in their establishment." In addition, "overspeeded industries" contributed greatly to labor turnover.[61]

The Bureau's work on unemployment was only a temporary effort, overwhelmed by the demands of wartime, which turned labor surpluses into labor shortages. The lasting effect of the work, however, was that the Bureau did undertake a statistical program to reflect changes in employment levels. Beginning with five industries in October and November 1915, the Bureau introduced the monthly series, "Amount of employment in certain industries," beginning publication in January 1916. This was the start of the Bureau's establishment series on employment and total payrolls. Meeker could say later that these were the only official figures on employment and unemployment.[62]

The work on unemployment also led the Bureau to the study of labor turnover. As Ethelbert Stewart explained, the Secretary directed the Bureau to study unemployment, and the Bureau found that the problem of unemployment was seriously complicated by "men hunting for jobs, by the shifting of the labor force."[63]

Labor turnover studies became integral elements of the Bureau's support of constructive employment practices by management. Meeker commented on the abysmal ignorance of employers regarding costs to their companies and to men and machines "of the ill-devised and shockingly wasteful system of 'hiring and firing' men in a steady stream with no attempt to try them out, fit them in, train them and keep them."[64]

Meeker and the Bureau actively supported those employers exploring avenues for the regularization of employment through the periodic national meetings of the Conference of Employment Managers, predecessor of the American Management Association. The Bureau published the conference proceedings from 1916 through 1918. Meeker said that, "Like all meritorious movements, this movement to promote the more intelligent treatment of laborers has spread until it has become nationwide."[65] He stressed that employers could derive the greatest benefit from their wage payments by "shortening the working-day, providing rest periods at convenient intervals, advancing piece and time rates, cutting out all over-time, re-creating in the employee an interest in the job he is doing and helping him to get the most out of his earnings and leisure."[66]

The Bureau made several additional early contributions to the study of turnover with work on the seasonality and irregularity of employment in the women's clothing industries, in support of an effort by those industries in New York City to obtain better information on the question. Extensive field investigations in 1915-16 and a wartime study in 1918 provided the basis for summaries later published in the *Monthly Labor Review* as "Mobility of Labor in American Industry."

In 1916-17, the Bureau collected information on corporate welfare plans from 430 employers in an effort to spread information on ways to reduce turnover by improving working conditions. Also, the

Review carried many articles on specific plans in various companies and industries.

Social insurance

Royal Meeker's interest in social insurance showed in much of his work at the Bureau, for he defined it very broadly to encompass most forms of protective legislation for workers. In 1916, he wrote the President to suggest "bold action on social insurance" that would include a model law for the District of Columbia and Federal employees as well as protection for all workers in interstate commerce. Pointing to the high infant mortality and accident rates, he urged establishment of national health insurance and made a strong appeal for support for safety programs.[67]

Workmen's compensation. As under Wright and Neill, the Bureau continued to publicize and encourage experiments and improvements in workmen's compensation programs. The Bureau regularly presented materials in the *Monthly Labor Review* covering State legislation and experience. In addition, it published a series of bulletins on workmen's compensation laws and programs in the United States and foreign countries.

Between 1908 and 1916, the Bureau had direct responsibility for administering the program of workmen's compensation for Federal employees. From his earliest days at the Bureau, Meeker sought to have this responsibility transferred. Meanwhile, he suggested improvements in the system. In his 1915 report to the Secretary, he listed several administrative reforms that should be enacted. He also wrote the President about shortcomings in the program. His complaints included administrative confusion, in that Congress had established three separate systems covering different groups of Federal workers. Yet he found "the most glaring inadequacy of the present law" to be its failure to include all employees of the government. The second greatest weakness, in his view, lay in the failure to cover occupational diseases. In 1916, after considering several proposals, Congress created the separate Federal Employees' Compensation Board to administer the system.[68]

Industrial safety and health. Actively continuing the efforts begun under Neill to improve industrial safety and health conditions,

Meeker combined research into effects and exposures with efforts to establish a uniform system of statistical reporting. In a letter to Presidential secretary Joseph Tumulty in February 1914, Meeker set forth his view of the Bureau's role: "It seems to me imperative that the Federal Bureau of Labor Statistics should act as a central clearinghouse for State agencies, for the purpose of standardizing accident and occupational disease statistics. This Bureau should be in a position to furnish at any time advice as to the best methods of preventing industrial accidents and occupational diseases."[69]

In Meeker's opinion, the Bureau, rather than any other agency or private firm, should be able to say where the hazard lay, just what the danger was, and how best to remedy the situation.

Meeker and Charles H. Verrill of the Bureau staff worked with a committee of the International Association of Industrial Accident Boards and Commissions to develop standard methods and definitions for reporting accidents. "No one State has yet published statistics that are at all adequate to its own needs, and no two States have produced results that are in any way comparable." To help remedy the lack of adequate statistics, the committee recommended systems for classification by industry; by cause, location, and nature of injury; and by extent of disability. The Bureau offered to tabulate and publish State accident statistics and also provided the committee with the benefit of its experience in developing severity rates for the iron and steel and machine-building industries.[70]

The Bureau established cooperative arrangements for reporting accidents with the States of Massachusetts, Ohio, and New York, hoping to extend such arrangements, and it continued the close relationship with the National Safety Council begun under Neill. Meeker at one time served as chairman of the Committee on Standard Forms for Accident Reporting, and, in 1916, he was elected chairman of the Governmental Section.

With the cooperation of insurance companies, Frederick L. Hoffman produced *Industrial Accident Statistics* in 1915, which presented data from the Prudential Insurance Company as well as from the Census Bureau, several States, and three foreign countries. In 1917, the Bureau published Louis I. Dublin's *Causes of Death by Occupation*, which gave figures from the Metropolitan Life Insurance Company's Industrial Department.

The Bureau also continued to publish pioneering studies by Alice Hamilton on exposure to industrial poisons, especially in the lead industry. Hamilton also wrote on industrial poisons in the rubber and explosives industries. The publication of the report on the explosives industry in 1917 proved especially opportune, coming as it did when "the enormous expansion in the industry. . . has drawn thousands of green workers into occupations which subject them to serious or fatal poisoning."[71]

In addition, the Bureau published a study by John B. Andrews on anthrax as an occupational disease, a report by Lucian W. Chaney and Hugh S. Hanna on the safety movement in the iron and steel industry, and one by Arthur R. Perry on preventable death in cotton manufacturing.

Meeker acknowledged, however, that much remained to be done. In 1920, shortly before leaving office, he told the Pennsylvania Safety Congress, "It is a shameful confession to be obliged to make, but we don't know whether the net result of our efforts to reduce industrial accidents has been more accidents or fewer accidents, a greater or a smaller loss in disability time." He then urged more effort to establish uniformity in definitions, statistics, coverage, and compensation, work which the Bureau continued.[72]

The second term: Statistics for wartime needs

When the United States entered the war in April 1917, the state of Federal statistics was "woefully incomplete and inadequate." Bernard Baruch, Chairman of the War Industries Board, later observed that "the greatest deterrent to effective action" during the war was the lack of facts.[73] Problems in gathering timely statistics were complicated by the competing demands of the many independent statistical bureaus. The multiplication of questionnaires became so great by mid-1918 that complaints from respondents mounted.[74]

The need for coordination became increasingly evident, but there was debate as to which agency should have the responsibility. Both Baruch's War Industries Board and the Labor Department's War Labor Policies Board, headed by Felix Frankfurter, discussed the issue. One proposal called for establishment of a temporary organization in the Bureau of Labor Statistics to collect, compile, and distribute labor statistics for the needs of the various departments and war agencies.

However, the gathering and distribution of industrial statistics—including labor statistics—was placed under the charge of the Central Bureau of Planning and Statistics of the War Industries Board, with arrangements for coordination between the Central Bureau and Meeker.[75] While BLS did not obtain the principal coordinating role, its responsibility for labor statistics was recognized and enhanced.

Cost-of-living studies and standard budgets

The demands of the wartime economy finally permitted Meeker to achieve his long-sought goal of a new, comprehensive consumer expenditure survey. Throughout the war, the government was concerned with the manner in which wages could be adjusted for the rising cost of living. Thus, the August 1917 agreement between the Emergency Fleet Corporation and the AFL Metal Trades Department, which established the Shipbuilding Labor Adjustment Board, stated that the Board would "keep itself fully informed as to the relation between living costs in the several districts, and their comparison between progressive periods of time."[76]

Great Britain had set an early example for revision of cost-of-living measurement during wartime. At first, wage adjustments were based on the retail prices of food, but these were found unsuitable in a time of rapidly changing prices, even with more frequent publication. In June 1916, the British Board of Trade produced a new index number covering all groups of expenditures and representing the "average cost of living of the working classes."[77]

In the United States, proposals for adjustments tied to an index figured prominently in policy discussions. Some means of achieving stability in purchasing power had been discussed by economists even before the war. Meeker and Irving Fisher had corresponded on the subject as early as 1912. At that time, Fisher had promoted the concept of a "stabilized" or "compensated" dollar to obtain constancy in purchasing power by adjusting "the number of grains [of gold] which go to make a dollar." The change would be determined, according to Fisher, "by index numbers of prices, such as those of. . . the United States Bureau of Labor."[78]

Fisher again promoted the idea as the war economy heated up, focusing on the use of a price index to adjust wages for the increased cost of living. In May 1917, he wrote Assistant Secretary of Labor Post to propose a "half-way" plan for salary adjustment. Fisher suggested that, since food prices rose twice as fast as general prices, adjustment should be set at half the rise in the Bureau's retail food price index number. This would, he argued, secure "rough justice." Meeker rejected the assumption that all items rose at one-half the increase in food prices, recommending instead that wages be adjusted up or down according to the full rise or fall in the food index. That is, until a further investigation into the retail prices of nonfood commodities could be made, the index numbers of retail prices of food should be considered as representing changes in the cost of living.[79]

In the meantime, Meeker pressed to begin work on surveys of the cost of living of families in shipbuilding centers for the Shipbuilding Board. In December 1917, he estimated his need at $50,000 to conduct the surveys, and the President allocated the sum from his National Security and Defense Fund. In May 1918, the President granted Meeker's request for another $25,000 to complete the surveys.[80]

During the early months of 1918, the Bureau scrambled to conduct the surveys in 18 shipbuilding centers, covering family expenditures in 1917 and 1918. The Shipbuilding Board put the results to immediate use in setting uniform national wage rates for most of the skilled shipyard trades.[81]

In February 1918, Henry R. Seager of the Shipbuilding Board wrote Post that the Board relied on the Bureau of Labor Statistics for authoritative data on changes in the cost of living and that it would seriously consider using index numbers if the Bureau decided officially to establish index numbers of changes in the cost of living of wage earners in different parts of the country. He noted, however, that Meeker was not yet prepared to undertake the task because of the technical difficulties and said that the Board would wait for the Bureau to take the initiative.[82]

In March, the policy was developed under which the tripartite National War Labor Board was to administer wartime labor-management relations. Strikes and lockouts were prohibited, and, of particular significance for the Bureau's programs, prevailing wages and working conditions in localities were to be considered in fixing wages. But the "right of all workers, includng common laborers, to a living wage" was declared, with minimum rates "which will insure the subsistence of the worker and his family in health and reasonable comfort."[83]

By August, the Secretary of Labor supported an indexing scheme as the way of standardizing and stabilizing wages. He wrote the President, expressing the need for "properly weighted family budgets prepared by the Bureau of Labor Statistics and a record made monthly of the changes in the cost of living, the wage rate to rise or fall during the ensuing month one cent per hour for each change of eight cents per day in the cost of living shown by the investigations made by the Bureau."[84]

By June, the National War Labor Board was calling for nationwide data on the cost of living, and the Bureau, with an allocation of $300,000 from the President, began on the larger task. Meeker pointed out how the new survey would provide much better information than the earlier surveys of shipbuilding centers. Those studies were done in haste, he said, with time not available to calculate new weights based on quantities consumed, so the old 1901 weights had been used. Also, the number of articles priced was not adequate; miscellaneous items of expenditure were not priced at all. Further, specifications for individual items had not been adequately developed to insure future pricing of identical or closely related items. And the shipbuilding centers were too few and too untypical to be representative of the country as a whole.[85]

The national study was conducted in 1918-19. Some 12,000 families with incomes of about $900 to $2,500 in 92 cities in 42 States were surveyed. More than 300 agents visited the homes of wage earners and "small" salaried workers, and, on the basis of interviews with housewives, obtained information on expenditures and income for a 1-year period between July 1917 and February 1919. Data were collected on quantities purchased, as well as costs, in contrast to the 1901 expenditure study, which had covered only costs. Information obtained by interview was frequently checked against daily expense accounts maintained by the housewives over at least a 5-week period.

The first results of the survey appeared in an article in the *Monthly Labor Review* in May 1919, with others following for the several regions. These presented "average yearly expense per family" for food, clothing, rent, fuel and light, furniture, and miscellaneous, along with "total average yearly expenses per family."

In releasing the results, Meeker acknowledged their shortcomings. It was unfortunate, he said, that the study had to be conducted in an abnormal period. "Many families not only economized on clothes and house furnishings but actually skimped themselves on food," Meeker stated, "both because of the high prices and because of the intense Liberty Loan drives."[86]

The data showed, Meeker stated, that there was no American standard of living that provided "all the necessaries, many of the comforts, and a goodly supply of the luxuries of life." Instead, there were many different standards depending on the income and size of families. The lot of lower income families was especially hard. They needed, he said, higher wages and cheaper food, clothing, houses, medical treatment, and insurance. He concluded, "Let us make the minimum living standard in America one that will support life in decency and health."[87]

While finding the cost-of-living report "generally illuminating," *The New York Times* disagreed with Meeker: "The Bureau of Labor Statistics cannot be accused of countenancing an unjust wage for the American workman. Quite the contrary, its tendency is to raise an ideal standard, a standard incapable of being realized in any nation, and especially in the present acute industrial crisis."[88]

In 1919, shortly after publishing the results of the expenditure survey, the Bureau issued its initial report on changes in the cost of living—its first comprehensive set of cost-of-living indexes for the Nation and for major industrial and shipbuilding centers. Thereafter, indexes were issued semiannually for the Nation as a whole and for 31 cities. Pricing for 1913-17, the period preceding the expenditure survey, was based on records of retail establishments in the 18 shipbuilding centers. Beginning with December 1917, the Bureau regularly collected data in the 31 major industrial and shipbuilding centers for about 145 commodities and services. Washington, D.C., was added in 1921.[89]

Later, an academic critique of cost-of-living studies in the *Journal of the American Statistical Association* concluded that, while economists had for several years debated the difficulties of constructing a cost-of-living index, the substantial correspondence of the Bureau's numbers with those of a wartime pilot study by the National Industrial Conference Board was the best proof that such a measure was practicable.[90]

Meeker described the purposes of the nationwide expenditure study as including the formulation of standard budgets for use by adjustment boards in setting minimum and fair wage awards. To determine the adequacy of the market basket utilized in constructing the cost-of-living indexes, he declared, "A standard minimum quantity budget must be agreed upon which will allow a sufficiency of all necessary commodities and services, food, clothing, housing, fuel, furniture, house furnishings, and miscellaneous to enable the standard family to live healthfully and decently."[91]

After the war's end, the Joint Commission of Congress on Reclassification of Salaries called on the Bureau to formulate standard budgets for government employees in the District of Columbia. The commission found, using the Bureau materials, that rates of compensation had not kept up with increases in the cost of living.[92] The main Bureau work for the commission was published in two articles in the *Monthly Labor Review* in 1919 and 1920. One presented a total budget, at market prices, necessary to sustain a level of health and decency for a government employee in Washington, D.C., with a family of five. The budget represented "a sufficiency of food, respectable clothing, sanitary housing, and a minimum of essential 'sundries'"; but did not include "many comforts which should be included in a proper 'American standard of living.'" No provision was made "for savings other than insurance, nor for vacations, nor for books or other educational purposes." The cost of the budget was estimated at $2,288 in October 1919. The second budget provided similar material for single men and women.[93]

The data from the 1918-19 expenditure survey were further used to develop a standard "minimum quantity budget necessary to maintain a worker's family of five in health and decency." Constructed with the assistance of the Department of Agriculture and the National Conference of Social Work, the standard reflected requirements for food, clothing, housing, heat and light, furniture and furnishings, and miscellaneous items. The costs of the budget were not calculated by the Bureau.[94]

The Bureau's cost-of-living and budget information was cited frequently and used extensively by parties to wage disputes and by Congress, Federal agencies, private companies, and international conferences. Its value was recognized by such groups as the Industrial Conference called by President Wilson in December 1919. In their report, the conference participants stressed that "it is vitally important that the government maintain and even extend its machinery for investigating and reporting" on changes in the cost of living. As important as the wartime investigations were, "Exact and reliable information is equally important during the period of reconstruction through which we are now passing."[95]

Yet, despite appeals by President Wilson and Meeker, Congress was determined to return appropriations to normal after the war. In 1919, the Bureau sought a deficiency appropriation of $475,000 for cost-of-living work. Congress allowed $12,000.[96] Meeker had developed the cost-of-living and budget programs to a most promising level of utility—only to have their future threatened by congressional budget cutting in the postwar retrenchment.

The industrial survey
Wartime demands intensified the need to speed and expand the gathering and tabulation of information on wages and hours, strikes and lockouts, and labor requirements. Requests came from various Federal agencies and from State wage adjustment committees and departments of labor. These requests, and especially those of the War Department for wage information in the vicinity of cantonments, required sending agents into localities not previously covered in the Bureau's wage surveys. Meeker's attempts to secure funds for expanded surveys between 1916 and 1918 were unsuccessful.

In October 1918, with the encouragement of the Central Bureau of Planning and Statistics of the War Industries Board, Meeker and others again stressed the need for more complete wage statistics. The Bureau's regular program permitted only about 10 industry studies on 2-year cycles, and these were largely of "historical or antiquarian interest" when finally published. Meeker proposed that 30 or more industries be surveyed at least once a year.[97]

Shortly thereafter, the President allotted $300,000 for an integrated study of occupational hours and earnings to reflect wartime conditions and help resolve disputes. Almost immediately, Meeker wrote that, while the work was being planned and organized as quickly as possible, "it is becoming increasingly difficult since the signing of the Armistice to get needed information from employers."[98] The information was obtained, however, and in May 1920 the Bureau presented the results of the survey, which covered wages and hours during 1918 and 1919 for 780 occupations in 28 industries, covering 2,365 establishments in 43 States. Unfortunately, as the Bureau acknowledged, with the sudden change in production requirements following the war's end, the data in the report reflected the unsettled conditions of postwar reconstruction.

The Bureau declared that it "could render no greater service to the country" than to have such information continuously available and pleaded for the support of "accurate, reliable, and strictly impartial" investigations such as the industrial survey. By that time, however, Congress had already refused further appropriations to maintain the program, and only the more limited wage survey program was continued.[99]

Administration

The many activities of the Bureau under Meeker were conducted with only modest increases in congressional appropriations (table 3). Limited funds made for low-paying job classifications and few opportunities for advancement, sources of constant complaint by Bureau officials and others. In surveying the Bureau's work, Wesley C. Mitchell wrote that the field work in collecting price and wage data was "better on the whole than the office work of making these data into finished bulletins." While the clerical force "stood on a level rather above that common to government offices," BLS lacked an "adequate staff of skilled statisticians." The weakness of the organization, as Mitchell explained it, arose from the fact that the Bureau could not offer a satisfactory career to capable men.[100]

In 1916, Stewart stated, "The one criticism always levelled at the Bureau of Labor Statistics is that the value of our material is greatly decreased and, as some of our very warm friends insist, destroyed by the lapse of time between the gathering and the final issuing of the material. Now, it is simply impossible for us to get our work out in reasonable time with the office force we have."[101] And Congress threatened action that would, in the Bureau's opinion, make matters worse by prohibiting employees from taking outside jobs for pay. Stewart stated that such an amendment would force "fifty percent of the best men in the Bureau" to resign.[102]

The wartime emergency increased the pressures. Late in 1917, Stewart commented that most of the Bureau's positions had not been re-rated since the founding of the Bureau in 1885 and that "our men who are able to supervise statistical work have left us or are leaving us for better pay in the war agencies." Turnover increased so much that,

Table 3.   Funding for Bureau of Labor Statistics, 1914–20
(in thousands)

| Fiscal year ended | Appropriations | | Special Presidential |
June 30 —	Total[1]	Salaries	funds
1914	$185	$102	–
1915	206	138	–
1916	209	138	–
1917	212	138	–
1918	213	148	$75
1919	243	173	[2]625
1920	322	217	–

[1]Includes miscellaneous and deficiency appropriations, but not allocations for printing and binding.

[2]$50,000 of this was returned.

SOURCES: National Archives Record Group 257, Bureau of Labor Statistics, Appropriations Ledger, 1887–1903. Legislative, Executive, and Judicial Appropriations.

whereas in 1916 it had been necessary to hire 150 people to fill the 101 permanent positions, in 1917, 222 people had to be hired to fill 108 positions.[103]

The extensive wartime studies on the cost of living and the industrial survey had been conducted through allocations from the President's special fund. The Bureau lost this source after the armistice and had to cut programs to meet its peacetime budget. In March 1920, a *Survey* article, "Let There Be Darkness," stated, "Apparently the Federal Bureau of Labor Statistics is to be hamstrung by Congress. Its appropriation has been so cut that some of its most important work must be stopped."[104]

Both Stewart and Meeker testified in favor of plans to solve some of the long-range personnel problems. In 1916, Stewart spoke in support of a pension system for civil servants, arguing that the government pays elderly, inefficient employees anyway, pension or no pension. Many corporations had established pension programs, he said, "because they had a water-logged pay roll that they had to fix up. In other words, they had a pension roll without a pension system, and they had to devise a pension system in self-defense."[105]

Congress did pass a wartime bonus for government employees, but Meeker noted that it did not cover the increase in the cost of living. He argued that wages should keep pace with living costs and with raises in private industry. In fact, he drafted a bill to provide automatic adjustment of government salaries to changes in the cost of living as measured by Bureau of Labor Statistics cost-of-living studies and retail price surveys.[106] Congress established a pension system in 1920, but it was many years before the concepts of comparability and periodic adjustment for government salaries were incorporated in statutes.

Publications

Meeker instituted a new publications policy in 1915 with the launching of a monthly journal to supplement the bulletins published on an irregular schedule. The Bureau had felt the need for some way to present materials that were important but too brief for publication as separate bulletins. Also, in introducing the *Monthly Review*, Meeker sought to give more frequent and wider publicity to labor-related activities. He asked officials of Federal, State, municipal, and private agencies to notify the Bureau of their business so notices and reports could be published in the *Monthly Review*. The periodical, he said, would present the current work of the Bureau, the Department, other Federal agencies, and the various State bureaus. In addition, it would publish materials from such bodies as State industrial commissions, factory inspection commissions, and temporary investigatory committees. Furthermore, one of its special features would be notes and summaries from foreign countries, particularly valuable in providing information on wartime labor policies and experience in the warring European nations. To emphasize the nature of the subject matter, the Bureau changed the name of the periodical to *Monthly Labor Review* with the issue for July 1918.[107]

The *Review* encountered difficulties during the war. In July 1918, the Joint Committee on Printing resolved, "That during the continuation of the war [the Public Printer] be directed to print only such publications as are required for the essential work of the Government and which do not delay necessary war printing." This attitude resulted in cuts in the BLS printing appropriations, and also in later charges that Congress tried to squelch publication of information about prices and the cost of living. Meeker complained that the cuts could force the discontinuance of the *Review* and asked for a deficiency appropriation. Secretary Wilson replied that the Department would cover the shortage from its funds rather than ask Congress for additional money.[108]

Despite the emergency pressures, the *Review* expanded greatly over its prewar size, publicizing the first results of new Bureau surveys on the cost of living, the new budget studies, and other original work as well much information on conditions in belligerent countries. Its popularity prompted a change in policy. With circulation up from the initial 8,000 in July 1915 to 19,000 in June 1920, the *Review* was put on a subscription basis in July 1920. Meeker citied the shortage of paper, the high cost of printing and supplies, and the necessity to econo-mize.[109]

During the war, the Bureau cooperated with another agency in the Department, the Woman in Industry Service, in the preparation of publications. The bulletins of both agencies were edited by the Bureau and issued as joint publications. Reporting on this arrangement to Secretary Wilson, Meeker cited the saving of cost and time and sug-gested that other departmental units also take advantage of the "expert Editorial Division in the Bureau of Labor Statistics."[110]

International activities

Interest in labor developments abroad, a concern of the Bureau from the time of its founding, increased during Meeker's tenure, although efforts at developing international standards for statistics were aborted by the war. In 1914, the Bureau issued a bulletin on labor laws and factory inspections in six major European countries and reported on how the start of the war affected food prices in 18 countries. From its beginning, the *Review* carried articles on the effect of the war on wages, hours, working conditions, and prices in European countries. In 1917, at the request of the Council of National Defense, the Bureau issued a series of bulletins on British munitions factories, covering hours of work, fatigue and health, welfare work, and industrial effi-ciency, as well as on the employment of women and juveniles and on industrial unrest.

These and other studies provided important background material for the establishment of war labor agencies and policies in the United States. The importance of the information was evidenced by the sta-tioning of a special representative in Great Britain to keep the Bureau in constant touch with developments there.[111]

After the war, at Frankfurter's request, the Bureau prepared reports on the labor situation in foreign countries for the use of the U.S. delegation to the Peace Conference. Early in 1919, Meeker went to England as economic adviser to a group of employers for a study sponsored by the Department of Labor on the British reconstruction experience. Ethelbert Stewart was also sent to England to help prepare for the Washington meeting of the International Labor Conference.

The U.S. contribution to the quasi-official International Association for Labor Legislation and its Labor Office through a congressional appropriation to the Bureau for the purpose was continued throughout the war. However, with the establishment of the League of Nations and its International Labor Office, Congress discontinued the subvention.[112]

Resignation

On May 5, 1920, Meeker wrote President Wilson of the "flattering offer" he had received to head up the Scientific Division of the International Labor Office to perform work similar to that of the Bureau. He felt that this was a fine opportunity to help organize the new ILO, a major office in the League of Nations. At the same time, he recommended Allan H. Willett of the University of Pennsylvania, who had directed the industrial survey, as his successor. In his formal letter of resignation to the President a month later, Meeker expressed his commitment to the Wilsonian ideal of a League of Nations. "I regret very much to sever myself from your Administration, but it seems to me that I can best serve the ideals for which you stand by accepting this position."[113]

President Wilson supported Meeker's decision to go to the ILO but reserved his decision on his successor. The President wrote that, after consultation with Secretary Wilson, he had "come to agree with him that a better appointment would be Mr. Ethelbert Stewart of Illinois." He went on to say, "I know you would be gratified by the terms in which the Secretary of Labor speaks of your own work at the head of the Bureau."[114]

In commenting on Meeker's resignation, Secretary Wilson described him "as an exceptionally efficient administrator of the Bureau of Labor Statistics." He cited as Meeker's accomplishments, in addition to the Bureau's regular fact-gathering, which "he has handled with sound judgment and quiet determination," first, coordination of the Bureau's work with that of the States and standardization of industrial terminology and methods; second, reorganization of the cost-of-living work on a family budget or market basket basis; and, third, his wartime studies of wages and living costs, accepted by all the wage boards. The Secretary concluded that, while Meeker's sympathies "were always with the workers, he never allowed these sympathies to distort the facts."[115]

Later years

Meeker continued his activities in social and labor economics for the next quarter century. From 1920 to 1923, he served as Chief of the Scientific Division of the International Labor Office of the League of Nations in Geneva. He returned to the United States to serve as Secretary of Labor and Industry for the Commonwealth of Pennsylvania under the Republican progressive Gifford Pinchot from 1923 to 1924. In 1924 also, he went to China under the auspices of the Institute of Social and Religious Research of New York as a member of the Commission on Social Research in China. In 1926 and 1927, he was a professor of economics at Carleton College in Minnesota. In 1930, he became associated with Irving Fisher as president of the Index Number Institute in New Haven, a position he held until 1936. During this period, he also directed a survey of aged persons for the State of Connecticut and became a special agent of the Connecticut Department of Labor. In 1941, he was named Administrative Assistant and Director of Research and Statistics of the Connecticut Department, from which he retired in 1946. He died in New Haven in 1953.

Chapter V.

Ethelbert Stewart: Holding the Fort

thelbert Stewart, appointed in June 1920, was the first Commissioner of Labor Statistics to come from the ranks. Carroll Wright had hired him as a special agent 33 years earlier, and he had served the Bureau in increasingly responsible positions for most of the period. Although he was 63 when he became Commissioner, he devoted 12 more years to the Bureau, serving during the administrations of Woodrow Wilson, Warren Harding, Calvin Coolidge, and Herbert Hoover.

During these years, the political climate was not a favorable one for the Department of Labor or the Bureau. Congressional and administration policies encouraged business interests, and the Department of Commerce, for 8 years headed by Herbert Hoover, grew in influence. Congress also gave some attention to the needs of farmers, who were suffering from depressed prices, by granting the Department of Agriculture additional funds, mainly for agricultural statistics. Other agencies, however, were subject to economy drives.

Following the brief recession of 1921, there was relative prosperity during much of Stewart's tenure, except in agriculture and in such "sick" industries as coal and textiles. The growth of the consumer

114

durable goods industries—automobiles, radios, refrigerators, and electric and gas stoves—contributed substantially as mass production, low prices, and installment credit brought these products increasingly into American households. Even with prosperity, however, there was constant unemployment, attributed largely to technological change.

For the first time in a period of prosperity, organized labor was unable to increase its membership or influence. A combination of factors contributed, including antiunion policies in the growing mass production industries, the continuing craft orientation of the American Federation of Labor, conservative Federal labor policies, and court decisions unfavorable to labor.

While Stewart fought for funds to modernize the Bureau's statistical and analytical work, he was usually rebuffed. Only when concern over unemployment mounted in the late 1920's did Congress provide additional funds. Under difficult circumstances, Stewart maintained the Bureau's independence and objectivity, standing firm against misuse of its reports for political purposes. He broke new ground in the field of productivity measurement and, with the encouragement and advice of the professional organizations, achieved some gains in the coverage and reliability of the Bureau's traditional employment, wage, and occupational safety programs.

The fourth Commissioner

Born in Cook County, Illinois, in 1857, Stewart spent his early years on the family farm. Because of a stammer, he was "practically barred" from any formal schooling, but he read voraciously and received some private tutoring. At 20, he moved to Lincoln, Illinois, to publish the *Lincoln County Republican*, but later sold his interest. After trying several jobs, he went to work at the Decatur (Illinois) Coffin Factory. While at the factory, Stewart joined a "workingmen's club" in Decatur and became involved in politics. In 1885, he ran for city clerk on a workingmen's ticket and served as an officer at the Illinois State Trades and Labor Convention; he was blacklisted by the coffin company for his activities.[1]

In 1885, Governor Richard J. Oglesby appointed Stewart Secretary to the Illinois Bureau of Labor Statistics, apparently at the suggestion of Henry Demarest Lloyd, financial editor of the Chicago *Tribune*. Stewart had visited Lloyd, impressed by his attacks on the monopolistic power exercised by the giant oil and railroad corpora-tions, and they had formed what was to be a lifelong friendship.

Also in 1885, Stewart became editor of the Decatur *Labor Bulle-tin*, having joined the Knights of Labor a few months earlier. For several years to follow, he held positions with various labor papers.

Stewart was reappointed as Secretary of the Illinois Bureau of Labor Statistics in 1887 and for successive 2-year terms through 1893. In this capacity he participated in a number of investigations of labor conditions in the State.

In 1887, he obtained a position as a special agent for the new Federal Bureau of Labor. In 1889, he wrote Wright about the possibil-ity of securing a permanent position, but the Commissioner appar-ently demurred then because of Stewart's speech problem. He continued to do fieldwork for the Bureau in the Midwest until 1910. Among other major studies, he worked on *Regulation and Restriction of Output* with John R. Commons. Under Neill, he planned and conducted the fieldwork for studies of the telephone and telegraph industries and the Bethlehem Steel Corporation.

In 1910, Stewart transferred to the Tariff Board and in 1912 to the Children's Bureau, serving as statistician of each agency.

He returned to the Bureau of Labor Statistics in 1913 to function simultaneously as Chief Clerk, Chief Statistician, and Deputy Com-missioner, Meeker's second in command. In addition to his extended Bureau responsibilities, he served the Department in a variety of capacities. Between 1913 and 1916, Secretary Wilson called upon him to investigate and mediate strikes in coal mining, the garment indus-try, and street railways. In 1917, the Secretary appointed him to a board of arbitration for wage adjustment in New York Harbor. During the war he served as chief of the Department's Investigation and Inspection Service, part of the War Labor Administration, conducting a number of brief surveys. In 1919, he went to London to help plan the League of Nations Labor Conference that met in Washington later that year. On returning from London, Stewart served as a technical adviser to the Bituminous Coal Commission. In 1920, as the special representative of the Secretary, he investigated deportation cases and, in that connection, advised on bail policy.[2]

In June 1920, the Secretary recommended Stewart to President Wilson for the position of Commissioner of Labor Statistics to suc-ceed Royal Meeker. Stewart had not been Meeker's first choice, but the Secretary thought him better qualified, and the President accepted his judgment, issuing a recess appointment. With the change in administrations imminent, the Republican Senate refused to confirm any of the Democratic President's appointees, including Stewart. The new Secretary, James J. Davis, renominated Stewart, writing to the incoming President, Warren G. Harding, "The position. . . is a technical and scientific one, and I have become entirely satisfied, from conferences I have held with men qualified to advise in such matters, that Mr. Stewart measures up fully to the standard."[3] The Senate confirmed Stewart in April 1921.

Stewart served under Secretary Davis for 10 years and more than fulfilled his expectations. On Stewart's 70th birthday in 1927, Davis wrote him, "You were represented to me as a fearless fighter for right and justice, and you have proved to be all of that and more. . . ." In 1930, Davis noted that he had watched the development of the Bureau with great interest and commented, "I am becoming more and more impressed, not only with the breadth and scope of the work of that Bureau, but by the industry, energy, and enthusiasm with which its work is conducted."[4]

Stewart's views

Stewart emphasized the practical over the academic or theoretical. Something of a muckraking newspaperman early in life, he retained that sense of the human, of the person behind the number. As he himself said, "For 30 years, I have been struggling to put some flesh upon the bony skeleton of mere tabulation." He cautioned against "this mania for statistics," warning that "the only things that make human life human do not lend themselves readily to the statistical method."[5]

In discussing the Bureau's cost-of-living surveys, Stewart once said, "It is accurate by any test to which you can put figures. But, like all similar attempts, it is of little value because it is impossible to put the necessities and aspirations of any family into figures. We can easily determine what they spend, but what they should have is a matter of widely varying opinion."[6] Similarly, the use of such surveys for setting wages only "perpetuates that standard, ossifies conditions, and paralyzes progress." As he expressed it, "there is one standard of the cost of living—that is the cost, whatever it may be, of living the maximum span of life and living it fully. This cannot be figured from the day's or the year's grocery bill."[7]

But statistics could shed light on the human condition, contributing to the understanding and remedying of economic and social problems. Indeed, progress had already been made. Textbooks carried facts and figures compiled by the bureaus, and such education and publicity stimulated passage of legislation to improve the condition of workers.

Statistics could also help in other ways. Stewart explained, "In the mad effort to produce and sell without any accurate information as to the amount of each commodity required by the people of this country or of the world, we run factories long hours and on night shifts, and the result is to produce unemployment and panics." Unemployment could be reduced by use of consumption statistics to guide production operations. The use of wage and cost-of-living data to establish a "fair day's work" and a "fair day's wage" could smooth industrial relations.[8]

Stewart expressed his view of the Bureau's independent role in replying to the Secretary regarding an editorial which had objected to the Bureau's reporting on old-age pensions. Stewart declared, "So long as the subject matter is of sufficient general interest to justify the publication of the facts, and so long as the Bureau of Labor Statistics sticks strictly to the question of facts, then all I have to say to this is that anybody [who] dislikes the facts is in hard luck."[9]

In reviewing the decade of the 1920's, Stewart pointed out the importance of the Bureau's studies of the impact of technology on employment, observing, "Never before did mechanical and industrial changes strike so many industries, processes, and occupations at one and the same time. The working people of the United States are entitled to know what the changing industrial conditions are, where they are, and the nature and extent of the occupational readjustment which is necessary to meet them without loss of earning power or industrial status."[10]

Earlier, in 1924, Stewart had analyzed some of the causes of discontent and dissatisfaction among workers—low wages, extensive unemployment and lost time, and plant inefficiency, or, as he put it, "the feeling that their power and energies are being frittered away, that their life and energy are being exhausted in inconsequential and unnecessarily laborious toil." Capitalism, he concluded, had brought increased physical comforts but had also "rendered life more hectic, more nerve-wracking, brain and soul wrecking, than any of the systems which preceded it."[11]

He stressed the importance of the broader social context when considering a particular social reform. In discussing the limitations of workmen's compensation laws, he wrote, "If we prize individualism so highly as an ism, let us think of the individual once in a while. . . . If from conditions inherent in an industry, a man loses wages because of an illness contracted by reason of and in the course of his employment, he is just as much entitled to compensation as if a flywheel split in two and injured his arm."[12]

Stewart favored proposed legislation to set wage standards on Federal construction projects. "Is the government willing, for the sake of the lowest bidder, to break down all labor standards and have its work done by the cheapest labor that can be secured and shipped from State to State?" And, when the Bureau developed wage data on municipal street laborers, he found these to reflect "sweatshop conditions," even though, as he said, "It is pretty generally agreed that the public, when it acts as an employer, should be a good employer."[13]

In regard to the effect of the minimum wage on the employment of women, he stated, "Anybody who handles the minimum wage law ought to realize that what we should consider is not industry, not administration, not legislation, but the social question, society; it is the question of whether our men are going to decrease 3 inches in height in 25 years as the men in France did. No industry has a right to mold women who are to be the mothers of our men in such a way as to deteriorate the race."[14]

In the same vein, he opposed the "family wage rate," an experiment popular in some European circles, in which the worker's earnings reflected the size of the family, arguing that this was too narrowly focused. Society as a whole should pay its share for replacing what he called "the raw material of which civilization is composed," so he supported a "social allowance" from the "political and social institutions." Given such relief from the costs of child rearing, more people would marry, and fewer mothers would work outside the home, thereby improving homelife.[15]

Commenting on the effects of automatic machine production, Stewart argued, "Let us change our point of view as to the object of existence. At present, it is work, work, work; produce, produce, produce; and sell, sell, sell. We have no education along other lines. We do not know what to do with our leisure." He warned, in recognition of the likely effects of technological developments, "The whole machinery of education should be turned at once toward a study of leisure, and toward teaching the coming generation the use and purpose of leisure, for, take it from me, they will have plenty of it."[16]

On the subject of leisure, Stewart received considerable newspaper coverage for his comments to the Second National Outdoor Recreation Conference in 1926. In discussing the need for public parks and the difficulties of conducting social life in boarding houses, Stewart observed, "I believe that a girl who works 9 hours in the spindle room of a cotton factory, or 8 hours a day in a boot and shoe factory at the speed rates which now prevail, can stand a little petting." This prompted headlines such as "Petting in City Parks Advocated by Labor Department Attache," "Let 'Em Pet in the Parks," and "Wants More 'Petting' and Fewer Policemen."[17]

Stewart was equally forthright in evaluating the problems confronting industry. Writing on the textile industry in the *American Federationist* in 1929, he pointed to overproduction, the loss of foreign markets, the decline in wages, and the rise in night work, coupled with inability to adjust readily to style changes and the hoary and inefficient commission or agent system of selling. His conclusion was, "In short, the situation in the textile industry is just as bad or worse than it is in the bituminous coal industry, and the problem is in the hands of men no more competent to solve it."[18]

The Bureau's work

Although the Bureau was recognized as a valuable and capable institution by technical experts and professional societies, it found few opportunities to modernize and improve its work during the 1920's. Only through increased cooperative arrangements with the professional associations and State agencies did the Bureau manage to expand some of its programs. Stewart maintained close relations with the International Association of Industrial Accident Boards and Commissions, the International Association of Public Employment Services, and the Association of Governmental Labor Officials, publishing their proceedings as Bureau bulletins. The Bureau also worked with the American Engineering Standards Committee, publishing an extensive series of its safety codes, and with the Personnel Research Federation and the National Conference on Outdoor Recreation.

The professional societies often came to the defense of the Bureau when its activities were threatened, as in 1922, when the Bureau of Efficiency recommended centralizing government statistical work in an enlarged Bureau of the Census. To be retitled the Bureau of Federal Statistics, it would take over the BLS programs of wages and hours, accident statistics, and prices. BLS, much reduced in function, would become the Bureau of Labor Economics.[19]

The American Economic Association and the American Statistical Association opposed the change. They pointed out that such an increase in responsibilities might swamp the Census staff, that there was in fact less duplication of statistical work than a "superficial survey" might indicate, and that friends of the Census Bureau should concern themselves more with securing larger appropriations to attract the best professional staff than with expanding its authority.[20] Talk of reorganization of statistical work subsided during the rest of the decade, and the Bureau's functions remained intact, although jurisdictional disputes flared from time to time.

Stewart and the Bureau also put considerable emphasis on developing cooperative relations with the State bureaus and establishing a nationwide network of reporting agencies. In this way, the Bureau was able to expand some of its programs despite congressional refusal to increase appropriations. Late in the decade, Stewart outlined several of the cooperative programs, specifically in employment, union wage, building permit, and accident statistics. Joining in one or more of the programs were New York, Illinois, Wisconsin, Massachusetts, Maryland, California, New Jersey, Michigan, and Pennsylvania.

In the business-oriented 1920's, the Bureau's relations with the business community were limited, but Stewart was fairly successful in obtaining cooperation in expanding regular, routine series on wages and employment. His contacts were mostly with research directors, safety experts, and personnel managers.

Cost-of-living and price indexes

Not long after he became Commissioner, Stewart was faced with a possible transfer of the cost-of-living work to another agency. In 1921, Secretary of Commerce Hoover, with President Harding's support, pressed to have the Census Bureau issue the cost-of-living reports.

121

Hoover claimed that the shift would result in greater accuracy, economy, and efficiency and complained that BLS was not cooperating with the Census Bureau. When *The New York Times* reported the proposed transfer, Secretary of Labor Davis indicated that no decision had been reached. Hoover, however, replied, "So far as I am aware, there is no dispute over this matter unless it arises from minor employees of the government who fear that, through any reorganization of method, their positions and authority might be curtailed."[21]

Stewart assured Secretary Davis that BLS was cooperating with the Census Bureau and would continue to do so in every way possible. No action was taken on Hoover's proposal.[22]

In appropriations hearings, Stewart regularly cited uses of the Bureau's cost-of-living index in wage adjustments. In 1923, he reported that more than half the settlements in wage controversies were based on the index. However, he was unable to obtain funds to maintain quarterly collection and publication. In his 1923 annual report, Stewart wrote, "It is very plain that the Bureau must continue to make these surveys every 3 months no matter at what cost, and the only immediate problem is how to answer the demand for such surveys from smaller cities and from a wider geographical distribution of industrial centers." But the director of the Bureau of the Budget responded that the President wanted BLS to live within its appropriation even if the surveys had to be curtailed. In May 1925, the work was put on a semiannual basis. [23]

In 1927, Stewart set forth the need for a new family budget study on which to base a revision of the cost-of-living index to reflect the changes in purchasing patterns, population distribution, and retail establishments since the last survey. He stated, "It is a very serious question as to whether or not the Bureau should continue to collect up-to-date prices to be applied to a 1918 quantity distribution of family purchases and call this an up-to-date cost of living." He proposed a new survey to cover a better variety of industrial centers, a larger number of smaller cities, a larger number of families, and families with a higher income level. Among the influences on consumers which such a study would reflect would be the increased purchase of automobiles and radios, the rise of installment payment plans, new types and locations of retail stores, and the growth of advertising.[24]

Support for a new study came from outside professional organizations, but Congress would not provide funds during Stewart's term.

However, a limited study was conducted in 1928, when Congress directed the Personnel Classification Board to formulate a wage scale for the government field service. The Board asked for BLS assistance, and the Bureau responded with a survey of the incomes and expenditures of the families of 506 Federal employees in Baltimore, Boston, New York, Chicago, and New Orleans. [25]

The Bureau also participated in an innovative cost-of-living inquiry conducted by the International Labor Office in 1930-31. The study originated with a request by the Ford Motor Company for information to help in setting wage rates of its employees in certain European cities to ensure the same general living standard as that of its employees in Detroit. The Bureau conducted the work in Detroit, covering a sample of 100 families. The Detroit budget was then used by the various European statistical agencies, with adjustment for differences in national consumption habits, government social insurance payments, and other factors, to determine the cost of living in those cities relative to Detroit. [26]

The Bureau did expand its collection of retail prices, a less costly and complex process than a consumer expenditure survey, so that by 1932, it included 42 articles of food in 51 continental cities of the United States and in Honolulu. The Bureau added electricity to the list of items priced—gas and coal for household use were already covered—but dropped dry goods.

The wholesale price index was revised and expanded several times during the period. In 1921, BLS completed a two-pronged improvement, regrouping the commodities and adding new articles and also shifting to the 1919 Census of Manufactures for weighting purposes. With data for August 1927, the Bureau issued a revised index in which the weighting base was changed from 1919 to 1923-25 and the price base was shifted from 1913 to 1926. At the same time, some new articles were added, such as automobiles, tires, rayon, and prepared fertilizer, and some old ones dropped, such as New York State hops and Bessemer steel billets and rails. With data for January 1932, BLS completed the third revision of Stewart's term, increasing the number of price series from 550 to 784, with adjustments back to 1926. At the same time, the Bureau began publication of a weekly index along with the regular monthly figures.

The wholesale price work was very popular. In 1922, the Bureau was providing data in advance of publication to such agencies as the

Federal Reserve Board, the Bureau of Standards, the Census Bureau, the Bureau of Markets, and the Federal Trade Commission. In the private sector, the *Review of Economic Statistics* based part of its Index of Business Conditions on BLS commodity prices.[27]

The wholesale price index became the focus of legislative proposals for stabilizing commodity price levels. A 1922 bill inspired by Irving Fisher would have pegged the quantity of gold weight in the dollar to a BLS index of wholesale prices to maintain constant purchasing power. In 1926, Stewart testified on a bill to amend the Federal Reserve Act to provide for the stabilization of the price level for commodities in general. The "price level" was defined as the price at wholesale as reflected in the BLS wholesale price index. Stewart gave considerable evidence on the index and supported the proposal, declaring that the responsibilities "are not burdensome and are entirely acceptable to the Department of Labor and to the Commissioner of Labor Statistics." In 1932, Stewart again testified on a proposal "for increasing and stabilizing the price level of commodities" by using data from the wholesale price index.[28]

With the onset of the depression, private research groups pointed out the need for better statistics on prices and living costs. In September 1931, the Social Science Research Council and the American Statistical Association sponsored a conference on improving the state of knowledge of price movements in the United States. The limits of the Bureau's cost-of-living index were noted, since pricing was based on 1918-19 family expenditures, as was the need for more comprehensive coverage for the retail and wholesale price indexes. The conference recommended construction of the official wholesale and retail price indexes by a single agency, with plans to be developed for a comprehensive family budget study when normal economic conditions were restored. Stewart agreed with many of the recommendations but noted the time and expense involved in carrying them out.[29]

Wages and industrial relations

Stewart expanded the collection of wage data, launching studies of the automobile, airplane, metal mining, cigarette, rayon, and Portland cement industries, among others. In the course of expanding coverage, the Bureau also focused on some new areas such as bonus systems and pay for overtime, Sundays, and holidays.

Stewart pointed out, however, that the limited funds permitted surveys of only about a dozen of the larger industries every 2 years at best, and that the importance of information on wages required at least annual reports, particularly for the newer industries. He cited the Bureau's embarrassment in meeting requests for data needed in tariff discussions with old information or with none at all.[30] The Bureau did continue annual publication of union scales of wages and hours, now grouped into about 12 trades and occupations in 67 cities.

A few new series were begun during Stewart's tenure. In the late 1920's, the Bureau started a monthly series on current general wage changes based on questionnaires sent to establishments and unions. Especially valuable were the series begun in 1932 on man-hours worked per week and average hourly earnings, obtained from reports of the establishments furnishing monthly employment data. Previously, only payroll totals had been available. The new information was an important addition to the Bureau's series, particularly for month-to-month changes.

Statistics on strikes and lockouts continued to be published quarterly until 1926, when they were issued monthly and supplemented by an annual report.

The Bureau also published much information on developments in collective bargaining. Bulletins on bargaining agreements were issued annually from 1925 through 1928. The *Monthly Labor Review* regularly carried information on labor agreements, awards, and decisions, and reports by Hugh L. Kerwin, Director of Conciliation, on the conciliation work of the Department of Labor. Other publications on industrial relations included studies of meatpacking, the West Coast lumber industry, bituminous coal mining, and apprenticeship systems in building construction. Studies relating to such aspects of welfare capitalism as the provision of recreational facilities by employers also presented information on vacations, sick leave, medical and hospital services, and group insurance.

Two editions of the *Handbook of American Trade Unions* were published. These listed union organizations and gave their history, jurisdiction, apprenticeship systems, benefits paid, and membership.

Employment and unemployment
The Bureau had published a monthly series on employment and payrolls since 1916. During the recession of 1920-21, in the absence of

measures of unemployment, the figures gained increased attention. In August 1921, the Senate directed the Secretary of Labor to report the number of unemployed, and Stewart prepared a response for Secretary Davis, reporting that "the best estimate that can be made from available sources of information is that there are at present 5,735,000 persons unemployed in the United States." He explained, "These figures relate to the differences in the numbers of employees carried on payrolls July 1921, as compared with the peak of employment in 1920," thus calling attention to the fact that the series was not a direct measure of unemployment, reflecting only "employment shrinkage."[31]

In transmitting Stewart's figures to the Senate, Davis alleged that the prewar unemployment situation had been worse, that more men and more breadwinners had been out of work in 1914. *The New York Times* supported the Secretary's position, pointing to farmhands drawn into the cities by the lure of silk-shirt pay but now returned to the farms, and to women factory workers who had returned to "the more normal life of the home." The *New Republic* however, vehemently disagreed, saying that Commissioners Wright and Neill and Secretary William B. Wilson had established a "tradition of accuracy and impartiality." It continued, "It remained for the present incumbent, in spite of the high standing of many of his bureau chiefs, to shatter this tradition. Manifestoes by the Secretary of Labor are no longer taken seriously in this country." [32]

In October 1921, at the urging of Secretary of Commerce Hoover, President Harding called a conference on unemployment, with Hoover as chairman. Varying estimates of the extent of unemployment were offered at the conference. The Bureau estimated the "shrinkage of employment" at 5.5 million. The U.S. Employment Service, which had been conducting its own surveys and issuing reports, estimated the number unemployed at 2.3 million. With such a range of estimates, the conference, as reported later, "merely voted to announce to the country that the number unemployed was between 3.5 million and 5.5 million, numbers startling enough to challenge attention."[33]

In 1922, after the conference adjourned, Assistant Secretary E. J. Henning directed the Employment Service to discontinue the publication of employment statistics in view of the function being performed by the Bureau. But despite agreements and directives, the Employment Service continued to collect such statistics. Stewart noted that both New Jersey and Pennsylvania refused to cooperate with the Bureau because of the duplication of requests from the two agencies. "It seems imperative," he said, "that unless the Employment Service gets out of the field, the Bureau of Labor Statistics must drop this feature of its work." In 1924, the Secretary again had to chastise the Employment Service, however, saying that its role was to match men with jobs, not to function as a statistical bureau. "Our Department already has one Bureau which devotes its energies to the gathering of statistics which affect labor."[34]

The matter did not end there. The Employment Service continued to issue reports on the general industrial situation, although it had stopped collecting payroll data from firms. The American Statistical Association warned in 1924 that these reports "tend to confuse the public mind, particularly when they are not in agreement with the more accurate statements based on payroll data put out by the State and Federal Bureaus of Labor Statistics."[35] Later, in the charged atmosphere of the Great Depression, such differences in unemployment estimates were to become politically explosive and were, in fact, to hasten Stewart's retirement.

An important outgrowth of the President's Conference on Unemployment was a committee appointed by Hoover to study the factors underlying employment and the practical measures that could be taken to prevent or mitigate unemployment. The committee called on the National Bureau of Economic Research for a study of business cycles and on the Russell Sage Foundation for a study of the adequacy of employment statistics. Under the direction of Wesley C. Mitchell, the National Bureau published *Business Cycles and Unemployment* in 1923, a comprehensive set of essays by noted economists. The American Statistical Association assumed the sponsorship of the study of employment statistics and appointed a committee on measurement of employment with Mary Van Kleeck of the Russell Sage Foundation as chairman. The full results of that study were published in 1926, representing the joint efforts and recommendations of the three organizations.

The report, *Employment Statistics for the United States*, was a landmark in the development of the role of professional advisory committees on government statistics. It recommended that BLS function as the coordinating agency for the publication of "a periodic report on employment throughout the nation," to include data made available by other Federal agencies and the States. It urged expansion of the employment series to include nonmanufacturing industries, information on hours worked, and additional data on characteristics of workers. It also recommended careful sampling.

The report acknowledged that employment statistics did not provide a measure of unemployment—they did not cover those who had never obtained employment, for example. And it pointed out the need for information on unemployment in local areas, since "the alleviation of distress can best be achieved in the locality where it is found."

The Bureau had already moved to expand its employment series, but the report served as encouragement and support for further work. By 1927, the Bureau's monthly reports provided employment and total payroll information for 54 manufacturing industries, covering about 11,000 establishments.

Outside experts were now examining the Bureau's data closely, and they pointed out some major shortcomings. For one thing, the series was still limited to manufacturing establishments and the railroads, and the shift of workers into distribution and service industries was not being captured. Further, Federal Reserve Board statisticians found a downward bias of nearly 2 percent a year in the factory employment figures when comparing them with the Census of Manufactures. The bias was attributed to the Bureau's slowness in picking up new industries, and new establishments in older industries. BLS was urged to adjust its data to the biennial census and to apply seasonal adjustment factors.[36]

In March 1928, with ominous signs of increasing unemployment, the Senate passed a resolution sponsored by Senator Robert F. Wagner calling on the Secretary of Labor to report the extent of unemployment and to devise a plan for periodic, permanent statistics. Secretary Davis responded, citing a BLS estimate of 1.9 million unemployed based on the "shrinkage in employment." Wagner and others were critical of the figure, claiming that the number unemployed was three times as large. He proposed three measures dealing with unemployment—expansion of BLS statistical programs, establishment of a nationwide system of employment offices, and creation of a Federal public works program.[37]

In May, Congress authorized $100,000 for expansion of the Bureau's employment series. With the funds, BLS would be able to double the number of manufacturing establishments covered and add establishments in agriculture, mining, building construction, and wholesale and retail trade. Data collection for some of these industries began in 1928.

In 1928 and 1929, the Senate held landmark hearings, chaired by Senator James Couzens of Michigan, on Wagner's comprehensive proposals on unemployment. Stewart testified on the "shrinkage of employment" and, as he had over the years, stressed that the Bureau's employment index was not an unemployment measure. He stated that a census of unemployment was necessary, from which the employment data could be adjusted to reflect current unemployment. To questions as to whether unemployment matters, including a count of the unemployed, were a State rather than a Federal Government function, Stewart responded that, while he did not intend the latter to assume all of the responsibility, it was the Federal Government's responsibility to undertake a complete survey. He pointed out that unemployment, in affecting purchasing power, affected commerce, which he saw as a Federal, not a State, concern. Furthermore, technological displacement of labor was a world problem.[38]

The Senate Committee had the benefit of advice from many technical advisers, including representatives of the American Statistical Association. Isador Lubin, later to become Commissioner of Labor Statistics, was economic adviser to the committee, on assignment from The Brookings Institution. Lubin and other technical witnesses supported Stewart's view of the need for a census of unemployment as a benchmark for the employment series, approved of the BLS effort underway to expand the reporting sample, and agreed that coverage of part-time employment should be added. [39]

Congress authorized the census of unemployment, and Secretary of Commerce Robert P. Lamont created an advisory committee to plan it. J. Chester Bowen, BLS Chief Statistician, served on the panel, as did William A. Berridge, of the Metropolitan Life Insurance Company and Aryness Joy, of the staff of the Federal Reserve Board. [40]

As public concern with unemployment intensified following the stock market crash of October 1929, the differing reports of the Bureau of Labor Statistics and the U.S. Employment Service again became a subject of debate. The Employment Service emphasized hiring prospects, and its figures showed a more optimistic forecast. The BLS data on employment and labor turnover provided a more accurate picture, but the figures appeared after the Employment Service releases. The administration highlighted the Employment Service figures, despite criticisms from New York State Industrial Commissioner Frances Perkins and others, and downplayed the more objective BLS data.[41]

Another incident grew out of President Hoover's request to Stewart for an experimental weekly employment index. In January 1930, basing his statement on the first weekly returns, President Hoover announced, "The tide of employment has changed in the right direction."[42]

A number of public figures attacked Hoover's statement. Frances Perkins said the numbers were based on too short a time period and did not correspond to data collected by her office. She further noted that the President had not quoted Stewart. Secretary Davis responded, "Unfortunately there is developing an inclination in some quarters to make politics out of our employment situation even to the extent of questioning the accuracy of the statement that the latest figures show an upward trend in employment." Senator La Follette, however, said of the administration that all it had done amounted to publishing "optimistic ballyhoo statements." In a February editorial, *The New York Times* noted that the Bureau's regular monthly numbers for January confirmed Perkins rather than Davis.[43]

Further incidents followed. In June, Secretary of Commerce Lamont released some very preliminary returns from the Census of Unemployment conducted in April. In a protest against what he viewed as attempts to reduce the unemployment count by separating those laid off from those with no jobs at all, Charles E. Persons, the man in charge of the Census tabulations, resigned. Perkins again complained of misleading interpretations given to the public. In July, following release of preliminary data on Greater New York City, Perkins declared that "a more accurate count" would have revealed more unemployment.[44]

These events, and the growing crisis, spurred action on improving employment statistics. In July, Congress enacted a bill sponsored by Senator Wagner directing the Bureau to "collect, collate, report, and publish at least once each month full and complete statistics of the volume of and changes in employment." Additional appropriations were provided.

At the same time, President Hoover announced the appointment of a committee on employment statistics to advise him "on methods by which we should set up statistics of employment and unemployment," later adding the consideration of "technological unemployment."[45]

Joseph H. Willits of the Wharton School of Finance and Commerce served as chairman of the committee, which included, among others, the Secretaries of Labor and Commerce, the Director of the Census, the Commissioner of Labor Statistics, representatives of the AFL and the National Association of Manufacturers, and academic experts. Among the technical advisers were W.A. Berridge, Meredith Givens, Ralph Hurlin, Bryce Stewart, and Ewan Clague. Thus, the committee constituted a "blue ribbon" panel of government and private compilers and users of such statistics.

After conducting several studies, the committee issued its report in February 1931. While noting the Bureau's efforts to expand the scope and samples of the series, the committee called for further improvements. In the manufacturing sector, it urged the Bureau to adjust its series to the Census of Manufactures to correct the downward bias reported by the Federal Reserve Board statisticians. It also called for data by city and State, especially where State agencies were not collecting such information. Sampling coverage should be improved to take account of the rise of new firms and new industries. The committee commended BLS for launching data collection in nonmanufacturing industries but called for further effort to include building construction and the growing "white collar" fields. On the measurement of hours worked and part-time employment, BLS should concentrate initially on manufacturing and railroads to gain experience for covering other industry sectors.[46]

The committee stressed the importance of accurate employment data for the measurement of unemployment. In the absence of some system of universal registration of the unemployed, nationwide unemployment censuses would provide the best measure, but these were costly and had other shortcomings. Therefore, the committee recommended the continuation of a decennial census of unemployment, possibly a quinquennial census, to which the employment series, with the recommended improvements, could be benchmarked.[47]

The committee gave considerable attention to the subject of technological unemployment, noting the difficulty of relating labor displacement to specific causes. Ewan Clague, who earlier had directed the development of industry productivity measures by the Bureau, was asked to prepare a preliminary survey. The committee stressed the importance of technological advance in any discussion of employment and unemployment, and recommended that fundamental data collection and case studies "should be a continuing part of the responsibility of the Federal Government and specifically of the Bureau of Labor Statistics."[48]

BLS had already begun many of the proposed programs. But the committee gave sanction and direction to a specific, comprehensive plan of action, and the Bureau's activities intensified rapidly. By 1932, summary reports covered 64,000 establishments in manufacturing and nonmanufacturing industries. With the assistance of several cities and States, the Bureau developed a series on construction industry employment, covering some 10,000 firms. Also, the Bureau developed a series showing the trend of employment in States, using data from State agencies to supplement BLS figures, as well as a series on employment in cities with a population of more than 500,000, covering 13 such cities by supplementing the monthly survey. However, an experimental survey of State, county, and city government employment and earnings proved unsatisfactory when reports declined substantially due to economy measures taken by those jurisdictions during the depression years. Federal civil service employment was reported beginning in 1932. The Bureau did not begin to benchmark its employment series to the Census of Manufactures until 1934.[49]

Industrial safety and health
The Bureau continued its campaign for improvement of industrial accident statistics. Its objective was to "do for the entire field what has been done for the iron and steel industry", referring to the Bureau's regular reports on accident rates in that industry begun in 1910. As Meeker had said earlier, Secretary Davis declared in 1923, "It is not greatly to the credit of our people that nobody knows with any substantial degree of accuracy how many industrial accidents occur annually in the United States. No one knows even the annual number of industrial fatalities. The difficulty in obtaining reliable data is due largely to the incomparability and incompleteness of the accident statistics published by the various States."[50]

Thus, the Bureau encouraged States and industries to adopt a uniform method of recording and reporting accidents. Stewart urged a strong statistical program to identify "where it will pay you to get busy."[51]

In the late 1920's, Stewart pushed for congressional authorization for a Division of Safety within the Bureau to act as a "clearinghouse for the information the States are gathering."[52] Although the authorization was never received, in 1926 the Bureau began an annual survey of industrial injuries in a group of manufacturing industries, based on State records and reports from establishments. With data for 1930 covering about 25 percent of the workers in some 30 manufacturing industries, it reported average frequency and severity rates.

Articles and bulletins covered a variety of related studies, including a survey of health in the printing trades and the mortality experience of union typographers, as well as several studies of industrial hygiene and industrial poisoning.

In addition, the Bureau cooperated with the American Engineering Standards Committee to write and publish safety codes. It also sponsored meetings such as the Industrial Accident Prevention Conference that convened in Washington in July 1926 with 33 States represented, a major step forward in cooperation. In 1926, the Bureau published a bulletin on phosphorus necrosis in the fireworks industry, the result of one of its investigations. Following this, through agreements with manufacturers, BLS was successful in eliminating the production and sale of small articles of fireworks containing white or yellow phosphorus.[53]

Social insurance
Social insurance and various forms of protective legislation continued to be an active interest of the Bureau. In the early 1920's, reports were published on workmen's compensation, family allowances, legal aid, cooperatives, a minimum wage, women workers, and child labor. Later in the decade, the Bureau concentrated on a relatively new field, pension and retirement systems. Following passage of amendments to the Federal retirement system in 1926, the Bureau launched a survey of 46 State and municipal plans, publishing the results in 1929 along with information on public service retirement systems in Canada and Europe. It followed with many other studies of domestic and foreign experiments.

The Bureau also published material in a related field, care for the elderly under private auspices. The *Review* presented articles on homes for the elderly operated by fraternal, religious, and nationality organizations, including one on homes for "aged colored persons."

The Bureau also cooperated with fraternal organizations in a survey of conditions in almshouses and "poor farms" around the country, developing the results in cooperation with the National Fraternal Congress.

Productivity and technological change
The study of productivity and the effects of technological change made important strides under Stewart. The Bureau had published studies on productivity in the lumber and shoe industries during Meeker's years, but, in general, as Stewart observed in 1922, "Few statistical subjects are more discussed, there is none upon which we know less."[54]

Productivity was an issue in labor-management relations in the 1920's. Wage adjustments recognizing the increased productivity of American industry became a goal of labor, formally stated by the AFL in 1925: "Social inequality, industrial instability, and injustice must increase unless the workers' real wages, the purchasing power of their wages, coupled with a continuing reduction in the number of hours making up the working day, are progressed in proportion to man's increasing power of production." [55]

Among spokesmen for management, there were divergent views on the role of productivity. Some contended that there were restrictions and inefficiencies in the work rules sought by labor; others reluctantly accepted the "economy of high wages" which would make for increased purchasing power to improve both standards of living and the demand for the increasing output of American industry.[56]

Stewart explained that the Bureau's work would not involve "what a man can do or what he ought to do. It is proposed simply to record what he does, as a matter of statistics." He had no sympathy with the use of such information "to drive men" in an "unreasonable speed-up," but believed that it was as important for industry to know "the time cost of production" as it was to know the labor cost or the material cost.[57]

In 1922, Stewart signed an agreement with the Babson Statistical Organization for a joint project on productivity, with the construction industry as the first subject. The study could not be carried out successfully, however, because of the great variation in materials among contractors and the lack of adequate records. Several other studies were completed and published—for longshoring and the shoe, brick, and paper boxboard industries—but the project was abandoned in 1924 because of a lack of funds and a shortage of staff equipped to handle the complex technical work.[58]

The groundwork for a more sophisticated program of industry productivity measures was laid in 1926, when Stewart brought Ewan Clague from the University of Wisconsin to direct a special project. For data on output, the work drew on the biennial Census of Manufactures supplemented by more current figures available from the Department of Commerce. Employment data came from the Bureau's monthly series. In 1926, the Bureau published output per man-hour measures for the steel, automobile, shoe, and paper industries. In 1927, measures were published for 11 additional industries. More extensive case studies of particular industries, such as the glass industry, also included output per man-hour measures.

Stewart cautioned that, while labor time was used as the unit for measurement, this did not mean that the increased output was due to the efforts of labor alone, or at all. "The increased output per man-hour in a given industry may have been due to more skillful and efficient labor, to new inventions, improved machinery, superior management, or any one of a number of factors; but the Bureau in these general summaries makes no attempt to determine the relative importance of these factors."[59]

Later, as concern grew over the effects on employment of increased productivity and technological change, the Bureau developed information on the displacement of workers. In the early 1930's, Bureau studies covered the effects of new technology in the telephone and telegraph industry; the amusement industry, in particular the effect of sound motion pictures; street and road building; agriculture; cargo handling; iron and steel sheet production; cigar making; and the automobile and tire industries.[60]

Administration

During Stewart's 12 years, the leadership of the Bureau changed little. Charles E. Baldwin was Stewart's second in command throughout, first as Chief Statistician and Chief Clerk, then as Assistant Commissioner. When Baldwin became Assistant Commissioner, J.C. Bowen succeeded him as Chief Statistician. Only two men served as Chief Editor under Stewart, Herman L. Amiss and Hugh S. Hanna. All four had been in the Bureau since at least 1909.

Stewart complained of underclassification of positions. As Commissioners had before him, he testified to Congress, "Clerks competent to do the work of the Bureau of Labor Statistics cannot be had at
these rates." This was one reason for the relatively poor attraction of
the Bureau for young professionals in these years.[61]

Perversely, even congressional attempts to improve pay for government employees affected the Bureau negatively. In 1927, Stewart
informed the House Committee on Appropriations that, although
Congress had increased the per diem paid to field agents, the Budget
Bureau had granted less than half the amount needed to cover the
increase. The liberalization resulted, he said, "in still further reducing
our possible field work."[62]

On one occasion, however, Stewart and Secretary Davis were
able to gain some ground in improving the status of Bureau personnel.
In September 1923, Stewart wrote Davis to complain that the Personnel Classification Board had rated BLS as a "minor bureau." In turn,
Davis wrote the Board, "There are four separate counts under each of
which it would appear a distinct injustice has been done in that the
real status of the Bureau has not been adequately considered. . . . I
cannot consent to the relegation of the personnel and work of the
Bureau of Labor Statistics to a Departmental clerical status." Concerned for the general treatment of economists, sociologists, and technical statisticians, the American Statistical Association, the American
Economic Association, the American Sociological Association, and
the American Association for Labor Legislation joined in protest.
Reversing itself, the Classification Board established the "Economic
Analyst Group" in the professional and scientific service.[63]

Congress routinely refused funds for expansion of the Bureau's
programs. In Stewart's first 4 years, the budget was at about its level in
1919 (table 4). In fact, Congress often reacted to Stewart's requests for
increased appropriations with suggestions for reductions instead. He
was pressed, for example, to justify the cost of field visits for data
collection in the wage and price programs when collection by mail
would be cheaper.

Table 4. Appropriations for Bureau of Labor Statistics, 1921–33
(in thousands)

Fiscal year ended June 30 —	Total[1]	Salaries
1921	$248	$173
1922	242	173
1923	242	173
1924	242	173
1925	288	215
1926	285	215
1927	294	220
1928	300	220
1929	[2]419	220
1930	396	273
1931	399	273
1932	[3]580	([4])
1933	450	([4])

[1]Includes salaries, miscellaneous, library, and deficiency and supplemental appropriations.

[2]Includes deficiency appropriations of $119,000.

[3]Includes supplemental appropriation of $140,000.

[4]Not available separately; total given as "salaries and expenses."

SOURCES: Legislative, Executive, and Judicial Appropriations. *The Budget of the United States Government.*

And the *Monthly Labor Review* was in jeopardy in 1921, when Congress, seeking to rein in government publications, put a requirement in an appropriations bill for specific congressional authorization for such journals. Approval for the *Review* was held up, and the need for economy was not the only reason given. Representative Stevenson of South Carolina, from the Joint Committee on Printing, declared that a Department of Labor pursuing its "legitimate functions" and publishing materials "legitimately to be used by the institutions of this country" would have no difficulties. However, "a magazine that reviews books and prints commendations of soviet literature and all that sort of thing . . . we do not propose that it shall be further published at the expense of the voters of the United States." Nevertheless, Congress passed the necessary authorization in May 1922.[64]

The disposition of Congress changed somewhat later in the decade. The Bureau's appropriation was increased by about 20 percent in 1925, with slight additional increases until 1929, when, with a weakening economy and growing unemployment, Congress granted a substantial deficiency appropriation for work on employment and unemployment statistics. Deficiency and supplemental appropriations were given for this work during the next years, but they often came too late in the fiscal year to be allocated, so that the Bureau of the Budget would delete the amount from new requests.[65]

International activities

The reporting of economic conditions abroad never flagged under Stewart. Bureau publications frequently presented statistics and reports on legislation and industrial developments in foreign countries. However, U.S. rejection of membership in the League of Nations in 1920 greatly limited BLS participation in international agencies. The Bureau moved to drop the annual allocation of $1,000 from its budget for the International Association for Labor Legislation. Stewart noted that the association had merged with the International Labor Organization, one of the constituent agencies of the League of Nations, to which the United States did not belong. Even so, the Bureau maintained "a friendly cooperation" with the ILO, especially while former Commissioner Meeker was there.[66]

Stewart did attend the meetings of the International Institute of Statistics in Rome in 1925 as a member of the U.S. delegation. He attended only one other international meeting, a session of the ILO Conference of Labor Statisticians in 1931. Stewart was there primarily because of the Bureau's work on the international study of wages and the cost of living for the Ford Motor Company. Stewart explained his reluctance to join in such functions: "If we send delegations to one of their conferences or conventions, I do not believe that we can escape the implication that we are as a country refusing to enter the League of Nations by the front door but are in fact crawling in through the back door."[67]

Retirement

On July 1, 1932, Commissioner Stewart, then 74 years old, was retired involuntarily under the Economy Act of 1932, which required automatic separation of retirement-age Federal employees after July 1932 unless specifically exempted by the President. Stewart's term ran until December 1933, but Secretary Doak's refusal to recommend an exemption resulted in his termination.

Observers generally attributed his retirement to factors other than age. The following incident, reported in *Time*, was also cited in other newspapers as the main reason: "Last spring, Secretary of Labor Doak told newsmen that he had been supplied departmental data which showed that employment was increasing throughout the land. Fooled before by such cheery statements from politically minded Secretaries, the reporters went to Commissioner Stewart to check up. The white crowned, white whiskered old man telephoned Secretary Doak that the statistics given him warranted no such declaration. Thereupon Secretary Doak recalled the newsmen, told them to disregard his earlier statement, and then, in front of them gave Statistician Stewart a tongue-lashing for daring to contradict his chief. It was Secretary Doak who refused to certify Mr. Stewart's indispensability to the President, thereby depriving him of his job."[68]

Stewart himself wrote that he had been considering retirement but "it was the cheap, boorish method employed that hurt me." The San Francisco *News* was more caustic: "In the city named for George Washington, it seems they fire people for telling the truth. Stewart has been in continuous government service for 45 years. He is recognized as one of the ablest men in his line in America, and his honest work on employment is particularly needed now. But, unfortunately for him and the country, he is too candid."[69]

For a year, from July 1, 1932 until July 6, 1933, Charles E. Baldwin served as the Acting Commissioner, and he tried to follow Stewart's policies.

Ethelbert Stewart died in 1936.

Chapter VI.

Isador Lubin: Meeting Emergency Demands

Isador Lubin was sworn in as Commissioner of Labor Statistics in July 1933, in the midst of the worst depression in the Nation's history. The Bureau expanded greatly during his tenure, first to meet the needs of the New Deal agencies set up to deal with the emergency and then to provide the information needed for guiding the economy during the war years. Through the force of his personality and the breadth of his knowledge and experience, Lubin provided the impetus for the Bureau's development into a modern, professionally staffed organization equipped to deal with the many tasks assigned.

The fifth Commissioner

Isador Lubin was born in 1896 in Worcester, Massachusetts, the son of Lithuanian immigrants. Helping out in his father's retail clothing business, Lubin learned of the uncertainties confronting factory workers in the early years of the century. He attended Clark College in Worcester and, with the goal of an academic career, accepted a fellowship at the University of Missouri. There he established a close relationship with Thorstein Veblen.

With U.S. entry into the war in 1917, Lubin, along with many other young academicians, was drawn into government service. For several months, he and Veblen were employed in the Food Administration, preparing studies dealing with food production and farm labor problems. In one study, they interviewed local leaders of the Industrial Workers of the World—widely viewed as radicals threatening the war effort—and reported that some of the grievances of the group were legitimate and that the agricultural workers involved were not receiving fair treatment.[1]

Lubin then joined the War Industries Board's Price Section at the invitation of its head, Wesley C. Mitchell. For a year, he was involved in studies analyzing wartime fluctuations in the prices of rubber and petroleum and their products, and the general effect of wartime government price floors and ceilings.

After his service in Washington, Lubin received an appointment as an instructor in economics at the University of Michigan and later was put in charge of the labor economics courses. He returned to Washington in 1922 to teach and conduct studies at the new Institute of Economics, which became The Brookings Institution in 1928. Among the studies he led were broad-gauged analyses of the American and British coal industries, dealing with the economic, social, and psychological influences on mine operators and unions, including the competitive effects of nonunion operations, national efforts at self-sufficiency in coal production, and alternative sources of energy.[2]

In the late 1920's, Brookings was a prime source of advice and research on the growing problem of unemployment. Lubin became a leading participant in studies of technological unemployment and of the British experience in dealing with unemployment. In 1928, he was assigned by Brookings to assist the Senate Committee on Education and Labor, which was considering legislation to deal with unemployment. He became economic counsel to the committee and, working closely with Senator James Couzens, the committee chairman, organized and directed the hearings, laying out the subject matter and selecting representatives of government, business, unions, and the economics profession to testify.

Brookings then assigned Lubin, at the request of Senator Robert Wagner, to assist in hearings on three bills in the spring of 1930. One called for expanded monthly reports on employment by the Bureau of Labor Statistics; another, for advance planning of public works to be activated during business depressions; and the third, for establishment of a Federal-State unemployment insurance system. Frances Perkins, New York State Industrial Commissioner, was among the witnesses Lubin assembled. Only the bill on employment statistics was enacted immediately.

Lubin helped organize the National Conference of Professionals held in Washington in March 1931 at the call of a bipartisan group of Senators led by Robert M. La Follette, Jr., to discuss a legislative program to combat the depression. The conference participants included governors, members of Congress, farm and labor leaders, businessmen, economists, social workers, and others. He also worked actively with Senators La Follette and Costigan in late 1931 and 1932 on bills proposing Federal relief and public works programs, again serving as economic counsel.

In August 1932, Senator Wagner asked Brookings to grant Lubin a leave of absence to work in his campaign for reelection. Lubin's 5 years of experience with measures to deal with unemployment proved valuable in Wagner's successful campaign, in which Wagner stressed his efforts to ease the burdens of the depression.[3]

In 1933, Frances Perkins, Secretary of Labor in the new Roosevelt administration, was looking for a Commissioner of Labor Statistics to fill the vacancy created by the retirement of Ethelbert Stewart. Lubin was on the list of candidates submitted by the American Statistical Association, and, knowing of his broad interests and experience, Perkins chose him as her nominee. Her biographer has stated, "When she offered him the post, she told him that he had been chosen because she thought he would remember that statistics were not numbers but people coping or failing to cope with the buffetings of life."[4]

Lubin's views

Lubin was prominent among those economists who saw the need for an increased role for government in economic affairs, particularly after the onset of the depression. As early as 1929, in reporting on the result of the study he conducted for the Senate Committee on Education and Labor, Lubin stressed that the so-called absorption of the "dispossessed" worker by "newer" industries was a "slow and painfully prolonged process." Further, many displaced workers were being forced into unskilled trades, with lower earnings and consequently reduced standards of living. "At the same time, they are being made to bear the burden of unemployment for which they are in no way responsible and over which they have no control." Lubin's assessment was that "unemployment is the result of industrial organization, and not of individual character."[5]

In testifying on unemployment insurance measures in 1931-32, Lubin stated that society was partly responsible for unemployment, resulting as it did "from the general disorganization of the economic system due to the fact that those persons who direct our system are not doing the job as well as it should be done." National corporations and industries and employed consumers benefiting from depressed prices should bear their share of the burden.[6]

It was his view that underconsumption resulting from the inequitable distribution of income had been a major factor contributing to the Great Depression. At the opening hearing of the Temporary National Economic Committee in 1938, Lubin stated, "A more equitable distribution is more than an ethical problem. . . . To me it is a problem of keeping the gears of the economic machine constantly in mesh." What was needed, he believed, was to so distribute income "that it will pull into our homes, through a higher standard of living, the goods, that is the clothing, food, entertainment, education, and so forth, which our economic machine must turn out at a rate considerably higher than at the present time. . . ."[7]

Lubin supported the establishment of minimum wages and maximum hours to protect the competitive system while making it possible for American workers to maintain a decent standard of living. In reviewing the industry codes established under the National Industrial Recovery Act, he frequently protested against the inadequate provisions on wages, hours, and child labor, and sought to include minimum standards for health and safety in the codes. With the establishment of adequate standards, Lubin stated, "Employers with a social conscience are assured that they will no longer be compelled to conform to the standards of competitors with blunted social sensibilities."[8]

At the final TNEC hearings in 1941, Lubin stressed the need for viewing the economy as a whole. "No set of measures that can be recommended will be adequate unless there is a fundamental underlying and continuing commitment that the goal of national economic policy is the full utilization of our resources, both of men and materials. . . ." When economic progress involved losses as well as gains, Lubin deemed it proper "that the cost of progress, which benefits the community as a whole, should be borne by the community. . . ." He called for defense contracts to require special dismissal funds to cover employees affected by cutbacks in defense industries in the postwar reconversion period.[9]

He believed events had demonstrated that government leadership and participation were required to meet violent economic dislocations, whether in peace or in war, since private enterprise did not adapt readily to such dislocations. No single program, neither the discouragement of economic concentration nor the indiscriminate spending of public funds, would bring a solution of these problems. "There is no panacea that will guarantee the creation of full employment in a free democracy."[10]

Lubin and the New Deal years

When Lubin assumed the leadership of the Bureau, he and Secretary Perkins were in agreement that the Bureau's staff and programs needed to be improved to keep up with the economic and social needs of the times. More and better information on employment and unemployment was of vital importance. More price data were needed by the agencies administering the National Industrial Recovery Act and the Agricultural Adjustment Act to determine whether consumers were being faced with unwarranted price increases. The National Recovery Administration also needed expanded and more current industry wage and hour studies for use in its code-formulating activities. And the new era of industrial relations ushered in by the National Labor Relations Act, as well as the division between the AFL and the CIO, called for more information on unions and collective bargaining developments.

Lubin added another dimension to the task: "Not only must raw data be improved but the Bureau must be enabled more fully to analyze the material it now has, so that evidence may be available as to where the recovery program is having the greatest effect and where it is falling down."[11]

Both Lubin and Perkins showed immediate interest in improving the Department's statistical program. Upon her appointment, Perkins called on the American Statistical Association to establish a committee for advice "regarding the methods, adequacy, usefulness and general program of the Bureau of Labor Statistics." This committee, whose membership included Ewan Clague and Aryness Joy, became part of the broader based Committee on Government Statistics and Information Services (COGSIS) sponsored by the Social Science Research Council and the ASA.[12]

Lubin readily acknowledged the role of outside experts in the "work of revision and self-criticism", reporting that "the Bureau has followed a consistent policy of consulting with recognized technical experts, and of constantly soliciting the opinions of employers and labor union officials regarding possible improvements to provide greater service."[13] At an informal meeting of labor union research staff members in 1934, Lubin announced the creation of a Labor Information Service for the use of local union officers and members. Relations with union research staff continued on an informal basis until June 1940, when a more formal relationship was established.

In mid-1934, Perkins reported that the Department's statistical work "is perhaps better than at any time during its history and represents the best technical standards, as to method, coverage and interpretation."[14]

Lubin and Perkins also were interested in improving the coordination of Federal statistical work. Immediately after his appointment in July 1933, Lubin participated in the setting up of the Central Statistical Board, which Roosevelt established by Executive Order at the end of July. Subsequently, Lubin and Perkins endorsed legislation for a permanent board, which was established by Congress in 1935 for a 5-year period to ensure consistency, avoid duplication, and promote economy in the work of government statistical agencies. The technical board was responsible to a Cabinet-level Central Statistical Committee composed of the Secretaries of Labor, Commerce, Treasury, and Agriculture. Lubin urged Perkins to press her claim as chairman of the committee with Roosevelt, and she was so designated. Lubin served as vice-chairman of the technical board.

While Lubin worked towards the improvement of statistical programs, Secretary Perkins encouraged a broader role for the Commissioner, giving him many special assignments, among them the chairmanship of a labor advisory board to the Public Works Administration. In this capacity, he dealt for almost 3 years with questions relating to the referral of union and nonunion workers to construction projects, job opportunities for Negro skilled workers in view of their exclusion from building trades unions, observance of arbitration awards, and determination of wages.

Lubin also served as chairman of a board set up to settle a strike of citrus workers in Florida in early 1934. The board included representatives of the National Recovery Administration, the National Labor Board, and the Department of Agriculture. The board's report called on the Department of Agriculture to insist that the marketing agreement approved for the citrus industry include provisions encouraging steady employment and recognizing the right of labor to organize and bargain collectively. In submitting the report to Agriculture Secretary Henry Wallace, Lubin urged that he establish an office to deal with agricultural labor problems. When Wallace took no action, Lubin proposed that the Bureau study the farm labor area. The effect of inadequate knowledge about these workers, according to Lubin, was their exclusion from all existing laws.[15]

When a strike threatened in the auto industry in November 1934, Leon Henderson, Chief Economist of the National Recovery Administration, asked Lubin's help in an investigation. The Bureau conducted a study of wages in the industry, including analyses of annual earnings, employment patterns, and seasonal fluctuations in production. Henderson and Lubin personally interviewed industry representatives. Among their recommendations was one accepted by the auto manufacturers, that new models be brought out in November, rather than in December, to achieve greater regularization of employment.[16]

Early in her administration, Perkins named Lubin chairman of a departmental committee to promote U.S. membership in the International Labor Organization. At the same time, she agreed to an ILO request to have Lubin serve on its advisory committee on labor statistics. Following U.S. entry into the ILO in August 1934, Lubin was the first U.S. delegate to its governing body. The Bureau was given responsibility for the administrative arrangements for continuing U.S. representation in Geneva, with funds for the purpose included in the Bureau budget.[17] Lubin continued to attend meetings of the governing body.

Perkins frequently asked Lubin to participate in economic discussions at the White House. He prepared analyses for her and for the

Central Statistical Committee she headed. Elected secretary to the committee, Lubin regularly prepared an economic report, which was abstracted for presentation to the National Emergency Council. In 1936, Perkins wrote the President that "the value of this arrangement would obviously be enhanced by Dr. Lubin's membership in the National Emergency Council. May I recommend and request that you designate him?"[18]

Lubin was soon given other White House assignments. He participated in the discussions the President held with business, labor, and government policy officials on measures for dealing with the major economic downturn of 1937. Soon after, he was the first witness in hearings on unemployment. In 1938, when Congress established the Temporary National Economic Committee to investigate monopolistic practices, the President asked Lubin to call off a lecture commitment to be on hand to help with preliminary arrangements.[19]

Lubin was designated as the Department of Labor representative to the TNEC, with A. Ford Hinrichs, the Bureau's Chief Economist, as alternate. Lubin had a large part in planning the work of the committee, in preparing analyses, and in making recommendations. The Bureau prepared several monographs for the committee, with Special Assistant Aryness Joy directing the staff work, which included both analytical and case study approaches.

Lubin's full-time direction of the Bureau came to an end in June 1940 when Secretary Perkins, at the request of Sidney Hillman, head of the Labor Division of the National Defense Advisory Commission, assigned Lubin to serve as Hillman's economic adviser. Lubin retained his position as Commissioner. In a memorandum to Hinrichs, named Acting Commissioner, Lubin stated, "In general, you are authorized on your own responsibility and without reference to me to represent the Bureau of Labor Statistics in any matters which may arise and to make any decisions that may be necessary either with reference to policy or internal administration." However, he would continue to be available to Hinrichs "on all matters of fundamental policy."[20]

Lubin's responsibilities grew under the Defense Advisory Commission, then under the Office of Production Management, and later under the War Production Board. Within a year, he was called to serve in the White House as special statistical assistant to the President. On May 12, 1941, Secretary Perkins wrote the President, "I am very glad to comply with your request to assign to your office and for your assistance Mr. Isador Lubin. . . . While Mr. Lubin will, I know, give you great assistance, his entire staff in the Department of Labor will be at his disposal to assist him in the inquiries he will make for you."[21]

Lubin remained as Commissioner on leave until his resignation from government service in 1946.

Hinrichs and the war years

Hinrichs served as Acting Commissioner for 6 years, supervising the wartime activities of the Bureau. He communicated with Lubin on a regular basis, but generally to meet Lubin's needs at the White House. His relations with Secretary Perkins were more formal than Lubin's had been.

A. Ford Hinrichs was born in New York City in 1899. He received his doctorate at Columbia University and taught there and at Brown University, where he was director of the Bureau of Business Research. In 1930 and 1932, he travelled to the Soviet Union, Italy, and Germany to study state economic planning.[22]

On his entry into the Bureau as Chief Economist, Hinrichs conducted a study of wages in the cotton textile industry requested by the National Recovery Administration for the development of industry codes. Later, he made a more intensive survey of the industry for the use of the Wage and Hour Administration. In early 1940, Hinrichs was designated Assistant Commissioner, shortly before becoming Acting Commissioner.

When Hinrichs took over the leadership of the Bureau in the midst of the national defense buildup, it had significantly enhanced its role as the factfinding agency of the Federal Government in the fields of employment, prices, wages, industrial relations, industrial safety and health, and productivity. It had an extensive file of data on economic trends and a staff trained to collect data accurately and economically.

With U.S. entry into the war, the agencies administering war production and stabilization programs needed a vastly more detailed body of economic data. Under Hinrichs, the Bureau became the factfinding arm of the Office of Price Administration, the National War Labor Board, the War Production Board, the War and Navy Departments, the Maritime Commission, and, to a lesser extent, other agencies. It supplied detailed information on employment conditions and provided estimates, by occupation and region, of the amount of labor needed to meet war production schedules. For price control and rationing programs, it provided data on wholesale and retail prices and the cost of living; for wage stabilization programs, it provided data on wages, hours, and the cost of living. Agencies such as the OPA and the WLB used the statistics from the Bureau to monitor the effectiveness of their administrative activities. The wartime work had a lasting impact on the Bureau's programs in improved quality, the expansion of regional and local data, and the development of more advanced statistical techniques.

The Bureau's work

The cost-of-living index
The Bureau's cost-of-living index figured in legislation immediately upon Roosevelt's entry into office. On March 20, 1933, Congress passed the Economy Act, which reduced Federal Government salaries by 15 percent on the basis of a drop of more than 20 percent in the cost of living since June 1928. Later in the year, as required under the act, the Bureau conducted a survey of the cost of living of Federal employees in the District of Columbia, comparing prices paid in 1928 and December 1933. Grouping expenditures for those earning under $2,500, over $2,500, and for single individuals living in rented rooms, the study found price declines averaging about 15 percent, except for the single individuals, for whom restaurant prices had not fallen as much as unprepared foods used at home.[23]

The national cost-of-living index underwent early improvement with the help of the Advisory Committee to the Secretary. By 1935, the index, still based on the 1917-19 expenditure survey, was published quarterly, calculated from food prices in 51 cities and other commodity and service prices in 32 of the large cities. Beginning in 1935, the national index was calculated by applying population weights to the data for the 51 cities. The number of food items was increased from 42 to 84, with a better representation of meats, fruits, and vegetables, and with weighting to make them representative of other foods whose pattern of price movements was similar. Pricing was based on written specifications, ensuring comparability from city to city and over time, and trained local personnel were employed on a contract basis to collect some of the data. The rent index was revised to make it more representative of wage earners and lower salaried workers.

Lubin pressed for authorization to conduct a new nationwide family expenditure survey and was able to obtain a special appropriation. Ethelbert Stewart had regularly, but unsuccessfully, asked for such authorization.

The expenditure survey was conducted in 1934-36, covering 12,903 white families and 1,566 Negro families in 42 cities with a population of 50,000 or more. Limited funds made it necessary to restrict the survey to large cities. The families included had incomes of at least $500 per year, were not on relief, and had at least one earner employed for 36 weeks and earning at least $300 or a clerical worker earning a maximum of $200 per month or $2,000 per year. The income of all the families averaged $1,524-$1,546 for white families and $1,008 for Negro families.[24]

The results showed a significant increase in expenditures for radios and used automobiles, and also reflected increased purchases of readymade clothing, gasoline, fuel oil, and refrigerators, better food and nutrition habits, better lighting in homes, use of dry cleaning and beauty shop services, and more automobile travel.

Data derived from the survey were incorporated in a revised cost-of-living index for wage earners and lower salaried workers in 33 large cities which was issued for the first quarter of 1940. One innovation was the inclusion of outlets representative of those patronized by Negro wage earners and salaried workers in cities where they constituted an important sector of the population.[25]

Almost simultaneously with the expenditure survey, BLS and the Bureau of Home Economics joined in a nationwide survey of expenditures of urban and rural consumers for the Works Progress Administration. The Central Statistical Board and the National Resources Committee sponsored the survey and led in the planning. At the opening of the TNEC hearings, Lubin called attention to the evidence from the survey that 54 percent of the 29 million American families had incomes below $1,250 a year.[26]

The requirements of the defense preparedness programs soon called for additional data on prices and the cost of living. In 1940, the National Defense Advisory Commission asked the Bureau to act as its statistical agency in the field of prices and to summarize price developments. Shortly thereafter, the Bureau was providing information on current price developments, special-purpose index numbers for war-associated products, additional pricing of such basic items as industrial chemicals and essential oils, cost-of-living price collection in additional cities and more rapid issuance of reports, and rent and housing surveys in defense production areas. Special studies were undertaken of commodities in short supply during the period of "voluntary" price regulations by the Office of Price Administration. The national index was now issued monthly, based on price and rent reports for 20 of the 34 large cities for which quarterly data were issued. By the end of the year, the Bureau also had initiated indexes for 20 additional representative small cities to compare changes in the cost of living in large and small cities.

In 1941, with the rising cost of living, the Bureau adopted a policy of keeping the index as up to date as possible. In 1942, consumer goods which were no longer available, such as refrigerators, automobiles, sewing machines, and new tires, were dropped. In 1943, the relative weights of rationed foods were changed to take account of their reduced availability. Also, commodity specifications were changed more frequently than in normal periods, and, with the introduction of Federal rent control, the Bureau began to obtain information from tenants rather than from rental management agencies. In addition, the Bureau conducted tests to determine whether the prices reported to field agents were those actually paid by consumers.

The validity of the cost-of-living index was further tested by an important economic study, the Survey of Family Spending and Saving in Wartime, notable for its use of probability sampling techniques. The survey was made primarily for the use of the Treasury Department in formulating its tax and war bond programs and for OPA and the War Production Board for decisions on rationing, price, and allocation policies. Data were obtained from a representative sample of 1,300 city families on income, spending, and savings in 1941 and the first part of 1942. The survey tested the relative weights in the cost-of-living index, establishing that they were substantially correct as of 1941. A smiliar study in 1945, covering 1944, resulted in minor changes in specifications and weighting patterns.[27]

The cost-of-living index had come in for review at the Bureau's annual conferences of union research directors from their inception in June 1940. Originally, these were basically technical reviews of the shortcomings of the index in view of changes in the availability and quality of commodities, additional expenditures by workers required to shift work locations, and rising prices in booming localities. Some participants called for a BLS pamphlet of questions and answers about the index, including what it showed and could not show. Lazare Teper, Research Director of the International Ladies' Garment Workers' Union, suggested that the Bureau point out that the index understated price rises due to quality deterioration and other wartime conditions, so that employers and unions could make appropriate adjustments in their negotiations.[28]

Later, when wage controls appeared imminent, some research directors asked the Bureau to either replace the index or supplement it by developing budgets for maintaining a working class family in "health and decency." Hinrichs contended that this was a matter for the War Labor Board to decide and not the Bureau. However, if the unions wished to press their case with the board, the Bureau was prepared to furnish them with the information on family income, expenditures, and savings from the survey conducted in 1941 and early 1942.[29]

The Bureau issued the pamphlet "Questions and Answers on the Cost-of-Living Index" in April 1942. The description of the index was relatively simple and clear. The pamphlet described the adjustments made for the disappearance and rationing of civilian goods. On the index's coverage, it stated, "A cost of living index can only measure the general change in the particular city of the goods and services *customarily* purchased by workers. It obviously cannot cover every conceivable increased cost which individual families experience." Among the costs which "by their nature cannot be covered in any measure of *average* living costs" were costs of maintaining the family at home while a wage earner worked at a distant job; commuting costs to distant jobs; higher costs, especially of rent and utilities, in cities to which workers migrated for defense jobs; and inconveniences caused by limited or disappearing goods.

Shortly after passage of the Economic Stabilization Act, in a letter to William H. Davis, chairman of the National War Labor Board, Hinrichs described the problems the Bureau faced in preparing the index. "You should be aware of the fact that we are experiencing considerable difficulty in the compilation of our indexes because of the many changes in kinds of consumer goods available. Moreover, as the rationing program is extended to more and more commodities, it will be necessary promptly to take account of the resulting changes in wage-earners' spending, if the cost of living is to be truly representative. We expect to make every effort to keep the index on the soundest possible basis and we will wish to discuss with your staff, from time to time, some of the policy problems which will arise in this connection."[30]

Davis replied, "We are much concerned that the Bureau's Cost-of-Living Index should not be open to attack on technical grounds. There have already been some comments by trade union representatives in cases before this Board, alleging that the index did not reflect the full rise in the cost of living. Our general policy is now based on the assumption that the cost of living will not rise substantially, and we must be in a position to prove that this is in fact the case by reference to an official index which is not open to serious question. While this is a technical problem that the Bureau must handle in its own way, it is very important to us that the index faithfully show changes in actual prices of wage earners' purchases under rationing or any other system of control of buying which may be instituted by the government."[31]

Unions had begun to collect retail price data in 1941 to demonstrate that tighter price controls were needed and that wage controls would reduce workers' real income. By late 1942, following the imposition of wage controls, the union studies were receiving much public attention. The Bureau and the standing committee of union research directors discussed the studies in December 1942, at which time it was decided to have two union research directors work with the Bureau to keep the unions and the public generally informed on the uses and limitations of the index.[32]

The effort at public education was extended in early 1943. Aryness Joy Wickens made trips to a number of cities where price surveys had been done, meeting with members of the public and union officials to explain the uses of the index, the methods of gathering and compiling price data, and the BLS materials available on changes in food prices. The Bureau gave advice on how to collect prices comparable to cost-of-living figures in cities it did not cover in the index. One result was that in Detroit, where union figures had differed substantially from BLS data, a new union survey following BLS techniques showed no significant divergence.[33]

By June 1943, in view of the 24-percent rise in the index over January 1941, as against the 15-percent general wage increase permitted by the Little Steel wage stabilization formula, the union research directors intensified their arguments. They now questioned the use of the cost-of-living index for wage adjustments, contending that what was needed were studies of workers' expenditures and a determination of the cost of an adequate standard of living. To those who insisted that the shortcomings of the index should be announced, and specifically to the labor members of the War Labor Board, Hinrichs replied, "If our index carries within it such serious shortcomings as to invalidate the policy conclusions based on it, then the thing to do is not to announce the shortcomings of the index, but to scrap it altogether or make it better. Our job is to make it better so that nobody else will scrap it." As to telling the War Labor Board members about the shortcomings, Hinrichs said he had not been invited to do so. "If asked, I am not going to avoid the question of any of the shortcomings. I have, of course, discussed our index with members of the staff of the War Labor Board, but it is not our function to ask for a formal discussion with the Board." He stressed that the unions should not put "all their eggs" in the cost-of-living basket and suggested that other BLS material could be used by the labor unions to support demands before the stabilization agencies.[34]

At Hinrichs' request, Secretary Perkins asked the American Statistical Association "to review and appraise the cost of living index with reference both to its construction and its uses." Frederick C. Mills, of Columbia University and the National Bureau of Economic Research, was appointed to head a committee of experts, which heard from labor organizations, employer associations, consumer groups, and government agencies. The committee also conducted special field studies and tests of Bureau procedures, utilizing Bureau staff.

The principal conclusions of the Mills Committee sustained the Bureau's position. These were: "First, that within the limitations established for it, the Cost of Living Index provides a trustworthy measure of changes in the prices paid by consumers for goods and services. Second, that many of the difficulties and doubts which have arisen concerning the index have their origins in attempts to use it uncritically for purposes for which it is not adapted."

The committee's assessment was that the index was useful for public policy dependent on measuring the average trend in consumer prices nationwide, but, for other policy uses, more specific indexes were required. If a policy of relating wage adjustments to actual living costs of workers were adopted, indexes for particular areas, industries, population groups, and income levels would be needed.[35]

The Mills Committee report was released in October 1943. Chairman Davis of the National War Labor Board wrote to Perkins, "I think this will be very helpful to the whole stabilization program. I was not only gratified to have my own conviction about the index confirmed, but I also think the committee's statement of the proper use to be made of the index will be helpful."[36]

The report was only the first stage in a prolonged scrutiny of wage stabilization policy and the cost-of-living index. With labor pressing for relaxation of the wage stabilization policy, President Roosevelt suggested that the War Labor Board set up a tripartite committee to explore the widespread "controversy and dispute as to what the cost of living is," and that agreement by such a committee could "have a salutary effect all over the country, because today all kinds of exaggerated statements are made."[37]

The board acted immediately to appoint the committee, known as the President's Committee on the Cost of Living, with Davis as chairman. At the initial meeting, the committee adopted a motion by George Meany of the AFL to investigate a number of specific questions: The cost of living in October 1943 compared with January 1, 1941, May 15, 1942, and September 15, 1942; how the index figure was arrived at; whether there were any changes in the methods of securing or computing the figures; and concrete suggestions for improving the securing of figures. The Bureau promptly provided the information, along with a description of the preparation of the index.[38]

In January 1944, the labor members of the War Labor Board submitted a report stating that, by December 1943, the true cost of living had risen at least 43.5 percent above January 1941, whereas the BLS index had risen only 23.5 percent. The report stressed that the BLS index understated price rises because of deterioration of quality and disappearance of low-priced merchandise. It also noted the absence of consideration of room rent, food bought in restaurants, and costs in moving from one city to another. In general, it charged that the index was inaccurate.[39]

The Bureau submitted a comprehensive statement in reply, observing that "there is conclusive evidence that they are absolutely wrong in asserting that the rise in the cost of living is nearly twice as great as the Bureau of Labor Statistics shows it to be." The Mills Committee reaffirmed the conclusions of its October report.[40]

The comments on the wide discrepancy of 20 percentage points impelled Davis to call on a committee of technical experts for an unbiased study. Wesley C. Mitchell, of the National Bureau of Economic Research, was designated as chairman. Other members were Simon N. Kuznets, of the War Production Board, and Margaret Reid, of the Budget Bureau's Office of Statistical Standards.

In June 1944, before the Mitchell Committee was ready with its report, the Bureau held its fifth annual conference with union research directors. While in previous years only research directors had been invited, this time other union officers also were included, among them George Meany. Meany addressed the conference. Meany's biographer has described what followed: "What he said was a bombshell, and a well-publicized one, for advance texts went to the press." He charged the administration with failing to keep down living costs and deciding that "the next best thing to do was to keep down the cost of living index. In this policy the Bureau of Labor Statistics obsequiously acquiesced. We are led to the inescapable conclusion that the Bureau has become identified with an effort to freeze wages, to the extent that it is no longer a free agency of statistical research."[41]

Shortly after the conference, the Bureau issued its regular monthly cost-of-living release, which now contained a brief explanatory statement: "The BLS index indicates average changes in retail prices of selected goods, rents, and services bought by families of wage earners and lower-salaried workers in large cities. The items covered represented 70 percent of the expenditures of families who had incomes ranging from $1,250 to $2,000 in 1934-36. The index does not show the full wartime effect on the cost of living of such factors as lowered quality, disappearance of low-priced goods, and forced changes in housing and eating away from home. It does not measure changes in *total* 'living costs'—that is, *in the total amount families spend for living*. Income taxes and bond subscriptions are not included."[42]

The release was greeted in the *American Federationist* with the headline, "BLS admits its index gives faulty view of true rise in living costs." The article continued, "Mr. Meany and other labor spokesmen had exposed the injustice of using the BLS figures as a guide to computing living costs and as a basis for establishing wage rates."[43]

The report of the Mitchell Committee also appeared at this time, stating, "Our examination of the methods used by the BLS and the other information we have gathered . . . leads us to conclude that the BLS has done a competent job, under very difficult market conditions, in providing a measure of price changes for goods customarily purchased by families of wage earners and lower-salaried workers living in large cities." The committee estimated that the Bureau's index in December 1943 understated hidden price rises by only 3 to 4 percentage points, mainly due to quality deterioration. The committee's one explicit recommendation was that the name of the index be changed.[44]

In November 1944, Davis submitted the report he had prepared as chairman of the President's Committee on the Cost of Living. In it, he drew on the Mitchell report in finding that "the accuracy of the index figures for what they were intended to measure is confirmed. They are entitled to the good reputation they have long enjoyed. . . . They are good basic figures for use in the formulation of fiscal and other governmental policies and for observing the effects of such policies." With the "searching" studies conducted for the committee, "no such substantiated criticism of BLS methods has survived." He did recognize that the 3 to 4 percentage points for the hidden increases, plus 0.5 of a point if small cities were also covered in the index, would bring the official rise of 25.5 percent in the index from January 1941 to September 1944 to about 30 percent. The industry members generally concurred in the chairman's conclusions, but the labor members issued separate statements. For the CIO, R.J. Thomas strongly endorsed changing the name of the index. For the AFL, Meany clarified the policy issues of the index, indicating that the AFL had never endorsed basing wages on the cost of living: "The established wage policy of this country has always been based on raising wages as increases in productivity made this possible."[45]

The findings of the President's Committee on the Cost of Living were an important element in the recommendations made in February 1945 to the Director of Economic Stabilization for maintaining the Little Steel formula as the standard for general wage increases for wage stabilization. In a dissenting statement, the AFL contended that wage earners had borne the brunt of the wartime anti-inflation program.[46]

In the early postwar period of continuing wage-price controls, the wage adjustment standard was relaxed. Regulations permitted adjustments for a 33-percent rise in the cost of living from January 1941 to September 1945, including a 5-point adjustment over the official cost-of-living index to allow for continued deterioration of quality and unavailability of merchandise. The Bureau explained the 5-point adjustment in its monthly release but did not include it in the index. In February 1947, in recognition of the disappearance of some of the wartime market factors, the Bureau discontinued the explanation.

Following Meany's appearance at the research directors' conference, Secretary Perkins ordered the annual conferences terminated. However, informal relations with the members of the former standing committee continued; Hinrichs actively sought and received their advice on Bureau programs. Formal relations were not reestablished until 1947, when Commissioner Clague set up both labor and business advisory councils.

Changing the name of the cost-of-living index as proposed by the Mitchell Committee was the subject of a conference with union research directors in January 1945, who, as early as 1940, had raised a question regarding the title. They agreed on a new title, "Consumer's Price Index for Moderate Income Families in Large Cities." Hinrichs submitted the proposal to Secretary Perkins, indicating that it met with Bureau approval. Perkins opposed any change, however, pointing out that the "Cost of Living" title was widely used in other countries and was well understood. She believed that the index under the new name would be no more acceptable to its critics and, in fact, would create even more confusion. In a few months, Secretary Perkins was succeeded by Lewis B. Schwellenbach, and, in July 1945, he agreed to the new title.[47]

Standard budgets

In 1936, the Works Progress Administration published two budgets giving quantities necessary for families for "basic maintenance" and for "emergency standards of living." These budgets were intended to appraise relief needs and set WPA wage rates. The Bureau updated the budgets periodically for 33 cities by applying changes in prices and rents reported to the Bureau for the cost-of-living index. In 1943, with the base of the estimates long out of date, they were discontinued.

In 1945, the House Appropriations Committee directed the Bureau to prepare a family budget based on current conditions, or to "find out what it costs a worker's family to live in large cities in the United States." A technical advisory committee of outstanding experts in the fields of nutrition and consumption economics helped develop the standards and procedures. The Bureau prepared the list of items and quantities to be included in the budget, priced them in 1946 and 1947, and developed dollar totals for 34 large cities. The results were published in 1948. As formulated, the budget for a city worker's family of four was an attempt to describe and measure a modest but adequate American standard of living.[48]

Wholesale prices

Lubin called for expansion of the Bureau's wholesale price work in 1933 to aid in the analysis of changes in the economy, both in specific industries and in major economic sectors. Immediate improvements included more detailed commodity specifications and broader commodity and industry coverage. In 1937, the index was changed from the "link-chain" formula used since 1914 to the "fixed-base" technique. Between 1933 and 1939, the number of individual commodities priced increased from about 2,300 to 5,000; the number of firms reporting increased from about 750 to 1,500.

The requirements of wartime gave a new orientation to the wholesale price program. The extensive use of the indexes in escalator clauses in large war contracts and in preparing price regulations made it necessary for the Bureau to hire price specialists with a thorough knowledge of particular commodity fields, to increase staff training, and to develop new techniques of price analysis. In a project conducted with the cooperation of the WPA, new groupings of commodities were developed, including separate indexes for durable and nondurable goods; producer and consumer goods; and agricultural and industrial goods.

Wages

The long-established program of periodic industry and union wage surveys continued under Lubin. In addition, the monthly series on average hourly earnings and average weekly hours in selected industries begun in 1932, based on the establishment survey, was expanded.

The Bureau had to recast its priorities to meet the urgent demands for information required to establish and administer the NRA codes. In place of the periodic studies of major industries, the Bureau had to conduct hurried and limited studies of industries such as cigars, cigarettes, tobacco, boys' hosiery, and silk. More comprehensive studies, dealing with working conditions as well as wages, covered such diverse subjects as the cotton textile and petroleum industries, the onion fields of Ohio, and editorial writers on newspapers.

With the end of the NRA, the regular program was resumed and new studies were undertaken. At the request of the engineering societies, the Bureau conducted a study of employment, unemployment, and income in the engineering profession. Also, special analyses were made to provide information on earnings and hours of Negro workers in the iron and steel industry and in independent tobacco stemmeries.

In its regular industry survey program, the Bureau made efforts to expand coverage to include annual earnings, earnings by age and length of service, and information on personnel policies. Annual earnings data proved difficult and costly to obtain, however, and this work was soon curtailed.

Several industry wage studies during the period included broad analyses of the industry's structure, including its competitive features, technology, demand, and profits. In his introduction to a study of cotton goods manufacturing, Lubin observed, "The more specific the economic application of the facts with reference to wages, the more intensive should be the preliminary study of the industrial background."[49]

The passage of the Walsh-Healey Public Contracts Act in 1936 and the Fair Labor Standards Act in 1938 resulted in a substantial increase in the wage program. The Bureau provided summary data on wages and hours to the Department's Wage and Hour and Public Contracts Divisions for the setting of minimum wages, and, during 1938 and 1939, developed frequency distributions of wages in about 45 industries, primarily low-wage consumer goods industries.[50]

Another reorientation of the Bureau's work was required when the defense program got underway in 1940. With the emphasis on war production, the Bureau shifted to occupational wage studies of heavy industries such as mining, smelting, and fabrication of nonferrous metals; shipbuilding; machinery; rubber; and aircraft. In addition, a number of disputes coming before the National Defense Mediation Board required the collection of wage data by occupation and locality.

Such data were increasingly needed by the National War Labor Board, especially after it was given wage stabilization authority in October 1942. In May 1943, the Director of Economic Stabilization authorized the board to establish, by areas and occupational groups, brackets based on "sound and tested going rates" for decisions in cases involving interplant wage inequity claims. Wage increases above the bracket minimum were permitted only in "rare and unusual" cases and cases of substandards of living.[51]

By agreement with the board, the Bureau was to be "one of the instrumentalities" for the collection of occupational wage rate data within various labor markets in each of the 12 War Labor Board regions. The Bureau was required to establish regional offices to serv- ice the needs of each board, with the program in the field subject to the general direction of the tripartite regional boards. The regional boards had authority to designate the occupations and industries to be covered and to interpret and evaluate the data. In practice, the boards relied substantially on the Bureau's expertise in the preparation of occupational patterns and job descriptions for the surveys.

The Bureau met the challenge of the board's requirements for occupational wage rate data by industry for virtually all U.S. labor markets. Within 6 months, with board funds, the Bureau collected data from over 60,000 establishments in 400 localities—an unprece- dented volume of information for such a short period of time. By 1945, pay rates in key operations had been collected from more than 100,000 establishments, and some 8,000 reports on an industry-local- ity basis had been transmitted to the board. The data collection included supplementary information such as overtime and shift-work provisions, the prevalence of union agreements, paid vacations, bonuses, insurance, and pensions. Using the summary reports, the regional boards established wage brackets covering tens of thousands of board determinations in interplant wage inequity situations.

A major issue arose over the board's proposal that "data secured by the Bureau in carrying out this project will be used and published, if at all, by or under the direction of the Board." Secretary Perkins, in opposing the rigid limitation on the Bureau's right to publish the material, cited the Bureau's mandate to make its information available as widely as possible, its importance for maintaining good public relations, and the use of its own funds for some of the work. The matter was finally resolved with the understanding that the Bureau would submit any proposed release or article to the authorized representative of the board, seeking advice on the content and timing of releases. Any disagreement would be referred jointly to the Secretary of Labor and the chairman of the NWLB.[52]

At first, the release procedure created problems for the Bureau. The unions contended that they needed the data in bracket-setting cases, even though they had been submitted to the War Labor Board. A satisfactory arrangement was developed whereby unpublished information was sent in response to requests, with the requesting party obliged to advise the Bureau of the intended use of the information in any wage negotiations or official procedure leading to wage determination, to insure that the Bureau's position was impartial.[53]

The occupational wage work provided the basis for developing an overall urban wage rate index to measure the impact of the stabilization program on basic wage rates. Data from the Bureau's regular programs were inadequate for the purpose. The weekly earnings series for example, failed to take account of the increased importance of payroll deductions. While estimates were made for these deductions, the series developed was affected by such factors as the effects of overtime pay; changes in the relative importance of regions, industries, and individual establishments; and changes in occupational structure. Gross average hourly earnings, subject to the same influences, were adjusted to eliminate the effects of overtime pay and interindustry shifts in employment, but the resultant straight-time hourly earnings index continued to be affected by changes in the relative importance of residual factors.

The urban wage rate index, first published in 1944, provided a better measure of basic wage rate changes. Field representatives collected the data directly for specific and well-defined key occupations; the same establishments were covered; and fixed weights were used for each occupation, industry, and area. The index was continued until 1947.[54]

As the war was coming to an end in 1945, plans were made to meet anticipated requirements for wage statistics during the reconversion period. The Bureau decided to conduct a large number of nationwide occupational surveys on an industry basis, including regional and locality breakdowns when feasible. Between 1945 and mid-1947, 70 manufacturing and 11 nonmanufacturing industries were studied.

Industrial relations

The great impetus given to union growth and collective bargaining by the NRA and the National Labor Relations Act stimulated the Bureau to gear up to provide information to ease the adjustment to new labor-management relationships. In 1934, the Bureau began publication of the *Labor Information Bulletin* and also established a separate Industrial Relations Division which began the collection and analysis of collective bargaining agreements. Within a few years, a file of 12,000 agreements was developed. Thereafter, efforts were made to improve the sample and to maintain it on a current basis. Strike statistics also were improved and made more current.

In conjunction with the National Labor Relations Board, the Bureau undertook a study of company unions in 1935. David Saposs, who had just completed a study on the subject for the Twentieth Century Fund, was hired as director of the study. At an informal meeting with BLS, AFL representatives expressed some reservations about the project, suggesting that the Bureau should place its emphasis on studying collective bargaining agreements rather than on what they viewed as merely "an arm of management."[55]

After the study was completed, Lubin reported to Secretary Perkins that union officials were urging him to issue the report as soon as possible. "Somehow or other a rumor has been spread that the bulletin may be suppressed."[56]

The preliminary report, appearing as an article in the *Monthly Labor Review* entitled "Extent and Characteristics of Company Unions," stirred up a tempest. The National Association of Manufacturers advised Lubin that some of its members, including those who had cooperated in supplying information to the Bureau, felt that in many respects the study "attempts to establish standards for employee representation plans which may result in misleading conclusions as to their functions and operations." They met with Lubin, and immediately thereafter the *Journal of Commerce* reported, "Although resentment in industrial circles against the recent study on company unions prepared by the BLS continues high, it now seems doubtful that an organized boycott will result."[57]

With the war emergency, the Bureau's ongoing analysis of collective bargaining provisions proved valuable to government agencies, employers, and unions as collective bargaining received encouragement under wartime policies. In 1942, the Bureau published *Union Agreement Provisions* (Bulletin 686). Based on the Bureau's file of several thousand agreements, it analyzed and provided examples of clauses for some 28 principal labor contract provisions. The demand for the bulletin was so great that it was reprinted four times.

During the war years, the War Labor Board called on the Bureau for special studies on the prevalence of certain contract provisions, including maintenance-of-membership clauses, seniority rules, and grievance procedures. The Bureau also developed statistics on strikes in defense industries and for specific cases before the board. It also provided considerable information to the War and Navy Departments, the Conciliation Service, and the War Production Board.

Employment and unemployment

Establishment data. The Bureau's employment statistics were of crucial importance in assessing the extent of the industrial recovery from the Great Depression and, later, in monitoring the defense and war programs. The monthly reports based on establishment payrolls were improved and expanded, incorporating recommendations of the Advisory Committee to the Secretary of Labor. Benchmarking to the biennial Census of Manufactures was finally implemented in 1934 and carried out on a regular schedule thereafter. In 1938, State, county, and municipal employment was included. Sampling was improved both on an industry and regional basis. Between 1933 and 1940, coverage increased from 70,000 representative private establishments employing 4.5 million workers to 148,000 establishments employing 8.4 million. By 1939, 17 States were cooperating in obtaining employment and payroll data in manufacturing establishments.

In 1937, in cooperation with the Women's Bureau, BLS began semiannual collection of separate data for men and women in those industries in which large numbers of women were employed. The information was analyzed and published by the Women's Bureau.

In 1940, with the growing defense program, Lubin pointed out the likely increase in the employment of women, as in the first World War. He called for wider collection and more detailed analysis of the employment conditions and earnings of women.[58] Regular monthly reporting on the employment of women in manufacturing industries was begun in June 1943. Separate turnover figures for women also were published.

Defense production programs required the expansion of industry coverage and reclassification to take account of industries manufacturing war materiel such as guns, tanks, and sighting and fire-control equipment. Sixty-seven industries were added to the 90 manufacturing industries previously covered. By 1945, reports were received from 180 industries covering 148,000 establishments and representing 12.5 million workers. Turnover rates were also compiled and analyzed for all employees and for women employees in 125 mining and manufacturing industries.

To aid in dealing with recoversion problems, the Bureau received a supplemental appropriation in 1945 permitting collection of data in all States for construction of State and area employment estimates comparable to the BLS national series. While the program was short lived, it served to develop close relationships with State agencies, facilitating establishment of the cooperative program that replaced it.[59]

Throughout the 1930's, the Bureau sought to provide additional measures which would serve as indicators of overall employment trends. Beginning in 1936, two series of estimates of nonagricultural employment were developed. The first, "total civil nonagricultural employment," showed the total number of individuals engaged in gainful work in nonagricultural industries, including proprietors and firm members, self-employed persons, casual workers, and domestic servants. The second, "employees in nonagricultural establishments," was limited to employees only. The totals for both series were benchmarked to the 1930 Census of Occupations, with periodic adjustments to the various industrial censuses and the newly developed Social Security tabulations. Persons employed on WPA and National Youth Administration projects, enrollees in the Civilian Conservation Corps, and members of the Armed Forces were not included. Beginning in 1939, similar estimates were prepared for each of the 48 States and the District of Columbia.[60]

Census of unemployment. The Bureau participated in an experimental census of unemployment in 1933 and 1934. Along with the Secretary's Advisory Committee and the Central Statistical Board, the Bureau provided professional direction for a trial household census in three cities. The Central Statistical Board set up an interdepartmental committee, chaired by Lubin, to supervise the study, which was conducted with resources provided by the Civil Works Administration. While the results were not published, the study was significant for its trailblazing application of methods by which the theory of sampling could be used under practical conditions for developing Federal economic and social statistics. The experience gained was to influence the development of techniques for measuring unemployment.[61]

Although the Advisory Committee recommended that the Bureau be responsible for unemployment estimates, later developmental work was carried on by the WPA, which, in 1940, initiated a national monthly sample survey of households, "The Monthly Report of Unemployment." Drawing on an innovation in the 1940 census, the survey made use of a new concept—the "labor force"—in place of the earlier "gainful workers" concept. The new concept included only persons who were actually working or seeking work; formerly, persons who had had a paid occupational pursuit were included whether or not they were at work or seeking work at the time of the survey.[62]

The Bureau contrasted the new series with its own nonagricultural employment series. It viewed the latter as providing "a means of throwing into proper perspective the significant fluctuations in basic industrial and business employment, where changes are measured currently with a high degree of accuracy." The WPA monthly sample survey of individual households, on the other hand, was viewed as the only satisfactory method of directly measuring the fluctuations in the size of the labor force and in unemployment, including in the employment total agricultural workers and such temporary and casual employment as the summer vacation employment of students not caught directly by BLS reporting techniques.[63]

With the termination of the WPA in 1942, the Bureau of the Budget transferred the work to the Census Bureau, which continued to publish the results, retitled the "Monthly Report on the Labor Force," until 1959, when responsibility for the survey was turned over to BLS.

Labor requirements studies. In association with its work in obtaining reports of employment and payrolls from contractors involved in the vast system of Federal public works projects, the Bureau obtained monthly reports of all expenditures for materials by the Federal Gov-

June 27, 1884.
CHAP. 127—An act to establish a Bureau of Labor.

Be it enacted by the Senate and House of Representatives of the United States of America in Congress assembled, That there shall be established in the Department of the Interior a Bureau of Labor, which shall be under the charge of a Commissioner of Labor, who shall be appointed by the President, by and with the advice and consent of the Senate. The Commissioner of Labor shall hold his office for four years, and until his successor shall be appointed and qualifed, unless sooner removed, and shall receive a salary of three thousand dollars a year. The Commissioner shall collect information upon the subject of labor, its relation to capital, the hours of labor, and the earnings of laboring men and women, and the means of promoting their material, social, intellectual, and moral prosperity. The Secretary of the Interior upon the recommendation of said Commissioner, shall appoint a chief clerk, who shall receive a salary of two thousand dollars per annum, and such other employees as may be necesary for the said Bureau: *Provided,* That the total expense shall not exceed twenty-five thousand dollars per annum. During the necessary absence of the Commissioner, or when the office shall become vacant, the chief clerk shall perform the duties of Commissioner. The Commissioner shall annually make a report in writing to the Secretary of the Interior of the information collected and collated by him, and containing such recommendations as he may deem calculated to promote the efficiency of the Bureau.

Approved, June 27, 1884

On June 27, 1884, President Chester A. Arthur signed the bill establishing a Bureau of Labor in the Department of the Interior.

William H. Sylvis, president of the iron molders union, first set the goal of establishing a national labor bureau at the 1867 convention of the National Labor Union.

Terence V. Powderly, as Grand Master Workman of the Knights of Labor, campaigned for establishment of a national bureau and sought the post of Commissioner.

Representative James H. Hopkins of Pennsylvania sponsored the bill establishing the Federal Bureau during the Presidential election year of 1884.

Samuel Gompers, president of the American Federation of Labor, counseled with and supported the Bureau while leading the fight to establish the Department of Labor.

Carroll D. Wright, Commissioner, 1885–1905

Charles P. Neill, Commissioner, 1905–13

Kellogg Building, first home of the Bureau of Labor

National Safe Deposit Building, home for 20 years, 1890–1910

G.W.W. Hanger, Acting Commissioner, 1913

Royal Meeker, Commissioner, 1913–20

BLS administration and finance office, 1920

Ethelbert Stewart, Commissioner, 1920–32   *Charles E. Baldwin, Acting Commissioner, 1932–33*

Department of Labor Building, 1917–35

Isador Lubin, Commissioner, 1933–46

A. Ford Hinrichs, Acting Commissioner, 1940–46

BLS tabulating room, about 1935

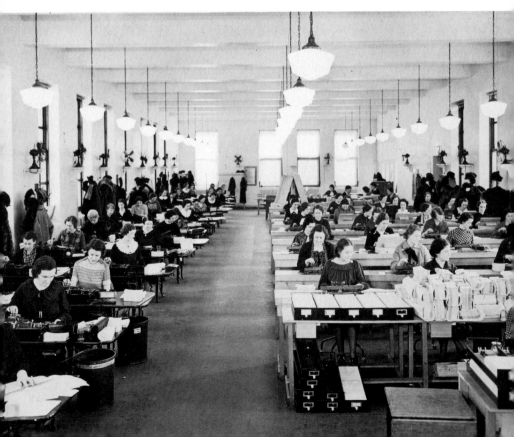

*Lubin and Senator O'Mahoney opening hearings
of Temporary National Economic Committee, 1938*

Top BLS staff, July 1946

Ewan Clague, Commissioner, 1946–65

Aryness Joy Wickens, Acting Commissioner, 1946 and 1954–55

Clague explains chart on wholesale prices.

Faith Williams (second from left),
Chief of the Office of Foreign Labor Conditions,
meeting with Swedish statistical group, 1950's

BLS tabulating room, 1950's

Arthur M. Ross, Commissioner, 1965–68

Geoffrey H. Moore, Commissioner, 1969–73

Ben Burdetsky, Acting Commissioner, 1968–69 and 1973

Julius Shiskin, Commissioner, 1973–78

Janet L. Norwood, Acting Commissioner
and Commissioner, 1978 to present

Norwood presents economic data
to Joint Economic Committee.

MONTHLY LABOR REVIEW

U.S. Department of Labor
Bureau of Labor Statistics
August 1984

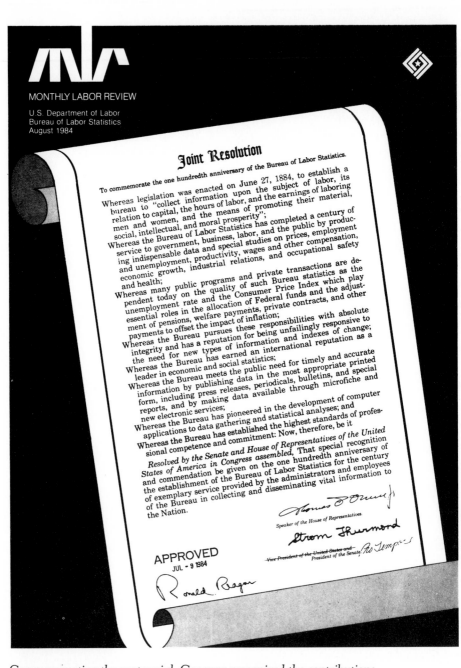

*Commemorating the centennial, Congress recognized the contributions
of the Bureau of Labor Statistics with a Joint Resolution,
featured on the cover of the Monthly Labor Review for August 1984.*

ernment or government contractors, in order to estimate the employment created by such public expenditures. Out of this developed studies of the indirect labor involved in the fabrication of certain basic materials, including steel, cement, lumber and lumber products, and bricks. Other studies covered the electrification of the Pennsylvania Railroad, several power projects, and houses constructed by the Tennessee Valley Authority.[84] The records of almost 40,000 federally financed construction projects completed between 1935 and 1940 were analyzed to determine the types and cost of labor and materials required to carry out a given dollar volume of construction contracts. The techniques developed in these studies proved useful in projecting labor requirements for planned expenditures for defense facilities.[65]

Occupational outlook studies. The defense effort also spurred the establishment of the Bureau's occupational outlook program. The original impetus came from the recommendation, in 1938, of President Roosevelt's Advisory Committee on Education that an occupational outlook section be set up in the Bureau to provide information to aid in career counseling. In 1940, under congressional authorization, the Occupational Outlook Service was established.

Soon, however, it was occupied with developing projections of manpower supply and needs for defense industries, including the aircraft industry. Calling attention to the need for authentic information on demand and supply of certain labor skills "to avoid all sorts of wild schemes which we may not be able to forestall and which may later rise to plague us," Lubin indicated that the recently authorized funds for occupational outlook investigations could be used legitimately for this purpose. In mid-1940, at Sidney Hillman's request, the President asked Congress to provide the Bureau with an additional $150,000 for the development of data on occupational skills needed by private industry in meeting military procurement needs.[66]

After the war, the occupational outlook program began to revert to its original function—studies for the guidance of young people. With demobilization, requests for outlook information came from the Army, the Navy, the Office of Education, and others. The Veterans Administration called on the Bureau for appraisals of the employment outlook for use in counseling veterans at its guidance centers. The Bureau developed analyses of over 100 occupations. Studies were also made of the occupational realignments during the war, which were used in planning the demobilization of the 11 million members of the Armed Forces and the 12 million workers in the munitions industries.

Research on postwar employment problems. The study of postwar labor problems was begun as early as 1941, when the House Appropriations Committee provided funds for research on the provision of jobs for workers displaced from war production. A division for research on postwar problems was established in the Bureau, which initially conducted studies of the impact of the war effort on employment in individual localities and industries. Subsequently, in the study of postwar full employment patterns, a major technical innovation—the "input-output" concept—was utilized. This involved the study of interindustry relationships throughout the economy in 1939, the last year before the expansion of munitions production. Funded by the Bureau, the work was conducted at Harvard University in 1942 and 1943 under Wassily Leontief and was then transferred to Washington. The input-output tables and techniques were utilized in developing both wartime attack targets and subsequent reparations policies for Germany; for estimates of postwar levels of output and employment in U.S. industries; and to forecast capital goods demand. The results of the program were published in 1947 as *Full Employment Patterns, 1950.* The study spread knowledge of the input-output concept within the government.[67]

Productivity and technological change

In 1935, the Bureau applied to the WPA for funds to conduct studies of productivity in 50 industries. The American Federation of Labor supported the proposal as filling a gap which had been experienced in developing the NRA codes and as necessary in collective bargaining for dealing with the problem of technological unemployment.[68] At about the same time, the WPA developed its own program. In cooperation with the WPA National Research Project on Reemployment Opportunities and Recent Changes in Industrial Techniques, the Bureau conducted several labor productivity surveys in important industries. By 1939, all of the surveys were completed.

Lubin's annual report for 1939 stated, "The Bureau expects to carry on further researches in the important field of labor productivity, in which it was a pioneer."[69] This resolve was underscored when, at the urging of the unions, Congress authorized the Bureau to "make continuing studies of labor productivity" and appropriated funds for the establishment of a Productivity and Technological Development Division, which was organized at the start of 1941. One of its earliest activities was to update the indexes constructed by the National Research Project.

During the war years, the division maintained annual indexes of productivity for some 30 industries and compiled collateral information on technological developments and other factors affecting employment and production in various industries. It provided information on technological developments in a monthly summary for the use of U.S. agencies and those of allied governments. Industrial establishments in 31 war industries were surveyed on the extent of absenteeism, with a monthly series continued for almost 2 years. Also, in the face of shortages, surveys of productivity were made in the rubber and gasoline industries.

Industrial safety and health
Compilation of data on the frequency and severity of industrial injuries had begun in 1926. When Lubin became Commissioner, about 1.4 million workers in 7,000 establishments were being covered. By 1944, 57,000 establishments were reporting annually. The much larger volume of reports was still being handled by the same number of staff members as in 1926; the enlarged coverage was made possible by radical changes in the methods of collecting and processing the data.

The impact of industrial accidents on war production, with the resultant loss of manpower, produced demands for more current information. The annual schedule on which reports had been issued previously could not meet this need. In 1942, the Bureau undertook to collect and publish monthly data on injuries in almost 10,000 establishments in industries of particular wartime importance. These were used by government agencies to pinpoint the plants and industries with high accident rates.

Several special studies were conducted during the war, including an examination of the effect of long work hours on efficiency, output, absenteeism, and accidents. A study of operations at the Frankford Arsenal in 1941 showed that, when extended hours required exertion beyond the normal physical strength of the workers, there were more accidents, greater spoilage of material, greater turnover, and decidedly less production in the extended hours than in the regular hours.[70] Further studies were made in 1943 and 1944.

The Bureau conducted detailed studies of accidents in the foundry, longshoring, and slaughtering and meatpacking industries. The Bureau's data were made available to the Department's Labor Standards Division, and to the Maritime Commission for safety drives.

Administration

Funding

The Bureau grew substantially under Lubin's direction. When he took over in 1933, the Bureau's budget had just been reduced in a governmentwide economy drive. Emergency funds made up for a further reduction in the regular budget in 1934. In succeeding years, congressional appropriations and funds transferred from other agencies permitted expansion and improvement of the Bureau's programs. By 1941, the regular budget had increased to over $1 million, more than double its level in 1934, and the staff had grown from 318 full-time employees to 810 (690 in Washington and 120 in the field).

There was a large increase in funding for the Bureau's activities during the war (table 5). Between 1942 and 1945, Bureau resources doubled, and at one point the number of full-time employees totaled almost 2,000. Congress maintained the regular appropriation for salaries and expenses at close to the prewar level but granted supplemental and national defense appropriations. In 1945, the Bureau received funds to expand its regional offices for the collection of State employment and payroll data comparable with national figures and also to cover occupational wage studies previously financed by the National War Labor Board. Both of these activities were terminated in 1946, however, when Congress failed to provide further funding.

As the war neared an end, the Bureau began planning for a reduction in its operations, and by 1946 had cut its staff by about 12 percent from the wartime peak. Supplemental appropriations, granted for expansion of work on foreign labor conditions, industrial relations, and productivity, partially made up for the reduction in wartime funds.

Table 5. Funding for Bureau of Labor Statistics, 1934–46
(in thousands)

Fiscal year ended June 30 —	Total[1]	Salaries and expenses	
		Regular	National defense
1934	$ 440	$ 414	–
1935	[2]949	528	–
1936	[2]1,284	885	–
1937	2,529	850	–
1938	1,114	784	–
1939	1,999	814	–
1940	3,215	1,012	–
1941	3,103	1,108	–
1942	2,677	1,081	$288
1943	4,292	1,207	1,001
1944	4,463	1,312	1,365
1945	5,507	1,312	2,672
1946	5,435	1,492	2,781

[1]Includes special and working funds in addition to appropriations for salaries and expenses.

[2]Includes special appropriation for revision of the cost-of-living index.

SOURCE: The Budget of the United States Government.

Staff

In the early days of the New Deal, the Bureau found itself without adequate staff to meet the vastly increased demand for data. When the National Recovery Administration called upon the Bureau for infor-mation needed to develop and assess the industry codes, personnel had to be detailed from inside and outside the Department. As Secre-tary Perkins stated at an appropriation hearing in 1933, "The Bureau of Labor Statistics has turned itself inside out in order to get this information and to make it available. . . in a form that was easily understood and readily used by people who had the responsibility of taking some action." Lubin added that every labor group involved in any NRA code had had to go to the Labor Department for informa-tion.[71]

Lubin indicated the lengths to which ingenuity had to be applied to make up for the shortage of staff: "I do not want to appear to boast, but I think I am one of the few officials who have actually gone out and borrowed people from other departments of the Government and put them to work during their spare time getting materials for which we would otherwise have to pay."[72]

In appropriation requests and in public statements, Lubin stressed the need to improve the professional qualifications of the Bureau's staff and to establish professional job categories at adequate levels to assure recruitment and retention of such personnel. He pointed out that he was the only trained economist on the Bureau's staff. The work of the Bureau's "highly efficient technical statisticians," he wrote the House Appropriations Committee, required the addition of economists to permit full analyses of the current economic problems facing the country.[73]

Lubin was always on the alert for capable staff. He brought into the Bureau persons of outstanding professional capacity who were authorities in their fields. Most had had advanced graduate study at top universities. A. Ford Hinrichs, director of Brown University's Bureau of Business Research, came as the Bureau's Chief Economist; Aryness Joy joined the staff from the Central Statistical Board. Throughout the period, there was internal training of the staff of a quality equal to that in the best American universities.

Lubin encouraged young economists to seek employment in government. Before the American Economic Association, he proselytised for the role of government economists. He contrasted the circumscribed environment of the academic researcher with the opportunities offered by Federal economic research for breaking down the barriers between economics, sociology, and political science.[74]

As a measure of his success in improving the Bureau's staff, he was able to report as early as 1937 that "more liberal appropriations by a Congress sympathetic with its work made possible a very considerable strengthening of its personnel."[75]

Organization

Lubin made several organizational changes just before he went on leave in 1940. To distribute the workload more evenly and reduce the pressure on top officials, he reorganized the Bureau into three, rather than two, principal areas. The former line positions of Chief Economist and Chief Statistician, each responsible for the activities of all the divisions of the Bureau in his field, were altered, with the Chief Statistican made a staff position and the other eliminated. Instead, the divisions were grouped under three branch chiefs who were to be responsible to the Assistant Commissioner, a new position. The three branches were Employment and Occupational Outlook, Prices and Cost of Living, and Working Conditions and Industrial Relations. During the war, when Hinrichs was Acting Commissioner, the position of Assistant Commissioner was not filled, however, and Hinrichs relied on the branch chiefs directly.

Wartime requirements resulted in the establishment of field offices. Before 1941, the only full-time field staff were those involved in the collection of retail prices. Between December 1941 and mid-1942, 8 field offices were established for price collection and 12 for wage analysis. All the activities in each region were consolidated under one regional director in 1944. Early in 1945, the collection of employment statistics was added to regional office duties, but this was discontinued in 1946 when Congress failed to renew appropriations. By the end of the war, the permanent value of the regional offices was well established.

Cooperation and consultation

Lubin's facility for inspiring confidence and gaining cooperation was of great value to the Bureau. His open and straightforward approach in his dealings with labor and business groups and the press made him influential in all of these areas. He maintained personal relationships with many corporate executives, and they exchanged views frankly on major issues of the day. He was intimately involved in resolving issues which might threaten the Bureau's activities, and, generally, his directness and persuasiveness kept the incidence of such occurrences low.

For example, he played a major role in resolving reporting problems arising from the role permitted trade associations by the National Recovery Administration. Companies were submitting their data directly to these associations, and some were refusing to continue to submit reports to the Bureau and other government agencies.[76] When, at Lubin's request, Secretary Perkins brought the problem to the attention of the NRA director General Hugh Johnson, Johnson ordered industries under NRA codes to furnish data directly to the Bureau and the Federal and State agencies cooperating with the Bureau.[77]

Some industry representatives questioned the order, contending that the code authorities—the trade associations—should be encouraged to get the information and provide it to the government.

Lubin addressed a meeting of trade association executives and explained that direct government collection was necessary in the interest of uniform and timely reporting.[78] Further, meeting with representatives of State governments and interested Federal agencies on the NRA order, Lubin cautioned on the need for maintaining and improving reporting relationships based on the established practices of voluntarism and confidentiality in reporting. While "under this order we have for the first time legal authority to secure these data," Lubin stated, "we don't want to use that power . . ., we would rather it would be a cooperative venture. . . . We have no intention of imposing any burdens on them that they couldn't easily handle. We expect, however, to continue on the old basis of absolute confidence. These data are confidential and not to be used for enforcement purposes."[79]

In another episode, in January 1936, the Automobile Manufacturers' Association advised the Bureau that information for individual companies in the industry would no longer be furnished directly to the Bureau, and that individual plants would not be identified, except by a code to make monthly comparisons for individual plants. The arrangement was a source of constant irritation to the Bureau.

Lubin wrote the association that he viewed this "as a one-way proposition, with the Bureau being placed in the position where it can have only what the association says it should have and not what it feels it needs for its own use. It seems queer that after 15 years of a cooperative relationship with the leading firms in the industry, they should suddenly stop giving us reports on their own initiative. It is hard for us to believe that they were not specifically told not to give us the reports." He went on to state, "I frankly cannot continue in the uncomfortable position I find myself in of warding off questions concerning our automobile figures." Lubin continued to press the matter.

The problem was finally resolved at the end of 1937, when the Automobile Manufacturers' Association authorized the forwarding of the individual reports to the Bureau. "I am sure this arrangement will prove to our mutual advantage," Lubin wrote.[80] Through his wide contacts with industry executives, he was also able to overcome other occasional reporting problems.

Lubin also worked to maintain good relations with labor groups. Early in his administration, he asked labor union research staff members to meet with BLS and the Advisory Committee to the Secretary of Labor. Relations with union research staff members continued on an informal basis until June 1940, when a formal advisory relationship was established.

Perkins and Lubin set the keynote for the relationship. Perkins saw this avenue of exchange of information as helping trade unions "to make contributions to the . . . solving of the industrial problem and the economic problem of the nation as a whole." Lubin urged the importance of continuing the relationship "so that we will have direct access to the people who are using our data."[81]

Annual conferences were held between 1940 and 1944. A standing committee was appointed each year and there were frequent discussions of the concerns of the research directors. The arrangement worked satisfactorily under Hinrichs until it came to an abrupt end in the midst of the controversy over the cost-of-living index.

Lubin and Hinrichs depart

Lubin resigned as Commissioner of Labor Statistics in January 1946, giving "personal obligations" as his reason for leaving government service. President Truman accepted his resignation but stated that he would continue to regard him "as a public servant whom I shall feel free to call upon whenever the occasion warrants. . . . For 13 years you have, without hesitation, given of your time and energy to the service of your government. You built up the Bureau of Labor Statistics into an institution that has commanded the respect of all recognized leaders in the field of economics and statistical science, as well as of labor and management throughout the country."[82]

Truman shortly appointed Lubin as the U.S. representative to the UN Economic and Social Council. In 1955, New York Governor Averell Harriman called on Lubin to serve as State Industrial Commissioner. In 1960, Lubin joined the economics faculty at Rutgers University. He served as economic consultant to the Kennedy and Johnson administrations, and to the Twentieth Century Fund. Lubin died in 1978 at the age of 82.

Ford Hinrichs had continued as Acting Commissioner during 1945 at the request of Secretary Perkins' successor, Lewis Schwellenbach. He had considered resigning when press reports cited the new Secretary as being critical of BLS, but Schwellenbach denied these as inaccurate and persuaded him to stay on. In September 1945,

Schwellenbach indicated he would recommend Hinrichs for the commissionership when Lubin left.[83]

On Lubin's resignation the following January, Philip Murray of the CIO submitted the name of Murray Latimer for the commissionership. AFL President William Green and some railway officials also supported Latimer. Some press reports indicated that Hinrichs was being replaced by a union-supported candidate; the cost-of-living controversy of 2 years earlier figured prominently in these stories and editorials.[84]

There was a groundswell of support of Hinrichs from the professional and academic community. Lubin urged Schwellenbach to nominate Hinrichs, advising, "Failure to nominate Hinrichs will, in my opinion, be grossly unfair to him as well as an admission by this administration that it has no faith in the Bureau." He also stressed that the commissionership had never been considered a political position.[85] Wesley Mitchell and Frederick C. Mills reiterated the findings of their technical committees on the Bureau's "highly competent" work under Hinrichs on the cost-of-living index, in the face of the "extraordinarily difficult" wartime conditions. Mitchell's description of Hinrichs' performance was characteristic: "His courage in countering the criticisms made by the labor union statisticians commanded my respect. He is a man of rare competence in his field and of rare integrity."[86]

Hinrichs again considered resigning but, at the urging of the Bureau staff, stayed on to avoid serious consequences to the Bureau's budget and operations. Schwellenbach also requested that he stay, again stating that his personal preference was to nominate Hinrichs, but that this was not immediately possible. In May, Hinrichs indicated that he could not appear before the Appropriations Committee in support of crucial postwar budgetary actions unless there were assurances that the forthcoming selection of the Commissioner would be based on professional competence and not on support by a special interest group. Schwellenbach responded in terms proposed by Hinrichs, giving "my full assurance that I will not recommend to the President the name of any person concerning whose professional competence and integrity there will be the slightest doubt, and that such recommendation will only be made after consultation with the President of the American Economic Association and the American Statistical Association."[87]

On July 1, 1946, Hinrichs tendered his resignation to Schwellenbach. In it, he noted that he had continued to maintain satisfactory informal relations with a number of unions, and that the establishment of a formal consultation procedure required careful consideration, one of the important problems calling for the prompt appointment of an excellent Commissioner. In accepting the resignation, Schwellenbach acknowledged that Hinrichs' appointment as Commissioner "now is not possible." He reiterated his assurance of the selection of the next Commissioner, "given as the result of firm conviction on my part that the Bureau of Labor Statistics shall be free and independent and one upon which everyone can rely."[88] At a press conference on his retirement, Hinrichs stressed the importance of maintaining the Bureau's nonpolitical and impartial position: "You can't run this organization under any political obligation from the outside. The man must be selected from the inside for his ability and competence. Later he should be cleared with the unions to be sure he enjoys their confidence."[89]

The search for the new Commissioner was already underway, with Edwin E. Witte of the University of Wisconsin canvassing the professional associations regarding the several men under consideration. By the end of July, there was agreement on Ewan Clague.[90]

Hinrichs subsequently served in the Economic Cooperation Administration and its successor agencies, as statistical adviser to the governments of Pakistan and Taiwan, and, later, as Director of Graduate Business Studies at Syracuse University. He died in 1979.

Chapter VII.

Ewan Clague:
An Expanding Role
for Economic Indicators

E wan Clague took office in August 1946, a difficult time for the Bureau. The legacy of wartime controversies, the appointment of a new Secretary of Labor, and the departure of Lubin and Hinrichs had created a stressful transition. Then the sweep of the Republican Party in the fall congressional elections brought government budget reductions in which the Bureau shared heavily. About 700 of its 1,700 employees had to be dismissed, a loss which removed a generation of middle management personnel.

The economy also was undergoing the strains of transition. With the end of the war, as workers faced reduced earnings and uncertainty over employment prospects, labor-management difficulties mounted, leading to the highest strike activity on record in 1946. The onset of inflation in 1947 after the removal of price controls intensified the economic uncertainty.

New opportunities as well as problems accompanied Clague into office. With passage of the Employment Act of 1946, Congress had created two agencies—the Council of Economic Advisers in the Executive Branch and the congressional Joint Economic Committee— which were to introduce the regular scrutiny of economic indicators to the highest levels of policymaking and thus heighten the importance of the Bureau's work. Further, the innovative agreement between General Motors and the United Auto Workers in 1948 calling for the use of the Consumer Price Index and productivity measures for adjusting wages increased public concern with the Bureau's statistics.

The growing use of statistics for government and private actions affecting millions of Americans was the subject of the 1952 presidential address to the American Statistical Association by Aryness Joy Wickens, the Bureau's Deputy Commissioner. She warned that the statistical profession was "scarcely prepared, and certainly not organized, to meet the serious responsibilities placed upon us by these new uses of statistics." She contrasted these "awesome" uses with the purely descriptive and analytical purposes for which they were created, and called upon the statistical and related professions not merely to be competent, fair, and honest, but "to be able to prove to a statistically unsophisticated public that, in fact, our statistics are trustworthy."[1]

Maintaining public confidence was a paramount consideration for Clague as he adapted and extended the Bureau's programs to meet changing needs during his long tenure. Almost immediately upon his appointment, he established formal advisory relations with the trade unions; contacts with the unions had been curtailed as a result of the wartime controversy over the cost-of-living index. And shortly thereafter, following expressions of interest from business organizations, he formed a business advisory committee. The committees consisted primarily of technicians in the fields of economics, statistics, and labor relations. Clague later suggested that it was through their experience with these advisory groups that General Motors and the Auto Workers gained sufficient confidence in the Bureau's statistics to adopt the CPI for wage escalation in 1948.[2]

Clague's success in keeping the Bureau's statistics trustworthy was attested by the findings of the various commissions, committees, and teams of experts which examined the Bureau during his many years in office and upheld the integrity and impartiality of its work.

The sixth Commissioner

Commissioner Clague came to office as a trained economist and an experienced civil servant, an outsider but one with roots and connections in the Bureau. His ties with the Bureau extended back some 20 years when he had joined the BLS staff to conduct pioneering productivity studies. In the early 1930's, he had participated in major examinations of Bureau activities, serving on President Hoover's Advisory Committee on Employment Statistics and Secretary Perkins' Advisory Committee to the Secretary of Labor.

Clague was born in Prescott, Washington, in 1896, the son of immigrants from the Isle of Man. He attended the University of Washington and, after serving as an ambulance driver during World War I, moved on to the University of Wisconsin where he studied under John R. Commons. On Commons' recommendation, Commissioner Ethelbert Stewart brought him to the Bureau in 1926 to help develop productivity indexes.

When that project ended, Clague worked under W.A. Berridge at the Metropolitan Life Insurance Company. He then joined the Institute of Human Relations at Yale University, where he studied the effects on workers of the shutdown of rubber mills in Hartford and New Haven. He moved to Philadelphia as Director of Research and Professor of Social Research at the Pennsylvania School of Social Work. While in Philadelphia, he made a number of studies for the Lloyd Committee on Unemployment Relief and the Philadelphia County Relief Board.

In 1936, Clague returned to Federal employment, serving first as Associate Director of Research and Statistics of the new Social Security Board and then as Director. In 1940, he became Director of the Bureau of Employment Security, a post he held until his appointment as Commissioner of Labor Statistics.

The Bureau's role

Clague gave as his first priority for the Bureau in 1947 "maintenance of the many recurrent statistical series," but he also noted the Bureau's continuing responsibility for a wide variety of comprehensive investigations dealing with many phases of American labor and industry.

And he referred to the Bureau's role as a special statistical service agency for Congress and other government agencies.[3]

Hoover Commission

Early in his administration, Clague's view of the role of the Bureau was affirmed and strengthened by the findings of the Hoover Commission—the Commission on Organization of the Executive Branch of the Government—established by Congress in 1947. The commission was set up to examine the amalgam of emergency agencies and expanded programs developed under the New Deal and during the war, with the charge to recommend organizational arrangements to provide economy, efficiency, and improved service.

The commission called on the National Bureau of Economic Research for a study of the various statistical agencies, which was conducted by Frederick C. Mills and Clarence D. Long. Mills and Long praised the cooperative program in which the Bureau, the Social Security Administration, and the State agencies joined to produce the employment statistics. They also spoke well of the reimbursable work the Bureau performed for other agencies which solved some problems of overlapping jurisdiction. However, they pointed out duplication in other areas and noted the competition between BLS and the Bureau of the Census over the monthly report on the labor force.[4]

The commission generally accepted the recommendations of the National Bureau. It called on the Office of Statistical Standards in the Bureau of the Budget to designate the responsibilities and fields of operation of each of the major special-purpose statistical agencies. Census was recommended as the service agency for the primary collection and tabulation of statistics on a repetitive basis "for which highly specialized knowledge of the subject matter is not required in the collection process." For the special role of BLS, the commission recommended transfer to the Bureau of the "prevailing wage" surveys conducted by other agencies in setting the pay of government blue-collar workers.[5]

Clague wrote the Under Secretary that the Bureau stood to gain from the recommendations and urged that he take action to secure the prevailing wage and labor force surveys. On the other hand, he strongly opposed any transfer to Census of responsibility for collecting statistics on the volume of construction, rents, or food prices.[6]

The Bureau in a growing Department

The Hoover Commission also provided support for the growth of the Department of Labor over the following decade. Following the commission's recommendations to restore lost functions and delegate new responsibilities to the Department, Congress transferred three agencies into the Department from the Federal Security Administration—the U.S. Employment Service, the Bureau of Unemployment Compensation, and the Employees' Compensation Appeals Board. The reorganization also strengthened the Secretary's authority over all the Department's agencies. Clague supported the reorganization and saw it as a formalization of existing operating relationships between the Bureau and the Secretary's office.

Soon after Secretary Mitchell's appointment in 1953, he set up a team of consultants to evaluate the Department's programs, administration, and organization. The team included J. Douglas Brown of Princeton University; Clark Kerr of the University of California; Eli Ginzburg of Columbia University; and Cyrus Ching, former Director of the Federal Mediation and Conciliation Service.

Reporting late in 1954, the consultants made extensive recommendations on the Department's programs. For BLS, they called for enhancement of the Bureau's series, increased appropriations for its work, and the designation of the Commissioner as the Secretary's chief statistical adviser. But, in commenting on the role of the Bureau in the Department, they observed that, while the Bureau devoted much of its efforts to the development of statistical materials which had some bearing on important departmental programs, "it has also proceeded in terms of its history, traditions, and inclinations, with the result that much of its work is not closely geared into the major programs of the Department."[7]

For better coordination within the Department, the consultants recommended the establishment of a Committee on Statistics and Research, to be headed by the Under Secretary. The committee would centralize decisionmaking and work towards eliminating duplication in statistical work. The committee was established but apparently met only twice. Mitchell did make Clague his statistical adviser, as recommended.[8]

Mitchell gave his own view of the Bureau in an article which followed the consultants' report. He pointed to the "high regard" and "fine reputation" which the Bureau had earned with employers, workers, and the general public. But he also stressed that "facts and figures must meet the growing needs of the country and the economy" and cautioned against "stagnation and self-satisfaction," concluding, "Our goal must be constantly to increase the usefulness of the work of the Bureau of Labor Statistics to all our people."[9]

At various times, Department officials suggested the establishment of a periodical which would absorb the Bureau's periodical, the *Monthly Labor Review*, arguing for a "popular" journal representing all the Department's activities. In 1957, following the report of another team of consultants which had stated, "We have encountered frequent expressions of hope that the MLR could be made more flexible and provocative of new ideas," George C. Lodge, Director of the Department's Office of Information, proposed recasting the *Review* as the Department's monthly periodical.[10]

Clague, expressing the view of the BLS executive staff, opposed the proposal on the grounds that it was inappropriate for the Office of Information to direct a research journal. The Under Secretary accepted this view while directing that the *Review* planning board include representatives from other agencies in the Department, which should be encouraged to publish in the *Review*. He later established a departmental publications committee to set general guidelines and provide oversight.[11]

The issue of making the *Review* a departmental publication arose again in the 1960's during a comprehensive review of departmental publications for reducing costs. In January 1964, Secretary Wirtz advised the Director of the Bureau of the Budget, "The *Monthly Labor Review*, heretofore a BLS publication, is being made a departmental publication." The move, he said, would save money by eliminating pressure for new periodicals and facilitating the consolidation of existing releases and reports. [12]

Assistant Secretary Daniel Patrick Moynihan, as chairman of the Department's advisory committee on publications, pursued the idea through various formulations. In December 1964, he reported to the Secretary's staff meeting that "a new proposal" had been developed "for transfer of the *Monthly Labor Review*" to the Office of the Assistant Secretary for Policy, Planning and Research. The *Review*, Moynihan argued, had become too closely associated with BLS and faced the danger of becoming isolated from the rest of the Department.[13]

Clague successfully opposed such a shift, charging that it would ruin the *Review's* reputation for objectivity, as it would become a policy and program organ for the Department. He did accede, however, to the creation of an expanded planning and advisory committee to counsel the Commissioner and the editor.

Meanwhile, the Department was expanding as Congress, concerned with manpower and labor relations issues in the late 1950's, passed the Welfare and Pension Plans Disclosure Act in 1958 and the Labor-Management Reporting and Disclosure Act in 1959—legislation for which the Bureau had conducted much of the early research. To administer the 1959 act, the Department created the Bureau of Labor Management Reports. BLS proposed a broad program of labor-management research, but the Commissioner of the new bureau decided instead to encourage private research by universities, a position from which BLS could not move him.[14]

In 1962, when the establishment of the Labor-Management Services Administration was under consideration in Secretary Arthur J. Goldberg's term, Clague again asserted the Bureau's role in basic factfinding in the field of labor-management relations. Later on, the Bureau was called upon for support services on a reimbursable basis.[15]

The formation of new agencies within the Department aroused heated controversy over jurisdiction, especially after the creation of the Office of Manpower, Automation, and Training and passage of the Manpower Development and Training Act of 1962. In 1963, Clague put the issue in stark terms. In referring to a draft of a departmental order establishing the Manpower Administration, he expressed the belief that BLS "has a most vital role to play in making certain that the new organization operated successfully" but that the proposed order "appears to be an attempt to restrict severely the role of this Bureau." Continuing, he posed the choice: The new agency could be primarily a coordinating and promotional organization or it could combine coordination with substantive research responsibilities. If the Department chose the latter, he argued, it faced the prospect that the agency would arrogate to itself "functions, personnel, and budget to the detriment of other Bureaus in the Department."[16]

As Robert J. Myers, Clague's Deputy Commissioner, described it later, the discussions resulted in an improved, although not entirely satisfactory, statement of BLS responsibilities. The establishment in 1964 of the Coordinating Committee on Manpower Research "has been quite useful in resolving jurisdictional questions and other problems that have arisen." Congress also had become concerned about jurisdictions, and a subcommittee of the House Appropriations Committee asked for a comprehensive statement from the Department. In February 1964, in "Programs in Manpower Research and Statistics," the Department laid out the responsibilities of the various agencies.[17]

With the launching of the "war on poverty" in 1964, the Department again gained new responsibilities. To meet the policy and administrative needs of the poverty programs, it called on the Bureau for data on the characteristics of the unemployed and the nature and extent of poverty. The Department considered cutting funds for the Bureau's regular programs, presumably without eliminating "absolutely essential economic data," to provide the resources for concentrating on the problem of unemployment.[18] The Bureau did establish an Office of Economic Research to examine such social issues as poverty and the condition of minorities. The office contributed substantially to Assistant Secretary Moynihan's much publicized report on the Negro family.

In 1965, the Department proposed another survey of BLS administrative procedures and programs. Clague asked for emphasis on the program aspect of the study, stressing that, for many years, the Bureau had faced competing demands from the Department of Labor, other Federal agencies, Congress, and the general public. The strain on the Bureau's resources had been intensified, Clague stated, by employment ceilings and limitations on average salaries and the number of supervisory personnel.[19]

A study was conducted by the management consultant firm of Booz-Allen and Hamilton, who later reported that Department officials had become "quite critical of the Bureau's capacity to respond to current economic and manpower problems and to supply innovative program ideas for their solution." Therefore, the report called for a "thoroughgoing examination of the Bureau with the objective of bringing its product more in line with the thrust and emphasis of current lines of social and economic advance."[20]

The climate within the Department at the time is suggested by Secretary Willard Wirtz's final report, for fiscal 1968, which provided an assessment of the Department's policies, programs, and administration over his 5-year term. The activist emphasis in the manpower program is evident in the following excerpt from his report: "Infinitely more than before, most of the gain was atmospheric, attitudinal: reflected in the identification of a 'manpower program' instead of an 'employment service,' in attacking not just 'unemployment' (as an economic fact) but 'poverty' (which is human) and in striking (even if only for one administrative generation) the phrase 'labor market' from the Department lexicon. It was, in any event, the unifying and dignifying theme in the history of the Department of Labor, 1963 to 1968, that wage earners—and those seeking that status—are people. Not statistics, not drones."[21]

Wirtz's appraisal of the administration of the Department also commented on the relationship between the "two governments" in the Federal Executive Branch—the political and the professional. It concluded: "(1) that a stronger central executive authority over both 'policymaking' and 'operations' was required, and (2) that better communications had to be developed between the two governments."

As Wirtz described the communications problem, particularly in regard to research activities, "Various efforts to develop a flow of ideas and suggestions up the lines have been largely unsuccessful. The prevailing notion is still that what is asked for will be supplied, but that volunteering anything is not worthwhile. Attempts by the Secretary's office to draw on the ideas incubating in the Bureau of Labor Statistics and in the research unit of the Manpower Administration are still disappointing. A first staff draft of testimony for a congressional committee hearing is characteristically sterile."[22]

Although these criticisms reflected the dissatisfaction of top policy officials with the Bureau's stance, and its position in the Department in terms of staff and budget was relatively diminished, the Bureau's reputation for integrity and technical competence was secure.

The Bureau's work

Employment and unemployment statistics
The Bureau had published national employment figures since 1916, based on surveys of payrolls of a sample of nonfarm establishments. In 1945, as part of the reconversion statistics program, the Bureau began to develop a national series that would yield estimates for each State. In some States, State agencies collected the data; in others, BLS

regional offices compiled the figures. All the data were sent to Washington for construction of the national series.

However, with the budget cuts of 1947, the Bureau shifted to complete compilation by State agencies under cooperative agreements. By 1949, all States were participating. BLS provided the technical guidance and standards and reimbursed the State agencies for half the direct personnel cost of the program. The Bureau of Employment Security also shared in the cost. In 1954, the program took over from the Federal Reserve Board the preparation of seasonally adjusted estimates of employment.[23]

Another source of data on employment was the monthly survey of the labor force, a survey of households which the Census Bureau had conducted since 1942. This survey, unlike the payroll survey, provided a direct measure of unemployment as well as employment. Increasingly, the publication and analysis of data from these two surveys, differing in concept and method, caused confusion and controversy. The substantial rise in unemployment in 1953 focused attention on the lack of coordination between the different agencies responsible for the figures. The matter came to a head when the Census Bureau had to reduce and restructure its survey program because of a cut in funds, and discrepancies cropped up even between its own new and old unemployment figures.

Noting these difficulties, the American Federation of Labor urged that BLS be given responsibility for the unemployment count, concluding, "We believe issuance by the Bureau of Labor Statistics of a single figure based upon statistically sound procedure will restore confidence in the measurement of unemployment and bring to an end the present uncertainty." The Joint Economic Committee called for better coordination and the Council of Economic Advisers also expressed concern. The confusion contributed to the formation of the Federal Statistics Users' Conference.[24]

The controversy also gave momentum to efforts to issue a joint monthly news release, a course urged, for example, by Wickens and Clague in February 1954. Secretary of Labor Mitchell and Secretary of Commerce Weeks agreed to a unified release, planned with the assistance of the Council of Economic Advisers and the Bureau of the Budget. The new report on employment and unemployment appeared in May 1954 with data for April. For the next 5 years, representatives of BLS, the Bureau of Employment Security, and the Census and Budget Bureaus met monthly to produce the release.[25]

Also in 1954, the Bureau moved to establish a Federal-State cooperative program for labor turnover statistics. For a number of years, BLS had published a national series based on turnover rates for selected industries which reported directly to the Bureau. Under the new agreements, as in the employment statistics program, the State agencies collected the data and transmitted the figures for the national series to BLS; BLS provided guidance and money; and the Bureau of Employment Security also allocated funds. The system proved popular, producing figures useful in both analysis and operations, and within 10 years all States were participating.

The recession of 1957-58 again stirred criticism of the occasional divergence of the figures of the various agencies in the unemployment release, and, in 1959, BLS finally achieved a long-sought goal. Secretary Mitchell negotiated an exchange between BLS and Census in which BLS gained responsibility for financing and analyzing the household survey (Current Population Survey) and publishing the results, while Census took over the BLS surveys on housing and construction activity.[26] Census continued to conduct the Current Population Survey under a contract with BLS. That same year, BLS instituted a formal press conference to release the monthly employment and unemployment figures.

With recurrent recessions, pressure mounted for a reexamination of the whole program of employment and unemployment statistics. In November 1959, the AFL-CIO complained that part-time and discouraged workers did not appear in the monthly totals and that, moreover, a national figure masked conditions in the severely depressed areas. In May 1960, Senator Gale W. McGee of Wyoming, speaking for the Senate Special Committee on Unemployment Problems, supported the BLS request for increased appropriations to expand surveys and conduct studies, citing the need for data on part-time and discouraged workers; on frictional, structural, and cyclical causes of unemployment; on the composition of the labor force; and on the effect of foreign trade on employment.[27]

Unemployment became a major issue in the 1960 election campaign. When organized labor and the Democrats blamed the incumbent Republicans for the high rate, Secretary Mitchell responded by pointing to the record level of employment and arguing that teenagers and those idled for short periods added considerably to the count of unemployed. Both Senator Henry M. Jackson of Washington, chairman of the Democratic National Committee, and George Meany, president of the AFL-CIO, asked the Department to release the October figure before the general election. Mitchell refused, saying that the normal schedule would call for a later release date.[28]

However, the October unemployment figure did became public before the election. Bernard D. Nossiter, writing in *The Washington Post* on November 3, 1960, noted that, in fact, in 1954, 1956, and 1958, President Eisenhower had announced favorable figures before the voting. Then Nossiter stated—correctly, as it turned out—that unemployment had reached 6.4 percent, the highest since the recession year of 1958.[29]

Clague promised a review of procedures "to develop better ways of keeping the confidentiality of the data under better control." And, during 1961, the Department began announcing the release dates for each month a year in advance.[30]

With unemployment mounting to almost 7 percent in 1961, Secretary of Labor Arthur J. Goldberg proposed various legislative programs to deal with the unemployment problem, focusing even more attention on the BLS figures. In the fall of 1961, *Reader's Digest* published an article accusing the Department of manipulating the data, charging that the Bureau exaggerated the figures to build support for the legislative agenda.[31] This prompted the Joint Economic Committee to call hearings and moved President Kennedy to establish the President's Committee to Appraise Employment and Unemployment Statistics. Under the chairmanship of Robert A. Gordon of the University of California, the committee made an extensive study of technical and program issues, including concepts and definitions, sampling, seasonal adjustment, State and local statistics, labor force dynamics, and comparison and reconciliation of the various series.

The Gordon Committee report, *Measuring Employment and Unemployment*, was issued in 1962. On the charge of manipulation, the committee "unanimously and categorically concluded that doubt concerning the scientific objectivity of the agencies responsible for collecting, processing, and publishing employment and unemployment statistics is unwarranted." The committee commended the Bureau for its policy of publishing release dates in advance, but it also called for a sharper distinction between the release of the statistics, with technical explanation and analysis, and policy-oriented comment, stressing the need to "publish the information in a nonpolitical context."[32]

For the household survey, the Gordon Committee also recommended implementation of sharper definitions and collection of more data on persons not in the labor force. It suggested developing questions to determine if a person had taken specific jobseeking steps within a definite time period and that BLS publish data on those working part time and whether that was voluntary.

For the establishment survey, the committee called for improvements in the benchmark data, strengthened sampling techniques, and preparation of estimates of standard error. In addition, the committee urged improvement of State and local statistics and development of job vacancy and occupational employment series.[33]

In January 1963, BLS and the Bureau of the Census added questions to the Current Population Survey designed to refine information concerning family relationships and availability for part-time work. In addition, BLS and Census undertook several research programs to develop and test other proposed changes.

Early in 1963, following up on the committee recommendation for a greater separation between technical explanations and policy-oriented comment, the Department announced that Bureau professionals would release the figures and that administration officials would make separate political statements.

Clague was obliged to protest to Secretary Wirtz on several occasions when President Johnson commented on favorable employment figures before their official release. On one such occasion, Gardner Ackley, Chairman of the Council of Economic Advisers, wrote members of the White House staff urging them to avoid "accidental premature" release and to respect the BLS procedures as recommended by the Gordon Committee, thus avoiding any political implications.[34]

Job vacancy statistics

Beginning in the 1950's, BLS conducted several studies to determine the feasibility of collecting statistics on job vacancies—twice at the urging of Arthur Burns, Chairman of the Council of Economic Advisers. In 1956, the Bureau surveyed about 100 plants to determine whether such information was available. Since only six were maintaining job vacancy data, it was found impractical to initiate a program.[35]

In the early 1960's, Burns returned to the idea, supported by a recommendation from the Gordon Committee, and in 1964 the Bureau again undertook feasibility studies. Clague personally surveyed programs in Israel and Great Britain, and the Division of Foreign Labor Conditions investigated reporting systems in Great Britain, the Netherlands, West Germany, and Sweden. In the summer of 1964, Secretary Wirtz proposed to the President and received approval for a series of pilot surveys on job vacancies in 20 labor market areas. BLS cooperated with the Bureau of Employment Security and State agencies to conduct the surveys, after which it concluded that collection was feasible and technical problems could be solved.[36]

The National Bureau of Economic Research and the National Industrial Conference Board actively supported the effort with their own conferences and projects. However, some criticisms of the program were voiced. The Bureau of the Budget, for example, objected to the combining of operating and statistical programs, the increased reporting burden on employers, and the high cost and hasty planning.[37]

The BLS Business Research Advisory Committee pointed to difficulties in establishing objective definitions and in obtaining accurate reports from employers and strongly opposed collaboration with the Bureau of Employment Security. The BLS Labor Research Advisory Committee expressed similar concern for defining terms and concepts and argued that vacancy statistics would be misused to "deflate" unemployment figures. The AFL-CIO opposed increased appropriations for the program, calling instead for continued research and investigation at the current level of funding.[38]

Secretary Wirtz responded to the allegation that the program provided "a device to centralize control of all job hiring in the U.S. Employment Service or to police compliance with Title VII of the Civil Rights Act of 1964." He stated that workers would be referred to employers only in response to a specific request, as in the past. The program, as Wirtz expressed it, had only one purpose—"to help reduce the still-too-high burden of unemployment on all sectors of our society."[39]

The request to expand the program was not approved by Congress, but the Bureau continued the experimental program and explored additional techniques.

Labor force studies

The many demands for new measurements and for improvements in concepts and methodology reflected increasing concern for manpower, or labor resource, issues. In the mid-1950's, analysts suggested that the traditional cyclical problems of the economy were being compounded by long-term structural problems of technological change and economic dislocation.[40] Secretary Mitchell encouraged research directed at the changing composition of the labor force, particularly the emerging problems of youth. In 1955, the Department published *Our Manpower Future, 1955-1965*, and, in 1960, its sequel, *Manpower—Challenge of the Sixties*. In 1960, the Bureau issued the results of a joint study with the Department, *School and Early Employment Experiences of Youth*. Also, at the request of the Senate Committee on Labor and Public Welfare, the Bureau updated and expanded *Employment and Economic Status of Older Men and Women*, which it had initially published in 1952. Moreover, BLS produced a number of studies as part of the Department's older worker program.[41]

In addition to its work on youth and older workers, BLS undertook studies of labor resource issues such as job mobility, the secondary labor force, labor surplus areas, and plant closings. Also, in line with its responsibility for the Monthly Report on the Labor Force, the Bureau began publishing data from the Current Population Survey on educational attainment, marital and family characteristics of workers, and multiple jobholders, among other topics.[42]

Meanwhile, at the request of the Armed Forces, the Bureau produced two projections of military manpower requirements. It also conducted several surveys of personnel resources in the sciences in cooperation with the Defense Department. Expanding activities in space research and technology, spurred by the Soviet challenge embodied in the launching of Sputnik in 1957, increased the demand for such information. In 1959, the Bureau joined with the National Science Foundation to launch an annual canvass of scientific and technical personnel.[43]

Consumer prices

Soon after the war, as goods reappeared on store shelves, BLS adjusted the weights and components of the Consumer Price Index. It also revised its calculations of food prices and, during the postwar inflationary surge, conducted special weekly telegraphic surveys of food prices for prompt release. However, as a result of budget cuts in 1947, the Bureau dropped a number of cities, eliminated some items, and reduced the frequency of pricing.[44]

The Bureau was saved from a further slash in its appropriation the following year by the General Motors-United Auto Workers contract, which stipulated the use of the Consumer Price Index for wage escalation. The importance of the Bureau's product to stability in this crucial industry was apparent even to congressional budget cutters.

In 1949, Congress approved funds for a major revision of the CPI. An important feature of the revision was a survey of dwelling units to correct for the acknowledged understatement of the rental component of the index arising from its failure to cover new units. The Bureau of the Budget proposed that BLS contract with the Census Bureau for the fieldwork in the dwelling unit survey, in line with the Hoover Commission recommendation that agencies use the Census Bureau to collect primary data. In response, BLS pushed for formulation of a governmentwide policy and posed three specific objections: The loss of training experience, the threat to confidentiality, and the delay the change would cause. Department support for the BLS position apparently settled the question for 20 years.[45]

Before the CPI revision was well underway, the outbreak of the Korean War and the subsequent rapid inflation required a change in the Bureau's plans. In October 1950, to avoid a repetition of the World War II controversy over the use of the CPI in adjusting wages, the Bureau announced a program for a temporary revision. It would draw on the field surveys already conducted on rents to ensure adequate coverage of new rental units and also on the results of several continuing expenditure surveys conducted between 1947 and 1949.

The Bureau held emergency discussions with its labor and business advisory committees, as well as with the American Statistical Association's technical advisory committee to BLS on prices. All agreed that the interim revision should produce improvements in the index, but there were differences on the particulars. The ASA and the business advisers suggested that the interim revised index should be linked to the existing series as of January 1950; the labor advisers asked for June 1950 and also preferred a more comprehensive revision. The Bureau adopted the January 1950 linking date and issued the interim revised indexes in February 1951, reflecting revision of city population weights, correction of the rent index, addition of new items, and revision of market basket weights.[46]

Shortly thereafter, in April, the United Electrical, Radio and Machine Workers, an unaffiliated union since its expulsion from the CIO for Communist domination, issued the "UE Cost of Living Index," threatening a repetition of the World War II cost-of-living controversy and disruption of the stabilization program. Attacking the "fundamental pro-employer, anti-labor character of the BLS index," the UE charged that the BLS index still had the shortcomings alleged in the earlier controversy and understated the substantially higher price level calculated by the union.[47]

As a result of the charges, the House Committee on Education and Labor established a special subcommittee to study the CPI, under the chairmanship of Representative Tom Steed of Oklahoma. The subcommittee heard testimony from Bureau officials and a variety of government, academic, business, and union representatives, including members of the Bureau's advisory committees. The hearings became a comprehensive examination of the development, concepts, construction, and use of the CPI. The relationship between the interim revision and the comprehensive revision was brought out, and there was a full discussion of the unresolved issues, including population coverage and the treatment of taxes, housing costs, quality changes, and new products.

Before the subcommittee issued its report, Soviet delegates to the United Nations Economic and Social Council in Geneva attacked the CPI, citing the UE report. U.S. delegate and former Commissioner Isador Lubin informed the Council of the situation. And Clague, writing to Representative Steed, pointed to Communist attacks on cost-of-living indexes in several western countries and predicted their continued criticism of such measures as part of the "party line."[48]

In its report, issued in October 1951, the Steed subcommittee noted several technical problems with the CPI and made a number of suggestions, including the development of estimates of place-to-place differences, annual sample surveys of family expenditures, and direct measures of homeowner costs. The report specifically rejected the UE criticisms, stating that the index was "the most important single statistic issued by the Government," meriting "the widespread confidence which the users have expressed in it." It concluded, "It is imperative that adequate financial support be given to the Bureau of Labor Statistics for this work."[49]

The Bureau came up against another problem when the time arrived to publish the new CPI and discontinue both the "interim index" and the "old series." In January 1953, in issuing the figures for December 1952, Clague noted that this was the last appearance of the old series, which had been published along with the interim index. The AFL, the railroad unions, and a number of manufacturers called for continuation of the old series to allow adequate time for parties to escalation agreements to convert to the new measure. The UAW, however, seeking to reopen the automobile contracts, opposed extension of the old series; the automobile manufacturers supported extension. The dispute finally came to President Eisenhower, who directed BLS to carry the old series for another 6 months and provided the funds.[50]

Later in 1953, BLS introduced the revised CPI. It covered a modernized market basket and an increased number of items. In addition, coverage had been expanded to include small urban places. Towns with a population as small as 2,500 were now included in the sample of cities priced; previously, no cities with a population under 50,000 had been included.

The treatment of housing costs also had been changed. The Bureau previously had used the rent index to approximate all changes in the cost of shelter, but, by 1950, 49 percent of the wage-earner and clerical-worker families owned their homes—up from 30 percent at the time of the previous survey in the 1930's—and the homes were much better equipped with "modern conveniences." Therefore, the Bureau began to measure all items connected with acquisition and operation of a home and calculated a housing index.[51]

The Bureau went to some lengths to make available to the public the detailed information from the consumer expenditure survey conducted as part of the revision program. When Congress rejected requests for appropriations to publish the results, the Bureau sought private financing and secured a grant from the Ford Foundation for work by the Wharton School, which published 18 volumes of statistical data.[52]

In 1953, to provide the opportunity for questions and clarification of the monthly CPI data, the Bureau began to hold a formal press conference for release of the figures.

In the late 1950's, shifting demographic and buying patterns prompted renewed criticisms of the CPI, especially as prices began to creep upward. Further, labor disputes in the steel industry, the 1957-58 recession, and debates over "administered" prices all focused attention on the index.[53]

Business economists, for example, complained that BLS included too many luxury items: "Actually, the index represents what the average urban family spends to live, not what it actually costs to supply its reasonable needs." In the process, the critics continued, BLS ignored the bargain-hunting and substitution habits of American consumers. They pointed to specific problem areas, such as treatment of quality change and introduction of new products.[54]

In view of these and other concerns—and just as BLS was starting another major revision—the Bureau of the Budget sponsored a comprehensive review of government price statistics by a committee of the National Bureau of Economic Research headed by George J. Stigler of the University of Chicago. The committee surveyed the Consumer Price Index, the Wholesale Price Index, and the Indexes of Prices Received and Paid by Farmers, studying such technical aspects as weight revision, specification pricing, sampling, and seasonal adjustment. In regard to the CPI, the committee discussed a broad range of issues such as the basic concept, population coverage, and treatment of quality change, government services, and taxes.[55]

The committee's report, issued in 1961, recommended periodic weight revisions, increased use of probability sampling, more prompt introduction of new commodities, and more funds for research. The committee also advocated restructuring the Wholesale Price Index and emphasizing actual transaction prices. As a major field of expansion, the group suggested the need for export and import price indexes.

For the CPI, the panel urged inclusion of single persons and nonfarm rural workers and renewed the call for development of a more comprehensive index for the entire population. Inclusion of single persons had been considered by BLS during planning for the 1953 revision but had been rejected because of the great heterogeneity within that population group.[56]

The committee also recommended additional research on two controversial and complex aspects of the CPI. First, it suggested that BLS investigate the feasibility of constructing an index based on rental housing units, but representative of owner-occupied houses, which could be substituted for the homeownership components introduced in the previous revision. This prompted a union economist to argue that the homeownership components measured "prices prevailing in the marketplace" and that use of a rental equivalent would introduce "subjective estimates."[57]

The second research area concerned the committee's recommendation to modify the CPI "in the direction of a welfare index"; that is, from the fixed-market-basket concept to the constant-utility or welfare or "true cost of living" approach. The committee urged research to develop such an approach to account more accurately for the introduction of new products; changes in product quality, consumer tastes, and relative prices; and product substitution by consumers. While recognizing that the complexities involved might require the production of both the CPI and a "true cost of living" index, the committee favored the continuous modification of the CPI to the extent that a welfare index could be produced on a monthly basis. Clague and the Bureau staff opposed outright any alteration of the CPI fixed market basket or replacement by a welfare index. They stressed the necessity of maintaining the CPI as a pure price index in view of the many purposes it served, arguing that hybridization by shifting toward the welfare concept would destroy "the usefulness of the index as an acceptable, unambiguous measure of change in consumer prices." However, Clague saw a welfare index, if one could be developed, as complementary to the CPI. [58]

By the time the committee made its report, BLS was deep into its revision program, but it did incorporate some of the committee's ideas in the new index issued in March 1964. It expanded population coverage to include single-person families, introduced probability sampling techniques in selecting items for pricing, and developed a system for measuring sampling error. It also established a division of price and index number research. And it returned to many of the unresolved issues in planning for the next CPI revision in the late 1960's.[59]

The usual local concerns arose during the planning for the 1964 revision. Writing to Clague in 1960, a top officer of the Department pointed to a particular difficulty. Noting that 32 cities would be dropped in the new sample, he pointed out that 8 of these were in districts which had Congressmen on the appropriations committee. "I have explored thoroughly the probability sampling technique, and I am not impressed by its purity to the extent that a little practicality cannot also be taken into consideration in the selection of cities." The official reminded the Commissioner of "the problems we encountered when cities were changed as a result of the last revision."[60]

Many letters over the period concerned New Orleans, San Diego, Phoenix, Denver, and others. As one response, BLS frequently tried to arrange for a local university to continue the work with BLS assistance. This avenue was used in responding to requests from Scranton and Portland in the early 1960's, but, after much discussion, the Secretary directed BLS to continue those surveys itself.

At one point, in view of the continuing controversies, Secretary Wirtz suggested eliminating all city indexes. In response, Clague noted that the national series depended on the city data, in that BLS first prepared the city indexes and then combined them to derive the national figure. The Commissioner recommended studying the issue in planning for the next comprehensive revision.[61]

Standard budgets

In 1945, the House Appropriations Committee had directed BLS to determine the living costs of workers in large cities and the differences between cities. In 1948, the Bureau published *Workers' Budgets in the United States*, reporting "a modest but adequate standard of living" for families of 4 persons in 34 cities in 1946-47. BLS priced the budget several times before discontinuing it in 1951, when the list of goods and the quantities had become obsolete.

In 1959, Congress authorized BLS to update its standard budgets. The Bureau priced its revised list of articles in the fall of the year in 20 large cities then included in the Consumer Price Index, publishing interim budgets for a city worker's family and a retired couple in 1960. Although based on a new list of commodities, the revisions were considered interim because the basic data reflected patterns in the 1950 consumer expenditure survey, soon to be replaced by the 1960-61 survey.

In 1963, recognizing the need to examine basic standard budget concepts while adjusting to the results of the more recent survey, BLS established the Advisory Committee on Standard Budget Research with representatives from industry, labor, State agencies, and academic and private research organizations. Publication of a new and greatly expanded series began in 1966 with *City Worker's Family Budget* (Bulletin 1570-1).[62]

Wholesale prices

During Clague's tenure, the Bureau regularly produced three measures of price movements in primary markets—the comprehensive monthly index, a weekly estimate of trends in the monthly series, and a daily commodity index. The Bureau completely revised the monthly program in 1952 and changed weights in 1955, 1958, and 1961. BLS had introduced the daily data for the Treasury Department during the 1930's and developed them into a series covering 28 commodities. With the 1952 revision, it issued a new series reporting prices for 22 items, either raw materials or commodities very close to the initial stage of production.[63]

In February 1952, BLS issued a revised Wholesale Price Index. Assisted by the advisory committee of the American Statistical Association, the Interagency Price Committee of the Bureau of the Budget, and its own business research advisory committee, the Bureau more than doubled the number of commodity series and shifted the base period from 1926 to an average of 1947-49. In the process, BLS added new major groups, split other groups into their component parts, and added new special-purpose indexes.

During the 1950's, BLS twice developed industry-sector price indexes—in 1953 as part of the input-output project and in 1959 for the Census Bureau.

In its 1961 report, the Stigler Committee criticized the Wholesale Price Index as having a universe that was never clearly defined, with ease of collection a major determinant of which prices to include. To provide a more meaningful concept for economic analysis, the committee proposed a revision to achieve three major objectives: To cover every important sector of the economy dealing in commodities; to provide maximum detail in price reporting; and to develop price indexes for the subgroups of commodities most useful in economic analysis. After the Stigler Committee recommendation, BLS launched a program to develop a time series of industry prices.[64]

Wages and industrial relations

For many decades, BLS had conducted studies of wage rates by occupation and industry, but experience during World War II emphasized the need for local labor market data. Thus, after the war, industry surveys gave greatly increased attention to local area information. Following the budget cuts of 1947, however, BLS severely reduced the number of industry surveys and restructured the program to produce two types of surveys: The longstanding industry surveys and a new series of community or area surveys. The industry surveys provided data on occupational levels and trends for the Nation as a whole and regions, while the community surveys covered several occupations common to a number of industries in a metropolitan area.[65]

In 1959, the Bureau announced a revamped and enlarged wage program. In the industry series, BLS proposed to cover 50 manufacturing and 20 nonmanufacturing industries on a regular cycle. The area program, previously limited to about 20 major labor markets, would be expanded to 80 areas chosen to represent all Standard Metropolitan Statistical Areas.

A stimulus for this expansion was the proposal for a pay comparability program for Federal civil service and postal employees which would require national data on white-collar salaries in private industry. An interagency committee established by the Bureau of the Budget concluded that the 80-area survey design was appropriate, and, in 1960, BLS conducted a survey of professional, managerial, and clerical occupations. With the enactment of the Federal Salary Reform Act of 1962, this National Survey of Professional, Administrative, Technical, and Clerical Pay, or "white collar" survey, was used as a basis for comparing the pay of Federal and private sector employees.[66]

Also as part of the community wage survey program, BLS provided other Federal agencies with information to assist in determining rates for blue-collar workers. In the late 1940's, concerned for duplication among various Federal wage-setting boards, the Bureau of the Budget had suggested that BLS serve as the collecting agency in communities where it made wage surveys. State and local governments used such data, too.[67]

The Bureau conducted a number of studies on the effect of the Federal minimum wage. After the rate rose from $0.40 to $0.75 per hour in January 1950, BLS worked with the Wage and Hour and Public Contracts Divisions of the Department on a project to survey the economic effects, covering industries such as southern sawmills, fertilizer, wood furniture, seamless hosiery, and men's dress shirts. When the rate rose to $1.00 in 1956, the Bureau again cooperated in a study. In the late 1950's, the two agencies sponsored a broad program of industry wage studies as part of a continuing appraisal of minimum wage legislation by the Wage and Hour Division and Congress.[68]

Congress called on BLS for a special study of earnings in retail trade to help in determining whether the industry should be covered by the Fair Labor Standards Act and, if so, what the minimum rate should be. Congress acted to increase the minimum wage but did not extend coverage. BLS published the results of its retail trade survey in late 1957.[69]

Health and other employee benefit plans were a growing area of study for the Bureau. During World War II and its aftermath, supplemental or "fringe" benefits increasingly were used to raise workers' pay. Wage controls restricted direct cash increases, and congressional failure to raise Social Security contributions prevented the system from providing health and other benefits. Therefore, labor unions pressed for health and welfare benefits in collective bargaining negotiations.

Early BLS benefit studies were largely descriptive rather than statistical. In the late 1940's, the Bureau conducted several sample surveys of health, insurance, and retirement plans as part of a joint program with the Social Security Administration and the Public Health Service. In 1953, BLS contracted with the National Bureau of Economic Research for a feasibility study on supplementary benefits. By 1959, the Bureau had worked out technical and conceptual problems to begin a program on employer expenditures for supplementary compensation. Starting with individual industries, reports later covered all employees in the private nonfarm sector. In the 1960's, as benefits continued to grow in importance, the Council of Economic Advisers asked for more frequent and detailed surveys. With departmental support, BLS put forward a plan to expand and refine its program, which was pending on Clague's retirement.[70]

In 1959, when Congress passed the Welfare and Pension Plans Disclosure Act, BLS expressed concern over whether the administrative regulations would assign the Bureau "responsibility for the conduct of substantive research in the field of employee benefits and pension plans, a responsibility which we now have and exercise in a modest way to the benefit of the Department."[71] Reports filed under the act with the Department's Bureau of Labor Standards provided a wealth of information. In cooperation with Labor Standards, BLS launched a regular program of sample studies of pension and retirement plans filed. It also published digests of health and welfare and pension plans derived from its industrial relations activities and analyses of collective bargaining agreements.

The provision of information on collective bargaining increased during Clague's tenure. With the rapid increase in prices and wages after the war and the need for the most current information on collective bargaining developments, the Bureau began to issue a monthly report, *Current Wage Developments*, which listed by company and union the negotiated changes in wages and supplementary benefits. In 1953, the list was limited to agreements affecting 1,000 or more production and related workers. Beginning in 1954, a statistical summary of wage changes was prepared on a quarterly basis to supplement the listing. In 1959, another statistical summary was introduced covering changes in wages and benefits in manufacturing for both union and nonunion workers.

The Bureau introduced a series of wage chronologies in 1948, each providing detailed information on changes in wages and benefits of a specific company and union, whether through collective bargaining or unilateral management decisions. During the Korean emergency, the Wage Stabilization Board found these and the *Current Wage Developments* reports particularly useful in their review of wage settlements.

Throughout the period, the Bureau maintained a file of collective bargaining agreements, as required by Section 211 (a) of the Labor Management Relations Act of 1947. Even before passage of the act, BLS had begun publication of in-depth studies on provisions of collective bargaining agreements, the Bulletin 908 series, continuing through 19 collective bargaining subjects before ending in 1950. Having issued many individual studies of contract provisions in the meantime, BLS launched a major new series in 1964 with a study of grievance procedures in major collective bargaining agreements (Bulletin 1425-1). In succeeding years, the Bureau produced studies on such subjects as severance pay, supplemental unemployment benefit plans, seniority, safety and health provisions, and wage-incentive provisions.

Productivity and technology
Under Clague, the Bureau resumed its work on productivity indexes for selected industries which had been interrupted by the war. A new

program of detailed industry reports, based on direct field surveys, supplemented the series. However, funding cuts in the early 1950's forced the Bureau to drop field collection and to rely on available secondary sources.

The General Motors-United Auto Workers contract of 1948, with its provision for wage adjustment based on an annual "improvement factor" as well as on the Consumer Price Index, was a major stimulus to the development of productivity measures for the economy as a whole. It was also a harbinger of the "guideposts" policy set forth by the Council of Economic Advisers in the 1960's. Both the Council and the Joint Economic Committee expressed continuing interest in the measurement of national productivity. The Bureau of the Budget and the AFL also pressed for such measures.

The Bureau's development of productivity measures for the economy was a long and arduous process, partly because productivity measurement was a very sensitive area of labor-management relations. Concern with the policy implications of the figures, in addition to the novelty and complexity of the technique and the lack of adequate data, made for extended discussions with the Bureau's business and labor advisory groups. One issue was the effect on collective bargaining of comparisons between economywide productivity indexes and the productivity developments in specific industries, particularly in the automobile and steel industries. Both labor and management in the auto industry were critical of the emphasis given to the broad measures, but the consensus within both of the Bureau's advisory groups was finally that such productivity measures were needed.

In 1955, the Bureau published its first productivity indexes for the manufacturing sector as a whole, reflecting the relationship of output to man-hours of production workers for the period 1939-53. Building on this experience, the Bureau worked toward development of indexes for the total private economy. These were published in 1959, covering the period 1909-58.[72]

The importance of productivity measurement was heightened in 1962, when the Council of Economic Advisers, in its annual report to the President, offered wage and price guideposts for noninflationary behavior in collective bargaining, basing them on the Bureau's data. The wage guidepost suggested was that "the rate of increase in wage rates (including fringe benefits) in each industry be equal to the trend rate of over-all productivity increase." On the price side, the Council suggested that price increases were warranted only if an industry's productivity rose less than the average for the economy.[73]

The labor requirements program authorized by Congress in 1959 added a significant new project to the Bureau's productivity work. In this program, BLS estimated the employment generated by—or labor hours required for—various types of government, or government-financed, construction, such as schools, hospitals, public housing, and college housing. This expanded the work begun in the 1930's to measure the volume of employment created by new construction.[74]

The role of labor costs in international trade was another subject of study for the Bureau. Increased competition in foreign trade, balance of payments problems, the outflow of gold, and other factors raised the question of whether the United States was pricing itself out of world markets. Bureau studies examined unit labor costs at home and abroad and the effects on collective bargaining and employment. As part of its activities, BLS also prepared materials for the "Kennedy Round" of tariff negotiations.

The Bureau was also called upon to study the effects of—and adjustments to—automation and technological change. It conducted a series of case studies on the introduction of automatic technology and also produced two major studies of office automation. Then, for the President's Advisory Committee on Labor Management Policy, it prepared a major study on technological trends in 36 industries. The Bureau also studied retraining programs and published case studies of workers displaced by the new technologies.

The continuing sensitivity of the productivity issue in labor-management relations was reflected in the Bureau's difficulty in conducting the automation studies despite the approval of its advisory groups. Management in the railroad and automobile industries proved reluctant to arrange for them. And Clague wrote of difficulties with union research directors who, feeling labor had an important stake in automation studies, demanded review of texts, participating companies, and other aspects of the work. In 1959, the research director of the Auto Workers attacked the BLS "surrender to big business" in the development of productivity materials, charging that the Bureau had succumbed to business pressures to "downgrade, obscure, and conceal" the facts, urging the Joint Economic Committee to investigate.[75]

Industrial safety and health
Continuing its long interest in industrial safety and health, BLS expanded its annual series of injury-frequency and injury-severity measures covering manufacturing and nonmanufacturing industries, and its monthly series (collected quarterly) for manufacturing. By 1966, the annual program covered over 650 industries and industry groups, and the monthly (quarterly) covered 140 manufacturing and industry groups. BLS also conducted intensive studies of injury rates and accident causes in selected industries, surveying about one industry a year.

Amendments to the Longshoremen's and Harbor Workers' Compensation Act passed in 1958 provided more work for BLS. These amendments authorized the Secretary of Labor to issue regulations protecting the health and safety of employees, including requirements to maintain records. The Secretary delegated the administrative functions to the Bureau of Labor Standards, and BLS acted as its agent in collecting and compiling data.[76]

International activities
During the late 1940's, the Bureau cooperated with various overseas projects of the U.S. Government. Working with the European Recovery Program, it planned and conducted a number of productivity studies and gave technical assistance to European governments for developing their own economic statistics. During 1950 and 1951, about 80 European labor statisticians took 3-month courses with BLS under arrangements made by the Organization for European Economic Cooperation and the Economic Cooperation Administration.

The Gift of Freedom, a Bureau publication which presented a wide range of statistics on the economic and social status of American workers, was reprinted in several foreign languages for distribution abroad.[77]

The Bureau published information on foreign labor conditions and statistics, introducing the monthly publication, Labor Developments Abroad, in 1956 and a series on labor law and practice in various countries in 1961. The Bureau also developed a considerable amount of material in collaboration with the International Cooperation Administration/Agency for International Development, including descriptions of labor conditions—primarily in developing countries—and a Foreign Labor Information Series. These were intended for the use of Foreign Service staff, labor specialists assigned abroad, and participants in technical and exchange programs, as well as businessmen and others.[78] BLS also developed several technical manuals, in cooperation with ICA/AID, to help foreign countries develop statistical programs relating to consumer prices and the labor force.[79]

In the early 1960's, BLS and the Department's Bureau of International Labor Affairs collaborated to publish *Labor Digest*, a series of brief notes on labor conditions around the world.

Economic growth studies

Since the 1930's, BLS had worked with Wassily Leontief of Harvard to develop "input-output" or interindustry analysis. Following the war, with W. Duane Evans heading the project, the Bureau projected employment patterns to 1950. Congress showed special interest in the BLS projections for steel, made in 1947.

At the initial request of the National Security Resources Board and the military establishment, the Bureau joined a cooperative program with other Federal agencies, universities, and research institutions which was later financed by the Air Force. As part of the project, BLS produced a 450-sector input-output table based on the 1947 Census of Manufactures.[80]

During the Korean War, the program became controversial when some employers called it state planning, a step toward a planned economy. With the armistice, the new administration sought ways to cut the defense budget, and Air Force funding was halted. Evans and BLS tried without success to arrange private financing for continuing studies. But in the late 1950's there was renewed interest in input-output studies as a means of analyzing economic problems.[81]

In 1962, the Bureau joined with other government agencies and private organizations in a wide-ranging program of studies for the analysis and projection of economic growth trends. The program represented an effort to develop a more comprehensive and integrated framework than had previously been available for analyzing the implications of long-term economic growth, particularly the implications for employment.

Other participants in the research program included the Office of Business Economics of the Department of Commerce, the Department of Agriculture, the Bureau of Mines of the Department of the Interior, Harvard University, George Washington University, the

Council of State Governments, and the National Planning Association. Guidance was provided by an interagency coordinating committee consisting of representatives from the Departments of Labor and Commerce, the Budget Bureau, and the Council of Economic Advisers. The chairman of the Council headed the committee.[82]

As one aspect of the research, BLS developed projections of the industrial distribution of employment based upon the input-output tables prepared by the Commerce Department. In late 1966, the Bureau published the 1970 projections of demand, interindustry relationships, and employment developed by BLS and the other participating agencies.[83]

Administration

Funding
After recovering from the slash in fiscal year 1948, the Bureau's regular appropriations for salaries and expenses showed little if any increase in the early 1950's. They began to rise in the late 1950's, then grew substantially in the 1960's with the expansion in the Bureau's programs (table 6). Congress provided separate funds for two revisions of the CPI within the period.

Outside funds, also called working funds or intragovernmental advances and reimbursements, added considerably to Bureau resources as other agencies funded statistical work done on their behalf. Normally providing from 4 to 7 percent of the Bureau's total budget, these payments mounted during the Korean War and later, in the 1960's, when the Department undertook new programs. The Atomic Energy Commission, the Air Force, the Office of Naval Research, the National Security Resources Board, the Veterans Administration, and the National Science Foundation, among others, underwrote Bureau activities.

Management
As had happened before in the Bureau's history, in 1950 Congress had occasion to investigate complaints lodged by employees and former employees of the Bureau. They alleged that the Division of Prices and Cost of Living "was overstaffed, poorly supervised, and steeped in an atmosphere of employee discontent." In the report presenting its findings, the House Subcommittee on Overstaffing in the Executive

Table 6. Funding for Bureau of Labor Statistics, 1947–65
(in thousands)

Fiscal year ended June 30 —	Total[1]	Salaries and expenses
1947	[2]$6,826	$6,268
1948	4,218	3,945
1949	4,579	4,362
1950	6,990	5,569
1951	8,702	5,722
1952	9,149	5,701
1953	7,077	5,766
1954	6,081	5,593
1955	5,974	5,441
1956	6,802	6,407
1957	7,481	6,875
1958	8,159	7,463
1959	8,597	7,989
1960	11,394	10,520
1961	13,350	11,118
1962	15,970	12,667
1963	17,655	14,590
1964	19,831	16,345
1965	20,373	18,542

[1]Includes appropriations for CPI revision (1950–52 and 1960–64) and miscellaneous, working, and trust funds.

[2]Includes $15,000 for a study of conditions in Hawaii.

SOURCE: *The Budget of the United States Government.*

Departments and Agencies concluded that funds for the revision of the CPI had been "dissipated through gross overstaffing, inferior planning, untrained supervision, and improvident administration."[84]

Secretary Tobin immediately wrote the subcommittee chairman of "the overall efficiency and economy of the Division's work" in turning out some of the country's "most important and most closely scrutinized statistics." While challenging the charge of dissipation of funds, Tobin acknowledged some problems of administration, which had been compounded by congressional delay in funding. He stated that, after great effort, the revision program was now back on schedule, and was urgently needed to avoid the controversy which had developed during World War II. Clague pointed out that an attitude survey had demonstrated that the vast majority of BLS employees were satisfied. Upon assurance that the Bureau would improve its management, the matter was dropped.[85]

Reconfirmation
Clague's administration was interrupted for about a year when Secretary Mitchell proposed his reappointment for a third term in 1954. Since Clague was a legal resident of Pennsylvania, his nomination required the assent of both Pennsylvania Senators, but Senator Edward Martin, the senior Senator, objected.

Senator Martin's objection centered on two pieces of information he had received about Clague's activities in the early 1930's—a newspaper clipping quoting Clague as saying that the economic future of the country would be state socialism, and his contribution to a college which the Attorney General had later listed as a Communist institution.

Delayed by Martin's objection, the appointment also became entangled with difficulties surrounding the appointment of another Department official, and confirmation proceedings were held up for almost a year. In the interim, Secretary Mitchell named Clague as his special assistant, and Aryness Joy Wickens, Clague's Deputy Commissioner, served as Acting Commissioner. A highly respected statistician, Wickens had had a long career in government before joining the Bureau in the late 1930's. Under Lubin, Hinrichs, and Clague, she had moved steadily upward, from Chief of the Price Division to Assistant Commissioner to Deputy Commissioner. During the year of Clague's absence, the work of the Bureau went on largely unaffected.

In July 1955, Clague finally had his confirmation hearing, and he was able to reply to Senator Martin's implied charge of association with radical causes. He informed the committee that the remark quoted—from an extemporaneous speech—was intended as a challenge to the audience and not as an espousal of socialism. His contribution to the college had been pledged in the 1920's to help provide education for poor students.[86]

Senator Martin had already informed the committee that he was no longer going to oppose the nomination. In addition, the committee had received letters from supporters. Stephen M. DuBrul, Executive-in-Charge of the Business Research Staff at General Motors, praised Clague's integrity, open-mindedness, courage, and determination. William F. Sullivan, President of the Northern Textile Association, noted Clague's "splendid record of accomplishment" as well as his objectivity and impartiality. Leo Teplow, Industrial Relations Consultant to the American Iron and Steel Institute, commented that Clague enjoyed "the wholehearted confidence of both management and labor."[87] Earlier, AFL President George Meany had spoken with Secretary Mitchell in support of reappointment.[88] Newspaper columnists and editorials also supported Clague. His confirmation took only half an hour.

Confidentiality

Early in his tenure, Clague reaffirmed the voluntary nature of the BLS reporting process and the necessity for strict confidentiality of the data provided by respondents. He saw the Bureau's dependence on voluntary cooperation as "a great asset in a democracy" rather than a limitation, as some others had viewed it. [89]

In the early 1960's, a serious challenge arose to the Bureau's policy of confidentiality. Under the provisions of the Public Contracts Act of 1936, government suppliers were required to pay at least the locally prevailing minimum wage, and the Secretary of Labor had been making determinations of the prevailing minimum in various industries from data collected in BLS wage surveys. Interested parties had won the right to judicial review of the Secretary's decisions. The Baldor Electric Company and 10 other suppliers in the electrical machinery industry brought the Department to court, challenging the Secretary's determination on the grounds that they had been denied access to documents underlying the BLS tables.

Throughout, the Bureau, supported by the Department, argued its fundamental policy that it operated on the basis of voluntary reporting, that granting access would break confidentiality and endanger its whole system of data collection. The Federal District Court and the Court of Appeals for the District of Columbia upheld the manufacturers, ruling that refusal of access to BLS documents breached their legal right to rebuttal and cross-examination.[90]

Rather than imperil the foundation of the Bureau's data gathering system, the Secretary revoked his determination, and none have been issued since. Over the years, the policy of confidentiality has been maintained, and other influences on wages, such as minimum wage setting under the Fair Labor Standards Act and the general extension of collective bargaining, have lessened the importance of the Public Contracts Act. It now serves mainly as a statement of the government's intent to be a good employer.[91]

Retirement

On September 14, 1965, Secretary Wirtz announced Ewan Clague's retirement, saying, "Ewan Clague has built his ideals and his competence and integrity into the traditions and strength of the Bureau of Labor Statistics and the Department of Labor. He stands preeminent in his field. His colleagues have paid him every honor they command. . . . The staff of the Bureau is both his compliment and his legacy to the future."[92]

Clague later described the understanding he had had with Secretary Wirtz: "When I was confirmed for a fifth term in August 1963, Secretary of Labor W. Willard Wirtz and I reached an agreement that we should be on the lookout for a successor. When Professor Arthur M. Ross of the University of California at Berkeley, one of the names on our joint list, became available in the summer of 1965, I submitted my resignation, and Ross was appointed Commissioner."[93]

Observers praised Clague and his accomplishments. Senator William Proxmire, a close observer of BLS from his post on the Joint Economic Committee, referred to his "19 immensely productive years," noting the "steady improvement in quality and the constantly more accurate and detailed picture of our economy" provided by BLS data during Clague's tenure. At Ross' nomination hearing, Senator Wayne Morse, veteran of economic stabilization programs and major labor-management crises, commented that he could always place complete reliance on Clague's work.[94]

The New York Times declared, "Integrity has been the dominant characteristic of the Bureau's approach to all its assignments." Under Clague, it continued, the Bureau had achieved "a remarkable degree of professional detachment and trustworthiness." *The Washington Post* editorialized in the same vein, commending Clague for his probity— his determination "to maintain the integrity of the BLS as an objective agency at times when there were pressures to twist results in conformity with political preconceptions."[95]

Clague had an active career for many years after his retirement. Initially, he served as a consultant to Secretary Wirtz. Later, he conducted and published research studies on labor force subjects, including the all-volunteer army, older workers, and coal miners. He has continued to be active in civic affairs.

Chapter VIII.

Four Commissioners: An Economy Going by the Numbers

There were four Commissioners of Labor Statistics in the two decades following Clague's departure as a variety of circumstances produced limited terms for Arthur M. Ross, Geoffrey H. Moore, and Julius Shiskin. Janet L. Norwood was well into her second term in 1984. Whatever the length of service, the head of the Bureau faced relentless demands as public interest in the Bureau's statistics heightened with continuous inflation, rising unemployment in four recessions, and the increased use of BLS data in evaluating national economic policies and distributing public and private funds.

The economic climate and escalating uses of statistics

In 1966, the chairman of the Joint Economic Committee stated, in introducing the hearings on government price statistics, that they would cast some light on "whether or not we have inflation. . . ." The annual rate of increase in consumer prices at that time was about 2 percent.[1] By the end of 1968, there was no longer any doubt about inflation—consumer prices had risen almost 5 percent over the year.

The inflationary boom of the late 1960's was accompanied by a drop in unemployment, which fell below the 4-percent goal set in the early 1960's. In 1969, however, unemployment started to rise, and the economy began to suffer from both inflation and high levels of unemployment at the same time. Moreover, labor disputes in longshoring, steel, and railroads compounded the problems.

In August 1971, when less drastic measures had failed to stem the inflation, President Nixon, having already moved to restrain excessive price and wage increases in the construction industry, imposed direct wage and price controls. During the freeze and the ensuing control period, the Bureau was called upon frequently to supply data to the stabilization agencies—the Cost of Living Council and the Pay Board.

Controls lapsed in 1974, and inflation resumed its upward course, accompanied by rising unemployment, as the oil embargo and world-wide food shortages helped push the country into the steepest recession in the postwar period. As the Council of Economic Advisers described the decade of the 1970's, "Each time inflation accelerated. . . a temporary boost in employment was achieved at the cost of a subsequent recession. Moreover, the recessions became more serious."[2]

In recognition of these economic conditions, Congress passed several countermeasures to stimulate the economy and enacted the Full Employment and Balanced Growth Act of 1978, which reaffirmed and enlarged on the commitment of the Employment Act of 1946. The 1978 act obligated the Government to reduce the rate of inflation while also reducing unemployment to 4 percent.[3] Meanwhile, another increase in oil prices led to a third inflationary wave, which lasted into 1982 before moderating.

The economy was also undergoing a variety of structural changes during the period. Commissioner Norwood, during her years in office, highlighted these trends: The larger number of young workers and the dramatic increase in the participation of women; the continued employment expansion in the service-producing sector and in white-collar occupations; the decline in the automobile, steel, and textile industries; and the general slowdown in productivity growth.[4]

The economic and social developments added to the importance of the Bureau's work in monitoring changes in the economy. And still other uses for the Bureau's data were developing which directly affected the pocketbooks of millions of Americans. With mounting inflation, pressures increased for indexation—tying money payments to price indexes—as a means of ensuring fairness. As President Nixon stated in 1969 in reference to social security benefits, "The way to prevent future unfairness is to attach the benefit schedule to the cost of living. . . . We remove questions about future years; we do much to remove this system from biennial politics; and we make fair treatment of beneficiaries a matter of certainty rather than a matter of hope."[5]

As early as 1962, Congress had linked Federal civil service retirement benefits to changes in the Consumer Price Index. This was followed by indexing arrangements for a growing number of Federal programs. All major retirement and disability plans came to be adjusted on the basis of the CPI, and components of the CPI were used to adjust payments for the food stamp program, the rent subsidy program, school meals, and nutrition programs for the elderly. In 1981, the Congressional Budget Office estimated that "almost a third of Federal expenditure is directly linked to the CPI or related price measures. . . . A one-percent increase in the CPI will automatically trigger nearly $2 billion of additional Federal expenditures, at 1981 program levels."[6]

In addition, wages of millions of workers under collective bargaining agreements were linked to the CPI. Also, under 1981 legislation, Federal income tax rate brackets were scheduled for linkage to the CPI beginning in 1985.

The Bureau's data also were used in Federal wage determinations. Under acts passed in 1962 and 1970, changes in the pay levels recorded in the BLS annual survey of professional, administrative, technical, and clerical pay in the private sector entered into the Federal pay-setting process. Area wage survey data played a role in setting wage rates for Federal blue-collar workers and for employees of government contractors. The BLS measure of changes in national average wages affected some benefits under the social security program and workers' compensation payments for longshore and harbor workers. In 1980, the Minimum Wage Study Commission recommended indexing the Federal minimum wage to this BLS measure.[7] Further, unemployment rates estimated by the States according to Bureau specifications determined the eligibility of States and local areas for funding under various Federal programs.

Additional proposals for indexation were made, although not everyone supported the automatic adjustment procedure. Its growth alarmed some policymakers and legislators, who held that indexing reinforced inflation and multiplied the problems arising from mushrooming Federal budget deficits. Whether or not indexation would continue to be adopted, the uses already established by legislation focused the public's attention on the Bureau's measures.[8]

The four Commissioners

The four Commissioners responded to the challenges facing the Bureau in different ways. Ross, a professor of labor-management relations, saw it as his mandate to shake up and modernize a staid, old-line organization, and he sought to develop more data and analysis pertinent to social policy. Moore, a foundation research economist and expert business cycle analyst, emphasized production of sound figures and their neutral, objective release. Shiskin, a civil servant with long experience in government economic and statistical activities, stressed maintenance of the integrity of the data and independence for BLS from the policy concerns of the Department. Norwood, also a career civil servant, protected and enhanced the quality and scope of the Bureau's core programs in the face of widespread budget cuts. With inflation mounting substantially and consequent controversy over the Consumer Price Index, Norwood addressed the criticisms on their technical merits, applying the findings of the Bureau's long-term study of the CPI in making revisions in the homeownership component. She stressed the impartial and independent public-service role of the Bureau in meeting these difficult problems, while giving the Bureau a more "human" face in her increased attention to data on minorities and women.

Arthur Ross, October 1965–July 1968

Arthur M. Ross succeeded Ewan Clague in October 1965. Ross had been a professor of industrial relations at the University of California at Berkeley and had served as director of its Institute of Industrial Relations from 1954 to 1963. For over 20 years, he had served on various public and private boards and commissions and as an arbitrator in several industries. Less of a bureaucrat than other Commissioners, one who had been a user rather than a producer of statistics, his philosophy was reflected in his comment that BLS products "will not simply be raw data but will be usable to labor, management, and to other customers."[9] Personally, Ross brought a concern for the disadvantaged and a commitment to social programs, pressing for research and surveys to identify and measure problems in slum areas.

From the beginning, Ross projected a new style and direction. In remarks at his swearing-in ceremony, he outlined six principal tasks for the Bureau, including maximum service to the Department;

increased analysis and interpretation; programs matched to new trends in the economy and labor force; improved technical quality, especially with enhanced computer capability; more effective communication of BLS activities; and development of new data and analysis on social issues and policy problems.[10] Supported by Secretary Wirtz in this determination to reinvigorate the Bureau, Ross used the results of extensive management surveys by the private firm of Booz-Allen and Hamilton to reorganize the Bureau's operations.

Ross' views made for a crowded agenda of activities for the program offices, ranging from new measures of poverty and related problems to a "master plan" to integrate and improve all the Bureau's price programs. The reorganization made for delay in putting the plans into practice, however, and they were not far along when, in the summer of 1968, Ross decided to return to academic life and accepted a post at the University of Michigan.

Rather than submit a new nominee in an election year, Secretary Wirtz named Deputy Commissioner Ben Burdetsky as Acting Commissioner. Burdetsky had been with the Department since 1955, and Ross had brought him into the Bureau in 1966 to manage the reorganization. Burdetsky served as Acting Commissioner until March 1969, when Geoffrey Moore was designated Commissioner.

Geoffrey Moore, March 1969–January 1973

Geoffrey H. Moore came to the Bureau from the National Bureau of Economic Research, where he had been the Vice President for Research. The immediate past president of the American Statistical Association, Moore had also lectured on economics at New York University and Columbia University.

Throughout his term, Moore worked closely with Arthur Burns and Julius Shiskin. Burns was Counselor at the White House and, later, Chairman of the Federal Reserve Board, while Shiskin was Chief Statistician of the Office of Management and Budget. Burns had been Moore's teacher at Rutgers. Shiskin and Moore had been classmates there and, afterwards, professional collaborators in the development of the Index of Leading Indicators.

Early in his tenure, Moore stated his aims for the Bureau: BLS data should be relevant, timely, accurate, and impartial. In keeping with these guidelines, Moore listed specific programs needing improvement, including local area data, public sector labor relations, the Wholesale Price Index, occupational safety and health statistics, and construction industry series. He also called for the development of a general wage index.[11]

Moore was able to make progress on many of these objectives during his term and, in addition, to integrate into the Bureau four programs on employment statistics that were transferred from the Manpower Administration in a governmentwide reorganization of statistical activities. But, as described later, he was faced with a succession of events during his last 2 years in office that put the Bureau and its staff in the midst of a political maelstrom.

Moore left office in January 1973, shortly before his first term was to end. President Nixon accepted his pro forma resignation, which had been requested along with those of other political appointees, including Secretary of Labor Hodgson, at the start of Nixon's second term.

With Moore's departure, Ben Burdetsky again served as Acting Commissioner. Moore returned to the National Bureau of Economic Research. While at the National Bureau, he also served as adjunct scholar at both the Hoover Institution and the American Enterprise Institute. In 1979, Moore started the Center for International Business Cycle Research at Rutgers University as part of the School of Business. In 1983, he moved the center to Columbia University as part of the Graduate School of Business. Moore has continued to write and testify on the quality of BLS data.

Julius Shiskin, July 1973–October 1978
Julius Shiskin, an economist and statistician, was appointed Commissioner in July 1973. He was already familiar with BLS operations and problems through his earlier work in the Office of Management and Budget and the Census Bureau. As head of the Office of Statistical Policy of OMB, he had sought to establish procedures for ensuring that the release of statistical data would be free of political considerations. He had also proposed the guidelines for the reorganization of government statistical activities in 1971.

At his nomination hearing, called upon for his view of the Commissioner's independence, Shiskin cited the 4-year term and promised, "I would not resign before that upon request." Later, in refusing to submit a pro forma resignation when Gerald Ford succeeded to the Presidency, Shiskin again noted the 4-year term and likened the position to that of Federal Reserve Governors. He reminded the committee that charges of politicization had followed the replacement of Moore and pointed out that Ewan Clague had served under four Presidents without submitting a resignation.[12]

Shiskin committed himself to improving the basic data and expanding the analytical work of the Bureau while maintaining the highest professional standards. In addition, he re-emphasized traditional BLS neutrality, observing, "Policy is not a role for professional statisticians."[13]

Shiskin served under three Presidents and four Secretaries of Labor. He encountered new and difficult problems, largely as a result of the Bureau's assumption of responsibility for local area unemployment statistics. He also faced contention on concepts and methodology in the revision of the Consumer Price Index.

Shiskin followed a policy of openness and full discussion of the Bureau's data and methods. Faced with charges of inadequacies in the unemployment data, he campaigned for a national commission to conduct a comprehensive review of employment and unemployment statistics, and he appeared before the Joint Economic Committee almost every month to provide the opportunity for questions about the Bureau's latest figures. He was closely associated with the establishment and funding of the program of continuing consumer expenditure studies.

Shiskin's success in improving the data and in maintaining the credibility of the Bureau was reflected in the support for his renomination in 1977.[14] With his reappointment by President Carter, Shiskin became the first Commissioner since Clague to start a second term. After a long period of illness, he died in office in October 1978.

Janet Norwood, May 1979—

Secretary Ray Marshall named Janet L. Norwood the Acting Commissioner during Shiskin's illness, and President Carter nominated her for Commissioner in March 1979. She was confirmed in May. A graduate of Douglass College of Rutgers University, Norwood received a Ph.D. at Tufts University. Subsequently, she taught at Wellesley and conducted research in international economics at Tufts.

The first woman to serve as head of the Bureau, Norwood was also the first Commissioner since Ethelbert Stewart to be appointed from the ranks. She had worked in the Bureau since 1963, primarily in the price office, where she renewed and redeveloped the international price program and managed the consumer price program. Moore had named her Associate Deputy Commissioner for Data Analysis in 1972, and, under Shiskin, she had become, first, Deputy Commissioner for Data Analysis in 1973 and, then, in 1975, the Deputy Commissioner. The Department recognized her professional accomplishments with the Secretary's Award for Distinguished Achievement (1972), the Secretary's Special Commendation (1977), and the Philip Arnow Award (1979). In 1984, the American Society for Public Administration and the National Academy of Public Administration honored Norwood with their National Public Service Award.[15]

Norwood stated that her role was not to theorize or predict the future, but to provide accurate statistics that were relevant to the country's economic and social needs. She warned the Bureau against a "built-in bias against change." "We ought to be the ones who are out there letting people know of changes which we think could be considered."[16]

During her tenure, the economic and political climate has kept public attention focused on BLS statistics. In her first term, inflation accelerated and unemployment rose to its highest level in more than 40 years. Members of the Carter administration criticized the Bureau's method of computing the CPI, claiming that it overstated the true rate of inflation. Candidate Reagan charged the President with "jimmying" the Producer Price Index, and President Reagan, referring to the seasonal adjustment of unemployment figures, complained that the statisticians in Washington had "funny ways of counting."[17]

Norwood was forced to rethink program priorities as both the Carter and Reagan administrations launched drives to cut government expenditures and employment. During fiscal year 1982, the Bureau suffered a 12-percent budget cut and lost about 10 percent of its work force through attrition. Norwood protected the Bureau's core programs—those relating to major national concerns—by winnowing out programs of more limited application, some of which required substantially more funding to bring up to Bureau standards of validity and reliability.

At the same time, Norwood obtained the resources needed to proceed with long-range plans for improving the scope and quality of data on consumer prices, producer prices, employment and unemployment, and wage and benefit costs. She put into effect many major recommendations of the National Commission on Employment and Unemployment Statistics. Moreover, she began work on two conceptually complicated programs—multifactor productivity measures and another comprehensive revision of the CPI. Also, under her leadership, the Bureau assumed responsibility for administering the resources for national labor market information programs.

In 1983, Norwood was reappointed by President Reagan, and the Senate confirmed her by voice vote without holding hearings. Secretary Donovan hailed the action as assuring that "the work of the Bureau will continue under the highest standards of professionalism and integrity." Facing her new term, Norwood commented, "The challenges will be even greater over the next 4 years."[18]

Public release of statistics

During Clague's tenure, the procedures for releasing BLS data had been changed from informal arrangements—primarily news releases and occasional press briefings at no set dates—to formal press conferences for the major Bureau series on dates scheduled in advance. Despite these new procedures, separating the release of BLS data from political considerations remained a continuing concern.

Just at the time Moore became Commissioner in 1969, Arthur Burns, as President Nixon's adviser, addressed the need to preserve the credibility of government statistics. Burns' view was reflected in a memorandum the President sent to the Office of Management and Budget within 3 weeks after taking office, stating, "The prompt release on a regular schedule of official statistics is a matter of vital importance to the proper management of both private and public affairs." In addition, it stipulated that "as a rule, new figures should be released through the statistical officer in charge."[19]

This program was vigorously pursued by the head of the Office of Statistical Policy of OMB, Julius Shiskin, who called for a rule, to be followed in all agencies, "that the written press release must come out at least 1 hour before any policy commentary."[20]

The BLS press conferences for technical briefings were also considered. Moore, Burns, and Shiskin agreed that these briefings should be discontinued, since they invited questions on economic policy and outlook—matters beyond the responsibility of career service statistical

officers. Shiskin drafted a memorandum recommending discontinuance, arguing, "The confidence of the public in the integrity of the
statistical agencies of the government can best be maintained if all the
statistics are routinely released on schedules in advance, in the form of
written press releases without press conferences." However, press
officers at the White House and the Department of Labor argued that
discontinuance during a period of inflation would be construed as
politically motivated, and the press conferences were continued.[21]

The issue took on new dimensions beginning in late 1970, when,
with the continuing rise in unemployment, the Bureau's assessment of
the contribution of the General Motors strike to an increase in the
unemployment rate differed from that of the administration. Then, in
February 1971, at the BLS monthly press briefing, a Bureau spokesman labeled the decline in the unemployment rate—from 6.2 to 6.0
percent—as "marginally significant." Secretary Hodgson, in a press
release issued simultaneously, characterized the decline as of "great
significance." The next month, the Secretary's press release called a
0.2 percentage point decline in the unemployment rate "heartening"
while the Bureau described the situation as "sort of mixed," since
employment and hours worked were also down.

Shortly after, Secretary Hodgson announced that there would be
no more monthly BLS press briefings. As Moore outlined the new
procedures, the statistics would be issued in written releases, reporters
could phone technicians to ask questions, and the Secretary would
wait at least an hour to make his statement.[22]

Moore and Shiskin, along with Hodgson, explained that these
arrangements would preserve the neutrality and objectivity of the
statistics and put the Bureau in conformity with the practices of other
statistical agencies.[23] However, there were immediate charges of
politicization, and these set off a round of congressional hearings and
reports, as well as investigations by the Joint American Statistical
Association/Federal Statistics Users' Conference Committee and by
the Industrial Relations Research Association.

Several other events also raised the charge of politicization. In
July 1971, now functioning without the press briefing, the Bureau
issued the unemployment data for June. The release warned that the
published figures possibly overstated the decline in unemployment
because of technical problems with the seasonal adjustment factors.
The warning, according to a later report of the Industrial Relations

Research Association, "evoked dismay and anger within the Administration. These reactions were duly reported in the press, and the Department of Labor was privately told of President Nixon's anger concerning the incident." Subsequently, the unemployment figures calculated with the revised seasonal adjustment factors showed a drop of half that originally reported.[24]

Shortly after the July incident, the Office of Management and Budget issued guidelines for the reorganization of Federal statistical activities, citing the proliferation of such activities and the recent recommendations of the President's Advisory Council on Executive Organization.[25] In the fall of 1971, in response to the OMB directive, Moore announced several changes in the Bureau's organization and personnel. The Office of Manpower and Employment Statistics, whose chief had been the Bureau spokesman at press briefings on the employment situation, was split into two separate units. In line with the OMB guidelines, the Bureau abolished the positions of Chief Economist and Chief Statistician, and the incumbents left the Bureau. In their place, two new offices were established, each headed by a Deputy Commissioner. The Deputy Commissioner for Statistical Operations and Processing was a Bureau staff member. The Deputy Commissioner for Data Analysis was new to the Bureau, having come from the President's Commission on Federal Statistics.

Moore characterized the reorganization as an effort to improve the management of the Bureau's programs and a refinement of earlier organizational changes made by Ross. But, coming on the heels of the termination of press briefings, the changes were attacked as politically inspired. Lawrence F. O'Brien, chairman of the Democratic National Committee, alleged that the White House was attempting to stack BLS with "political appointees." *The Washington Post* editorialized, "The Nixon Administration is bringing hand-picked political appointees into the Bureau of Labor Statistics." As the *Post* noted, the reorganization appeared to many as retribution.[26]

With the termination of the press briefings, the Joint Economic Committee began monthly hearings on the employment situation. At the first several of these, the committee heard testimony from officials of the Bureau, the Department, and the Office of Management and Budget relating to the press briefings and the reorganization. It received reports from the American Statistical Association and the Industrial Relations Research Association, and also called upon Ewan

Clague and Robert A. Gordon, who had been chairman of the President's Committee to Appraise Employment and Unemployment Statistics in the early 1960's.

The House Committee on Government Operations concluded, based on a study and hearings by a subcommittee, that the reasons given for terminating the press briefings were unpersuasive and recommended that Hodgson immediately reinstitute the briefings and "make it clear in a departmental directive that the traditional objective role of the BLS must be maintained." In "additional views," 4 of the committee's 16 Republican members supported Moore's view that the new procedures should be given an opportunity to be tested before reaching final judgment on the termination.[27]

The Committee on Post Office and Civil Service also issued a report, following an investigation by the staff of its Subcommittee on Census and Statistics. The staff had interviewed 65 individuals interested in Federal statistics, including present and former employees of government agencies, users of Federal statistics, labor representatives, news media, and members of congressional staffs. While accepting the subcommittee finding that there was "no supportive evidence of conspiratory politicization of Federal statistics," the committee held that an incumbent administration under the decentralized statistical system could "politically influence and utilize the various statistical agencies." This warranted "constant vigil, to insure the continuation of public confidence in the reliability and validity of Federal statistics and to avoid creating a credibility gap in government information." The staff also recommended studying "the feasibility and desirability of establishing one central independent agency to. . . reduce the opportunity for an incumbent administration to exercise a partisan effect," among other reasons.[28]

Moore welcomed the report as supporting the Bureau "on every point that had been raised." Hodgson reiterated his commitment to the "scientific independence and integrity" of the Bureau and pointed to the procedures established to protect them.[29]

Shortly thereafter, however, Moore was involved in a political issue which was unprecedented for a BLS Commissioner. In November 1972, following his landslide reelection victory, President Nixon called on all Presidential appointees to submit their resignations. Although his term extended to March 1973, Moore, believing he had no option, submitted his. Contrary to his expectations, it was accepted, becoming effective in January.

Moore's removal caused an immediate outcry. Senator Proxmire, pointing to the traditionally nonpolitical nature of the commissionership, warned, "If the preparation of our basic statistics becomes further tainted with suspicion of political manipulation, it could lead to a serious credibility crisis." The Industrial Relations Research Association viewed the acceptance of Moore's resignation "with particular concern. . . because this termination under these circumstances represents a sharp break with the long-established tradition that this position has not been regarded as a political appointment."[30]

The Committee on the Integrity of Federal Statistics, a joint committee of the American Statistical Association and the Federal Statistics Users' Conference, reported, "During the past 2 years, the integrity of the Federal statistical system has come into question. . . . Specific steps should be taken to allay the growing fears concerning politicization. . . and to ensure and maintain a high level of credible, professional, statistical work." Among the specific recommendations were that "heads of statistical agencies should be career professionals of demonstrated competence. . . free of political influence," and that they have direct control of their program planning, budgetary priorities, and publications.[31]

Soon after these events, the Office of Management and Budget developed further the requirements for separating the technical release process from policy and political statements through a succession of directives added to the one first issued in 1969. The rule requiring a 1-hour delay between the technical release and any policy statement, already widely in effect, was formally stipulated by OMB in April 1972, along with the requirement for written releases. In October 1974, the circulation of data before their official release (BLS data had been given in advance to the White House and several agencies) was restricted to the Chairman of the Council of Economic Advisers specifically for briefing the President; other principal advisers would be notified at the same time as the media, subject to the 1-hour rule on political comment. These provisions were continued in later revisions of the directive.[32]

The procedure for clearance of Bureau releases within the Department of Labor paralleled the OMB requirements. In 1969, the Bureau was given authority for final clearance, although in the early

1970's departmental officials participated in the clearance procedure. In 1970, for example, Secretary Hodgson asked Moore to hold review meetings in the Secretary's office as a convenient way to "keep himself informed." After several months, the meetings were moved to the Commissioner's office, with the departmental group attending.[33]

Then, in 1974, in a move complementing a revision of the original OMB directive, Secretary Brennan specified that data should not be "available to me or any other official of the Department of Labor outside the BLS until it is released to the press about one hour before public release." In 1981, an OMB directive specifically included the Secretary as one of the principal economic advisers to receive indicators at the same time as the press. Norwood testified in 1979, "There is no further review outside the Bureau."[34]

The Bureau's work

Consumer prices

In 1964, under Clague, the Bureau had completed a major revision of the CPI. In 1966, Commissioner Ross presented to the Joint Economic Committee's Subcommittee on Economic Statistics a "master plan" for a comprehensive system of price indexes which included improvements in the CPI to fill gaps, update statistical techniques, and extend coverage to the entire population. In addition, the proposal provided for review—between major revisions—of such elements as outlet and reporter samples and item and specification samples, with appropriate reweighting. Furthermore, it called for experimentation with new approaches to shelter costs, substitution, new products, quality change, taxes, and annual consumer surveys.[35] Planning for the next CPI revision, started in 1968, reflected extensive discussion of such issues.

The issue of quality change had already been brought to Ross' attention in several controversies involving the automobile industry. The United Auto Workers, with automatic cost-of-living adjustments in their contracts, kept close watch on the CPI. In 1966, with contracts up for renewal the following year, UAW President Walter Reuther attacked the "Big Three" automakers for their use of BLS data for "unjustified price increases" and called for improvement in the BLS technique of adjusting the CPI for quality change.[36] In 1967, Senators Warren Magnuson and Walter Mondale also questioned the

BLS technique in their efforts to determine the cost of higher safety and pollution standards for automobiles. They also criticized the position of the manufacturers in maintaining that they could not provide Congress with cost estimates, although they had furnished them to the Bureau. The Bureau refused to give Congress details and specific figures because the industry had submitted them in confidence, but it did offer summary data. In addition, it moved to refine the quality adjustment process with a continuing research program.[37]

Implementation of the plans for the CPI revision began under Moore. In 1970, the Office of Management and Budget directed that the Census Bureau—rather than BLS, as before—conduct the prerequisite consumer expenditure survey, hoping that this would increase efficiency since the Census Bureau was the agency specializing in the collection of data from households. In another change from previous procedures, data were collected at quarterly intervals during the year rather than in a single annual review on the assumption that consumers would be more likely to recall details of their expenditures over the shorter time span. The quarterly interviews involved about 20,000 families. A separate sample of about 20,000 families was asked to complete a 2-week diary to provide additional detail. These innovations and other factors complicated and delayed the project, and data collection was not completed until 1973—approximately 2 years later than planned. A "point-of-purchase" survey, to improve item and outlet samples by determining where people bought various goods and services, was conducted in 1974, covering some 23,000 families.

Commissioner Shiskin had to resolve several major conceptual problems before the revision of the CPI could be carried through. One concerned the population to be covered. From its inception, the CPI had been based on the expenditures of urban wage earners and salaried workers. There had been proposals, notably from the Stigler Committee, for extending coverage to the entire urban population, in view of the expanded use of the CPI as a broad economic indicator. The growing use of the CPI for indexation also pointed up the need for wider coverage.

In April 1974, Shiskin announced plans to proceed with an index representing all urban consumers and to drop the traditional index. The announcement sparked a lively controversy. The BLS Labor Research Advisory Council, while not opposing the broader index, strongly objected to the discontinuance of the traditional measure.

The Business Research Advisory Council supported the broader concept but suggested that the Bureau explore the possibility of publishing more than one index.[38]

George Meany of the AFL–CIO criticized Shiskin's decision, maintaining, "The CPI should remain firmly grounded in the experience and needs of low- and middle-income workers. . . . We have no objection to the Bureau of Labor Statistics developing a separate index covering additional occupational categories, if funds are available." Leonard Woodcock, of the United Auto Workers, also attacked the decision and further complained of the "secretive" way in which BLS reached its determination, alleging that the labor advisory group had only been given one opportunity to discuss the question.[39]

Senator Proxmire introduced a bill requiring BLS to produce the traditional CPI, whether it compiled other indexes or not. Citing the role of the CPI in collective bargaining, he stated, "If the BLS is allowed to dismantle the present Consumer Price Index in favor of a more broadly based index, it will create absolute chaos." Shiskin, while acknowledging the problem, responded that, after all, the unions would have 3 years to adjust agreements to the new index. Moreover, he continued, BLS would produce "a whole family of indexes" if Congress would provide the money.[40]

The Subcommittee on Economic Statistics of the Council on Economic Policy supported the broader coverage and recommended that BLS compile both the broad and the traditional CPI for a period of 3 years before deciding the next step.

Shiskin then sent the Secretary a revised plan for congressional action to allow for the production of two indexes, a new Consumer Price Index for All Urban Consumers (CPI–U) and the traditional Consumer Price Index for Urban Wage Earners and Clerical Workers (CPI–W), both to be calculated for at least 3 years. Congress provided an increased appropriation for the additional work in the fiscal year 1976 budget.[41]

In 1978, the Bureau published the new CPI–U along with the traditional, though revised, CPI–W. The CPI–W was based on the buying patterns of about 40 percent of the civilian noninstitutional population; the CPI–U, on about 80 percent. The CPI–U added coverage of the self-employed; professional, managerial, and technical workers; short-term and part-time workers; and the unemployed, retirees, and others not in the labor force.

Even before the work was completed, the Office of Management and Budget sought legislation making CPI–U the index for government programs, arguing that it "is the best measure that we now have in the country in a technical sense." And later, the General Accounting Office also recommended the change. Congress did require use of the CPI–U to escalate tax rate brackets starting in 1985. However, most Federal programs and collective bargaining agreements continued to make use of the traditional CPI–W.[42]

Another thorny problem facing Shiskin was the method of measuring homeownership costs. In the 1953 revision, the Bureau had changed from a rent-based method to an "asset" formulation based on five specific costs associated with homeownership: House prices, mortgage interest, property taxes, insurance, and maintenance and repair costs. Then, the Stigler Committee had recommended investigating the development of an index based on rental housing representative of owner-occupied homes.

The Bureau was already studying the issue of which method to use for the upcoming revision when, in the late 1970's, house prices and mortgage interest rates rose more than other market-basket costs. This focused increasing attention on the BLS method of measurement. Critics felt that the investment aspects of homeownership should be removed from the cost of shelter. Furthermore, BLS found that the data provided by the Federal Housing Administration on home prices and interest covered only 6 percent of the housing market—a small and unrepresentative sample.

In planning the revision, the Bureau explored alternatives to measure only the "flow of services" and to exclude the investment aspects of homeownership. One alternative, the so-called user-cost approach, included the prices for all five components but adjusted the result for appreciation and the cost of equity. Another approach, rental equivalence, provided for a survey of a sample of rented homes similar in type and location to owned homes, using the rental price to represent the cost of shelter.[43]

Neither of the Bureau's research advisory groups found these proposals acceptable. As one labor adviser wrote in 1975, "To price only the 'services' is to price an abstraction which has no concrete existence and for which there are no market transaction prices." Such a procedure, the economist continued, was at variance with the character of the index and even with the treatment of other durable goods.

Specifically, she contended that the rental equivalence measure depended on faulty assumptions, since the rental market and the home-purchase market differed greatly. And the user-cost measure also rested on many theoretical assumptions.[44]

During 1976, at the Commissioner's request, the Bureau's advisory groups formed a Joint Technical Group on Homeownership in the Revised CPI. The panel met four times between March and December 1976, and its spokesman reported to Shiskin: "We believe BLS has not yet found a satisfactory user-cost approach. . . . Further research on user cost should be continued." The Subcommittee on Economic Statistics also failed to reach a consensus. In April 1977, citing "widespread disagreement," Shiskin announced that BLS would continue the existing treatment while also continuing research.[45]

In 1978, soon after the revised CPI was issued, the Bureau received authorization and funds for a continuing, rather than a periodic, consumer expenditure survey, a goal it had sought for 25 years. It also was able to institute a continuing point-of-purchase survey, planned to cover one-fifth of the CPI areas each year, thereby updating the entire sample of outlets for pricing within 5 years.[46]

Labor advisers had expressed fears that a continuing consumer expenditure survey would be used to revise the CPI market basket too frequently, violating the concept of a fixed market basket. They argued that, out of economic necessity in periods of rapid inflation, workers would substitute products—"trade down"—and, therefore, frequent revision would "understate price increases."[47] Responding to this argument, Shiskin saw the continuing survey as having both immediate pertinence and a longer range use in deciding when a major revision of the CPI would be called for. He insisted that the data would only be used for a revision after an appropriate number of years. He also urged the continuing survey as a means of avoiding the substantial startup costs of periodic surveys. The Subcommittee on Economic Statistics of the Council on Economic Policy gave the project top priority, saying that a continuing survey would facilitate revision of the CPI, help keep weights and market baskets more current, assist in revising family budget estimates, and provide valuable data for analysis of spending patterns.[48]

The resurgence of inflation in 1978—about the time Norwood became Acting Commissioner—and its acceleration in the following 2 years intensified concern about the rising costs of the indexation process. Attention centered on the CPI, and specifically on its home-ownership components. In 1979 and 1980, the Council of Economic Advisers pointed out that shelter costs, which had a substantial weight in the index, were rising faster than most other components of the CPI and questioned the Bureau's treatment of the purchase of homes and the associated costs of home financing. The Council described the Bureau's exploration of alternative treatments of this component and the failure of any of these to satisfy major users of the CPI. It suggested that using a rent index to represent the costs of using the services of a house might provide a better measure of changes in the cost of living to the average consumer, particularly in periods of sharp changes in costs of homes and home financing.[49]

At hearings of the House Budget Committee's Task Force on Inflation in December 1979, government, labor, and management witnesses discussed the housing component. In her testimony, Commissioner Norwood discussed the problems of altering the index at that time. The following month, Norwood announced that, although no change would be made in the official index, the Bureau would publish five experimental measures for the CPI in the monthly release, using alternative approaches to homeownership costs. Based on the extensive staff analysis for the CPI revision, these included three flow-of-services measures—one based on rent substitution and two on outlays.[50]

The treatment of homeownership continued to be debated. Some members of Congress urged President Carter to appoint a special panel of economists to study the homeownership issue. Others, especially in the Senate, suggested shifting from the CPI to some other measure as the indexing mechanism. Alfred Kahn, chairman of the Council on Wage and Price Stability, frequently attacked both the homeownership component and congressional inaction on severing the linkage, between the CPI and the entitlement programs.[51] President Carter's last economic report in January 1981 stated that the CPI had overstated significantly the actual rise in the cost of living because of the way it treated housing and mortgage interest costs.[52]

The New York Times exhorted Carter to change the housing measure: "Since the index has been overstating inflation, it has triggered billions in excessive increases in wages and pensions. Thus the index not only measures inflation but contributes to it." Early in 1981, the General Accounting Office recommended that BLS substitute for the homeownership component some measure of the cost of consuming housing services—either rental equivalence or nominal outlays.[53]

Norwood testified before several congressional committees examining the effect of the CPI on Federal expenditures. During the debate, she maintained: "It is for the Congress—Congress and the administration—to determine what the purpose of the indexation should be." She noted that escalation "sometimes produces results that were not anticipated." As to the CPI itself, she pointed out that BLS had raised the housing issue during the revision process but had been unable to obtain a consensus among its advisory groups and users. Summarizing, she concluded, "Some people would like an index that doesn't go up so much, and other people would like an index that goes up more. And when they don't have that which they want, they feel there must be something wrong with the indicator itself."[54]

In October 1981, Norwood announced that BLS would shift to the rental equivalence approach for the housing component. Noting that BLS had called attention to the issue over a period of 10 years, she cited immediate factors requiring implementation of the change before the next overall revision of the index. There had been changes in the financial markets affecting the availability, arrangement, and rate of mortgage money. In addition, the FHA sample caused increasingly serious estimation problems. Furthermore, the Economic Recovery Tax Act of 1981 directed use of the CPI-U to adjust income tax brackets. This, Norwood said, obliged the Bureau to produce "a CPI which reflects the experience of consumers to the fullest extent possible."[55]

The change, Norwood said, would be implemented at different times in the two CPI's. It would be introduced into the CPI-U with the data for January 1983, largely because the Economic Recovery Tax Act mandated advance announcement of tax bracket changes by December 15, 1984, based on CPI-U data for the prior 2 years. For the CPI-W, widely used in collective bargaining, the shift would be delayed until January 1985 to provide time to adjust the provisions of labor-management contracts.[56]

Both the change and the split timetable sparked controversy. Almost immediately, bills were introduced in Congress, one requiring continuance of the current methods for 5 years beyond the change dates and another requiring congressional approval of changes that would cause "reduction of benefits to retirees and disability programs."[57]

Business spokesmen generally supported the changes as "a welcome improvement in the accuracy of the CPI that is long overdue." The BLS Business Research Advisory Council favored the shift but recommended that the Bureau produce "one single measure at the earliest possible date." Labor union representatives, still critical of the rental equivalence approach, welcomed the 2-year grace period that allowed further study and evaluation.[58]

The complete implementation of the rental equivalence approach, following full public discussion and improvement of the rental sample, was carried out on schedule and without further controversy.

In fiscal year 1984, the Bureau received funds to begin another major revision of the CPI, scheduled for completion in 1987. As planned, the CPI for January 1987 would include a new market basket and reflect data from the 1980 Census of Population; improved measures of price change, especially homeownership and rental costs; modernization of the computer system; and enhanced error measurement and quality control.[59]

Standard budgets

BLS issued new standard—or family—budgets during 1967 and 1968 for a family of four and for a retired couple, using data from the 1960-61 consumer expenditure survey. Each of these budgets was calculated at three levels—a medium or moderate standard, a lower, and a higher. Federal and State governments wrote the budgets into legislation on social security, unemployment insurance, public welfare, and employment and training programs.

The Bureau, however, increasingly questioned its role in making the normative judgments underlying the series. As Moore wrote in 1969, "I do not think the BLS should set itself up as an authority on what is adequate or inadequate, what is a luxury and what is not, etc., no matter how reasonable the position may seem to us." Thus, in 1971, Moore proposed to suspend preparation of the estimates for a few years until data from the next consumer expenditure survey became available. At that time, suggested Moore, the Bureau would "expand its program of publishing and analyzing data on actual spending patterns for families of different sizes and types at different incomes and expenditure levels and for different regions and sizes of place."[60]

"Consistent and considerable pressure" forced BLS to continue issuing estimates for use in a variety of social programs. For example, Nelson A. Rockefeller, Governor of New York, wrote, "The possibility that the Bureau of Labor Statistics will discontinue periodic publication of family budget data threatens New York and many other States with the loss of a valuable, irreplaceable administrative tool." Therefore, Moore suggested that either the Office of Management and Budget or an interagency committee set the standards for which BLS could collect the prices. Later, Shiskin argued that an operating agency such as the Department of Health, Education, and Welfare should develop the standards, rather than a statistical agency. Although OMB accepted the idea, HEW refused to take the responsibility.[61]

Moreover, a lack of funds compounded the problem. Shiskin posed the dilemma faced in 1974: "The Bureau's professional reputation and credibility are dependent on the maintenance of data of high quality. Yet, in this case, the Bureau has no resources with which to protect the quality of this program."[62]

In 1978, after considering a number of alternative approaches to the standards issue, the Bureau contracted for a complete review of the family budget program with the Wisconsin Institute for Research on Poverty, which then appointed the Expert Committee on Family Budget Revision. In its 1980 report, the committee, recognizing the problem confronting the Bureau, recommended four new budget standards to be defined on the basis of actual expenditures of families at different income levels, rather than the older procedure based on judgments as to the adequacy of quantities and expenditures. In 1981, however—as part of a substantial program reduction required during the fiscal 1981 budget cycle—Norwood decided to halt the production of these data for lack of the additional resources needed either to implement the recommendations of the Expert Committee or to bring the quality of the budgets up to Bureau technical standards.[63]

Wholesale prices
In 1976, BLS started the first comprehensive revision of the Wholesale Price Index by surveying index users to determine their needs and their views of shortcomings in the measure. The Bureau had substan-

tially revamped procedures twice, in 1914 and 1952; it had instituted a major expansion and reclassification in 1967; and it had most recently reweighted the index in January 1976. But BLS wanted a "general price index" that would be more broadly based and more accurate, utilizing probability sampling.[64]

Critics had pointed to inadequacies from time to time. Jules Backman and Martin Gainsbrugh, in 1966, had noted several shortcomings. Others wrote of out-of-date weights, double and triple counting, and list (rather than transaction) prices. Also, such groups as the National Association of Wholesaler Distributors pushed for a change of name to more accurately describe the data. In 1975, Albert Rees, director of the Council on Wage and Price Stability, attacked the index for presenting "totally inadequate data" and announced that Richard Ruggles of Yale would lead an examination. Ruggles issued his report in 1977, proposing a number of improvements in the program.[65]

The outside recommendations for improvement in the index were taken into account in the extensive planning for the multiyear revision of the series. To set the measure on a firmer theoretical foundation, the revision plans were based on a model of a fixed-input output price index. The new system consisted of four major components: Industry output price indexes, detailed commodity price indexes, stage-of-processing price indexes, and industry input price indexes. It rested on collection of actual transaction prices, expansion of coverage, and elimination of multiple counting of price changes.[66] In 1978, to emphasize that the index was a measure of change in selling prices received by producers at the level of the first significant commercial transaction in the United States, the Bureau changed its name from Wholesale to Producer Price Index.

The Bureau continued to introduce new producer price indexes, with the goal of covering all 493 industries in the mining and manufacturing sectors. By 1983, the Producer Price Index Revision program covered 191 industries, accounting for almost 60 percent of the value of all domestic mining and manufacturing production, with over 18,000 price quotations for over 3,500 commodities. BLS used probability sampling techniques to select companies by size and location and to identify individual items and transaction terms for the firms. Estimates of sample error were also being constructed. Budget cuts, however, postponed completion of the project as well as further developmental work on new indexes for the services sector.

Petroleum prices. On several occasions during 1973, when major petroleum exporting countries imposed an oil embargo, the New England congressional caucus complained to the Secretary of Labor of the failure of BLS to provide "adequate wholesale or retail price data" on petroleum products—even at a time of acute shortages. The Secretary initially responded by noting that BLS had been working on the problem for more than a year, contacting companies and helping them develop reporting procedures, but that response had so far been disappointing. In December, the Secretary reported that the first data would soon be published. Indeed, on December 21, with the release of CPI figures for November, BLS presented the expanded and improved gasoline component, along with monthly retail gasoline price measures.[67]

But continued difficulties in developing voluntary reporting from the companies—especially on wholesale prices—at a time of shortages and embargoes encouraged those demanding mandatory reporting of energy statistics. In March 1974, the Joint Economic Committee recommended, "Unless corporations producing petroleum products provide full and immediate cooperation with the requests of the Bureau of Labor Statistics, Congress should provide BLS with authority to require submission of corporate data with appropriate safeguards to prevent competitive injury."[68]

However, following considerable discussion, the Bureau's Business Research Advisory Council upheld the principle of voluntary reporting and offered to encourage increased participation. The petroleum industry representative to the Business Advisory Council on Federal Reports made a similar offer.[69]

In June 1974, in presenting the Wholesale Price Index for May, the Bureau introduced improved data for refined petroleum products. Even so, the New England congressional caucus still complained of the lack of detail specific to their region. Commissioner Shiskin explained that more detail was not feasible, as BLS collected statistics from a sample and would not issue numbers that would identify reporters.[70]

Export and import prices
Following World War II, BLS had started development of indexes of prices for U.S. exports and imports, but had terminated the work in 1948 due to budget cuts. Research on concept and methodology resumed in the late 1960's. The Bureau published export price indexes in 1971 and import price indexes in 1973. As of June 1982, coverage accounted for 71 percent of the value of exports and 96 percent of the value of imports. By the end of 1983, BLS had expanded coverage to 100 percent of the value of products in U.S. foreign trade—but with less detail than originally planned because of budget reductions.[71]

Employment and unemployment statistics
The Gordon Committee—set up in 1961 to review employment and unemployment data—had called upon the Bureau for major improvements in its statistics. During the next 20 years, recurring recessions and the legislation passed to alleviate them increased the demand for more detailed and accurate employment data. In addition, the reorganization of government statistical activities gave the Bureau added responsibilities; in 1972, it took over from the Manpower Administration the preparation and publication of local area unemployment statistics, occupational employment statistics, employment and wage data for workers covered by unemployment insurance, and data on the characteristics of the unemployed. The Bureau also expanded its analysis and publication of labor force data relating to minorities, women, and families.

In the 1980's, the Bureau worked to carry out the recommendations of another group of experts empaneled to review the government's statistics—the National Commission on Employment and Unemployment Statistics. The National Commission, headed by Sar Levitan, issued its report, *Counting The Labor Force*, in 1979, after extensive public hearings, preparation of 33 background papers, and much discussion. "By and large," the commission stated, "the most important national statistics are timely, objective, and reasonably accurate, and they have unquestionably played a crucial role in guiding policy formulation. The commission's review of existing data, however, has led it to several areas in which the information system might be improved." The commission's 90-odd recommendations covered all the Bureau's employment and unemployment statistics programs.[72]

Secretaries of Labor Ray Marshall and Raymond Donovan, as required by the law establishing the commission, submitted reports to Congress evaluating the desirability, feasibility, and cost of each recommendation. Under Norwood, a number of major recommendations were put into effect, but others were found to be too costly or impractical, and implementation of others awaited the results of testing and the development of programs.

Current Population Survey. In January 1967, the Bureau put into effect some of the major recommendations of the Gordon Committee for the CPS. It introduced sharper definitions; a minimum age of 16, rather than 14; and a larger sample.

One element of the new definitions proved controversial. Under the new terminology, persons were classified as unemployed only if they had searched for work within the previous 4 weeks and were currently available for work. If no job search had been conducted, a person was classified as "not in the labor force" rather than unemployed.

Union economists charged that the new procedure, which had been tested in a survey of 13,000 households in September 1966, would aggravate the "existing undercount" of unemployment by excluding those who were discouraged—those who were no longer searching because they believed no work was available. They advocated increased efforts to identify and learn more about discouraged workers. Although the new definition of unemployment remained in force, the Bureau did add a series of questions to the CPS designed to collect data on discouraged workers. The results were published quarterly thereafter.[73]

The size of the CPS sample, increased in 1967, had to be decreased in 1971, but the Bureau obtained funds to increase it substantially in 1978 and again in 1980, largely to provide the detail needed to improve State and local estimates. In 1981, the sample had to be reduced again but remained considerably higher than it was before 1980. New methods of seasonal adjustment were introduced in 1973 and refined in 1980.

In 1976, the Bureau—to allay outside criticism of the unemployment concept—began to publish in its monthly release on the employment situation an array of unemployment rates, U-1 through U-7, each based on a different definition. The U-5 rate remained the official definition, but, as Shiskin explained, "No single way of measuring unemployment can satisfy all analytical or ideological interests."[74]

As the National Commission had recommended, the Bureau added military personnel stationed in the United States to the national labor force and employment figures, although not to the State and local data, and included them in the computation of the overall unemployment rate. Further, all industry and occupational data in the CPS were classified according to a new system developed for the 1980 census. In addition, the estimation methods were revised along the lines the commission had recommended.

BLS also added monthly questions to the CPS on the school attendance of 16- to 24-year-olds, another recommendation of the commission, to learn more about their work and school choices and their labor market attachment. The commission had also recommended improving the identification of discouraged workers by collecting more specific information on recency of job search, current availability, and desire for work, but the Bureau postponed this work indefinitely because tests of the feasibility of introducing pertinent questions into the CPS questionnaire were inconclusive. Discouraged workers continued to be counted as outside the labor force and excluded from the official unemployment figure, in line with the commission's recommendation reached after much debate.

The commission had called upon BLS to prepare an annual report containing national data on economic hardship associated with low wages, unemployment, and insufficient participation in the labor force. The Bureau issued the first report, _Linking Employment Problems to Economic Status_, in January 1982, with annual reports thereafter. Congress, in the Job Training Partnership Act of 1982 (PL97–300), specifically authorized the Secretary of Labor to develop such information.

In the early 1980's, the Bureau started a major project to redesign the CPS in cooperation with other Federal sponsors of household surveys and the Census Bureau. By July 1985, an entirely new sample will have been phased in, based on materials from the 1980 census.[75]

Establishment survey. The Bureau continued to expand its monthly series on employment, hours, and earnings in nonagricultural establishments. In 1965, it had covered a sample of 135,000 establishments; by 1975, the sample had grown to 160,000 and by 1983, to 190,000.

In 1979, the National Commission criticized the sample design and other basic statistical underpinnings of the establishment survey, but urged caution in making major changes that might disrupt economic series essential for current analyses and as building blocks for important indicators. Basic shortcomings noted by the commission included inadequate sample size, poor documentation, and lack of quality control measures. With the support of the Secretary, BLS established a long-range project for a full-scale modernization of the survey. Major changes would await development of an overall systematic redesign.

The commission specifically recognized the inadequacy of industry detail for the large and growing service-producing sector of the economy, and the Bureau moved to improve the sample. Cooperating State agencies responded with a buildup of coverage so that, by 1984, BLS expanded publication of industry detail in the service sector by 82 additional industries.[76]

Occupational employment statistics. The Vocational Education Act of 1963 required the States to develop information on future occupational requirements for use in planning education and training programs. To help State officials, the Bureau prepared a series of occupational projections for the year 1975, published in *Tomorrow's Manpower Needs* (1969).

Also, at the urging of the Gordon Committee, the Bureau began to develop occupational statistics through industry studies. Then, in 1971, BLS mailed questionnaires to 50,000 manufacturing establishments, marking the start of the Occupational Employment Statistics survey conducted in cooperation with the Employment and Training Administration and the State employment security agencies. Between 1971 and 1981, the Bureau completed three survey cycles for manufacturing; various nonmanufacturing and service industries; and government services. By 1982, 48 State agencies had joined the effort.

Since 1980, the survey has been an important source of data for the Bureau's national industry-occupational matrix, one of its basic tools for occupational employment projections and occupational outlook studies.

Local area unemployment statistics. Among the Bureau's most intractable problems has been the inadequacy of local area unemployment data. Before the program was turned over to the Bureau, the figures had been used primarily to identify areas of labor shortage or surplus by the Bureau of Employment Security and its successor agencies. They had been developed through a complicated series of computations—the 70-step or Handbook method—relying heavily on data derived from administrative records of the unemployment insurance system. Beginning with passage of the Comprehensive Employment and Training Act (CETA) in 1973 and later under additional legislation, these data were incorporated in the formula used for the regular and direct distribution of Federal funds to States and local areas. The Bureau, assigned technical and publication responsibility for the data, found them of questionable quality for the new purpose.

Shiskin summarized the difficulties: "These unemployment statistics have been severely criticized because they lack conceptual uniformity and consistency, are of uneven reliability, and cannot be fully reconciled with data from the national survey of employment and unemployment."[77]

In 1974, BLS instituted new procedures to improve the data, including benchmarking the annual estimates to the Current Population Survey and improving the Handbook procedures to provide greater uniformity among the States in concepts and methods. States facing reduced CETA funding challenged the new procedures. New Jersey attacked the methodology, Maryland attacked the implementation, and both charged specifically that the Secretary of Labor, in instituting the changes, had violated the advance-notice requirement of the Administrative Procedures Act and had exceeded his authority.

The Bureau's statistical methods were upheld in the New Jersey case. In the Maryland case, a lower court upheld the Department position that it was not required to give advance notice in the *Federal Register* of changed methods for gathering unemployment statistics, but the decision was reversed by the U.S. Court of Appeals for the District of Columbia. In so ruling, the court found that "the development of statistics no longer serves merely informational purposes" in view of their use in allocating billions of dollars under the CETA program.[78]

The Bureau continued efforts to improve the data, although it recognized the limited possibilities in view of the lack of funds. Shiskin acknowledged many shortcomings, stating in 1977, "When you get to those very small areas we're talking about, we worry about whether we're giving any better than random numbers." He estimated that accurate State-by-State figures would require an additional annual appropriation of $40–$50 million—which still would not provide dependable city and county data.[79]

In 1978, BLS again introduced improvements. The monthly unemployment rates for 10 States and 2 metropolitan areas were now drawn directly from the Current Population Survey. With these revisions, Congress, in reauthorizing CETA, provided that the Secretary should ensure that areas within Standard Metropolitan Areas and central cities would not lose funds as a result of changes in statistical methodology.[80] In addition, the Bureau and the States began work to standardize the underlying unemployment insurance claims data to provide greater consistency with the concept of unemployment used in the CPS.

In 1979, after reviewing the local area unemployment statistics program, the National Commission concluded, "There is no way, at reasonable cost, to produce accurate employment and unemployment statistics for thousands of areas every month." Thus, it suggested "only incremental" improvements: Expansion of the CPS, enhancement of the Handbook procedures, and congressional review of the allocation formulas.[81]

The very large sums of money required for a major overhaul constituted a critical obstacle. Even so, in 1982, Norwood commented, "The local unemployment statistics program is one which clearly needs more work."[82] The Bureau continued an intensive research effort.

Job vacancy statistics. The Bureau continued its efforts to develop job vacancy statistics, although methodological and conceptual problems and budget restraints plagued the program from the beginning. In 1967, the Bureau began collection of job vacancy data in Phoenix and Oklahoma City in connection with the regular labor turnover survey. At about the same time, however, funding for the turnover program was cut in half as part of general budget reductions.[83]

Shortly after assuming office in January 1969, President Nixon, at the urging of Arthur Burns, directed BLS to develop plans for a national system of job vacancy statistics. Building on the Bureau's earlier efforts, Commissioner Moore developed a Federal-State cooperative program of statistics on job openings and labor turnover. The first data on job openings were published in 1970. BLS had to terminate the program in 1974, however, after the Manpower Administration withdrew its supporting funds on the basis that the data were not useful to the placement activities of the State employment security agencies.[84]

In the late 1970's, Congress authorized the Bureau to plan for a survey of job openings. A pilot study demonstrated that, while a national program could be developed, the cost would be "in excess of $25-$30 million a year"—twice the budget for the national household survey. Then, the labor turnover program, which had been the vehicle for the pilot study, became a casualty of the 1982 budget cut, in view of its overall technical limitations, particularly its failure to cover service industries, where turnover rates were highest.[85]

This checkered history reflected the difficult and controversial nature of job vacancy statistics. The Labor Research Advisory Council expressed grave reservations because of the difficulty in defining basic terms and the belief that industry would use vacancy statistics to "deflate" unemployment figures. Somewhat more supportive of the program, the Business Research Advisory Council nevertheless opposed connections with local employment offices and sought assurances that the Employment Service would not use vacancy data to direct referrals. In its report, the National Commission "found no evidence that useful job vacancy statistics can be collected in a cost-effective manner."[86]

Poverty and urban problems

BLS accomplished some of its most innovative work in special surveys related to poverty and urban problems. In February 1966, the Bureau canvassed food prices in six large cities for the National Commission on Food Marketing and also for Esther Peterson of the President's Committee on Consumer Interests on the question, "Do the Poor Pay More?"[87]

At about the same time, the Bureau launched a new quarterly series of data on conditions in urban poverty neighborhoods. Beginning with data from the Current Population Survey of March 1966, the Bureau compiled special tabulations of poverty tracts and compared the findings with characteristics of other city dwellers. Census had developed the classification system for the Office of Economic Opportunity, basing it on 1960 census data for cities of 250,000 population or more and for a range of variables such as income, education, skills, housing, and family conditions.

Then, in response to a directive of Secretary Wirtz that the Bureau and the Manpower Administration "provide the information necessary for a concerted attack on individual and social problems," the agencies conducted a series of pilot projects. The Manpower Administration financed a joint BLS–Census survey of slum areas in six large cities covering the period July 1968 through June 1969, a study specifically designed for use in the President's Concentrated Employment Program of jobs and training activities. In October 1969, BLS published *Urban Employment Survey: Employment Situation in Poverty Areas of Six Cities*, following with special articles in the *Monthly Labor Review*. The Bureau conducted a second urban employment survey but, despite its desire to continue the work, was unable to reach agreement with the Manpower Administration on methodological issues and policy priorities.[88]

In 1971, Moore announced that BLS would suspend production of the quarterly series on poverty areas the following year to improve accuracy by allowing for introduction of 1970 census data when they became available. The suspension was criticized by Senator Hubert Humphrey and George Meany because it would occur in a Presidential election year. Roy Wilkins, chairman of the Leadership Conference on Civil Rights, wrote the Secretary, "The BLS has enjoyed a deserved reputation for integrity. Recent developments have raised doubts. . . . The decision to abandon the ghetto unemployment data . . . reinforces these doubts and raises new questions of political interference with BLS."[89] In 1973, once data from the 1970 census had been introduced, BLS resumed publication of the quarterly data but based solely on an income definition of poverty.

Earnings statistics

Since 1947, BLS had published a series on gross and spendable average weekly earnings based on the establishment survey. Spendable earnings were derived by adjusting average gross weekly earnings of all production or nonsupervisory workers for Federal taxes and Social Security payments for a worker with no dependents and for one with three dependents. Adjusted by changes in the CPI, "real" gross and spendable earnings series were developed to indicate changes in the purchasing power of money earnings. In 1982, the spendable earnings series was discontinued because of conceptual inadequacies. Many critics—among them former Commissioner Moore—had faulted the series as "misleading" because it rested on the unwarranted assumption that a worker with three dependents had the same weekly earnings as the average for all workers. The National Commission had recommended discontinuance, explaining, "This hybrid figure does not measure what it purports to measure."[90]

Instead, the commission urged development of earnings statistics derived from the Current Population Survey. BLS then published quarterly reports of median earnings of workers and their families derived from the CPS. Some observers characterized these statistics as "soft," noting that they were based on subjective, oral responses, in contrast to the "hard" numbers derived from establishment reports. Furthermore, the CPS samples were rather small, with a substantial nonresponse rate, and the statistical variance for earnings was relatively high.[91]

Earnings data were also derived from the reports filed by employers covered by the unemployment insurance program. From these reports, BLS developed and published statistics on average annual pay by State and industry. The data were used by the Employment and Training Administration and State agencies to construct projections of total and taxable wages and by the Commerce Department in developing the personal income estimates in the gross national product accounts.

For a number of years, up to data for 1975, BLS also published another series on annual earnings, developed from a 1-percent random sample of the records of the Social Security Administration and the Railroad Retirement Board.

Wages, benefits, and industrial relations
In 1965, the Bureau's wage program included three principal types of surveys which produced occupational wage information: Area wage surveys, industry wage surveys, and the national survey of professsional, administrative, technical, and clerical pay (the PATC or white-collar survey). Although differing in industrial, geographic, and occupational coverage, and originating for different purposes at different times, they were developed into an integrated program based on common concepts and definitions, a common set of administrative forms, and a single manual of procedures.

In the area wage survey program, statistical techniques were improved in the early 1970's. By 1982, the program included about 70 Standard Metropolitan Statistical Areas, statistically selected to represent all metropolitan areas of the United States, excluding Alaska and Hawaii.

The Bureau also conducted wage surveys in 86 areas on behalf of the Employment Standards Administration for use in administering the Service Contract Act of 1965. The act required payment of the prevailing wage by employers providing services to the Federal Government under contracts of $2,500 or more.

For several years after World War II, BLS added detail to its area wage surveys for use by the Department of Defense and other agencies in setting wage rates for their blue-collar employees. However, in 1965, President Johnson directed the Civil Service Commission to work towards developing a uniform system for all Federal agencies. In the negotiations that followed, BLS rejected proposals that it actively participate in these surveys, noting a potential conflict of interest and violation of confidentiality, since representatives of employee unions and agency management customarily participated in the detailed planning and conduct of the surveys. Therefore, under the Coordinated Federal Wage System, established administratively in 1968 and enacted into law in 1972, BLS provides some statistical support, but local wage survey committees, consisting of management and labor representatives, conduct the studies.[92]

Various groups have suggested that BLS become the data collection agency for both the white- and blue-collar pay systems. This was the recommendation of the Federal Job Evaluation and Pay Review Task Force in 1971. In 1979, the General Accounting Office recommended that BLS work with the Office of Personnel Management to improve the system.[93]

Industry wage surveys, conducted in each industry on a 3- or 5-year cycle, covered about 40 manufacturing and 25 nonmanufacturing industries by 1982. Following the budget cuts for fiscal year 1982, the program was reduced to 25 manufacturing and 15 nonmanufacturing industries.

The PATC survey was made the basis for carrying out the principle of comparability of Federal and private-sector pay under legislation passed in 1962 and 1971. The Bureau acts as the data collector for the

President's Pay Agent, which sets the specifications for the survey and makes the recommendations on pay adjustment.[94]

Several investigations of the Federal pay system have touched on matters relevant to the Bureau's role. In 1973, the General Accounting Office, after a review of the comparability process, emphasized the need to expand the coverage of the PATC survey and to clarify the definitions and terminology. In 1975, the President's Panel on Federal Compensation (Rockefeller Panel) called for the inclusion of data from State and local governments, a change which would require amending the Federal pay laws. Also at that time, the Council of Economic Advisers urged the separation of managerial or political interests—those of the President's Pay Agent and the Federal Employees Pay Council—from the technical side of pay comparability, with the Bureau assigned responsibility for developing a mechanism for determining the wage rates and benefits of workers doing "comparable work" to that of government employees.[95]

With increases in appropriations, BLS extended the occupational coverage of the PATC survey from 72 occupational work levels in 1975 to approximately 100 such categories in 1982. However, critics still complained that the survey covered mainly large, high paying firms, and also objected to the continued exclusion of State and local government workers.[96]

The review groups also had recommended that the Federal pay comparability system be expanded to include benefits. The Office of Personnel Management, in developing its Total Compensation Comparability project, called on the Bureau to gather data on benefit plans in the private sector. The Bureau conducted a pilot project in 1979 and then developed an annual survey of the incidence and characteristics of employee benefit plans in medium and large firms.

The Bureau added another type of occupational wage survey in 1970 with a program of surveys of wages and benefits of municipal government employees. The series eventually covered 50 occupations in 27 large cities before it was eliminated in the budget cuts of fiscal year 1981.

Economic policymakers had long felt the need for a current, broadly based measure of change in wage costs in the economy, comparable in scope to the consumer price and employment measures. The urgency increased with the wage-price spiral of the Vietnam era. In 1969, the Bureau asked Albert Rees of Princeton University to make recommendations for improving its measures of wage change. While questioning whether a new series could be developed on a cost-effective basis, Rees suggested that the Bureau develop an index from the existing data on average hourly earnings in the establishment survey, adjusted to exclude overtime payments in manufacturing and employment shifts between high- and low-wage industries. He also stressed the importance of obtaining information on the changes in the earnings of government employees.[97]

The Hourly Earnings Index was developed in 1971, responding to the Rees suggestion. While it represented a step forward, the index was limited to earnings of production workers, excluded supplementary benefits, did not adjust for part-time workers, and did not provide separate detail for occupational groups.

Pressure continued for the development of a broad, general wage measure to serve as an economic indicator. Shiskin explained that government officials responsible for monitoring the economy and evaluating the effectivenesses of economic policies had pressed BLS to produce a measure which included benefits. Although the labor advisers questioned the proposed measure, complaining of the lack of "a well-constructed, theoretical framework," they participated in the technical development of what came to be called the Employment Cost Index.[98]

The Employment Cost Index, measuring quarterly changes in wages and salaries, was first published in 1976. Designed as a fixed weight index at the occupational level, it eliminated the effects of employment shifts among occupations. Developed in stages, the ECI included benefits in 1980 and, by 1981, presented indexes by occupational group and industry division for State and local government workers as well as for the private nonfarm sector. It also provided detail by collective bargaining status, region, and area size. In October 1980, the Office of Management and Budget designated the ECI a "Primary Federal Economic Indicator."[99]

The series on current changes in wages and supplementary benefits agreed to in collective bargaining continued as an indicator in this more limited but significant sector. Since 1982, BLS has followed about 1,900 bargaining situations involving actions covering 1,000 workers or more. Initially limited to wage adustments, the series now covers changes in total compensation in agreements covering 5,000 workers or more in all industries and 1,000 workers or more in construction. Also, beginning with 1979, BLS has published data on total compensation under negotiated agreements covering 5,000 workers or more in State and local government employment.

Bureau wage programs of long standing were eliminated during the budget tightening of 1979–82, however. The series of wage chronologies, which provided a continuous record of wage and benefit changes negotiated in about 30 major firms or associations of firms, was discontinued, along with the series on union wage rates and benefits in the building and printing trades, in local transit and trucking, and in grocery stores.

Industrial relations programs were also substantially affected. The Bureau's file of collective bargaining agreements was maintained only for contracts covering 1,000 workers or more, and, while the file continued as a basis for BLS reports on wage negotiations, in-depth studies of contract provisions were no longer conducted. The directory of unions and employee associations was discontinued, and strike statistics were reduced in coverage.

Productivity and technology
Economic conditions focused increasing attention on the productivity of U.S. industry and its workers. Concern over the consequences of technological change and foreign competition, the use of productivity improvement factors in collective bargaining agreements, and the implementation of wage-price guidelines as national economic policy gave productivity measurement heightened importance. With the slow rate of productivity increase during the 1970's, productivity measures remained in the spotlight.

To meet the demand for more information, the Bureau's ongoing work on productivity measures was expanded. The number of industries for which BLS prepared productivity indexes increased to 116 over the period, reflecting in part extended coverage in trade and services. Productivity measures for the economy as a whole and major sectors, first published on an annual basis in 1960, were introduced quarterly in 1968.

Innovative work was stimulated by the National Academy of Sciences Panel to Review Productivity Statistics, which recommended in 1979 that BLS "experiment with combining labor and other inputs into alternative measures of multifactor productivity." The General Accounting Office seconded the suggestion in a 1980 report.[100]

In 1983, the Bureau published its first multifactor productivity indexes for major sectors of the private economy, covering the period 1948–81. These estimates measured the annual change in output per unit of combined labor and capital input. The Bureau explained that this "more inclusive measure" represented the first step in trying to quantify the contribution of a number of major factors underlying productivity change. Comparing movements of the multifactor index with those of the more familiar measure—output per hour of all persons—would indicate how much of the growth or falloff in output per hour was due to changes in the use of capital—capital productivity—and how much was due to a combination of the other factors, i.e., changes in technology, shifts in the composition of the labor force, changes in capacity utilization, and so forth.[101]

The Bureau also played a leading role in developing statistics on productivity in the Federal Government. The Joint Economic Committee initiated the project in 1970 by asking the General Accounting Office, the Office of Management and Budget, and the Civil Service Commission to establish a task force to collect information and construct indexes. BLS provided assistance and, in 1973, assumed full responsibility for collecting data and developing measures. By 1982, the program covered about 450 organizational units in almost 50 Federal departments and agencies.[102]

Meanwhile, BLS continued its interest in the impact of automation and technological change. In 1966, it released an expanded and updated version of its study of 36 major industries. It followed with new studies on computers, railroads, and energy, while continuing to update the earlier work in a series of publications.

The Office of Productivity did lose one of its programs in the latter part of the period. Since 1959, the Bureau had surveyed various types of federally assisted construction to determine labor and materials requirements in order to estimate the total employment generated. Over the years, it had conducted some 28 studies, covering, for example, highways, hospitals, college housing, Federal office buildings, and sewers—extending the scope to include private housing construction. The data were used in projecting training needs and occupational outlook, shortages and surpluses in labor supply, material demands, and input-output matrixes. During the 1982 budget austerity, BLS eliminated the program, largely because of the time lag between survey dates and publication and the extensive use of estimation and imputation.[103]

Economic growth and employment projections

Since the 1960's, the Bureau had produced projections of the labor force, industry output, and employment. The Bureau prepared projections on a 2-year cycle covering five areas: Labor force, aggregate economic performance, industry final demand and total production, industry employment levels, and occupational employment by industry.[104]

The Bureau continued to publish revised editions of the *Occupational Outlook Handbook*, a comprehensive reference volume for career guidance first produced in 1949 at the urging of the National Vocational Guidance Association and with the financial support of the Veterans Administration. In 1957, BLS had added the *Occupational Outlook Quarterly* to supplement the biennial *Handbook*.

The projections work was coordinated with the occupational outlook programs, although the functions were located in separate offices. In November 1979, the Bureau brought the work together under the umbrella of the Office of Economic Growth and Employment Projections, making for closer integration of the work on labor force, industry output, employment, and occupational projections.[105]

Industrial safety and health

Historically, BLS had conducted frequent studies of occupational safety and health problems and had worked closely with safety and inspection groups. By 1966, it was publishing both quarterly and annual statistics on the frequency and severity of work injuries in many industries.

Passage of the Occupational Safety and Health Act of 1970 greatly altered the field of industrial safety statistics. The act directed the Secretary of Labor to issue regulations requiring covered employers to maintain accurate records of work-related deaths, injuries, and illnesses. In 1971, the Secretary delegated to BLS the responsibility for developing the underlying statistical system, in coordination with the Assistant Secretary for Occupational Safety and Health.

The Bureau moved quickly to construct a cooperative Federal-State program to gather statistics necessary under the new law, providing grants to States for planning and development. The specialized treatment formerly accorded the collection of data on occupational injuries of longshore workers was discontinued, superseded by the more comprehensive program. By 1976, the annual survey of occupational injuries and illnesses had become the largest annual sample survey conducted by the Bureau. In the following years, BLS sought to reduce the reporting burden on employers while refining the survey. In 1982, it sampled about 280,000 establishments in 48 participating States.

The Bureau also developed procedures to provide additional information from State workers' compensation records on the characteristics of the injuries and illnesses and the workers involved. The Supplementary Data System, introduced in 1976, became fully operational in 1978, and by 1982, 34 States were participating in the cooperative program.[106]

In addition, to help fill gaps in the knowledge of how and why on-the-job accidents occur, in 1977 the Bureau began a series of direct surveys of injured workers. Each survey in the Work Injury Report program was designed to cover a specific type of accident being studied by the Occupational Safety and Health Administration and the National Institute for Occupational Safety and Health. From 1978 on, the Bureau conducted four such studies each year, publishing, for example, *Accidents Involving Eye Injuries* and *Back Injuries Associated with Lifting*.

International activities

In the 1960's, with the growing importance of foreign trade and concern for competition in world markets, the Bureau published two studies presenting international comparisons of unit labor costs, one for the manufacturing sector as a whole and the other covering the iron and steel industry. The Bureau also participated in a joint project of the Department of Labor and the Japanese Ministry of Labor, a comparative study of wages in Japan and the United States. Janet Norwood, as Chief of the Wage and Labor Cost Section of the Office of Foreign Labor and Trade, led BLS activities for the project.[107]

However, in 1969, BLS dismantled the Office of Foreign Labor and Trade and distributed its constituent units throughout the Bureau. Then in 1972, as a result of budget cuts and staff reductions, one of the units was abolished and the periodical *Labor Developments Abroad*, begun in 1956, was suspended. To fill the gap, the *Monthly*

Labor Review expanded its coverage of foreign labor conditions. The Office of Productivity and Technology continued the work on international comparisons of employment, earnings, and productivity.

The Bureau continued to provide training and technical assistance to developing countries. The training programs for foreign technicians were restructured in the early 1970's, when it became apparent that the developing countries no longer needed basic statistical training as much as they needed more advanced training on practical applications. At the recommendation of a 1972 task force representing the U.S. Agency for International Development and the Department of Labor, BLS instituted short-term seminars on specific topics in applied labor statistics. By the early 1980's, about a dozen seminars of 4 to 8 weeks duration were being held each year. Moreover, the BLS international training program held two seminars overseas in 1977. Since then, about 20 such seminars have been conducted throughout the world on various topics in labor statistics.

Administration

Funding
Generally, the Bureau's budget fared relatively well until Federal appropriations tightened in the 1980's. BLS appropriations increased about eightfold between 1966 and 1985, although this reflected mandated salary increases in addition to growth in programs and personnel (table 7). The number of staff positions increased by one-third over the period. In 1983, the Bureau was given full financial responsibility for the labor market information system, and an initial sum of $20.4 million in unemployment insurance trust funds was included in the Bureau's budget for fiscal year 1984.

With the tightening of the Federal budget in the 1980's, Norwood gave priority to assuring the quality and adequacy of the Bureau programs providing major national indicators. Other programs were trimmed to accommodate to the loss of funds. In fiscal year 1982, when Congress added a cut of 4 percent to the 12 percent proposed by the administration, the Bureau considered furloughing its work force as other agencies had done, but managed to avoid that step through advance planning of new hires and replacements. With support from labor and business groups and the Joint Economic Commit-

Table 7. Funding for Bureau of Labor Statistics, 1966–85
(in thousands)

Fiscal year ended—	Total[1]	Salaries and expenses
June 30 —		
1966	$21,995	$19,967
1967	23,519	20,588
1968	24,311	20,985
1969	27,071	21,933
1970	30,433	24,653
1971	32,644	28,096
1972	42,033	37,300
1973	48,874	44,451
1974	53,261	48,635
1975	62,324	54,422
1976	75,841	65,846
September 30 —		
1977[2]	90,363	75,617
1978	93,410	84,015
1979	103,869	94,752
1980	124,395	102,890
1981	121,792	111,081
1982	120,170	113,067
1983	130,001	121,743
1984	157,740	137,340
1985	173,260	152,860

[1]Through fiscal year 1984, includes the direct appropriation together with advances and transfers of Federal funds and payments from trust funds. For fiscal years 1984 and 1985, includes, in addition to the direct appropriation, the trust fund supplement of $20.4 million transferred to BLS for management of the labor market information program. The 1985 figure does not include other advances and transfers.

[2]Includes funds for transition quarter.

SOURCE: *The Budget of the United States Government.*

tee, Congress appropriated supplemental funds to restore the initial administration levels.

Management
In 1966, Secretary Wirtz's management consultants, Booz-Allen and Hamilton, recommended that BLS become "a more integral part of the Department." Also, characterizing BLS as too compartmentalized and inflexible to meet new demands, the consultants suggested stronger central leadership for the Bureau, with a Chief Economist

responsible for products and planning and a Chief Statistician responsible for standards and techniques.[108] Ross accepted these recommendations and put them into effect, also separating the operations functions from the program and planning functions in the Bureau's regional offices.

Implementing another Booz-Allen recommendation, the Bureau established a central Office of Publications to help the Commissioner and the program offices plan, prepare, and disseminate public information. The Office used computer languages created by the Bureau's systems staff to generate photocomposed statistical tables, charts, and text, making the Bureau a pioneer in the photocomposed production of statistical publications from existing data bases.[109] Moreover, BLS now makes available major data series at the time of initial release through electronic news releases and, more comprehensively, through magnetic tape.

Indeed, the Bureau had emphasized improving its electronic information systems. Booz-Allen had stressed the need for broader and more aggressive use of electronic data processing and had recommended the centralization of all data collection and processing, which were then being conducted separately in the various program offices. BLS had installed a second-generation computer system in 1963. Under Ross, the Bureau encouraged computer language training for its professionals to promote expanded use of the computers for analysis and interpretation and worked with the Department to plan a system based on a third-generation facility.

During the early 1970's, the Office of Systems and Standards developed Table Producing Language (TPL), a system designed to select, restructure, cross-tabulate, and display data. Installations around the world have acquired this tabulating system, including commercial enterprises, State and municipal agencies, major universities, and other national statistical agencies. In fiscal year 1978, BLS initiated LABSTAT (LABor STATistics), its greatly expanded data base or general pool of statistical information which gives users direct on-line computer access to more than 150,000 time series.

Meanwhile, the Bureau had moved into time-sharing on mainframe computers at the National Institutes of Health and, later, with a commercial computer center. This boosted processing capabilities in major programs and greatly increased opportunities for analytical research, while also facilitating transmissions between BLS headquarters and the field offices—without committing scarce resources to expensive and soon-outdated equipment.

Having already reorganized under Ross, the Bureau largely conformed with proposals issued by the Office of Management and Budget several years later for improving the organization of all Federal statistical activities. In 1971, when OMB called for centralized data collection and processing activities within the statistical agencies and the establishment of separate units for planning and data analysis, Moore replaced the positions of Chief Economist and Chief Statistician with two Deputy Commissioners, one in charge of data analysis and the other in charge of statistical operations. Shiskin altered the arrangement somewhat by establishing a single Deputy Commissioner in 1975.[110]

During her term, Norwood refined the BLS organizational structure. She enlarged the role of the Office of Research and Evaluation, which she expanded in 1982, reflecting increased interest in mathematical statistics and concern for improving the quality of the Bureau's data. In 1982, she also created the position of Deputy Commissioner for Administration and Internal Operations. In 1983, she announced the recombination of the two program offices dealing with employment statistics, forming the Office of Employment and Unemployment Statistics.[111]

Field operations

The tremendous growth in demand for local data and the accompanying expansion of Federal-State cooperative programs enhanced the role of the Bureau's regional offices. In 1967, as part of the Department's effort to establish uniform regional organizations and boundaries, BLS changed the location of one of its regional offices from Cleveland to Kansas City. In 1968, it established new offices in Philadelphia and Dallas, for a total of eight.

The incoming Nixon administration pushed decentralization of government activities, prompting the Department to issue orders to its agencies to delegate authority to the field. In 1973, when the Bureau's regional directors were designated Assistant Regional Directors, Shiskin complained of the "apparent subordination of the Bureau staff to political appointees," namely the Department of Labor Regional Directors.[112] In 1975, Secretary Dunlop made a change, establishing Regional Commissioners along with Regional Solicitors and Regional

Administrators. At about the same time, Shiskin created the position of Assistant Commissioner for Field Collection and Coordination in the national office.

The regional offices now exercise several basic functions: They collect and process primary data required for the Consumer Price Index, the Producer Price Index, the Employment Cost Index, the international price program, and the occupational wage survey program. They supervise and assist cooperating State agencies in collecting labor force and occupational safety and health statistics and also assist in the preparation of area estimates of labor force, employment, and unemployment. In addition, they disseminate Bureau publications and data. The Regional Commissioners represent the Commissioner and the Bureau in the regions and advise the Department's Regional Director.

Advisory groups
The Business and Labor Research Advisory Councils, established in 1947, continued to play active roles as advisers and disseminators of the Bureau's data. Most recently, Norwood has stressed the importance of their role and her desire to see that they become more helpful to the Bureau in carrying out its mission.

Over the years, there have been proposals for extending the Bureau's formal advisory arrangements. Moore proposed setting up some means of obtaining advice from the staffs of universities and research institutes, but these were not implemented. In 1979, the final report of the National Commission on Employment and Unemployment Statistics contained a proposal for a panel "broadly representative of the data-using community." In his comments on the report, Secretary Marshall noted that BLS sought means of obtaining advice from State, county, and municipal leaders, as well as CETA prime sponsors, State employment security agencies, and others interested in State and local statistics. However, in his report on the National Commission recommendations, Secretary Donovan rejected the suggestion for a "new permanent advisory council."[113]

Chapter IX.

History as Prologue: The Continuing Mission

The mission of the Bureau of Labor Statistics since its founding 100 years ago has been to collect information on economic and social conditions and, in the words of Carroll Wright, the first Commissioner, through "fearless publication of the results," to let the people assess the facts and act on them. It was the belief of its founders that dissemination of the facts would lead to improvement of the life of the people.

On the occasion of the Bureau's centennial, Janet L. Norwood, the tenth Commissioner, summed up the Bureau's past—and continuing—role: "The Bureau stands for—

—Commitment to objectivity and fairness in all of its data gathering and interpretive and analytical work;
—Insistence on candor at all times;
—Protection of confidentiality;
—Pursuit of improvements;
—Willingness to change; and
—Maintenance of consistency in the highest standards of performance."

These principles, Norwood stressed, must be steadfastly applied in monitoring "our programs to ensure that they remain accurate, objective, and relevant. We must modernize our statistical techniques because a statistical agency that does not constantly move ahead in the use of new techniques quickly moves backward."

As an institution, the Bureau has evolved from the original and sole labor agency in the Federal Government, with a broad factfinding scope, to one among many specialized labor agencies. Serving as a quasi-Department of Labor during its first two decades, it was called upon to study and report on issues such as the violent strikes and lockouts of the period and the harsh conditions of employment for women and children. Today, the Bureau is a general-purpose statistical agency, gathering, analyzing, and distributing information broadly applicable to labor economics and labor conditions.

While the focus and perspectives of Bureau studies have changed over the years, most areas of investigation have remained germane— the course of wages and prices, the state of industrial relations, problems of unemployment and the effects of technological and demographic change, and safety and health conditions in the workplace. Some areas of study, such as child labor, have been rendered unnecessary by legislation. In others, newer, specialized agencies have taken over the work the Bureau began.

The Bureau's role has been to provide data and analyses that contribute to the development of policy without crossing the line into policy formulation, but the line is a fine one. Certainly Neill and Lubin, through their personal relations, advised Presidents and Secretaries on specifics of labor and economic policy. And at times the Bureau has found itself in the midst of controversy, its findings and objectivity challenged by one set of partisans or another. Wright's wage and price studies were attacked as products of political manipulation, and, during World War II, labor unions challenged the cost-of-living index because of their dissatisfaction with the government's wage stabilization policies.

Professional integrity is essential to a government agency which provides information for public and private policy needs, and the Bureau's institutional probity has been a constant concern of the Commissioners and their staffs. Over the years, the Bureau's objectivity has been affirmed and reaffirmed upon review of its work by congressional committees, Presidential commissions, and professional associations of economists and statisticians. All noted areas needing improvement, but none found reason to question the independence and integrity of the Bureau.

For the first half-century of its existence, the Bureau's appropriations changed only when special funding was provided for particular programs, such as the woman and child study of 1907–09, and development of a cost-of-living index during World War I. The emergency demands of the depression of the 1930's and the accompanying social legislation also led Congress to increase appropriations to expand and improve the Bureau's statistics. And, similarly, World War II needs generated increased resources and programs.

After the war, the climate was vastly different. Government policy concerns required data produced on a frequent and regular basis. The Employment Act of 1946, which established the congressional Joint Economic Committee and the Council of Economic Advisers, epitomized the new conditions. As government social and economic policies developed and expanded, legislation frequently incorporated Bureau statistics as escalators or other administrative devices. There was now a regular demand for new and improved statistics, with support for resources to make them available. While increases in resources have not always been forthcoming, and programs have been cut on occasion to make room for new and expanded series, the postwar trend has been one of provision of funds for such expansion and improvements.

Bureau programs have changed to meet changing conditions. Ongoing statistical series such as the Consumer Price Index have been adjusted periodically to assure that concepts and coverage reflect altered societal patterns. Along with regular planned revisions, the Bureau has made interim revisions, as in the case of the treatment of the homeownership component in the CPI. New series, including the Employment Cost Index and the multifactor productivity indexes, have been developed.

Meeting these vastly increased requirements has been made possible through the development of sophisticated statistical techniques of sampling and the computerization of statistical operations. Bureau personnel now include mathematical statisticians, computer programmers, and computer systems analysts as well as economists and clerical staff.

In addition, close coordination with other Federal agencies and with the States, evolving from Wright's early efforts, has improved the quality of the data and efficiency in collection and processing.

Bureau respondents generally have given their full cooperation because of the assurance of confidentiality for reported information, a guarantee which has been assiduously enforced. In its communication with the public, the Bureau has emphasized frankness regarding limitations of the data and the provision of detailed information on concepts and methods. There has been a constant striving to improve the timeliness, regularity, and accuracy of the data and their public presentation.

While well established, the principles have needed regular reiteration, particularly during unsettled times. There have been many occasions when the messenger has been buffeted by the storms of rapid economic and social change. This has been especially true when the Bureau's data have been used in implementing and monitoring policy, as in the wartime use of its cost-of-living index for wage stabilization. On other occasions, Bureau staff efforts to explain technical limitations have collided with policymakers' unqualified use of the data. In such circumstances, the Bureau has been sustained by the widespread recognition that its nonpartisanship and objectivity must be assured and protected. Congress, successive Secretaries of Labor, the Bureau's labor and business advisory groups, the professional associations, and the press have supported the independence and impartiality of statistical research in government agencies.

The roots of this independence and professionalism are deep and strong. The tradition of impartiality has been underwritten by both Democratic and Republican administrations over the century of the Bureau's existence, during which Commissioners have been selected for their technical competence without regard to partisan considerations.

The Bureau faces great challenges in the years ahead as the phenomena it measures grow in complexity in the dynamic economy of the United States. It will require openness to new methods and techniques and adherence to the standards already set to carry out its mission during the next century.

Appendix:

BLS Publications

From its beginning, the Bureau of Labor Statistics has conducted a substantial publications program. Initially, the Bureau published annual reports, issuing 25 volumes for the years 1885–1910. Each presented the comprehensive findings of a specific survey or study, covering such topics as strikes and lockouts, convict labor, industrial education, and technological displacement of workers.

Supplementing these, the Bureau conducted special investigations, frequently at the direction of Congress, producing 12 special reports between 1889 and 1905. These covered such subjects as marriage and divorce, slum condititions, social insurance, and labor legislation.

The Bureau also provided Congress with reports on such topics as labor disputes and pension systems, later published as House or Senate documents. Two notable examples were the 19-volume *Report on Condition of Woman and Child Wage-Earners in the United States* (1910–13) and the 4-volume *Report on Conditions of Employment in the Iron and Steel Industry* (1911–12).

From 1895, when Congress authorized publication of a periodical, until 1912, the Bureau issued the bimonthly *Bulletin*. This presented original work, digests of State reports, summaries and digests of foreign labor and statistical papers, and summaries of current legislation and court decisions.

In 1912, the Bureau discontinued the annual reports and the bimonthly *Bulletin*, issuing instead a series of bulletins, published irregularly, each covering a specific program area. In 1915, BLS introduced the *Monthly Review*, changing the name to *Monthly Labor Review* in 1918.

Over the years, BLS added such periodicals as *Labor Information Bulletin* and *Labor Developments Abroad* and published such special volumes as *Activities of the Bureau of Labor Statistics in World War II* (1947), *The Gift of Freedom* (1949), and *BLS Centennial Album* (1984).

At present, BLS publishes bulletins, numbered continuously from 1895; reports, a series started in 1953; and one quarterly and five monthly periodicals. These periodicals, reflecting the importance of the major recurring statistical series, are *CPI Detailed Report, Current Wage Developments, Employment and Earnings, Monthly Labor Review, Occupational Outlook Quarterly*, and *Producer Price Indexes*.

In addition, BLS issues some 200 national and 1,300 regional news releases each year and summaries of survey results in advance of fuller publication in bulletins, providing timely distribution of the Bureau's latest data.

There have been several special sections in the *Monthly Labor Review* giving historical perspective: "50 Years' Progress of American Labor" (July 1950), "Seventy Years of Service—The Story of BLS" (January 1955), and "Fifty Years of the MLR" (July 1965). The Bureau has published subject indexes for the MLR—Bulletins 695 (1941), 696 (1942), 1080 (1953), 1335 (1960), 1746 (1973), and 1922 (1976). In addition, there are indexes to each volume, now presented annually in the December issue.

The Bureau also has produced numerical listings and subject indexes for the bulletins and reports, including *BLS Publications, 1886-1971*, Bulletin 1749 (1972) and *BLS Publications, 1972-77*, Bulletin 1990 (1978).

Periodically, BLS has published bulletins explaining its statistical methods and procedures, beginning with *Methods of Procuring and Computing Statistical Information of the Bureau of Labor Statistics*, Bulletin 326 (1923). In the 1950's, the Bureau issued two editions of

Techniques of Preparing Major BLS Statistical Series, Bulletin 993 in 1950 and Bulletin 1168 in 1954. Under the title *BLS Handbook of Methods,* the Bureau continued with Bulletins 1458 (1966), 1711 (1971), 1910 (1976), and 2134-1 (1982) and 2134-2 (1984).

BLS published *Handbook of Labor Statistics,* Bulletin 439, in 1927 as a compendium of historical data, issuing the most recent edition, Bulletin 2217, in 1985.

In sheer volume, the largest number of bulletins have presented wage data, published currently as Industry Wage Surveys and Area Wage Surveys (previously Occupational Wage Surveys). Two major series on contract provisions were the 19-volume set, *Collective Bargaining Provisions,* Bulletin 908 (1947-50), and the 21-volume series, *Major Collective Bargaining Agreements,* Bulletin 1425 (1964-82). In 1947, the Bureau issued the first *Directory of Labor Unions in the United States,* Bulletin 901, publishing the last edition in 1980.

One of the Bureau's most popular bulletins is the *Occupational Outlook Handbook,* which it revises every 2 years—most recently as Bulletin 2205 (1984).

In recent years, BLS has expanded its analysis and publication of labor force data on women, minorities, and families. For example, in 1978, it introduced the quarterly report *Employment in Perspective: Working Women* and, in 1980, another quarterly report, *Employment in Perspective: Minority Workers,* with data on blacks and Hispanics.

Source Notes

Chapter I. Origins

[1] James C. Sylvis, *The Life, Speeches, Labors and Essays of William H. Sylvis* (Philadelphia: Claxton, Remsen & Haffelfinger, 1872), p. 74.

[2] Terence V. Powderly, *Thirty Years of Labor* (Columbus, Ohio: Excelsior Publishing House, 1889), pp. 302–303.

[3] U. S. Congress, House, Select Committee on Depression in Labor and Business, *Investigation Relative to the Causes of the General Depression in Labor and Business* (46C, 2S, 1879), pp. 8–9, 118–119.

[4] American Federation of Labor, *Proceedings, 1881*, p. 4, and *Proceedings, 1883*, p. 14; Joseph P. Goldberg and William T. Moye, "The AFL and a National BLS," *Monthly Labor Review*, March 1982, pp. 21–29.

[5] U. S. Congress, Senate, Committee on Education and Labor, *Labor and Capital* (48C, 1885), Vol. I, pp. 87, 271, 327, 382, 790–791, 1142.

[6] Ibid., pp. 570–571; ibid., Vol. III, pp. 278–280.

[7] *Congressional Record* (48C, 1S), Apr. 19, 1884, p. 3140.

[8] *Congressional Record* (48C, 1S), Mar. 7, 1884, pp. 1675–1676; Apr. 19, 1884, p. 3139; May 14, 1884, p. 4157.

[9] *The New York Times*, Feb. 10, 1884, p. 6; Apr. 10, 1884, p. 8.

[10] *Journal of United Labor*, May 25, 1884, p. 702; Powderly, *Thirty Years*, pp. 314–315.

[11] National Archives Record Group (NARG) 48, Secretary of the Interior, Appointments Division, Powderly to President Arthur, June 30, 1884.

[12] NARG 48, Secretary of the Interior, Appointments Division, Anonymous, re. labor question and appointment of a Commissioner, stamped received Mar. 16, 1885; *The New York Times*, July 24, 1884, p. 4; July 29, 1884, p. 4; Aug. 15, 1884, p. 5; Nov. 27, 1884, p. 1.

[13] AFL, *Proceedings, 1884*, p. 14.

[14] *The New York Times*, July 1, 1884, p. 4.

[15] NARG 48, Secretary of the Interior, Appointments Division, Henry Feuerbach to President Arthur, Aug. 14, 1884.

[16] NARG 48, Secretary of the Interior, Appointments Division, Wright to Secretary, Aug. 26, 1884; Anonymous, Mar. 16, 1885; and National Labor Convention, July 30, Chicago, received Oct. 18, 1884.

[17] *The New York Times*, Jan. 20, 1885, p. 4.

Chapter II. Carroll Wright

[1] James Leiby, *Carroll Wright and Labor Reform: The Origin of Labor Statistics* (Cambridge: Harvard University Press, 1960), pp. 204–205.

[2] Joseph Dorfman, *The Economic Mind in American Civilization*, Vol. III, *1865–1918* (New York: Viking Press, 1949), pp. 123–130.

[3] Wendell D. Macdonald, "The Early History of Labor Statistics in the United States," *Labor History*, Spring 1972, p. 275; Read Bain and Joseph Cohen, "Trends in Applied Sociology," in George A. Lundberg, Read Bain, and Nels Anderson, eds., *Trends in American Sociology* (New York: Harper and Brothers, 1929), p. 350.

[4] Carroll D. Wright, *The Relation of Political Economy to the Labor Question* (Boston: A. Williams and Co., 1882), pp. 11-12, 16-17.

[5] Massachusetts Bureau of Statistics of Labor, *Eighth Annual Report, 1877*, p. vii; Wright, *Popular Instruction in Social Science* (Boston: Geo. E. Crosby & Co., 1886), p. 11.

[6] Wright, "The Factory System as an Element of Civilization," *Journal of Social Science*, December 1882, p. 125; Massachusetts Bureau, *Sixteenth Annual Report, 1885*, p. 26.

[7] Wright, "Factory System" (1882), p. 110.

[8] Wright, *Outline of Practical Sociology* (New York: Longmans, Green and Co., 1909, seventh edition, revised), pp. 251, 256-257.

[9] Wright, "The Relation of Invention to Labor," *The Liberal Club, Buffalo* (Buffalo: The Matthews-Northup Co., 1893), p. 32; Wright, "The Factory as an Element in Social Life," Catholic University *Bulletin*, January 1901, p. 64.

[10] Wright, *Relation of Political Economy*, pp. 25, 27; Wright, "Why Women Are Paid Less Than Men," *Forum*, July 1892, p. 637.

[11] Wright, "Does the Factory Increase Immorality?" *Forum*, May 1892, pp. 344-349.

[12] Wright, *Outline*, p. 295.

[13] Wright, *The Battles of Labor* (Philadelphia: G.W. Jacobs & Co., 1906), pp. 174, 176.

[14] Wright, *Battles of Labor*, p. 186; Wright, *Outline*, p. 299.

[15] Massachusetts Bureau, *Eighth Annual Report, 1877*, p. vi.

[16] Wright, "The Working of the United States Bureau of Labor," *Bulletin* (54), September 1904, p. 978.

[17] John R. Commons, *Myself* (New York: The Macmillan Co., 1934), p. 93.

[18] Walter F. Willcox, "Development of the American Census Office since 1890," *Political Science Quarterly*, September 1914, p. 11; S.N.D. North, "The Life and Work of Carroll Davidson Wright," American Statistical Association *Journal*, June 1909, p. 461.

[19] Wright, "The Working," pp. 976-977.

[20] Great Britain, Royal Commission on Labour, *Fourth Report, 1893-1894*, Vol. XXXIX, Pt. 1, *Minutes of Evidence* (c.7063.1) (London: Her Majesty's Stationery Office, 1893), pp. 478, 491, 493.

[21] Wright, "The Working," p. 977.

[22] National Archives Record Group 257, BLS, Telegrams, 1897-1902, Wright to J. B. Crockett, Mar. 30, 1898.

[23] E.R.L. Gould, "The Progress of Labor Statistics in the United States," International Statistical Institute *Bulletin* (Rome, 1892), p. 188.

[24] Wright, "A Basis for Statistics of Cost of Production," ASA *Journal*, June 1891, p. 258.

[25] *American Federationist*, June 1897, p. 76.

[26] Wright, "The Work of the U.S. Bureau of Labor," Association of Officials of Bureaus of Labor Statistics, *Proceedings, 1885*, pp. 129, 132-133.

[27] Leiby, *Carroll Wright*, pp. 80-82.

[28] Henry Jones Ford, *The Cleveland Era* (New Haven: Yale University Press, 1921), pp. 131-132; Denis Tilden Lynch, *Grover Cleveland* (New York: Horace Liveright, Inc., 1932), p. 328.

[29] *National Labor Tribune*, Feb. 25, 1888, p. 1; June 30, 1888, p. 1; *Journal of United Labor*, Sept. 20, 1888, p. 2702.

[30] Terence V. Powderly, *The Path I Trod*, ed. by Harry J. Carman, Henry David, and Paul N. Guthrie (New York: Columbia University Press, 1940), pp. 230-232; *Journal of United Labor*, May 5, 1888, p. 2672.

[31] U. S. Congress, House, Select Committee on the Tenth Census, *Result of the Tenth Census* (House Report 2432, 48C, 2S, 1884), p. 3; House, Committee on the Census, *Permanent Census Bureau* (House Rept. 262, 57C, 1S, 1902), Appendix A, Part 1, Historical Summary.

[32] Wright with William C. Hunt, *The History and Growth of the Untied States Census* (Washington: Government Printing Office, 1900), p. 81; U.S. Congress, Senate (52C, 1S, 1891), Senate Executive Document No. 1, Letter from the Secretary of the Interior, *A Permanent Census Bureau*, pp. 65-66.

[33] Willcox, "Development," pp. 444-445.

[34] S.N.D. North, "The Life," p. 459.

[35] Willcox, "Development," p. 443.

[36] Ibid., pp. 445-446; Wright and Hunt, *The History and Growth*, pp. 82-83; House, Committee on Appropriations, *Hearings, Permanent Census* (54C, 2S, 1897), pp. 3, 7, 11.

[37] Senate, Committee on the Census, *Permanent Census Service* (54C, 2S, 1897), p. 28; House, Committee on Appropriations, *Report: The Twelfth and Subsequent Censuses* (House Rept. 2909, 54C, 2S, 1897), p. 2; House, Committee on the Census, *Permanent Census* (House Rept. 262), Historical Summary.

[38] *Congressional Record* (55C, 2S), Jan. 5, 1898, p. 316; Feb. 21, 1898, p. 1965.

[39] Ibid., pp. 1965, 1967.

[40] Ibid., p. 1965.

[41] Wright and Hunt, *The History and Growth*, p. 84.

[42] Albert K. Steigerwalt, *The National Association of Manufacturers, 1895-1914* (Ann Arbor: Bureau of Business Research, Graduate School of Business Administration, University of Michigan, 1964), pp. 83-84.

[43] American Federation of Labor, *Proceedings, 1896*, p. 81; *Proceedings, 1897*, p. 22; Library of Congress, American Federation of Labor Papers, Samuel Gompers Letterbooks, Gompers to Frank Hall, New Orleans, Feb. 10, 1899.

[44] U.S. Department of Commerce and Labor, *Organization and Law of the Department of Commerce and Labor* (Washington: Government Printing Office, 1904), pp. 501 and 520; Henry F. Pringle, *Theodore Roosevelt* (New York: Harcourt, Brace & Co., 1931), pp. 244-246; Thomas Beer, *Hanna* (New York: Octagon Books, 1973), p. 275.

[45] AFL, *Proceedings, 1901*, p. 27; *Congressional Record* (57C, 1S), Jan. 22, 1902, p. 863.

[46] House, Committee on Interstate and Foreign Commerce, *Hearing, Department of Commerce* (57C, 1902), pp. 30, 40, 105.

[47] Ibid., p. 34.

[48] Ibid., pp. 6, 22.

[49] Ibid., pp. 506, 547–548, 552.

[50] Ibid., p. 501.

[51] Ibid., pp. 492, 495; NARG 257, BLS, Letters Sent, Wright to Fawcett, Jan. 31, 1902.

[52] Francis E. Rourke, "The Department of Labor and the Trade Unions," *The Western Political Quarterly*, 1954, p. 660.

[53] *The Works of Theodore Roosevelt, Presidential Addresses and State Papers* (New York: P.F. Collier & Son Publishers), Vol. III, pp. 126–127.

[54] Wright, "The Working" (1904), p. 975.

[55] Wright, "The Working of the Department of Labor," *Cosmopolitan*, June 1892, p. 236.

[56] House, Committee on Appropriations, *Hearings, Legislative, Executive, and Judicial Appropriations*, FY 1897 (54C, 1896), p. 83; ibid., FY 1903 (1902), p. 290.

[57] U.S. Commissioner of Labor, *First Annual Report, Industrial Depressions* (1886), pp. 290–293.

[58] Wright, "The Working," *Cosmopolitan*, p. 233.

[59] AFL, *Proceedings, 1887*, p. 9.

[60] Richmond Mayo-Smith, "The National Bureau of Labor and Industrial Depressions," *Political Science Quarterly*, September 1886, p. 441.

[61] Commissioner of Labor, *First Annual Report*, p. 291; Alvin H. Hansen, *Business Cycles and National Income* (New York: W.W. Norton & Co., Inc., 1951), pp. 64–65, 222–224.

[62] Commissioner of Labor, *Thirteenth Annual Report, Hand and Machine Labor* (1898), pp. 5–6.

[63] Macdonald, "Carroll D. Wright and His Influence on the BLS," *Monthly Labor Review*, January 1955, p. 8.

[64] *Locomotive Firemen's Magazine*, August 1896, pp. 99–100.

[65] *Locomotive Firemen's Magazine*, September 1903, pp. 457, 460–461.

[66] Senate, *A Report on Labor Disturbances in the State of Colorado, from 1880 to 1904, Inclusive* (Senate Doc. 122, 58C, 3S, 1905). Also, NARG 257, BLS, Letters Sent, May 17 to July 20, 1904, G. W. W. Hanger to President, June 15, 1904; and July 21 to Sept. 24, 1904, Wright to President, Sept. 8, 1904.

[67] Commissioner of Labor, *Eleventh Special Report, Regulation and Restriction of Output* (1904), p. 27.

[68] Clyde O. Fisher, *Use of Federal Power in Settlement of Railway Labor Disputes*, Bulletin 303 (Bureau of Labor Statistics, 1922), pp. 18–19.

[69] U. S. Strike Commission, *Report on the Chicago Strike of June–July, 1894* (1895), pp. 194–201.

[70] Ibid., p. 52.

[71] *American Federationist*, December 1894, p. 231.

[72] House, Committee on Labor, *Carriers Engaged in Interstate Commerce* (House Rept. 1754, 53C, 3S, 1895), Wright to L. E. McGann, Feb. 1, 1895, p. 4; *Locomotive Firemen's Magazine*, March 1895, p. 262.

[73] House, Labor, *Carriers* (1895), p. 4.

[74] *Congressional Record* (54C, 2S), Feb. 26, 1897, pp. 2388–2389.

[75] House, Committee on Labor, *Carriers Engaged in Interstate Commerce and Their Employees* (House Rept. 454, 55C, 2S, 1898), pp. 2–3.

[76] United Mine Workers of America *Journal*, Sept. 11, 1902, pp. 1, 2, 4.

[77] "Our Splendid Labor Commissioner," *Current Literature*, December 1902, p. 689; "Colonel Wright's Inconsistent Awards," *American Federationist*, November 1903, p. 1156; *UMWA Journal*, April 21, 1904, p. 4.

[78] Commissioner of Labor, *Fourth Annual Report, Working Women in Large Cities* (1888), p. 10.

[79] Ibid., pp. 70, 73.

[80] Association of Officials of Bureaus, *Proceedings, 1895*, p. 21.

[81] Commissioner of Labor, *Eleventh Annual Report, Work and Wages of Men, Women and Children* (1895–96); H. L. Bliss, "Eccentric Official Statistics, III," *American Journal of Sociology*, November 1897.

[82] Commissioner of Labor, *Seventeenth Annual Report, Trade and Technical Education* (1902), p. 10.

[83] *Congressional Record* (52C, 1S), May 20, 1892, p. 4474.

[84] Wright, *Relation of Political Economy*, p. 33.

[85] Commissioner of Labor, *Fourteenth Annual Report, Water, Gas, and Electric-Light Plants Under Private and Municipal Ownership* (1899), p. 7; Association of Officials of Bureaus, *Proceedings, 1902*, p. 77.

[86] Wright, "The Industrial Progress of the South," Association of Officials of Bureaus, *Proceedings, 1897*, pp. 116–117; Leiby, *Carroll Wright*, p. 107.

[87] NARG 257, BLS, Letters Sent, Jan. 2 to Feb. 26, 1901, Wright to Reuben S. Smith, Washington, D.C., Feb. 8, 1901.

[88] NARG 257, BLS, Letters Sent, Aug. 11 to Oct. 28, 1903, Wright to Du Bois, Aug. 24, 1903.

[89] Dorfman, *The Economic Mind*, pp. 350–351.

[90] John Higham, *Strangers in the Land* (New York: Atheneum, 1971), pp. 90–91.

[91] Senate, Committee on Finance, *Retail Prices and Wages* (Senate Rept. 986, 52C, 1S, 1892), p. I.

[92] 25 Stat. 183.

[93] Senate, Committee on Finance, *Retail Prices and Wages; and Wholesale Prices, Wages, and Transportation* (Senate Rept. 1394, 52C, 2S, 1893).

[94] "Retail Prices under the McKinley Act," *Quarterly Journal of Economics*, October 1892, p. 105; "Notes and Memoranda," *Quarterly Journal of Economics*, October 1893, p. 104; Frank W. Taussig, "Results of Recent Investigations on Prices in the United States," *ASA Journal*, December 1893, pp. 487–488; Mayo-Smith, *Science of Statistics*, part II, *Statistics and Economics* (New York: Columbia University Press, 1899), pp. 207, 316–317.

[95] Frederick C. Waite, *Prices and Wages* (Washington, 1894), pp. 7–12. An address delivered before the National Statistical Association at the Columbian University in November 1894.

[96] Roland P. Falkner, "Wholesale Prices: 1890 to 1899," *Bulletin* (27), March 1900, p. 270; Taussig, in "Notes and Memoranda," *Quarterly Journal of Economics*, May 1900, p. 432.

[97] "Course of Wholesale Prices, 1890 to 1901," *Bulletin* (39), March 1902, p. 234.

[98] Wesley C. Mitchell, "The Making and Using of Index Numbers," *Index Numbers of Wholesale Prices in the United States and Foreign Countries*, Bulletin 284 (Bureau of Labor Statistics, 1921), p. 127.

[99] Commissioner of Labor, *Eighteenth Annual Report, Cost of Living and Retail Prices of Food* (1903); "Retail Prices of Food, 1890 to 1904," *Bulletin* (59), July 1905.

[100] Commissioner of Labor, *Nineteenth Annual Report, Wages and Hours of Labor* (1904); "Wages and Cost of Living," *Bulletin* (53), July 1904, p. 703; "Wages and Hours of Labor in Manufacturing Industries, 1890 to 1904," *Bulletin* (59), July 1905, pp. 1–3; Harry M. Douty, *The Development of Wage Statistics in the United States* (Ithaca: Cornell University, New York State School of Industrial and Labor Relations, Bulletin No. 64, 1972), pp. 11, 18–19.

[101] "Wages and Cost Living," 1904, pp. 722–723; *The New York Times*, Aug. 8, 1904, p. 5; UMWA *Journal*, Dec. 29, 1904, p. 4; Amalgamated Meat Cutters and Butcher Workmen, *Official Journal*, August 1904, p. 22.

[102] International Association of Machinists, *Machinists' Monthly Journal*, September 1904, pp. 776–777, 823.

[103] Ernest Howard, "Inflation and Prices," *Political Science Quarterly*, March 1907, p. 81.

[104] Mitchell, "Methods of Presenting Statistics of Wages," ASA *Journal*, December 1905, pp. 328, 330; and "The Trustworthiness of the Bureau of Labor's Index Number of Wages," *Quarterly Journal of Economics*, May 1911, p. 613; National Civic Federation, *Monthly Review*, Sept. 15, 1904, p. 8.

[105] E. H. Phelps Brown and Margaret H. Browne, "Carroll D. Wright and the Development of British Labour Statistics," *Economica*, August 1963, pp. 279–280.

[106] Wright, "The Evolution of Wage Statistics," *Quarterly Journal of Economics*, January 1892, pp. 185–186; G.W.W. Hanger, "Bureaus of Statistics of Labor in Foreign Countries," *Bulletin* (54), September 1904, p. 1023.

[107] Great Britain, Royal Commission (c.7063.1), *Minutes of Evidence*, pp. 435–464.

[108] Brown and Browne, "Carroll D. Wright," p. 283; House, Committee on Labor, *Report, Bulletins of the Department of Labor* (House Rept. 1752, 53C, 3S, 1895), Wright to L. E. McGann, Feb. 1, 1895, p. 1.

[109] James Myers, "American Relations with the International Labor Office, 1919–1932," *Annals of the American Academy of Political and Social Science*, March 1933, p. 135.

[110] Hanger, "Bureaus of Statistics," pp. 1080–1086; *Historical Survey of International Action Affecting Labor*, Bulletin 268 (Bureau of Labor Statistics, 1920), pp. 54, 87, 89–90.

[111] Massachusetts, Committee on Relations Between Employer and Employee, *Report* (1904).

[112] Massachusetts, Commission on Industrial and Technical Education, *Report* (1906); Wright, "The Work of the National Society for the Promotion of Industrial Education," *Annals of the American Academy of Political and Social Science*, January 1909, p. 13.

[113] Wright, "The Working" (1904), pp. 987–989.

Chapter III. Charles Neill

[1] Theodore Roosevelt, *The Letters of Theodore Roosevelt*, selected and edited by Elting E. Morison and others (Cambridge: Harvard University Press, 1952), Vol. VI, p. 1301, to P. H. Grace, Oct. 19, 1908.

[2] U. S. President, *Message, Beginning of the First Session of the Fifty-ninth Congress* (Dec. 5, 1905), pp. 14–15.

[3] President, *Message, Beginning of the First Session of the Fifty-seventh Congress* (Dec. 3, 1901), pp. 10 and 12.

[4] President, *Message, Beginning of the Third Session of the Fifty-eighth Congress* (Dec. 6, 1904), p. 5.

[5] William Howard Taft Papers, Manuscript Division, Library of Congress, Charles P. Neill to Rudolph Forster, Assistant to Secretary to President, Sept. 12, 1911.

[6] U.S. Congress, House, Committee on Agriculture, *Hearings: Beveridge Amendment* (59C, 1S, 1906), pp. 94–95.

[7] George M. Kober, compiler, *Charitable and Reformatory Institutions in the District of Columbia* (69C, 2S, Senate Document 207, 1927), pp. 9–11, 20; Constance McLaughlin Green, *Washington, Capital City, 1879–1950* (Princeton: Princeton University Press, 1962), p. 73.

[8] Catholic University, Charles P. Neill Papers, Neill—Articles, Neill, "The Economic Evolution of Soceity," in "The Evolution of Industry" (Washington: The University Extension Committee, Civic Center Lectures, 1900); Green, *Washington*, p. 71; Walter F. Dodd, *The Government of the District of Columbia* (Washington: John Byrne & Co., 1909), p. 269.

[9] Roosevelt, Theodore *Roosevelt, An Autobiography* (New York: The Macmillan Co., 1919), p. 509; Richard G. Balfe, "Charles P. Neill and the United States Bureau of Labor," Ph.D. dissertation (University of Notre Dame, 1956), pp. 38–39.

[10] Balfe, "Charles P. Neill," p. 58; Catholic University, Neill Papers, Correspondence, 1895–1942, Edward A. Moseley to Marshall Cushing, Nov. 22, 1904; and *Review of Reviews*, January 1905, p. 9.

[11] National Conference of Charities and Correction, *Proceedings, 1901*, p. 376.

[12] Neill, "Standard of Living," *Charities and Commons*, July 22, 1905, pp. 942–943.

[13] Neill, "Child Labor at the National Capital," in *Annals of the American Academy of Political and Social Science*, March 1906, pp. 270 ff.; *Charities and Commons*,

Mar. 3, 1906, pp. 795 ff.; and National Child Labor Committee, *Child Labor, A Menace to Industry, Education, and Good Citizenship: Proceedings, 1906,* pp. 12 ff.

[14] Neill, "The Prospects of Industrial Peace," *Collier's Weekly,* Aug. 22, 1903, p. 9.

[15] Neill, "Some Ethical Aspects of the Labor Movement," in his *The Social Application of Religion* (Cincinnati: Jennings and Graham, 1908), pp. 69–70, 76, 83.

[16] *Review of Reviews,* July 1906, pp. 6–12; and William H. Harbaugh, *Power and Responsibility, The Life and Times of Theodore Roosevelt* (New York: Farrar, Straus and Cudahy, 1961), pp. 255–260.

[17] Roosevelt, *The Letters,* Vol. V, p. 190, to James Wilson, Secretary of Agriculture, Mar. 22, 1906; Theodore Roosevelt Papers, Manuscript Division, Library of Congress, Roosevelt to "My Dear Commissioner Neill," Mar. 22, 1906; Balfe, "Charles P. Neill," pp. 79–82.

[18] *Current Literature,* July 1906, pp. 1–9.

[19] U. S. Congress, House, Special Committee to Investigate the Conditions in the Stock Yards of Chicago, *Conditions in Chicago Stock Yards* (59C, 1S, House Doc. 873, 1906); House, Agriculture, *Hearings: Beveridge,* pp. 261–271.

[20] House, Agriculture, *Hearings: Beveridge,* p. 128.

[21] *Current Literature,* July 1906, p. 8.

[22] *American Federationist,* May 1906, pp. 293–296; Roosevelt, *The Letters,* Vol. V, pp. 190–191, to Frank Morrison, Mar. 22, 1906.

[23] Roosevelt, *The Letters,* Vol. V, pp. 379–380, to Neill, Aug. 21, 1906; Theodore Roosevelt Papers, Neill to the President, Aug. 16, 1906, and Press Release, Sept. 19, 1906; Taft Papers, Neill to Taft, Aug. 28, 1907.

[24] Amalgamated Meat Cutters and Butcher Workmen, *Butchers' Journal,* September and October 1906, p. 1.

[25] International Association of Machinists, *Machinists' Monthly Journal,* November 1906, p. 981.

[26] Roosevelt, *The Letters,* Vol. V, p. 323, to Neill, June 28, 1906; and Balfe, "Charles P. Neill," pp. 116–119.

[27] Naomi Wiener Cohen, *A Dual Heritage, The Public Career of Oscar S. Straus* (Philadelphia: The Jewish Publication Society of America, 1969), pp. 158–160; Oscar S. Straus Papers, Manuscript Division, Library of Congress, Correspondence, Roosevelt to Straus, Jan. 18, 1907.

[28] Straus Papers, Diary Materials, Vol. I, 1906–1907, p. 54, Mar. 12; Balfe, "Charles P. Neill," pp. 116–118.

[29] Taft Papers, Neill to Charles D. Hilles, Secretary to the President, Apr. 10, 1911; House, Committee on Appropriations, *Legislative, Executive, and Judicial Appropriation Bill for 1910, Hearings,* p. 12.

[30] American Federation of Labor, *Proceedings,* 1907, p. 40.

[31] U. S. Department of Commerce and Labor, *Labor Conference* (Washington: Government Printing Office, 1909), p. 26; Neill, "Distribution of Immigrants," *National Civic Federation Review,* March–April 1907, p. 10.

[32] Taft Papers, Neill to the President, Sept. 11, 1909.

[33] U. S. Commissioner of Labor, "Third Report of the Commissioner of Labor on Hawaii," *Bulletin* (66), September 1906, p. iii; and "Fourth Report of the Commissioner of Labor on Hawaii," *Bulletin* (94), May 1911, pp. 762–763.

[34] Selig Perlman and Philip Taft, *History of Labor in the United States, 1896–1932*, Vol. IV, *Labor Movements* (New York: The Macmillan Co., 1935), pp. 262–265; *The New York Times*, Sept. 7, 1909, p. 1, and Sept. 11, 1909, p. 1.

[35] AFL, *Proceedings, 1909*, p. 209.

[36] Perlman and Taft, *Labor Movements*, pp. 139–143; Taft Papers, Neill to the President, Sept. 11, 1909, and Taft to Neill, Sept. 13, 1909.

[37] U.S. Bureau of Labor, *Report on Strike at Bethlehem Steel Works, South Bethlehem, Pennsylvania* (61C, 2S, Senate Doc. 521, 1910), pp. 10–16.

[38] IAM, *Monthly Journal*, June 1910, p. 499; *The New York Times*, May 12, 1910, p. 9.

[39] Bureau of Labor, *Report on Conditions of Employment in the Iron and Steel Industry* (62C, 1S, Senate Doc. 110).

[40] IAM, *Monthly Journal*, September 1911, p. 836.

[41] "Report on Wages and Hours in the Iron and Steel Industry, Issued by the U. S. Bureau of Labor," *American Federationist*, March 1912, p. 227; Samuel Gompers, *Seventy Years of Life and Labor* (New York: E. P. Dutton, 1925), Vol. II, pp. 129–130.

[42] Bureau of Labor, *Report on the Miners' Strike in Bituminous Coal Field in Westmoreland County, Pa. in 1910–11* (62C, 2S, House Doc. 847, 1912), pp. 5–10, 14–18.

[43] Bureau of Labor, *Report on Strike of Textile Workers in Lawrence, Mass. in 1912* (62C, 2S, Senate Doc. 870, 1912), pp. 7–9; House, Committee on Rules, *The Strike at Lawrence, Mass., Hearings* (62C, 2S, 1912), p. 3.

[44] Balfe, "Charles P. Neill," p. 150.

[45] *Survey*, Dec. 30, 1911, p. 1407; Jan. 13, 1912, p. 1563; Mar. 9, 1912, p. 1898; President, *Message Concerning the Work of the Interior Department and Other Matters* (Feb. 2, 1912), pp. 11, 12; House, Committee on Labor, *Hearings: Industrial Commission* (62C, 2S, 1912), pp. 25–26.

[46] Timothy Shea, "The Southern Pacific Strike," Brotherhood of Locomotive Firemen and Enginemen, *Locomotive Firemen and Enginemen's Magazine*, February 1907, p. 265.

[47] House, Committee on Interstate and Foreign Commerce, *The Erdman Act, Hearings on Amendments* (62C, 2S, 1912), p. 38; Samuel P. Orth, "The Battle Line of Labor," *The World's Work*, November 1912, p. 60.

[48] Martin A. Knapp, "Government Mediation in Railroad Labor Disputes," National Civic Federation, *Proceedings, 1912*, pp. 29, 31.

[49] Dept. of Commerce and Labor, *Reports, 1912*, pp. 15–16; Neill, "Mediation and Arbitration of Railway Labor Disputes in the United States," *Bulletin* (98), January 1912, p. 26.

[50] House, Committee on Interstate and Foreign Commerce, *Erdman Act* (1912), pp. 21, 42.

[51] Frederick L. Hoffman, "Industrial Accidents," *Bulletin* (78), September 1908, p. 417.

[52] National Safety Council, *Transactions, 1912*, pp. 3–8; and *1913*, pp. 75–79 and 101–103.

[53] International Association for Labor Legislation, *Report of the 5th General Meeting, Lucerne, 1908*, Appendix No. 1, "Report of the Board," p. 47.

[54] National Archives Record Group 40, Dept. of Commerce, Office of the Secretary, Secretary Cortelyou to Dr. H. Scherrer, President, International Association for Labor Legislation, May 2, 1904.

[55] John B. Andrews, "Phosphorus Poisoning in the Match Industry in the United States," *Bulletin* (86), January 1910, pp. 31, 145–146; House, Committee on Interstate and Foreign Commerce, *Hearings: Health Activities of the General Government* (61C, 2S, 1910), pt. VI, p. 408.

[56] NARG 40, Dept. of Commerce, Office of the Secretary, Nagel to Neill, Apr. 21, 1910.

[57] *Survey*, June 11, 1910, p. 427; Dec. 23, 1911, p. 1397; NARG 40, Dept. of Commerce, Office of the Secretary, Taft to Nagel, May 16, 1910, and P. Tecumseh Sherman to Neill, May 27, 1910; and Don D. Lescohier, *Working Conditions*, Vol. III of *History of Labor in the United States, 1896–1932* (New York: The Macmillan Company, 1935), pp. 361–362.

[58] *Survey*, Apr. 13, 1912, p. 86; and Lescohier, *Working Conditions*, p. 362.

[59] International Association for Labor Legislation, *Report, Lugano, 1910*, p. 14; Andrews, "Report of Work: 1910, American Association for Labor Legislation," *American Labor Legislation Review*, January 1911, pp. 96–98.

[60] AFL, *Proceedings, 1910*, pp. 41 and 274.

[61] Isaac M. Rubinow, "Accident Compensation for Federal Employees," *Survey*, Aug. 16, 1913, pp. 624–627.

[62] NARG 257, BLS, General Letter Book, Vol. I, Jan. 3, 1905–May 16, 1905, p. 303, Neill to Lawrence O. Murray, Mar. 21, 1905; Vol. III, Oct. 28, 1905–May 5, 1906, pp. 209–210, Neill to Sophonisba P. Breckinridge, Jan. 29, 1906; and House, Appropriations, *Legislative, Executive, and Judicial Bill for 1907, Hearings* (Feb. 24, 1906), pp. 622–623.

[63] House, Appropriations, *LEJ for 1907*, p. 621.

[64] Roosevelt Papers, ca. Jan. 15, 1907, C. P. Neill, "Memo on Child Labor."

[65] House, Appropriations, *LEJ for 1907*, p. 617; *Congressional Record* (59C, 2S), Jan. 21, 1907, p. 1458.

[66] House, Appropriations, *LEJ for 1907*, pp. 617–618.

[67] *Congressional Record* (59C, 2S), Jan. 21, 1907, pp. 1457–1458.

[68] Balfe, "Charles P. Neill," p. 130.

[69] Roosevelt, *The Letters*, Vol. V, pp. 594–595, to Oscar S. Straus, Feb. 20, 1907.

[70] NARG 40, Dept. of Commerce, Office of the Secretary, Straus to Tawney, Feb. 21, 1907.

[71] *The New York Commercial*, May 22, 1907, p. 1, quoted in Balfe, "Charles P. Neill," p. 133.

[72] National Child Labor Committee, *Third Annual Report, 1907*, p. 11; *American Federation of Labor Records: The Samuel Gompers Era* (Microfilming Corporation of America, 1979), Convention Files, 1909 Convention, Res. 67, Woman and Child Labor, Gompers to Executive Council, Dec. 21, 1909.

[73] Bureau of Labor, *Report on Conditions of Woman and Child Wage-Earners in the United States* (61C, 2S, Senate Doc. 645), Vol. I, Cotton Textile Industry (1910), pp. 14–15, 192–195.

Source Notes

[74] Catholic University, Neill Papers, Bureau of Labor Data, Mary McDowell to Neill, Sept. 28, 1907.

[75] *Summary of the Report on Condition of Woman and Child Wage Earners in the United States*, Bulletin 175 (Bureau of Labor Statistics, 1915), p. 32.

[76] Ibid., pp. 28–29.

[77] *Report on Condition*, Vol. XVI, *Family Budgets of Typical Cotton-Mill Workers* (1911), p. 9.

[78] Ibid., pp. 25, 133–137, and 178.

[79] Thomas R. Dawley, Jr., *The Child that Toileth Not, The Story of a Government Investigation* (New York: Gracia Publishing Co., 1912); Daniel J. B. Mitchell, "A Furor Over Working Children and the Bureau of Labor," *Monthly Labor Review*, October 1975, pp. 34–36.

[80] Judson MacLaury, "A Senator's Reaction to Report on Working Women and Children," MLR, October 1975, pp. 36–38; *Congressional Record* (62C, 3S), Jan. 24, 1912, p. 1249, and Feb. 26, 1912, p. 2438.

[81] NARG 174, Dept. of Labor, Charges vs. Chas. P. Neill, Original Transcript, Mar. 15, 1913, pp. 36–41.

[82] Ibid., p. 30.

[83] *Congressional Record* (62C, 3S), Jan. 24, 1912, p. 1249.

[84] "More Reports Needed," *Survey*, Aug. 5, 1911, p. 638.

[85] Warren M. Persons, "Recent Publications on Women in Industry," *Quarterly Journal of Economics*, May 1911, pp. 601, 602, 608.

[86] AFL, *Proceedings, 1911*, p. 35.

[87] "Seventh Annual Report, 1911," *Child Labor Bulletin*, June 1912, p. 200.

[88] NARG 174, Dept. of Labor, Charges vs. Chas. P. Neill, Original Transcript, p. 44.

[89] Ibid., p. 48.

[90] Ibid., pp. 46–51; *Retail Prices, 1890 to 1911*, Bulletin 105, part 1 (Bureau of Labor, 1912), p. 4; *Retail Prices, 1907 to December 1914*, Bulletin 156 (Bureau of Labor Statistics, 1915), p. 359.

[91] *Retail Prices*, Bulletin 105, pp. 4–6; *Retail Prices, 1890 to June 1912*, Bulletin 106 (Bureau of Labor, 1912), pp. 5–6; *The Consumer Price Index, History and Techniques*, Bulletin 1517 (Bureau of Labor Statistics, 1966), p. 2.

[92] NARG 174, Dept. of Labor, Charges vs. Chas. P. Neill, Original Transcript, p. 51.

[93] Ibid., pp. 51–52.

[94] NARG 40, Dept. of Commerce, Committee on Statistical Reorganization, "Replies to the Questions of the Interdepartmental Statistical Committee," p. 7.

[95] NARG 257, BLS, General Correspondence, 1908–15, probably by Neill in January 1910.

[96] NARG 40, Dept. of Commerce, Office of the Secretary, Assistant Secretary and Solicitor to Secretary, Dec. 13, 1909.

[97] NARG 174, Dept. of Labor, Charges vs. Chas. P. Neill, Exhibits, Exhibit A, Geo. A. Traylor to Sen. Lee S. Overman, Mar. 3, 1913, with "Summary of Charges Preferred Against Charles P. Neill."

[98] NARG 174, Dept. of Labor, Charles P. Neill, William S. Waudby to William B. Wilson, Mar. 11, 1913.

[99] NARG 174, Dept. of Labor, Charges vs. Chas. P. Neill, Tillman to W. B. Wilson, Mar. 8, 1913; and Neill, Overman to President, Mar. 21, 1913.

[100] NARG 174, Dept. of Labor, Charges vs. Chas. P. Neill, Report, "preliminary" dated Mar. 20, 1913, and "final" dated Mar. 27, 1913.

[101] *AFL Records* (MCA), Executive Council Records, Minutes, Jan. 22, 1913, p. 42; NARG 174, Dept. of Labor, Neill, A. B. Garretson, telegram to W. B. Wilson, Mar. 7, 1913.

[102] NARG 174, Dept. of Labor, Neill, editorial, *Washington Times*, Mar. 11, 1913.

[103] Ibid., A. J. McKelway, telegram to President, Mar. 11, 1913; National Child Labor Committee, *Proceedings, 1913*, p. 155.

[104] Taft Papers, President to Sen. Borah, Feb. 27, 1913.

[105] NARG 174, Dept. of Labor, Neill, Ralph M. Easley, telegram to W. B. Wilson, Mar. 6, 1913.

[106] Ibid., Clinton Alvord, President, Worcester Loom Company, to the President, Mar. 15, 1913.

[107] Woodrow Wilson Papers, Manuscript Division, Library of Congress, Wilson to B. R. Tillman, Mar. 21, 1913; NARG 174, Dept. of Labor, Neill, Commission, dated Mar. 22, 1913.

[108] Woodrow Wilson Papers, Tillman to Wilson, Mar. 24, 1913; Catholic University, Neill Papers, Correspondence re Charges, B. R. Tillman to Prof. D. D. Wallace, Mar. 13, 1913; NARG 174, Dept. of Labor, Neill, James M. Barker, Secretary, Senate, May 1, 1913.

[109] *The New York Times*, May 14, 1913, p. 2; NARG 174, Dept. of Labor, Neill, Neill to the President, May 12, 1913, and Neill to the Secretary of the same date.

[110] NARG 174, Dept. of Labor, Neill, Secretary to Neill, May 14, 1913.

[111] Isaac F. Marcosson, *Metal Magic, The Story of the American Smelting & Refining Company* (New York: Farrar, Straus and Company, 1949), p. 264.

[112] National Civic Federation, *National Civic Federation Review*, Dec. 1, 1913, p. 2.

[113] Marguerite Green, *The National Civic Federation and the American Labor Movement, 1900–1925* (Washington: The Catholic University of America Press, 1956), pp. 456, 457; *Review of Reviews*, November 1922, p. 467.

[114] Anthracite Board of Conciliation, *Addresses by John L. Lewis and J. B. Warriner at 50th Anniversary Dinner*, delivered Oct. 1, 1953 (Hazleton, Pennsylvania), pp. 16, 19.

[115] Catholic University, Neill Papers, Correspondence, 1895–1942, Supreme Court of the District of Columbia to Dr. Charles P. Neill, Jan. 9, 1920.

[116] John O'Grady, *Catholic Charities in the United States, History and Problems* (Washington: National Conference of Catholic Charities, 1930), pp. 336–338 and 340–341.

Chapter IV.   Royal Meeker

[1] Royal Meeker, "The Relation of Workmen's Compensation to Old Age, Health, and Unemployment Insurance," International Association of Industrial Accident Boards and Commissions, *Proceedings, 1916*, Bulletin 210 (Bureau of Labor Statistics, 1917), p. 248.

[2] Woodrow Wilson Papers, Manuscript Division, Library of Congress, Meeker to Wilson, May 10, 1905; Wilson to Meeker, Sept. 13, 1911, and Jan. 3, 1912; and National Archives Record Group 174, Dept. of Labor, Meeker, Meeker to W. B. Wilson, Aug. 21, 1913, and Aug. 28, 1913.

[3] Wilson Papers, Wilson to Meeker, Dec. 3, 1912; Meeker to the President, Mar. 21, 1913; and the President to Meeker, Mar. 26, 1913; also Ray Stannard Baker, *Woodrow Wilson, Life and Letters: President, 1913–1914* (Garden City, New York: Doubleday, Doran & Co., Inc., 1931), pp. 146–147.

[4] Wilson Papers, President to Meeker, June 23, 1913.

[5] *The New York Times*, July 23, 1913, p. 6; NARG 257, Bureau of Labor Statistics, General Correspondence, 1908–15, C. H. Verrill to Mrs. Elizabeth L. Otey, Oct. 10, 1913.

[6] NARG 174, Dept. of Labor, Meeker, Meeker to W. B. Wilson, June 23, 1913.

[7] Ibid., Meeker to W. B. Wilson, July 7, 1913; Wilson Papers, President to Meeker, June 23, 1913.

[8] Meeker, "The Promise of American Life," *Political Science Quarterly*, December 1910, pp. 689, 695, 697, 699.

[9] Meeker, "The Work of the Federal Bureau of Labor Statistics in Its Relation to the Business of the Country," *Annals of the American Academy of Political and Social Science*, January 1916, pp. 265 and 271.

[10] Ibid., pp. 263 and 265.

[11] Ibid., p. 264.

[12] Meeker, "Address," *Proceedings of the American Association of Public Employment Offices*, Bulletin 192 (Bureau of Labor Statistics, 1916), pp. 42–47.

[13] U. S. Congress, Joint Committees on Labor, *Hearings, National Employment System* (66C, 1S, 1919), pp. 326, 333.

[14] Meeker, "Social Insurance in the Untied States," National Conference of Social Work, *Proceedings, 1917*, pp. 528, 534–535; comments, *Proceedings of the Conference on Social Insurance*, Bulletin 212 (Bureau of Labor Statistics, 1917), p. 912; and "Distributing the Burden of Sickness," *American Labor Legislation Review*, June 1918, p. 158.

[15] Meeker, comments, *Proceedings of the Conference on Social Insurance* (212), pp. 911–912.

[16] Congress, House, Appropriations Committee, *Legislative, Executive, and Judicial Appropriation Bill, 1915, Hearings*, p. 770; Meeker, "Lacks in Workmen's Compensation," *American Labor Legislation Review*, March 1919, pp. 35, 39–44; "Social Insurance," National Conference, *Proceedings, 1917*, pp. 531–533; and "The Relation of Workmen's Compensation," pp. 245–247.

[17] Meeker, "Minimum Requirements in Compensation Legislation," IAIABC, *Proceedings, 1919*, Bulletin 273 (Bureau of Labor Statistics, 1920), p. 14 (also in *Monthly Labor Review*, November 1919, pp. 280 ff).

[18] Senate, Committee on the District of Columbia, *Hearings, Child Labor in the District of Columbia* (66C, 2S, 1920), pp. 59, 61.

[19] Meeker, "Compulsory Civic Service," *The New York Times*, Apr. 6, 1913, V, 4.

[20] Meeker, "The Connection of Our School System and Our Prison System," n.d., pp. 5–6.

[21] Meeker, "Compulsory Civic Service."

[22] Meeker, "A Plan for More Effective Cooperation Between State and Federal Labor Offices," Association of Governmental Labor Officials of the United States and Canada, *Proceedings, 1915*, p. 83; "The Promise of American Life," p. 697.

[23] Meeker, "Employees' Representation in Management of Industry," *American Economic Review*, March 1920 (Supplement), pp. 96 and 101.

[24] NARG 174, Dept. of Labor, Department Committee on Correlation, Minutes of Meeting, Apr. 1, 1914, p. 2; Intermediate Report No. 2, May 28, 1914, p. 2; Memorandum, W. B. Wilson, Secretary, Aug. 14, 1914.

[25] Senate, *Report, Bureau of Labor Safety* (Senate Rept. 712, 63C, 2S, 1914); House, Committee on Labor, *Report, Bureau of Labor Safety* (House Rept. 44, 64C, 1S, 1916), p. 1; NARG 174, Dept. of Labor, Bureau of Labor Safety, "Activities of the Federal Government Along the Lines of Safety and Sanitation," apparently by F. H. Bird, marked C. M. E. 12.15.14.

[26] NARG 174, Dept. of Labor, Bureau of Labor Safety, Secretary to Rep. David J. Lewis of Maryland, Aug. 27, 1913.

[27] NARG 174, Dept. of Labor, Women's Bureau, Secretary to Miss Agnes Nestor of National Women's Trade Union League, May 24, 1916: Miss Zip S. Falk to the Secretary, July 19, 1916; Edith Abbott, review, *Summary of the Report on Condition of Woman and Child Wage Earners in the United States* (that is, Bull. 175, 1916), *American Economic Review*, September 1916, pp. 663–664.

[28] NARG 174, Dept. of Labor, Women's Bureau, Stewart to Secretary, June 27, 1916, transmitted by Secretary to Rep. Lewis, June 28.

[29] NARG 174, Dept. of Labor, Women's Bureau, Secretary to Rep. Lewis, July 26, 1916.

[30] House, Committee on Labor, *Woman's Division in Department of Labor* (House Rept. 1205, 64C, 2S, 1916), pp. 3–4.

[31] NARG 257, BLS, General Correspondence, 1916–24, Meeker to Mary Van Kleeck, Dec. 15, 1916.

[32] House, Appropriations, *LEJ for 1918*, p. 495; Joint Committees on Labor, *Hearings, Women's Bureau* (66C, 2S, 1920), p. 40.

[33] Wilson Papers, Meeker to Tumulty, Oct. 20, 1913.

[34] House, Appropriations, *LEJ for 1915*, p. 750; Wilson Papers, Meeker to President, Aug. 15, 1914; Senate, Appropriations, *LEJ for 1916*, p. 227.

[35] NARG 174, Dept. of Labor, Dept. Committee on Correlation, Stewart, "Report on Jurisdictional Conflict Between the Bureau of Labor Statistics and the Public Health Service, A Bureau in the Treasury Department," pp. 1, 7, 14; Advisory

Council, Meeker, for the Secretary, June 24, 1918; Senate, Appropriations, *LEJ for 1916*, p. 228.

[36] Wilson Papers, Meeker to Tumulty, Feb. 4 and Feb. 6, 1914.

[37] NARG 174, Dept. of Labor, Child Labor Law, Stewart to Secretary, Sept. 12, 1916.

[38] Wilson Papers, Meeker to President, Feb. 16, 1915.

[39] U. S. Dept. of Labor, *Report Relating to Section 10 of Act Creating the Department of Labor* (64C, 2S, House Document 1906, 1917).

[40] Meeker, "Address," National Safety Council, *Proceedings, 1914*, p. 76; comments, "The Statistical Work of the United States Government," *American Economic Review*, March 1915 (Supp.), p. 173.

[41] Meeker, "A Plan for More Effective Cooperation," p. 80.

[42] Meeker, "Introduction," IAIABC, *Proceedings, 1916* (210), p. 6.

[43] Meeker, "Address," *American Association of Public Employment Offices* (192), pp. 46–47.

[44] Meeker, comments, "The Statistical Work," p. 174.

[45] *Retail Prices, 1907 to December 1914*, Bulletin 156 (Bureau of Labor Statistics, 1915), pp. 357, 364.

[46] Irving Fisher, assisted by Harry G. Brown, *The Purchasing Power of Money* (New York: Macmillan Co., 1913), pp. 203, 228; Wesley C. Mitchell, "The Making and Using of Index Numbers," Bulletin 173 (Bureau of Labor Statistics, 1915), pp. 112–113.

[47] Meeker, "On the Best Form of Index Number," *American Statistical Association Journal*, September 1921, p. 915.

[48] Senate, Appropriations, *LEJ for 1915*, p. 92; Wilson Papers, Meeker to President, Mar. 23, and July 8, 1914.

[49] NARG 174, Dept. of Labor, Stewart to Secretary, Jan. 9, 1914; Senate Appropriations, *LEJ for 1916*, p. 185; *Union Scale of Wages and Hours of Labor, May 1, 1915*, Bulletin 194 (Bureau of Labor Statistics, 1916), p. 222; House, Appropriations, *Further Urgent Deficiency Bill, FY 1916* (64C, 1S, 1916), p. 240.

[50] House, Appropriations, *LEJ for 1915*, pp. 741, 743.

[51] Senate, Committee on Education and Labor, *Report, Cost of Living in the District of Columbia* (Senate Rept. 377, 63C, 2S, 1914), pp. 1–2.

[52] House, Committee on the District of Columbia, *Hearing, Authorizing and Directing the Department of Labor to Make an Inquiry into the Cost of Living in the District of Columbia* (64C, 1S, 1916), p. 25.

[53] House, Committee on the District of Columbia, *Hearings, Minimum Wage for Women and Children* (65C, 2S, 1918), p. 14.

[54] "Cost of Living in the District of Columbia, Second Article: Summary of Family Expenditures," MLR, November 1917, p. 2; "Cost of Living in the District of Columbia, Fourth Article: Wage-Earning Women, Who They Are and What They Do." MLR, January 1918, p. 7; William F. Ogburn, "Analysis of the Standard of Living in the District of Columbia in 1916," *ASA Journal*, June 1919, p. 389.

[55] International Association on Unemployment, *Reports, Ghent: Statistics of Unemployment*, pp. 83–84.

[56] American Federation of Labor Papers, Samuel Gompers Letterbooks, Manuscript Division, Library of Congress, Gompers to Meeker, Sept. 9 and Sept. 12, 1914.

[57] House, Appropriations, *LEJ for 1915*, p. 759.

[58] "Committee to Deal with Unemployment," *Survey*, Dec. 12, 1914, p. 281; "New York's Program for Unemployment," *Survey*, Dec. 26, 1914, p. 329; *Unemployment in New York City, New York*, Bulletin 172 (Bureau of Labor Statistics, 1915), pp. 6–8.

[59] *Unemployment in the United States*, Bulletin 195 (Bureau of Labor Statistics, 1916), p. 6; NARG 257, BLS, General Correspondence, 1908–15, Shillady to Stewart, July 7, 1915.

[60] Meeker, "The Work," *Annals*, January 1916, p. 268; "A Problem in Eclipse," *The Annalist*, Jan. 3, 1916, p. 9.

[61] House, Committee on Labor, *Hearings, National Employment Bureau* (64C, 1S, 1916), pp. 29–30; *Proceedings of the Conference on Social Insurance* (212, 1917), p. 838.

[62] Meeker, "The Cost of Industrial Accidents," MLR, April 1920, p. 9.

[63] Stewart, "Informal Remarks," *Proceedings of the Conference of Employment Managers' Association of Boston, Mass., Held May 10, 1916*, Bulletin 202 (Bureau of Labor Statistics, 1916), p. 8.

[64] Meeker, "The Work," *Annals*, January 1916, p. 267.

[65] Meeker, "Introduction," *Proceedings of Employment Managers' Conference*, Bulletin 196 (Bureau of Labor Statistics, 1916), p. 5.

[66] Meeker, "Introduction," *Proceedings of the Employment Managers' Conference, Philadelphia, Pa., April 2 and 3, 1917*, Bulletin 227 (Bureau of Labor Statistics, 1917), p. 5.

[67] Wilson Papers, Meeker to President, Mar. 3, 1916.

[68] House, Committee on the Judiciary, *Hearings, Federal Employees' Compensation* (63C, 2S, 1914), p. 19; *Hearings, Federal Employees' Compensation* (64C, 1S, 1916), pp. 29–30; Dept . of Labor, *Reports of the Department of Labor, 1915*, pp. 97–98; Wilson Papers, Meeker to President, Nov. 15, 1915.

[69] Wilson Papers, Meeker to Tumulty, Feb. 6, 1914.

[70] Meeker, "Introduction," IAIABC, *Proceedings, 1916* (210), p. 5; *Report of Committee on Statistics and Compensation Insurance Cost*, Bulletin 201 (Bureau of Labor Statistics, 1916), pp. 8–9; Dept. of Labor, *Reports of the Department of Labor, 1916*, pp. 146–147.

[71] Dept. of Labor, *Reports of the Department of Labor, 1917*, p. 167.

[72] Meeker, "The Cost of Industrial Accidents," p. 4.

[73] Joseph Dorfman, *The Economic Mind in American Civilization*, Vol. III, 1865–1918 (New York: Viking Press, 1949), p. 477.

[74] NARG 1, War Labor Policies Board, War Industries Board, Memorandum Regarding Conference on Industrial Survey, Oct. 5, 1918; Bernard M. Baruch, *American Industry in the War, A Report of the War Industries Board* (Washington: Government Printing Office, 1921), p. 45.

[75] NARG 1, WLPB, Committees, Statistics Committee, Meetings of June 5, 13, and 19, 1918; Bureau of Labor Statistics, etc., Frankfurter to Gay, June 29, 1918; and

Zenos L. Potter, "The Central Bureau of Planning and Statistics," ASA *Journal*, March 1919, pp. 275–276.

[76] Willard E. Hotchkiss and Henry R. Seager, *History of the Shipbuilding Labor Adjustment Board, 1917 to 1919*, Bulletin 283 (Bureau of Labor Statistics, 1921), p. 10.

[77] George E. Barnett, "Index Numbers of the Total Cost of Living," *Quarterly Journal of Economics*, February 1921, p. 241.

[78] Wilson Papers, Fisher to Meeker, Oct. 7, Oct. 24, Nov. 1, Nov. 9, Nov. 12, Nov. 22, and Dec. 11, 1912; Fisher, "A Compensated Dollar," *Quarterly Journal of Economics*, February 1913, pp. 214, 220–221.

[79] NARG 174, Dept. of Labor, Fisher to Post, May 15, 1917; Meeker to Assistant Secretary, July 21, 1917.

[80] Wilson Papers, Meeker to President, Nov. 27, 1917; Nov. 28, 1917; Dec. 1, 1917 with initials "WW" dated Dec. 5, 1917; and May 8, 1919; NARG 257, BLS, Appropriations Ledger, 1913–19.

[81] Hotchkiss and Seager, *History* (283,1921), pp. 24, 33, 39, and 44; U. S. Shipbuilding Labor Adjustment Board, *Decision as to Wages, Hours and Other Conditions in Pacific Coast Shipyards* (Oct. 1, 1918), pp. 1, 3, 5–6.

[82] NARG 174, Dept. of Labor, Seager to Post, Feb. 27, 1918.

[83] *National War Labor Board*, Bulletin 287 (Bureau of Labor Statistics, 1921), pp. 31–33.

[84] NARG 174, Dept. of Labor, Wage Stabilization Conferences, Secretary to President, Aug. 7, 1918; Secretary to John R. Alpine, Acting President, AFL, Sept. 13, 1918; and Frankfurter to Secretary, Oct. 15, 1918.

[85] Meeker, "The Possibility of Compiling an Index of the Cost of Living," *American Economic Review*, March 1919 (Supp.), pp. 109–115.

[86] Meeker, "What Is the American Standard of Living?" National Conference of Social Work, *Proceedings, 1919*, p. 165.

[87] Ibid., p. 172.

[88] "The American Standard," editorial, *The New York Times*, Oct. 29, 1919, p. 12.

[89] Hugh S. Hanna, "Summary of Increased Cost of Living, July 1914 to June 1919," MLR, October 1919, pp. 989–996; "Index Numbers of Changes in Wages and Cost of Living," MLR, November 1919, pp. 191–193; "Changes in Cost of Living in the United States," MLR, June 1920, pp. 76–79.

[90] Barnett, "A Critique of Cost-of-Living Studies," ASA *Journal*, September 1921, p. 909.

[91] Meeker, "What Is the American Standard?" National Conference, *Proceedings, 1919*, pp. 164–165; "Need for and Uses of a Standard Minimum Quantity Budget," National Conference of Social Work, *Proceedings, 1920*, p. 83.

[92] House, Congressional Joint Commission on Reclassification of Salaries, *Report* (66C, 2S, 1920, House Rept. 686), pp. 40–41, 178–179, 196.

[93] "Tentative Quantity-Cost Budget Necessary to Maintain Family of Five in Washington, D.C.," MLR, December 1919, pp. 22–25; "Quantity-Cost Budget Necessary to Maintain Single Man or Woman in Washington, D.C.," MLR, January 1920, pp. 35 ff.

[94] "Minimum Quantity Budget Necessary to Maintain a Worker's Family of Five in Health and Decency," MLR, June 1920, pp. 1–18.

[95] Dept. of Labor, *Annual Report, 1920*, p. 263.

[96] U. S. President, *Address, The Cost of Living* (Aug. 8, 1919), p. 8; Senate, *Secretary of the Treasury, Letter: Estimate of Appropriation to Investigate Cost of Living* (Senate Rept. 108, 66C, 1S, 1919), p. 2; NARG 174, Dept. of Labor, Monthly Report of Bureau, Louis F. Post, Memorandum for the Secretary, Sept. 27, 1919.

[97] NARG 1, WLPB, War Industries Board, Meeker and Lamson, "Memorandum in re the Need for More Complete Wage Statistics," Oct. 28, 1918.

[98] Ibid., Secretary of Labor and Chairman, War Industries Board, to President, Nov. 4, 1918, and Meeker to Secretary, Nov. 5, 1918; Bureau of Labor Statistics, etc., Meeker to Gay, Nov. 26, 1918.

[99] *Industrial Survey in Selected Industries in the United States, 1919, A Preliminary Report*, Bulletin 265 (Bureau of Labor Statistics, 1920), pp. 5, 24.

[100] W. C. Mitchell, comments, "The Statistical Work," *American Economic Review*, March 1915 (Supp.), p. 182.

[101] House, Appropriations, *LEJ for 1918*, pp. 490–491.

[102] NARG 257, BLS, General Correspondence, 1916–1924, Stewart to Hon. Reed Smoot, Feb. 15, 1917.

[103] House, Appropriations, *LEJ for 1919*, pp. 1011–1013; *LEJ for 1920*, p. 589.

[104] *Survey*, Mar. 27, 1920, p. 798.

[105] House, Committee on Reform in the Civil Service, *Hearing, Retirement of Employees in the Federal Classified Service* (64C, 1S, 1916), pp. 7–8.

[106] NARG 257, BLS, General Correspondence, 1916–1924, Meeker to Senate Committee on Appropriations, Jan. 22, 1919.

[107] "Introductory," MLR, July 1915, p. 6.

[108] *The Official Bulletin*, July 8, 1918, p. 9; NARG 174, Dept. of Labor, Secretary's Cabinet, Meeker, Memorandum for the Secretary, Aug. 10, 1918; Bureau of Labor Statistics, 1916–21, Secretary, Memo for the Commissioner, Oct. 5, 1918.

[109] NARG 257, BLS, General Correspondence, 1916–1924, Meeker to Secretary, May 15, 1920; Meeker, "Announcement," MLR, July 1920, p. ii.

[110] NARG 174, Dept. of Labor, Meeker to Secretary, May 24, 1919.

[111] Dept. of Labor, *Reports of the Department of Labor, 1919*, pp. 216–217.

[112] House, Appropriations, *LEJ for 1922*, p. 1275.

[113] Wilson Papers, Meeker to President, May 5, 1920; Meeker to President, June 16, 1920.

[114] Wilson Papers, W. Wilson to Meeker, June 19, 1920.

[115] "Announcement," MLR, August 1920, p. II.

Chapter V. Ethelbert Stewart

[1] Chester McA. Destler, "A Coffin Worker and the Labor Problem, Ethelbert Stewart and Henry Demarest Lloyd," *Labor History*, Summer 1971.

[2] National Archives Record Group 174, Department of Labor, Chief Clerk's File, Louis F. Post, Assistant Secretary, to All Officers and Employees of the Bureau of

Source Notes

Immigration and Immigration Service in the Department of Labor, Mar. 11, 1920, and various correspondence between Post and Stewart in March and April 1920.

[3] Warren G. Harding Papers, Manuscript Division, Library of Congress, Ohio Historical Society Microfilm, James J. Davis to the President, Mar. 17, 1921.

[4] Ethelbert Stewart Papers, University of North Carolina, Southern Historical Collection (Microfilm), General Correspondence, Apr. 22, 1927; James J. Davis Papers, Manuscript Division, Library of Congress, "Introductory Statement of Secretary of Labor James J. Davis before the Meeting of the Advisory Committee on Employment Statistics, Oct. 22, 1930."

[5] Stewart, "The Value of Labor Statistics," International Association of Governmental Labor Officials, Proceedings, 1918, pp. 64–65.

[6] Gilbert E. Hyatt, "A Human Statistician," The Locomotive Engineers Journal, January 1927, p. 17.

[7] Stewart Papers, Speeches and Essays, Undated, "Cost of Living For What?" pp. 4, 6.

[8] Stewart, "The Value," IAGLO, Proceedings, 1918, pp. 62–63; "The Future of Labor Statistics," IAGLO, Proceedings, 1921, pp. 15, 19, 21.

[9] NARG 257, Bureau of Labor Statistics, Correspondence with Secretary of Labor, 1925-27, 1929, Commissioner, Memo for Secretary, Aug. 8, 1929.

[10] Stewart, "Need for Statistics as a Measure of Industrial Changes," American Federationist, January 1930, pp. 89–90.

[11] Stewart, "The Value," p. 64; "The Wastage of Men," IAGLO, Proceedings, 1924 (also Monthly Labor Review, July 1924), p. 4; Stewart Papers, Speeches and Essays, Undated, "The Wage System and the Interest System," pp. 3–4.

[12] Stewart, "Occupational Diseases and Workmen's Compensation Laws," MLR, February 1930, p. 95.

[13] Stewart, "Long Working Hours of Certain Municipal Employees," MLR, August 1929, p. 1; U.S. Congress, House, Committee on Labor, Employment of Labor on Federal Construction Work, Hearings (71C, 2S, 1930), pp. 16–17.

[14] Stewart, "Discussion: Women and Children in Industry," IAGLO, Proceedings, 1923, p. 41.

[15] Stewart, "A Family Wage-Rate vs. A Family Social Endowment Fund," Social Forces, September 1927, pp. 121, 123-125.

[16] Stewart, "Ultimate Effects of Automatic Machine Production," MLR, March 1929, p. 49.

[17] Stewart Papers, Speeches and Essays, "Report to Second National Outdoor Recreation Conference," p. 6; Baltimore Sun, Jan. 21, 1926; Washington Daily News, Apr. 16, 1926; Jefferson County Union, Fort Atkinson, Wis., Apr. 23, 1926.

[18] Stewart, "Present Situation in Textiles," American Federationist, June 1929, p. 690.

[19] Bureau of Efficiency, Report on the Statistical Work of the United States Government, 1922, pp. 5-16.

[20] "Final Report of the Joint Committee of the American Statistical and American Economic Associations to the Director of the Census, 1922," American Statistical Association Journal, March 1923, pp. 641-642.

283

[21] *The New York Times*, May 11, 1921, p. 3; Jan. 11, 1922, p. 11; "The Labor Department Attacked," *Survey*, June 25, 1921, pp. 426-427.

[22] NARG 174, Department of Labor, Chief Clerk's File, Herbert Hoover to the Secretary, June 18, 1921; Stewart, Memorandum for the Secretary, June 20, 1921; Secretary to the Secretary of Commerce, June 21, 1921.

[23] Department of Labor, *Annual Report, 1923*, p. 59; NARG 174, DOL, Chief Clerk's File, Lord to Secretary, May 22, 1925, and Stewart to Chief Clerk, May 26, 1925.

[24] Dept. of Labor, *Annual Report, 1927*, pp. 59-61.

[25] U.S. Personnel Classification Board, *Closing Report of Wage and Personnel Survey*, 1931, pp. 231-232; *Report of Wage and Personnel Survey, Field Survey Division* (70C, 2S, House Doc. 602, 1929), pp. 365-367.

[26] Hugh S. Hanna, "The International Cost of Living Inquiry," *Annals of the American Academy of Political and Social Science*, March 1933, pp. 162-164.

[27] House, Appropriations, *Departments of Commerce and Labor Appropriation Bill, FY 1923, Hearings* (67C, 2S, 1922), p. 780; Warren M. Persons and Eunice S. Coyle, "A Commodity Price Index of Business Cycles," *The Review of Economic Statistics*, November 1921; and articles in subsequent years.

[28] House, Committee on Banking and Currency, *Stabilization, Hearings* (69C, 1S, 1926), pp. 605, 615, 619-621; *Stabilization of Purchasing Power of Money, Hearings* (67C, 4S, 1922); *Stabilization of Commodity Prices, Hearings* (72C, 1S, 1932), p. 262.

[29] "A Constructive Program for Price Statistics," *ASA Journal*, March 1932, pp. 74-78; Senate, Committee on Manufactures, *Establishment of National Economic Council, Hearings* (72C, 1S, 1931), pp. 583 ff.

[30] Commissioner of Labor Statistics, *Annual Report, 1930*, p. 26.

[31] *Congressional Record* (67C, 1S), Aug. 5, 1921, p. 4695; NARG 174, DOL, Chief Clerk's File, Stewart to Secretary, Aug. 12, 1921, and Secretary to President of the Senate, Aug. 12, 1921.

[32] *The New York Times*, Sept. 15, 1921, pp. 14 and 29; "'Normalcy' in Unemployment," *New Republic*, Oct. 11, 1922, p. 163.

[33] Ralph G. Hurlin and William A. Berridge, eds., *Employment Statistics for the United States* (New York: Russell Sage Foundation, 1926), pp. 24-30.

[34] NARG 174, DOL, Chief Clerk's File, Henning to Director General of Employment Service, June 3, 1922, and Secretary, Memorandum for Mr. Jones, Mar. 4, 1924; NARG 257, BLS, General Correspondence, 1916-1924, Stewart to Henning, Aug. 2, 1922.

[35] "Committee on Governmental Labor Statistics of the American Statistical Association, Report for 1924," *ASA Journal*, March 1925, p. 96.

[36] Paul H. Douglas, review of *Employment Statistics for the United States, Journal of Political Economy*, August 1928, p. 523; Royal Meeker, "The Dependability and Meaning of Unemployment and Employment Statistics in the United States," *Harvard Business Review*, July 1930, p. 396; Miriam E. West, *Employment Indexes in the United States and Canada* (American Statistical Association, Committee on Governmental Labor Statistics, 1929), p. 8; "Miscellaneous Notes," *ASA Journal*, September 1928, pp. 324-325; Berridge, "Employment and the Buying Power of Consumers," *The Review of Economic Statistics*, November 1930, pp. 186, 187n.

[37] *Congressional Record* (70C, 1S), Mar. 26, 1928, pp. 5337-5338; *The New York Times*, Feb. 16, 1928, p. 2; Mar. 27, 1928, p. 1; Mar. 28, 1928, p. 13; and Apr. 21, 1928, p. 16.

[38] Senate, Committee on Education and Labor, *Unemployment in the United States, Hearings* (70C, 2S, 1929), pp. 179-187; also *Causes of Unemployment, Report* (70C, 2S, Sen. Rept. 2072, 1929), p. XV.

[39] Senate, Education and Labor, *Unemployment*, pp. 491-517.

[40] *The New York Times*, July 14, 1929, p. 20, and July 16, 1929, p. 12; Dept. of Labor, *Annual Report, 1930*, p. 89.

[41] Joseph W. Duncan and William C. Shelton, *Revolution in United States Government Statistics, 1929-1976* (U.S. Department of Commerce, Office of Federal Statistical Policy and Standards, 1978), pp. 23-24; John Bruce Dudley, "James J. Davis, Secretary of Labor Under Three Presidents, 1921-1930," Ph.D. dissertation (Ball State University, 1971), p. 275.

[42] *The New York Times*, Jan. 22, 1930, p. 1; Mary Van Kleeck, "Employment Statistics," IAGLO, *Proceedings, 1931*, pp. 77-78; Berridge, "The Employment Situation," *New York Times Annalist*, Feb. 21, 1930.

[43] *The New York Times*, Jan. 23, 1930, p. 11; Jan. 24, 1930, p. 35; Feb. 9, 1930, p. 1; Feb. 20, 1930, p. 24.

[44] *The New York Times*, June 28, 1930, p. 17; July 16, 1930, p. 15; "An Expert on Hoover's 'Experts,'" *New Republic*, Aug. 20, 1930, p. 4.

[45] *The New York Times*, July 30, 1930, p. 5; Aug. 3, 1930, p. II, 18; Aug. 4, 1930, p. 14; Aug. 21, 1930, p. 40.

[46] U.S. Advisory Committee on Employment Statistics, *Report*, 1931, pp. 6-7, 9-12, 16-18.

[47] Ibid., pp. 19, 22.

[48] Ibid., pp. 24-25.

[49] Commissioner of Labor Statistics, *Annual Report, 1932*, pp. 1-5; *Revised Indexes of Factory Employment and Payrolls, 1919 to 1933*, Bulletin 610 (Bureau of Labor Statistics, 1935).

[50] Dept. of Labor, *Annual Report, 1923*, pp. 59, 61.

[51] Stewart, "Need of a More Definite Background for Statistics in the Chemical Industry," National Safety Council, *Transactions, 1926*, pp. 541, 544; Charles E. Baldwin, "How to Make Statistics Uniform," IAGLO, *Proceedings, 1925*, p. 149.

[52] House, Committee on Labor, *Division of Safety, Hearings* (69C, 1S, 1926), p. 16.

[53] *Congressional Record* (69C, 2S), Jan. 27, 1927, p. 2392.

[54] Stewart,, "Efficiency of American Labor," IAGLO, *Proceedings, 1922*, p. 7.

[55] Irving Bernstein, *The Lean Years: A History of the American Worker, 1920-1933* (Boston: Houghton Mifflin, 1960), p. 103; American Federation of Labor, *Proceedings, 1925*, p. 271.

[56] Don D. Lescohier, *Working Conditions*, Vol. III of *The History of Labor in the United States, 1896-1932* (New York: The Macmillan Co., 1935), p. 334; Joseph Dorfman, *The Economic Mind in American Civilization*, Vol. IV, *1918-1933* (New York: Viking Press, 1959), pp. 66-67.

[57] Stewart, "Efficiency of American Labor," p. 7, 17; "Labor Efficiency and Production," *MLR*, August 1922, p. 110.

[58] Stewart, "Labor Productivity and Costs in Certain Building Trades," *MLR*, November 1924, p. 1; Dept. of Labor, *Annual Report, 1924*, p. 155.

[59] Dept. of Labor, *Annual Report, 1927*, p. 61.

[60] Commissioner of Labor Statistics, *Annual Report, 1932*, pp. 6–11.

[61] House, Appropriations, *Hearings, Legislative, Executive, and Judicial Appropriation Bill, 1922* (66C, 3S, 1920), p. 1272.

[62] House, Appropriations, *Appropriations, Department of Labor, 1928, Hearings* (69C, 2S, 1927), pp. 22–23.

[63] NARG 257, BLS, General Correspondence, 1916–1924, Commissioner to Secretary, Sept. 17, 1923; Secretary to F. J. Bailey, Chairman, Personnel Classification Board, Jan. 21, 1924; "Classification of Statistical Workers in Government Service," *ASA Journal*, March 1924, pp. 91–92; "Report of the Committee on Personnel Classification in the Federal Government," *ASA Journal*, March 1925, p. 118.

[64] "The Labor Department Attacked," *Survey*, June 25, 1921, p. 426; *Congressional Record* (67C, 2S), Dec. 7, 1921, p. 119.

[65] House, Appropriations, *Department of Labor Appropriation Bill for 1933, Hearings* (72C, 1S, 1932), pp. 31–34.

[66] House, Appropriations, *Appropriation, 1922*, p. 1275.

[67] NARG 174, DOL, Chief Clerk's File, Stewart, Memorandum to The Acting Secretary, June 2, 1928.

[68] "The Cabinet: Tin Can," *Time*, July 11, 1932, p. 7; "Looking for a Job, Ethelbert Stewart Retired After 45 Years," *The Evening Star* (Washington), July 2, 1932; *The New York Times*, July 3, 1932, p. 3.

[69] Stewart Papers, General Correspondence, Stewart to von Klein Smid, undated draft, July 1932; Clippings, "Honesty Penalized," San Francisco *News*, July 14, 1932.

Chapter VI. Isador Lubin

[1] Isador Lubin, "Recollections of Veblen," in C.C. Qualey, ed., *Thorstein Veblen: The Carleton College Veblen Seminar Essays* (New York: Columbia University Press, 1968), pp. 139–141.

[2] Lewis Lansky, "Isador Lubin: The Ideas and Career of a New Deal Labor Economist," Ph.D. dissertation (Case Western Reserve University, 1976), pp. 50–60; Isador Lubin, *Miners' Wages and the Cost of Coal* (New York: McGraw-Hill, 1924); Lubin and Helen Everett, *The British Coal Dilemma* (New York: The Macmillan Co., 1927).

[3] Lansky, "Lubin," pp. 100–102.

[4] George Martin, *Madam Secretary: Frances Perkins* (Boston: Houghton Mifflin Co., 1976), pp. 302–303.

[5] U.S. Congress, Senate, Committee on Education and Labor, *Unemployment in the United States, Hearings* (70C, 2S, 1929), pp. 491–517.

[6] Senate, Select Committee on Unemployment Insurance, *Unemployment Insurance, Hearings* (72C, 1S, 1932), pp. 475–486.

[7] U.S. Congress, Temporary National Economic Committee, *Investigation of Concentration of Economic Power, Hearings*, Part 1, *Economic Prologue* (75C, 3S, 1939), p. 79; *The New York Times*, Dec. 21, 1938.

[8] Senate, Education and Labor, *Fair Labor Standards Act of 1937, Joint Hearings* (75C, 1S, 1937), pp. 309-363.

[9] TNEC, *Investigation of Concentration of Economic Power, Final Report and Recommendations* (77C, 1S, Senate Doc. 35, 1941), pp. 517-557.

[10] Ibid., pp. 51-52.

[11] Department of Labor, *Annual Report, 1933*, p. 41.

[12] Advisory Committee to the Secretary of Labor, "Interim Report," April 1934, pp. 1-2; Social Science Research Council, Committee on Government Statistics and Information Services, *Report on Government Statistics* (New York: SSRC, 1937), pp. 77-78.

[13] Dept. of Labor, *Annual Report, 1935*, p. 64.

[14] Dept. of Labor, *Annual Report, 1934*, p. 9.

[15] National Archives Record Group 257, Bureau of Labor Statistics, Lubin letters to Secretary Wallace, Mar. 26, Apr. 13, Apr. 16, 1934.

[16] "Report on Labor Conditions in the Automobile Industry," *Monthly Labor Review*, March 1935; Lewis L. Lorwin and Arthur Wubnig, *Labor Relations Boards* (Washington: The Brookings Institution, 1935), pp. 367, 380-381; N. A. Tolles and M. W. LaFevver, "Wages, Hours, Employment and Annual Earnings in the Motor-Vehicle Industry, 1934," *MLR*, March 1936, pp. 521-553; Senate, Education and Labor, *Fair Labor Standards*, p. 336.

[17] NARG 257, BLS, Lubin to Perkins, Nov. 22, 1933; *The New York Times*, Aug. 21, 1934; Jan. 30, 31, 1935. This continued for a dozen years, until a separate Bureau of International Affairs was established in the Department in 1946.

[18] NARG 174, Department of Labor, Perkins Files, Perkins to Roosevelt, Mar. 30, 1936.

[19] *The New York Times*, Nov. 9, 11, 14, 1937; Jan. 4, 5, 1938; NARG 257, BLS, Roosevelt to Lubin, June 16, 1939.

[20] NARG 257, BLS, Lubin to Hinrichs, July 1, 1940.

[21] NARG 174, DOL, Perkins File, Perkins to President Roosevelt, May 2, 1941.

[22] A. Ford Hinrichs and William A. Brown, Jr., "The Planned Economy of Soviet Russia," *Political Science Quarterly*, September 1931, pp. 362-402.

[23] "Adjustment of Federal Salaries to the Cost of Living," *MLR*, February 1934, pp. 376-379.

[24] Faith M. Williams and Alice C. Hanson, *Money Disbursements of Wage Earners and Clerical Workers, 1934–36, Summary Volume*, Bulletin 638 (Bureau of Labor Statistics, 1941), p. 1.

[25] "Changes in Cost of Living from December 15, 1939 to March 15, 1940," *MLR*, July 1940, p. 139; "The Bureau of Labor Statistics' New Index of Cost of Living," *MLR*, August 1940, p. 383.

[26] TNEC, *Hearings*, p. 79; *The New York Times*, Dec. 21, 1938.

[27] *Family Spending and Saving in Wartime,* Bulletin 822 (Bureau of Labor Statistics, 1945); "Expenditures and Savings of City Families in 1944," MLR, January 1946.

[28] Bureau of Labor Statistics Annual Conference with Research Directors of National and International Unions, *Proceedings, 1941,* p. 62.

[29] BLS Annual Conference with Research Directors, *Proceedings, 1942,* pp. 43, 69.

[30] NARG 257, BLS, Hinrichs to William H. Davis, Oct. 16, 1942.

[31] NARG 257, BLS, Davis to Hinrichs, Oct. 21, 1942.

[32] Kathryn S. Arnow, *The Attack on the Cost-of-Living Index* (Washington, D.C.: Committee on Public Administration Cases, 1951), p. 61.

[33] Ibid., pp. 61–62.

[34] BLS Annual Conference with Research Directors, *Proceedings, 1943,* p. 64.

[35] Special Committee of the American Statistical Association, "An Appraisal of the U.S. Bureau of Labor Statistics Cost-of-Living Index, Released Oct. 10, 1943," *American Statistical Association Journal,* December 1943, pp. 387–405.

[36] NARG 257, BLS, Davis to Perkins, Oct. 19, 1943.

[37] Office of Economic Stabilization, *Report of the President's Committee on the Cost of Living,* 1945, p. 2.

[38] Ibid.

[39] Ibid., p. 3; George Meany and R. J. Thomas, *Cost of Living, Recommended Report for the Presidential Committee on the Cost of Living* (Washington: Congress of Industrial Organizations, 1944), p. 4.

[40] Office of Economic Stabilization, *Report,* pp. 3–4.

[41] Joseph C. Goulden, *Meany* (New York: Atheneum Publishers, 1972), pp. 113–114.

[42] "Cost of Living in Large Cities, May 1944," MLR, July 1944, p. 180; Arnow, *The Attack,* p. 134.

[43] *American Federationist,* Weekly News Service, June 20, 1944.

[44] "Report of the Technical Committee Appointed by the Chairman of the President's Committee on the Cost of Living, June 15, 1944," in Office of Economic Stabilization, *Report,* pp. 261–263 and 295.

[45] Office of Economic Stabilization, *Report,* pp. 12–35.

[46] William Green, "America's Wage Policy," *American Federationist,* March 1945, pp. 3–4.

[47] NARG 257, BLS, Hinrichs to Perkins, Jan. 31, 1945; Perkins to Hinrichs, Memo of February 8, 1945.

[48] *Workers' Budgets in the United States: City Families and Single Persons, 1946 and 1947,* Bulletin 927 (Bureau of Labor Statistics, 1948).

[49] A. F. Hinrichs, *Wages in Cotton-Goods Manufacturing,* Bulletin 663 (Bureau of Labor Statistics, 1938), p. XI.

[50] Dept. of Labor, *Annual Report, 1936,* p. 77; *1939,* pp. 74–75.

[51] *Federal Register,* May 18, 1943, p. 6490.

[52] NARG 174, DOL, Perkins Files, Davis to Perkins, June 1, 1943, and Perkins to Davis, June 16, 1943.

[53] NARG 257, BLS, Standing Committee of Union Research Directors, Subcommittee on the Release of Wage Information, Aug. 26, 1943.

[54] Robert J. Myers, Harry Ober, and Lily Mary David, "Wartime Wage Movements and Urban Wage-Rate Changes," *MLR*, October 1944, pp. 684–705; *Activities of the Bureau of Labor Statistics in World War II* (Bureau of Labor Statistics, 1947), pp. 90–92; H. M. Douty, "A Century of Wage Statistics: The BLS Contribution," *MLR*, November 1984, p. 21.

[55] NARG 257, BLS, A. F. Hinrichs to Lubin, Apr. 2, 1935.

[56] NARG 257, BLS, Lubin to Perkins, Sept. 3, 1935.

[57] "Extent and Characteristics of Company Unions: Preliminary Report," *MLR*, October 1935, pp. 865–876; NARG 257, BLS, Noel Sargent, Secretary, National Association of Manufacturers to Lubin, Oct. 11, 1935, and Lubin to Sargent, Oct. 14, 1935; *Journal of Commerce*, Oct. 15, 1935.

[58] Dept. of Labor, *Annual Report, 1940*, p. 100.

[59] *Procedures Used in Compiling Monthly Statistics Relating to Employment and Pay Rolls* (Bureau of Labor Statistics, May 1945), p. 1; Dept. of Labor, *Annual Report, 1946*, p. 57.

[60] *Handbook of Labor Statistics*, Bulletin 694 (Bureau of Labor Statistics, 1942), pp. 182–183.

[61] Joseph W. Duncan and William C. Shelton, *Revolution in United States Government Statistics, 1926–1976* (U.S. Department of Commerce, Office of Federal Statistical Policy and Standards, 1978), p. 38.

[62] Lester R. Frankel and J. Stevens Stock, "On the Sample Survey of Unemployment," *ASA Journal*, March 1942; John E. Bregger, "The Current Population Survey, A Historical Perspective and BLS' Role," *MLR*, June 1984, pp. 8–9.

[63] *Handbook*, pp. 183–184.

[64] For example, Herman B. Byer, "Employment Created by PWA Construction," *MLR*, October 1936, pp. 838–845.

[65] Dept. of Labor, *Annual Report, 1941*, pp. 82–83.

[66] NARG 257, BLS, Lubin to Secretary, Jan. 26, 1940; President to Secretary, Jan. 26, 1940; William H. McReynolds to Sidney Hillman, June 21, 1940.

[67] Jerome Cornfield, W. Duane Evans, and Marvin Hoffenberg, "Full Employment Patterns, 1950," Part 1, *MLR*, February 1947; Part 2, *MLR*, March 1947; Duncan and Shelton, *Revolution*, pp. 109–111; *Activities in World War II*, pp. 81–84.

[68] NARG 257, BLS, Boris Shishkin to Lubin, Aug. 23, 1935, enclosing copy of letter from William Green to Perkins, Aug. 20, 1935.

[69] Dept. of Labor, *Annual Report, 1939*, p. 77.

[70] *Activities in World War II*, p. 144.

[71] House, Appropriations Committee, *Department of Labor Appropriation Bill for 1935, Hearing* (73C, 2S, 1934), p. 11.

[72] Ibid., p. 55.

[73] Ibid., pp. 71–72.

[74] Lubin, "Government Employment as a Professional Career in Economics," *American Economic Review*, March 1937 (Supplement).

[75] Dept. of Labor, *Annual Report, 1937*, p. 77.

[76] NARG 174, DOL, Perkins Files, Secretary to the President, Aug. 23, 1933; Secretary to Hugh Johnson, Aug. 7, 1933; Resolution of the Central Statistical Board, Aug. 14, 1933.

[77] Ruth Aull, *The Content of NIRA Administrative Legislation, Part A, Executive and Administrative Orders* (Office of National Recovery Administration, Division of Review, Work Materials No. 35, 1936), p. 18.

[78] NARG 257, BLS, Roscoe Edlund, Association of American Soap and Glycerine Producers, Inc., to Lubin, Mar. 22, 1934; Lubin to Edlund, Apr. 4, 1934.

[79] NARG 257, BLS, transcript of meeting May 19, 1934.

[80] NARG 257, BLS, Lubin to Andrew Court, Apr. 13, 1936; Lubin to Stephen DuBrul, General Motors, Apr. 13, 1936; DuBrul to Lubin, July 28, 1937; Lubin to DuBrul, July 30, 1937; Court to Lubin, Aug. 17, 1937; Lubin to Court, Aug. 21 and Sept. 11, 1937; Lubin to W. J. Cronin, Dec. 2, 1937.

[81] BLS Annual Conference with Research Directors, *Proceedings, 1940*, p. 1.

[82] NARG 174, DOL, Schwellenbach Files, Lubin to President, Jan. 22, 1946, and President replies, Jan. 24, 1946.

[83] Martin, *Madam Secretary*, pp. 464–465; NARG 257, BLS, Office of Publications, Statement of Lewis B. Schwellenbach for release Sept. 6, 1945.

[84] NARG 174, DOL, Schwellenbach Files, Murray to Schwellenbach, Jan. 29, 1946; *The New York Times*, Jan. 26, 1946; Mar. 29, 1946, p. 42; Mar. 30, 1946, p. 14; *New York Herald Tribune*, Feb. 25, 1946.

[85] NARG 174, DOL, Schwellenbach Files, Lubin to Schwellenbach, Feb. 26, 1946; and Lubin to Jim Abrahamson, Feb. 27, 1946.

[86] NARG 174, DOL, Schwellenbach Files, Letters to Schwellenbach from Wesley C. Mitchell, Feb. 27, 1946; Frederick C. Mills, Feb. 28, 1946; other letters from Royal Meeker, Mar. 13, 1946; William A. Berridge, Metropolitan Life Insurance Co., Mar. 4, 1946; Senator Wayne Morse, Mar. 29, 1946; J. J. Moran, American Union of Telephone Workers, Apr. 2, 1946; and Morris L. Cooke to the President, Mar. 19, 1946.

[87] NARG 174, DOL, Schwellenbach Files, Memorandum from Hinrichs to the Secretary, May 22, 1946; Schwellenbach to Hinrichs, May 23, 1946.

[88] NARG 174, DOL, Schwellenbach Files, Hinrichs to Schwellenbach, July 1, 1946; Schwellenbach to Hinrichs, July 2, 1946.

[89] *The Washington Post*, July 3, 1946.

[90] NARG 174, DOL, Schwellenbach Files, Edwin E. Witte to Schwellenbach, July 26, 1946.

Chapter VII.   Ewan Clague

[1] Aryness Joy Wickens, "Statistics and the Public Interest," *American Statistical Association Journal*, March 1953, pp. 1–14.

[2] Ewan Clague, *The Bureau of Labor Statistics* (New York: Frederick A. Praeger Publishers, 1968), p. 26.

[3] Clague, "The Program of the U.S. Bureau of Labor Statistics," International Statistical Conference, *Proceedings: International Statistical Institute*, 1947, pp. 182–183.

[4] Frederick C. Mills and Clarence D. Long, *The Statistical Agencies of the Federal Government* (New York: National Bureau of Economic Research, 1949), pp. 54, 57–59, 97–99, and 128–129.

[5] U.S. Commission on Organization of the Executive Branch of the Government, *Department of Labor*, March 1949, pp. 16–17.

[6] National Archives Record Group 257, Bureau of Labor Statistics, Ewan Clague to the Under Secretary, Feb. 10, 1950.

[7] NARG 174, U.S. Department of Labor, Mitchell, 1954, Leo Werts to John J. Gilhooley, Nov. 4, 1954, covering "Recommendations of Program & Organization Consultants, 1954," including "Recommendations Concerning Employment and Unemployment Statistics (9/13/54)."

[8] NARG 174, USDOL, Deputy Under Secretary, Mitchell, Secretary's Instruction No. 57, "Responsibility for Statistical Standards," July 14, 1955; Records of Deputy Under Secretary Millard Cass, Samuel R. Pierce, Jr., to Cass, Aug. 31, 1955, and Under Secretary to Cass, May 12, 1960, covering "BLS Statement on Consultants' Recommendations."

[9] James P. Mitchell, "A Prefatory Note," *Monthly Labor Review*, January 1955, p. II.

[10] NARG 257, BLS, Dept. of Labor Publications Program, "The Scope of this Report" (apparently November 1956) and Lodge and Cass, "Department of Labor Publications Program," Feb. 26, 1957.

[11] NARG 257, BLS, MLR Planning Committee, 1951—, Under Secretary to Clague, "*Monthly Labor Review*," Oct. 18, 1955; Dept. of Labor Publications Program, Lawrence R. Klein to Philip Arnow, "Oct. 3, 1957, Meeting of the Departmental Publications Committee," Oct. 4, 1957.

[12] NARG 174, USDOL, W. Willard Wirtz, 1964, "Introduction, The Cost of Departmental Publications" (apparently John W. Leslie, Jan. 8, 1964); NARG 257, BLS, Dept. of Labor Publications Policy, Wirtz, memorandum for Kermit Gordon, Director, Bureau of the Budget, Jan. 23, 1964.

[13] NARG 174, USDOL, Wirtz, 1964, "Notes on Secretary's Staff Meeting, Dec. 28, 1964"; NARG 257, BLS, *Monthly Labor Review*, "Minutes of Discussion on Proposal Relating to Monthly Labor Review, March 17, 1965."

[14] NARG 257, BLS, Robert J. Myers to Assistant Secretary Daniel P. Moynihan, Nov. 3, 1964, "The Research Program of BLMR"; Clague to Morris Weisz, Mar. 12, 1965, "BLMR History—your memorandum of Dec. 30."

[15] NARG 257, BLS, Division of Wages and Industrial Relations, 1951–1964, Clague to Werts, "Labor-Management Relations Program for the Department," Sept. 27, 1962.

[16] NARG 257, BLS, Clague to Werts, "Draft No. 3—Manpower Administration," Jan. 21, 1963.

[17] NARG 257, BLS, Myers to Arthur M. Ross, "Secretary's Orders Governing Manpower Research," Oct. 8, 1965; U.S. Congress, House, Subcommittee of Appropriations, *Hearings, Departments of Labor and Health, Education, and Welfare Appropriations for 1965* (88C, 2S, 1964), pp. 291 ff, "Programs in Manpower Research and Statistics."

The First Hundred Years

18 NARG 174, USDOL, Wirtz, 1964, Moynihan, Memorandum for the Secretary, Nov. 27, 1964.

19 NARG 257, BLS, Clague to Werts, Feb. 23 and May 7, 1965.

20 Booz-Allen and Hamilton, *Bureau of Labor Statistics, General Review* (confidential report), 1966, pp. 7 and 14.

21 U.S. Dept. of Labor, *Annual Report, 1968*, p. 23.

22 Ibid., p. 6.

23 John P. Wymer, "Industry Employment Statistics in the United States, Fifty Years of Development," *Employment and Earnings*, January 1966, pp. viii-x.

24 House, Subcommittee of Appropriations, *Hearings, Departments of Labor and Health, Education, and Welfare Appropriations for 1955: Testimony of Members of Congress, Interested Organizations, and Individuals* (83C, 2S, 1954), p. 37, statement of National Legislative Committee, American Federation of Labor; NARG 174, USDOL, Mitchell, 1954, Clague to Secretary, "Statistics of employment and unemployment," Mar. 15, 1954.

25 NARG 257, BLS, Div. of Manpower and Employment Statistics, Clague for the Secretary, Feb. 12, 1954, and News Release, "Combined Employment Release Announced," for April 25, 1954; Office of Program Planning, Wickens to Clague, Feb. 15, 1954.

26 Mitchell, General Order No. 99, May 18, 1959, "Operation of the Monthly Report on the Labor Force"; NARG 257, BLS, MRLF—Historical File on Combined Release and Transfer of Functions to BLS, Maurice H. Stans, Bureau of the Budget, Memorandum for Secretary Strauss and Secretary Mitchell, "Construction and Labor Force Statistics," signed by Mitchell and Strauss on Nov. 18, 1958; USDOL, BLS, News Release (USDL 2864), July 14, 1959, "The Employment Situation: June 1959."

27 NARG 257, BLS, Productivity, Clipping, *Wall Street Journal*, Nov. 20, 1959, "Agency Urged to Revise Way It Figures Jobless"; Senate, Subcommittee of Appropriations, *Hearings, Labor-Health, Education, and Welfare Appropriations for 1961* (86C, 2S, 1960), pp. 1034, 1037–1039; *Daily Labor Report* (230), Nov. 25, 1959, p. BB1; (133), July 12, 1961, pp. B1–B3.

28 *The New York Times*, following dates in 1960: Aug. 2, p. 20; Aug. 17, p. 64; Sept. 21, p. 26; Oct. 16, p. 1; Oct. 29, p. 12; Nov. 2, p. 80; Nov. 4, p. 23; Nov. 8, p. 19; Nov. 11, p. 1.

29 Bernard D. Nossiter, "Delay Seen for Unemployment Report," *The Washington Post*, Nov. 3, 1960, p. 25; clipping, "Delayed Report Shows Rise in Unemployment."

30 NARG 257, BLS, Clague to the Under Secretary, Nov. 9, 1960; and Release of Statistics I, Clague to the Under Secretary, Feb. 20, 1961.

31 James Daniel, "Let's Look at Those 'Alarming' Unemployment Figures," *Reader's Digest*, September 1961.

32 DLR (219), Nov. 13, 1961, pp. A5 and A7; U.S. President's Committee to Appraise Employment and Unemployment Statistics, *Measuring Employment and Unemployment*, 1962, pp. 12, 20, and 212.

33 *Measuring Employment*, pp. 14–15, 17, 23, 25–26, 151–152.

34 NARG 174, USDOL, W. Willard Wirtz, 1964, Wirtz, Memorandum for the President, not sent, filed June 4, 1964; Wirtz, 1965, Clague to Secretary, June 10, 1965,

and Gardner Ackley, Memorandum for Members of the White House Staff, July 2, 1965.

35 NARG 257, BLS, Job Vacancy Statistical Program I, Seymour L. Wolfbein to Clague, Jan. 12, 1956, and Clague to Charles Stewart, Nov. 6, 1956, covering Clague to Under Secretary, Nov. 6, 1956.

36 Ibid., Clague to Moynihan, July 18, 1963; Clague to Moynihan, Oct. 28, 1963; Myers to Moynihan, July 7, 1964; and Wirtz to the President, July 28, 1964; President's Committee, *Measuring Employment*, pp. 199–202; Raymond A. Konstant and Irvin F. O. Wingeard, "Analysis and Use of Job Vacancy Statistics, Part I," *MLR*, August 1968, pp. 22–23; "Part II," September 1968, p. 21.

37 NARG 257, BLS, Job Vacancy Statistical Program I, Clague to Moynihan, Dec. 17, 1963; Kermit Gordon to Wirtz, Sept. 5, 1964.

38 Ibid., BLS statement, "Job Vacancy Research Program," June 9, 1964, and Van Auken, Memorandum to the Job Vacancy Files, Nov. 9, 1964; *DLR* (112), June 11, 1965, pp. A4–A5.

39 NARG 257, BLS, Job Vacancy Statistical Program I, Secretary, Memorandum to All Employers, Nov. 5, 1964.

40 J. E. Morton, *On the Evolution of Manpower Statistics* (Kalamazoo, Mich.: The W. E. Upjohn Institute for Employment Research, 1969), p. 64.

41 Dept. of Labor, *Annual Report, 1959*, p. 8; BLS bulletins, *Employment and Economic Status of Older Men and Women*, Bull. 1213 (1956), p. III; *Older Workers under Collective Bargaining, part I, Hiring, Retention, Job Termination*, Bull. 1199-1 (1956); *Older Workers under Collective Bargaining, part II, Health and Insurance Plans, Pension Plans*, Bull. 1199-2 (1956).

42 Among the reports were: Vincent F. Gegan and Samuel H. Thompson, "Worker Mobility in a Labor Surplus Area," *MLR*, December 1957; Robert L. Stein, "Unemployment and Job Mobility," *MLR*, April 1960; *Impact on Workers and Community of a Plant Shutdown in a Depressed Area*, Bull. 1264 (Bureau of Labor Statistics, 1960).

43 BLS bulletins, *Military Manpower Requirements and Supply, 1954–60*, Bull. 1161 (1954); *Military Manpower Requirements and Supply, 1959–63*, Bull. 1262 (1959); *Scientific Research and Development in American Industry, A Study of Manpower and Costs*, Bull. 1148 (1953); *BLS Handbook of Methods for Surveys and Studies*, Bull. 1458 (1966), p. 41; *Employment of Scientific and Technical Personnel in Industry, 1962*, Bull. 1418 (1964).

44 *Techniques of Preparing Major BLS Statistical Series*, Bull. 993 (Bureau of Labor Statistics, 1950), pp. 1 and 5; *The Consumer Price Index*, Report 517 (Bureau of Labor Statistics, 1978 rev.), p. 4; Dept. of Labor, *Annual Report, 1947*, p. 54; House, Committee on Education and Labor, Special Subcommittee, *Hearings, Consumers' Price Index* (82C, 1S, 1951), p. 19.

45 NARG 257, BLS, CPI, Revision of, Wickens to Secretary, Sept. 23, 1949.

46 NARG 257, BLS, Cost of Living, Clague to the Secretary, Sept. 25, 1950; George W. Brooks to Clague, Nov. 3, 1950; Price Division, "Statement by the Commissioner on the Interim Adjustment of the Consumers' Price Index," Feb. 20, 1951, and BLS statement, "Interim Adjustment of Consumers' Price Index," Apr. 11, 1951.

[47] NARG 257, BLS, Price Division, Clague to the Secretary, Apr. 24, 1951; "UE Calls U.S. Price Index 'Fraud'; Asks Senate Probe," *UE News*, Apr. 30, 1951, p. 1; Harvey A. Levenstein, *Communism, Anticommunism, and the CIO* (Westport, Conn.: Greenwood Press, 1981), pp. 299–301.

[48] NARG 257, BLS, Price Division, Lubin to Clague, cable, Aug. 6, 1951; also Clague to Lubin, cable, Aug. 6, 1951; Clague to Rep. Tom Steed, Aug. 8, 1951.

[49] House, Subcommittee of Education and Labor, *Hearings, Consumers' Price Index*, pp. 202, 207–208, 275, 278, 280–282, and 358 and *Report, Consumers' Price Index* (82C, 1S, Subcommittee Rept. No. 2, 1951), pp. 32–33, 35, 36, and 39; Senate, Committee on Public Welfare, Subcommittee on Labor and Labor-Management Relations, *Report, Study of Wage and Price Indexes* (82C, 1S, Committee Print, 1951).

[50] NARG 257, BLS, Clague, "Statement Concerning the Resumption of the 'Old Series' Consumers' Price Index," before Senate Committee on Appropriations, Feb. 23, 1953 (typed); Price Division, Walter P. Reuther to Secretary (wire), Jan. 26, 1953; "First Labor Issue Put to Eisenhower," *The New York Times*, Jan. 29, 1953.

[51] Helen Humes Lamale, "Housing Costs in the Consumer Price Index," *MLR*, February 1956, pp. 189–191; U.S. Congress, Joint Committee on the Economic Report, *Report, The Consumers' Price Index* (80C, 2S, Joint Committee Print, 1949), p. 6.

[52] Dept. of Labor, *Annual Report, 1953*, p. 63; NARG 257, BLS, Price Division, "Efforts to Secure Outside Financing for the General-Purpose Tabulations of the Bureau of Labor Statistics 1950 Study of Consumer Expenditures," Jan. 12, 1954; NARG 174, USDOL, Mitchell, 1956, W. Duane Evans to Secretary, Oct. 8, 1956.

[53] NARG 257, BLS, Price Division, Clague, "What Consumer Price Index Really Is," *Journal of Commerce*, Aug. 16, 1956, with introductory note by H. E. Luedicke; clipping, "The Cost of Living, The Index is Misleading & Incomplete," *Time*, Nov. 11, 1957; Joint Economic Committee, *Hearings, Relationship of Prices to Economic Stability and Growth* (85C, 2S, 1958), and *Hearings, Employment, Growth, and Price Levels* (86C, 1S, 1959).

[54] NARG 257, BLS, Price Division, Clipping, J.R.W., "Newsletter: Commodity Report—Price Indices Not Telling Real Story," *Journal of Commerce*, Aug. 8, 1956; *DLR* (179), Sept. 14, 1960, p. A10.

[55] Joint Economic Committee, Subcommittee on Economic Statistics, *Hearings, Government Price Statistics, Part I* (87C, 1S, 1961), p. 2, with report and papers from Price Statistics Review Committee following: *The Price Statistics of the Federal Government, Review, Appraisal, and Recommendations*.

[56] Joint Economic Committee, *Hearings, Price Statistics, I*, pp. 5–6; *The Consumer Price Index: History and Techniques*, Bull. 1517 (Bureau of Labor Statistics, 1966), pp. 8–9; NARG 257, BLS, CPI, Revision of, Hollander to Clague, June 14, 1951; Hollander to Clague, May 26, 1952, "Treatment of single-person consumer units in the revised Consumers' Price Index."

[57] Joint Economic Committee, *Hearings, Price Statistics, I*, pp. 47–48; *Hearings, Price Statistics, II*, p. 680.

[58] Joint Economic Committee, *Hearings, Price Statistics, I*, pp. 52 and 55; *Hearings, Price Statistics, II*, p. 560.

[59] NARG 257, BLS, Consumer Price Index—General, BLS statement, "Major Changes in the Consumer Price Index," Mar. 3, 1964; *The Consumer Price Index*, Rept. 517, p. 5.

[60] NARG 257, BLS, Revision of the CPI, James E. Dodson to Clague, Sept. 14, 1960.

[61] NARG 257, BLS, Price Division, Herbert Bienstock to Walter G. Keim, Jan. 3, 1964; John R. Howard to Sen. Maurine Newberger, Feb. 20, 1964; W. Willard Wirtz, Memorandum to Clague, Nov. 10, 1964; Clague to Secretary, Nov. 18, 1964; Clague to Secretary, Feb. 4, 1965, "Elimination of Consumer Price Index for Individual Cities."

[62] NARG 257, BLS, Price Division, BLS statement, "The Budgets in Their Historical Perspective," January 1965; *City Worker's Family Budget For a Moderate Living Standard, Autumn 1966*, Bull. 1570-1 (Bureau of Labor Statistics, 1967), pp. vi-vii.

[63] NARG 257, BLS, Price Division, BLS, "Review of the BLS Wholesale Price Index," Oct. 24, 1957; Allan D. Searle, "Weight Revisions in the Wholesale Price Index, 1890-1960," MLR, February 1962, p. 180; *Techniques of Preparing Major BLS Statistical Series*, Bull. 1168 (Bureau of Labor Statistics, 1954), pp. 82 and 93; *BLS Handbook of Methods for Surveys and Studies*, Bull. 1910 (Bureau of Labor Statistics, 1976), p. 127.

[64] Joint Economic Committee, *Hearings, Price Statistics*, I, p. 64; *Handbook*, Bull. 1910, p. 123.

[65] H.M. Douty and Toivo P. Kanninen, "Community Approach to Wage Studies," MLR, October 1949, pp. 366-367 and 369; *Techniques*, Bull. 1168, p. 97.

[66] Kanninen, "New Dimensions in BLS Wage Survey Work," MLR, October 1959, pp. 1081 and 1083-1084; NARG 257, BLS, DWIR, Douty to Clague, June 19, 1959, covering additional materials; and Bureau of the Budget, "Design for a Survey of White-Collar Pay in Private Industry," Sept. 17, 1959.

[67] Clague, *The Bureau*, pp. 99-100; Joseph P. Goldberg, "The Government's Industrial Employees, part II, Consultation, Bargaining, and Wage Determination," MLR, March 1954, p. 253; NARG 257, BLS, DWIR, Cass to Holleman, "State Wage Collection Programs," Mar. 9, 1962.

[68] Harry S. Kantor, "Economic Effects of the Minimum Wage," MLR, March 1955, pp. 307-308; L. Earl Lewis, "75-Cent Minimum Wage: Effects on Fertilizer Industry," MLR, January 1951; Norman Samuels, "Effects of the $1 Minimum Wage in Seven Industries," MLR, March 1957; *Factory Workers' Earnings, May 1958*, Bull. 1252 (Bureau of Labor Statistics, 1959); *Industry Wage Survey, Hotel and Motels, June 1961*, Bull. 1328 (Bureau of Labor Statistics, 1962); *Industry Wage Survey, Eating and Drinking Places, June 1963*, Bull. 1400 (Bureau of Labor Statistics, 1964).

[69] NARG 174, USDOL, Mitchell, 1956, Mitchell to Sen. Paul H. Douglas, Jan. 31, 1956; NARG 257, BLS, DWIR, BLS statement (no date), "Retail Trade Wage Survey"; House, Subcommittee of Appropriations, *Hearings, Second Supplemental Appropriation Bill, 1956* (84C, 2S, 1956), p. 341; *Employee Earnings in Retail Trade in October 1956, Summary Report*, Bull. 1220 (Bureau of Labor Statistics, 1957).

[70] *Problems in Measurement of Expenditures on Selected Items of Supplementary Employee Remuneration, Manufacturing Establishments, 1953*, Bull. 1186 (Bureau of

Labor Statistics, 1956), p. iii; *Employer Expenditures for Selected Supplementary Remuneration Practices for Production Workers in Manufacturing Industries*, Bull. 1308 (Bureau of Labor Statistics, 1962); NARG 257, BLS, DWIR, William J. Carson to Albert L. Moore, Jr., Aug. 26, 1953; Division of Wages and Industrial Relations, 1965–1971, Walter W. Heller to Wirtz, Nov. 11, 1964; Clague to Moynihan, Dec. 4, 1964; Wirtz to Ackley, "Statistical Program of Fringe Benefits," Dec. 28, 1964.

[71] NARG 257, BLS, Division of Wages and Industrial Relations, 1951-1964, Douty to Clague, July 22, 1958, "Review of draft."

[72] Joseph W. Duncan and William G. Shelton, *Revolution in United States Government Statistics, 1926–1976* (U.S. Department of Commerce, Office of Federal Statistical Policy and Standards, 1978), pp. 96–97; Clague, *The Bureau*, pp. 117–119; *Trends in Output per Man-Hour and Man-Hours per Unit of Output—Manufacturing, 1939–53*, Rpt. 100 (Bureau of Labor Statistics, 1955); *Trends in Output per Man-Hour in the Private Economy, 1909–1958*, Bull. 1249 (Bureau of Labor Statistics, 1960).

[73] *Economic Report of the President*, January 1962, together with the Annual Report of the Council of Economic Advisers, pp. 186-190.

[74] NARG 257, BLS, Reorganization of the Productivity Division, Leon Greenberg to Henry J. Fitzgerald, Sept. 11, 1959; *Techniques*, Bull. 1168, p. 30; *Labor Requirements for School Construction*, Bull. 1299 (Bureau of Labor Statistics, 1961); *Labor and Material Requirements for College Housing Construction*, Bull. 1441 (Bureau of Labor Statistics, 1965).

[75] NARG 257, BLS, Division of Productivity and Technological Change, 1953–63, Nat Weinberg to Clague, Apr. 8, 1953, and Clague to Walter C. Wallace, Dec. 10, 1959; Productivity Division, Clague to Cass, Feb. 27, 1957; Productivity; UAW Controversy—BLS Productivity Report, "The Bureau of Labor Statistics' Surrender to Big Business."

[76] *Handbook*, Bull. 1458, p. 208.

[77] Dept. of Labor, *Annual Report, 1949*, pp. 69 and 75; *Annual Report, 1951*, pp. 208-209.

[78] *Foreign Labor Publications*, mimeograph (Bureau of Labor Statistics, 1962) pp. i-ii; *Labor Law and Practice in Honduras*, Rpt. 189 (1961); "Summary of Labor Conditions in Burma," mimeograph (December 1952); *Foreign Labor Information: Labor in Argentina*, mimeograph (June 1959); *Labor in the Sudan*, Rpt. 182 (Bureau of Labor Statistics in cooperation with International Cooperation Administration, 1961).

[79] Each prepared by BLS for Agency for International Development: *The Forecasting of Manpower Requirements*, Rpt. 248 (1963); *Conducting a Labor Force Survey in Developing Countries*, Rpt. 263 (1964); *Computation of Cost-of-Living Indexes in Developing Countries*, Rpt. 283 (1964).

[80] Dept. of Labor, *Annual Report, 1947*, p. 59; *Annual Report, 1950*, p. 177; Duncan and Shelton, *Revolution*, p. 111.

[81] Clague, *The Bureau*, pp. 128–130.

[82] Ibid., pp. 130–131; Duncan and Shelton, *Revolution*, p. 114; *Handbook*, Bull. 1458, pp. 220–221.

[83] *Projections 1970, Interindustry Relationships, Potential Demand, Employment*, Bull. 1536 (Bureau of Labor Statistics, 1966).

[84] NARG 257, BLS, Division of Prices and Cost of Living, 1950-1964, Edward D. Hollander, File Memorandum, July 6, 1950; House, Committee on Post Office and Civil Service, Subcommittee on Overstaffing in the Executive Departments and Agencies, "Investigation of Employee Utilization in the Executive Departments and Agencies," Preliminary Report, part II, "The Prices and Cost of Living Division, Department of Labor" (81C, 2S, 1950, Committee Print), pp. 49 and 55.

[85] NARG 257, BLS, Division of Prices and Cost of Living, 1950-1964, Maurice J. Tobin to Rep. John Bell Williams, Dec. 21, 1950; Hollander to Clague, et als., "Results of Employee Attitude Survey," Feb. 7, 1951.

[86] Senate, Committee on Labor and Public Welfare, *Hearing: Nomination of Ewan Clague* (84C, 1S, 1955), pp. 2-4, 6, and 8.

[87] Ibid., pp. 12, 15, and 18.

[88] NARG 257, BLS, Bert Seidman to Ewan Clague, Sept. 7, 1954.

[89] Clague, "The Program," 1947, p. 179.

[90] "Appeals Court Delays Order Setting Aside Walsh-Healey Determination," *DLR* (76), Apr. 18, 1963, p. A7; "Appeals Court Affirms Injunction Against Walsh-Healey Determination," *DLR* (128), July 1, 1964, p. A1.

[91] "Wirtz Revokes Motors-Generators Wage Determination Struck Down by Courts," *DLR* (187), Sept. 24, 1964, p. A10; Herbert C. Morton, *Public Contracts and Private Wages, Experience under the Walsh-Healey Act* (Washington: The Brookings Institution, 1965), pp. 89, 114, and 131.

[92] *DLR* (176), Sept. 14, 1965, pp. A9-A10.

Chapter VIII.   Four Commissioners

[1] U.S. Congress, Joint Economic Committee, Subcommittee on Economic Statistics, *Government Price Statistics, Hearings* (89C, 2S, 1966), p. 3.

[2] *Economic Report of the President, February 1984*, together with the Annual Report of the Council of Economic Advisers, p. 201.

[3] *Economic Report of the President, January 1979*, together with the Annual Report of the Council of Economic Advisers, pp. 167-169.

[4] U.S. Department of Labor, Bureau of Labor Statistics, Janet L. Norwood, *Statement before the Subcommittee on Economic Stabilization, Committee on Banking, Finance, and Urban Affairs, House of Representatives* (Feb. 17, 1983), pp. 2, 4, 5, 6, and 16.

[5] *Weekly Compilation of Presidential Documents*, Sept. 29, 1969, pp. 1319-1320.

[6] U.S. Congress, Congressional Budget Office, *Indexing with the Consumer Price Index: Problems and Alternatives*, June 1981, p. xiii; Norwood, *Statement before the Appropriations Subcommittee, House of Representatives, FY 1984 Appropriations* (Mar. 15, 1983), p. 2.

[7] Minimum Wage Study Commission, *Report*, May 24, 1980, p. 84.

[8] For a detailed and comprehensive catalog of indexation, see U.S. Congress, Senate, Committee on the Budget, *Indexation of Federal Programs* (97C, 1S, Committee Print, 1981), prepared by the Congressional Research Service.

[9] *Daily Labor Report* (182), Sept. 21, 1965, p. A4; U.S. Congress, House, Subcommittee of Appropriations, *Hearings, Departments of Labor and Health, Education, and Welfare Appropriations for 1967* (89C, 2S, 1966), pp. 677 and 681.

[10] *DLR* (204), Oct. 21, 1965, pp. E1–E2.

[11] Geoffrey H. Moore, "Long-Range Program Objectives for BLS," *Monthly Labor Review*, October 1969, pp. 3–6.

[12] Senate, Committee on Labor and Public Welfare, *Hearing, Nomination of Julius Shiskin* (93C, 1S, 1973), p. 12; National Archives Record Group 257, BLS, Under Secretary, Shiskin, Memo for the Secretary, "*Pro Forma* Resignation," Aug. 13, 1974.

[13] Senate, Labor and Public Welfare, *Hearing, Shiskin* (1973), pp. 3, 8.

[14] Office of Publications files, Shiskin, (photocopy) May 19, 1977, Senator Proxmire to the President; Senate, Committee on Human Resources, *Hearing, Nomination of Julius Shiskin* (95C, 1S, 1977), pp. 1–2, 26.

[15] Senate, Labor and Human Resources, *Hearing, Nomination of Dr. Janet L. Norwood* (96C, 1S, 1979), pp. 8–9.

[16] Ibid., p. 6; *Forbes*, June 11, 1979, p. 155; Philip Shabecoff, "She Takes Her Computers Home," *The New York Times*, July 22, 1979.

[17] "Republican Claims Index Was Manipulated," *Washington Star*, Oct. 7, 1980, p. A1; "Fact and Comment: Unfortunately that Price Index Drop Is a Phony," *Forbes*, Oct. 27, 1980, p. 25.

[18] *DLR* (114), June 13, 1983, p. A2.

[19] "Release of Statistics by Federal Agencies: The President's Memorandum to the Director of the Bureau of the Budget, Feb. 8, 1969," in *Weekly Compilation of Presidential Documents* (Feb. 14, 1969), p. 248.

[20] Joint Economic Committee, *Current Labor Market Developments, Hearings* (92C, 1S, 1971), pp. 338–339.

[21] NARG 257, BLS, Release of Statistics I, draft, July 22, 1969, "Policy on the Presentation and Interpretation of Government Statistics," signed by Shiskin, with holograph note: "Used at mtg. 7/28/69—w/Herb Klein, M. Mann, and J. Shiskin," with typed note attached, "Proposal made to Dr. Burns (with minor revisions)."

[22] NARG 257, BLS, Discontinuance of Press Briefings, Moore, memorandum for the Secretary, "Proposed Procedure for Handling BLS Price and Employment Releases," Mar. 15, 1971; Senate, Subcommittee on Appropriations, *Hearings, Department of Labor and Health, Education, and Welfare and Related Agencies Appropriations for Fiscal Year 1972* (92C, 1S, 1971), pp. 113–114.

[23] NARG 257, BLS, Discontinuance of Press Briefings, GHM, "Statement by Secretary Explaining Change in Procedure for Releasing Price and Employment Statistics," Mar. 16, 1971; Senate, Subcommittee of Appropriations, *Hearings, Appropriations for Fiscal Year 1972*, pp. 113–114.

[24] Joint Economic Committee, *Federal Statistical Programs, Hearings* (93C, 1S, 1973), p. 26.

[25] NARG 257, BLS, Reorganization, October 1971 I, Shultz (OMB) to Secretaries, "Reorganization," July 15, 1971.

[26] *DLR* (189), Sept. 29, 1971, p. A16; NARG 257, BLS, Reorganization, October 1971 I, (copy) "Nixon Ousting Labor Analysts," *Washington Post*, Sept. 29, 1971.

[27] House, Committee on Government Operations, *Report, Discontinuance of Monthly Press Briefings by the Bureau of Labor Statistics, Department of Labor* (92C, 1S, House Report 92-759, 1971), p. 10.

[28] House, Committee on Post Office and Civil Service, Subcommittee on Census and Statistics, *Report, Investigation of Possible Politicization of Federal Statistical Programs* (92C, 2S, House Rept. 92-1536, 1972), letter of transmittal and pp. 1–2, 8–9, and 11–12.

[29] Dept. of Labor, BLS, News Release (USDL 72-693), Oct. 6, 1972, "Statement by Commissioner of Labor Statistics;" James D. Hodgson, "Statement of Policy by the Secretary of Labor Concerning the Role of the Bureau of Labor Statistics," Nov. 10, 1972.

[30] "Secretary of Labor, Remarks of Press Secretary, Nov. 29, 1972," in *Weekly Compilation*, Dec. 4, 1972, pp. 1707–1708; DLR (242), Dec. 14, 1972, p. A6; (244), Dec. 18, 1972, p. A9; (5), Jan. 8, 1973, p. A12; Daniel J. Balz, "Civil Servant, Statistician Named Chief of Troubled Bureau of Labor Statistics," *National Journal*, July 7, 1973, p. 995.

[31] NARG 174, USDOL, Brennan, 1973, Secretary to John H. Aiken, Mar. 21, 1973, covers "Maintaining the Professional Integrity of Federal Statistics, Final Report," American Statistical Association/Federal Statistics Users' Conference Committee on the Integrity of Federal Statistics, 1973.

[32] NARG 257, BLS, Discontinuance of Press Briefings, Bureau of the Budget, Circular A-91, "Prompt Compilation and Release of Statistical Information," Feb. 12, 1969; Moore, Memo for the Secretary, "Proposed procedure," Mar. 15, 1971; OMB Circular A-91, Revised, Apr. 26, 1972.

[33] NARG 257, BLS, Reorganization, October 1971 I, Moore to Robert A. Gordon, Dec. 9, 1971.

[34] NARG 174, USDOL, Brennan, 1974-5, Secretary to Senator Proxmire, Oct. 30, 1974; Senate, Labor and Human Resources Committee, *Hearing, Norwood* (1979), p. 22.

[35] Joint Economic Committee, Subcommittee on Economic Statistics, *Price Statistics* (1966), p. 3; DLR (102), May 25, 1966, pp. B22–B24.

[36] NARG 257, BLS, CPI—Quality Change I, Walter P. Reuther to Secretary, Sept. 27, 1966.

[37] Ibid., Magnuson and Mondale to Ross, July 28, 1967; Magnuson and Mondale to Ross, Oct. 2, 1967; Ross to Magnuson and Mondale, Oct. 12, 1967.

[38] NARG 257, BLS, CPI Revision #4, Mark Roberts to Members of the Labor Research Advisory Council, Mar. 29, 1974; Dept. of Labor, BLS, News Release, Apr. 5, 1974, "Revised Consumer Price Index to Reflect Expenditures of More Americans;" *The Consumer Price Index: Concepts and Content Over the Years*, Report 517 (Bureau of Labor Statistics, 1978), p. 10.

[39] DLR (61), Mar. 28, 1974, p. A5; (68), Apr. 8, 1974, pp. A12–A13.

[40] DLR (68), Apr. 8, 1974, p. A11; (79), Apr. 23, 1974, pp. A17 and A19.

[41] NARG 257, BLS, CPI Revision #4, Gary L. Seevers, Chairman, Subcommittee on Economic Statistics, Council on Economic Policy, Memo for Shiskin, "Family Definition in the Consumer Price Index, Apr. 16, 1974;" Seevers (CEA), Edgar Fiedler (Treasury), Jack Carlson (OMB), and Joseph Duncan (OMB), Memo for The Troika,

"Coverage in the Revised CPI," May 10, 1974; Shiskin, Memo for the Secretary, "A Revised Plan for the 1977 CPI," May 14, 1974; NARG 174, USDOL, Usery, 1976–77, Secretary to Hon. James T. Lynn, Jan. 18, 1977; DLR (101), May 23, 1974, p. A4.

[42] House, Committee on Government Operations, *Hearings, Consumer Price Index for All-Urban Consumers* (95C, 2S, 1978), p. 6; U.S. Comptroller General, *A CPI for Retirees Is Not Needed Now But Could Be in the Future* (General Accounting Office, GGD 82-41, 1982), p. iii.

[43] Norwood, *CPI Issues*, Report 593 (Bureau of Labor Statistics, 1980), pp. 1–2; *Consumer Price Index* (Rpt. 517, 1978), pp. 13–14.

[44] NARG 257, BLS, CPI Revision—Homeownership Component, Roberts to Shiskin, July 7, 1975, enclosing Anne Draper to Roberts, "Labor Criticisms of Flow of Services Pricing of Homeownership Component of Consumer Price Index;" Joseph P. Goldberg to Members of the Price Committee of the Labor Research Advisory Council, Mar. 31, 1977, covering Draper to Roberts, "Homeownership Component of the Consumer Price Index," Mar. 21, 1977.

[45] Ibid., Noel A. McBride to Shiskin, Jan. 6, 1977; K. G. Van Auken, Jr., to Members of the Business Research Advisory Council and Its Committee on Consumer and Wholesale Prices, Jan. 12, 1977; Shiskin to Lyle E. Gramley, Council of Economic Advisers, Apr. 15, 1977.

[46] *BLS Handbook of Methods*, Bulletin 2134-1 (Bureau of Labor Statistics, 1982), p. 38; NARG 257, BLS, Consumer Expenditure Surveys, Helen H. Lamale to Chase, "Plans for Continuing Expenditure Surveys," Mar. 14, 1966.

[47] NARG 257, BLS, CPI Revision #5, Roberts, Lazare Teper, and Draper, July 29, 1974, attention: Joseph P. Goldberg, "June 1974 BLS Paper on CEX."

[48] NARG 257, BLS, CPI Revision #7, Shiskin to Robet Ferber, Oct. 24, 1975; Division of Prices and Cost of Living, 1973–1975, Burton G. Malkiel, Council of Economic Advisers, Memo for Rudy Penner, "The Continuing Consumer Expenditure Survey," Nov. 1, 1975.

[49] *Economic Report of the President, January 1979*, pp. 43–44; *Economic Report of the President, January 1980*, pp. 39–40.

[50] DLR (14), Jan. 21, 1980, pp. X1ff.

[51] DLR (242), Dec. 14, 1979, p. A11; (37), Feb. 22, 1980, p. A15; (40), Feb. 27, 1980, p. A9; (47), Mar. 7, 1980, p. A8; (67), Apr. 4, 1980, p. A2.

[52] *Economic Report of the President, January 1981*, p. 10.

[53] "Take a Parting Shot at Inflation" (editorial), *The New York Times*, Dec. 4, 1980, p. A30; Comptroller General, *Measurement of Homeownership Costs in the Consumer Price Index Should Be Changed* (General Accounting Office, PAD 81-12, 1981), pp. iv, v, and 55.

[54] Dept. of Labor, News Release (USDL 80-303), May 9, 1980, "Norwood Urges Users to Become Better Informed About Indexation;" House, Appropriations, *Hearings, Departments of Labor, Health and Human Services, Education, and Related Agencies Appropriations for 1982* (97C, 1S, 1981), pp. 1072–1073.

[55] Dept. of Labor, News Release (USDL 81-506), Oct. 27, 1981, "Statement of Dr. Janet L. Norwood."

[56] USDOL News Release (USDL 82-327), Sept. 17, 1982, "Norwood Says CPI Change Will Improve Inflation Measure."

57 *DLR* (238), Dec. 11, 1981, pp. A13–A14.

58 Dr. James A.Clifton, for Chamber of Commerce of the United States, "Statement," before Senate Committee on Governmental Affairs, Apr. 20, 1982, p. 1; *DLR* (28), Feb. 9, 1983, pp. A11–A12.

59 House, Appropriations, *Hearings, Departments of Labor, Health and Human Services, Education, and Related Agencies Appropriations for 1984* (98C, 1S, 1983), pp. 306–307.

60 NARG 257, BLS, Standard Budgets, Moore to Popkin, "Measuring Retired Couples' Living Costs in Urban Areas," Dec. 2, 1969; Moore to Users of BLS Budgets and Interarea Living Cost Indexes, "Improved Program for the BLS Family Budget Estimates and Interarea Indexes of Living Costs," Dec. 15, 1971.

61 NARG 257, BLS, Standard Budgets III, Nelson A. Rockerfeller, Governor of New York, to Secretary, Oct. 4, 1972; Moore, Memo to Shiskin, "Standard Family Budgets," Oct. 27, 1972; Shiskin to William A. Morrill, May 22, 1973; Morrill to Shiskin, Aug. 14, 1973; Under Secretary, Burdetsky, Memo for the Under Secretary, "Backlog and Priorities," May 19, 1973.

62 NARG 257, BLS, Under Secretary, Shiskin, Memo to Under Secretary Schubert, "BLS Family Budget Program," Sept. 6, 1974.

63 NARG 257, BLS, Standard Budgets III. W. John Layng to Norwood, "Revision of Family Budget Program," Apr. 27, 1976; Harold W. Watts, "Special Panel Suggests Changes in BLS Family Budget Program," *MLR*, December 1980, pp. 3–10.

64 John F. Early, "Improving the Measurement of Producer Price Change," *MLR*, April 1978, pp. 7 and 9; Council on Wage and Price Stability, *The Wholesale Price Index*, June 1977; *DLR* (115), June 14, 1977, p. A10.

65 Joint Economic Committee, Subcommittee on Economic Statistics, *Inflation and the Price Indexes* (89C, 2S, Joint Committee Print, 1966), p. 38; *Government Price Statistics, A Report* (89C, 2S, 1966), pp. III, 16–17; *DLR* (101), May 23, 1975, p. A12; (131), July 8, 1975, p. A6.

66 *Handbook of Methods* (1982), p. 43; Early, "Improving the Measurement," pp. 7ff.

67 NARG 174, USDOL, Brennan, 1973, Thomas P. O'Neill, Jr. and Silvio O. Conte to Secretary, May 31, 1973; Secretry to O'Neill and Conte, June 25, 1973; O'Neill and Conte to Secretary, Oct. 29, 1973; Secretary to O'Neill and Conte, Dec. 5, 1973; Dept. of Labor, News Release (USDL 73-601), Dec. 21, 1973.

68 Joint Economic Committee, *Report, A Reappraisal of U.S. Energy Policy* (93C, 2S, Joint Committee Print, 1974), pp. 2 and 27.

69 *DLR* (40), Feb. 27, 1974, p. A1; NARG 257, BLS, Wholesale Price Index II, Robert H. Stewart, Jr., to Petroleum Industry Advisers, Mar. 18, 1974.

70 "A New Oil Index Creates Confusion," *Business Week*, June 22, 1974; NARG 174, USDOL, Usery, 1976–77, Edward P. Boland and Silvio O. Conte to Secretary, Feb. 23, 1976; Shiskin to Boland and Conte, Mar. 16, 1976.

71 *The Department of Labor during the Administration of President Lyndon B. Johnson, November 1963–January 1969*, chap. V, "Data Collection and Analysis" (typescript, USDOL Historian's Office), p. 585; *Handbook of Methods* (1982), p. 62; Dept. of Labor, *Annual Report, 1982*, pp. 22–23.

[72] National Commission on Employment and Unemployment Statistics, *Counting the Labor Force* (1979), p. 2.

[73] DLR (234), Dec. 2, 1966, pp. A10–A11; Paul O. Flaim, "Persons Not in the Labor Force: Who They Are and Why They Don't Work," MLR, July 1969.

[74] Shiskin, "Employment and Unemployment: The Doughnut or the Hole?" MLR, February 1976, p. 4.

[75] Senate, Subcommittee of Appropriations, *Hearings, Departments of Labor, Health and Human Services, Education, and Related Agencies Appropriations for Fiscal Year 1982* (97C, 1S, 1981), p. 429; John E. Bregger, "Labor Force Data from the CPS to Undergo Revision in January 1983," MLR, November 1982, pp. 3–4.

[76] National Commission, *Counting*, pp. 153–55 and 158–59; Thomas J. Plewes, "Better Measures of Service Employment Goal of Bureau Survey Redesign," MLR, November 1982; Harvey R. Hamel and John T. Tucker, "Implementing the Levitan Commission's Recommendations to Improve Labor Data," MLR, February 1985.

[77] NARG 257, BLS, Under Secretary, Shiskin, Memo for Under Secretary, "Unemployment Statistics for State and Local Areas," Feb. 1, 1974.

[78] DLR (66), Apr. 4, 1974, pp. A4–A5; (171), Sept. 2, 1980, p. A10; MLR, October 1977, p. 72; April 1978, p. 52.

[79] House, Committee on Government Operations, *Hearings, Intergovernmental Antirecession Assistance Act of 1977* (95C, 1S, 1977), p. 94; *The New York Times*, May 25, 1977, p. VI,5.

[80] Norwood "Reshaping a Statistical Program to Meet Legislative Priorities," MLR, November 1977, pp. 6–11; Martin Ziegler, "Efforts to Improve Estimates of State and Local Unemployment," MLR, November 1977, pp. 12–18; 92 Stat. 1952.

[81] National Commission, *Counting*, p. 15.

[82] Myron Struck and Kenneth E. Jolin, "Labor Department Statistics Found Less and Less Reliable," *Washington Post*, Sept. 17, 1982, p. A13.

[83] *The Department during Johnson*, chap. V, "Data Analysis," pp. 564–567.

[84] NARG 257, BLS, JOLTS IV, President to Secretary, Jan. 30, 1969; Budget Write-up, Feb. 28, 1969; Moore, for the Under Secretary, Nov. 21, 1972; *The Department of Labor History During the Administration of Presidents Richard M. Nixon and Gerald R. Ford, January 1969 to January 1977*, vol. II, chap. V, "Data Collection and Analysis" (typescript USDOL Historian's Office), p. 23.

[85] Senate, Appropriations, *Hearings for Fiscal Year 1982*, pp. 455 and 472; Dept. of Labor, Secretary of Labor, *Final Report on the Recommendations of the National Commission on Employment and Unemployment Statistics*, October 1981, p. 3; Dept. of Labor, *Annual Report 1982*, p. 22.

[86] NARG 257, BLS, Job Vacancies II, Chester E. Johansen to Lester S. Kellogg, Jan. 18, 1965; DLR, (99), May 20, 1966, Special Supplement, pp. 1–2; National Commission, *Counting*, p. 122.

[87] NARG 174, USDOL, Wirtz, 1966, Esther Peterson to the Secretary, "Briefing Memo—BLS Survey to Determine to What Extent 'the Poor Pay More'," Jan. 10, 1966; NARG 257, BLS, Division of Prices and Cost of Living, 1965-1968, June 12, 1966, USDOL, BLS, "A Study of Prices Charged in Food Stores Located in Low and Higher Income Areas of Six Large Cities, February 1966."

[88] James R. Wetzel and Susan S. Holland, "Poverty Areas of Our Major Cities," MLR, October 1966, p. 1105; NARG 257, BLS, Survey Program for Urban Poverty Areas #2, Wirtz to Stanley Ruttenberg and Ross, July 12, 1966; Ross to Secretary, Dec. 22, 1967; Malcolm R. Lovell, Jr., to Philip M. Hauser, July 17, 1970; Daniel S. Whipple, "Employment Among the Poor of Six Central Cities," MLR, October 1973.

[89] DLR (204), Oct. 21, 1971, pp. A8–A9; The New York Times, Oct. 26, 1971, p. 66; NARG 257, BLS, Survey Program for Urban Poverty Areas, Roy Wilkins to Secretary, Nov. 22, 1971.

[90] Flaim, "The Spendable Earnings Series, Has It Outlived Its Usefulness?" MLR, April 1982, p. 86; DLR (178), Sept. 11, 1980, p. A12; National Commission, Counting, p. 206.

[91] National Commission, Counting, pp. 206–208.

[92] BLS Handbook of Methods for Surveys and Studies, Bulletin 1458 (Bureau of Labor Statistics, 1966), p. 114; Harry A. Donoian, "A New Approach to Setting the Pay of Federal Blue-Collar Workers," MLR, April 1969, pp. 30 and 32; Comptroller General, Determining Federal Compensation, Changes Needed to Make the Processes More Equitable and Credible (General Accounting Office, FPCD 80-17, 1979), p. 29.

[93] President's Panel on Federal Compensation, Report to the President, 1975, pp. 23–24; Comptroller General, Wages for Federal Blue-Collar Employees Are Being Determined According to the Law, But Improvements are Needed (General Accounting Office, FPCD 80-12, 1979).

[94] 84 Stat. 1946 (Jan. 8, 1971), also as 5 U.S.C 5305.

[95] Comptroller General, Improvements Needed in the Survey of Non-Federal Salaries Used as Basis for Adjusting Federal White-Collar Salaries (General Accounting Office, B-167266, 1973), pp. 2 and 30; President's Panel, Report (1975); NARG 257, BLS, White Collar (PATC) II, Paul MacAvoy, Council of Economic Advisers, to Shiskin, Sept. 23, 1975; George L. Stelluto, "Federal Pay Comparability, Facts to Temper the Debate," MLR, June 1979, p. 20.

[96] NARG 257, BLS, White Collar (PATC) II, James L. Blum, Memo for Shiskin, "Follow-up on PBRC Decision on PATC Survey," Sept. 14, 1973; Shiskin to David P. Taylor (OMB) and Raymond Jacobson (CSC), Jan. 8, 1974; Handbook of Methods (1982), p. 69; Dept. of Labor, News Release (USDL 82-241), July 12, 1982, "White-Collar Salaries, March 1982."

[97] NARG 257, BLS, Rees Review of Wage Program, Albert Rees (Princeton University), "Improving Measures of Wage Changes," August 1969; DLR (160), Aug. 19, 1969, p. A12.

[98] NARG 257, BLS, Employment Cost Index, Roberts to Shiskin, Mar. 25, 1975, covering Roberts, Oswald, and Burkhardt to Joseph W. Duncan (OMB), Mar. 25, 1975; NARG 174, USDOL, Usery, 1976–77, Shiskin to Senator Roman L. Hruska.

[99] Victor J. Sheifer, "Employment Cost Index, A Measure of Change in the 'Price of Labor'," MLR, July 1975; "How Benefits Will Be Incorporated Into the Employment Cost Index," MLR, January 1978.

[100] Rees, "Improving the Concepts and Techniques of Productivity Measurement," MLR, September 1979, p. 23.

[101] Dept. of Labor, BLS, News Release (USDL 83-153), Apr. 6, 1983, "Bureau of Labor Statistics Introduces Its First Measures of Multifactor Productivity;" Trends in

Multifactor Productivity, 1948–81, Bulletin 2178 (Bureau of Labor Statistics, 1983), p. 2.

[102] *Handbook of Methods* (1982), p. 101.

[103] Robert Ball, "Employment Created by Construction Expenditures," MLR, December 1981, pp. 39, 42; *Labor and Material Requirements for Hospital and Nursing Home Construction*, Bulletin 2154 (Bureau of Labor Statistics, 1983), pp. iii, 37, 63; Dept. of Labor, *Annual Report, 1982*, pp. 23, 31.

[104] *Employment Projections for 1995*, Bulletin 2197 (Bureau of Labor Statistics, 1984), p. 10.

[105] "Brief History of Bureau of Labor Statistics Projections," MLR, August 1981, p. 14.

[106] Norman Root and David McCaffrey, "Providing More Information on Work Injury and Illness," MLR, April 1978; Root and Michael Hoefer, "The First Work-Injury Data Available from New BLS Study," MLR, January 1979.

[107] Senate, Labor and Human Resources, *Hearing, Norwood* (1979), p. 9.

[108] Dept. of Labor, *Annual Report, 1968*, pp. 2, 4; Booz-Allen and Hamilton, *Bureau of Labor Statistics, General Review* (confidential report, Mar. 22, 1966), pp. 76, 78; Booz-Allen and Hamilton, *U.S. Department of Labor, The Organization and Management of the Bureau of Labor Statistics* (December 1966), pp. 5, 14, 61–62.

[109] Discussion of computers at BLS is based on *The Development and Uses of Table Producing Language*, Report 435 (Bureau of Labor Statistics, 1975), and *Information Processing at BLS*, Report 583 (Bureau of Labor Statistics, 1980).

[110] NARG 257, BLS, Reorganization, October 1971 I, Shultz (OMB) to Secretaries, "Reorganization," July 15, 1971; DLR, (189), Sept. 29, 1971, p. A16; (202), Oct. 19, 1971, p. A10.

[111] Dept. of Labor, BLS, Norwood, "Management Decision, Memorandum #8," June 26, 1982; Norwood, Memorandum, "Organizational Changes," Jan. 4, 1983.

[112] NARG 257, BLS, Asst. Regional Director Classification, Shiskin to Under Secretary, Aug. 22, 1973.

[113] National Commission, *Counting*, p. 272; Secretary, *Interim Report on the Recommendations of the National Commission on Employment and Unemployment Statistics*, Mar. 3, 1980, p. 43; Secretary, *Final Report* (1981), p. 6.

Index

Index

Index

Index